KILLER B's

The 237 Best Movies on Video (probably) You've ^ Never Seen

KILLER B's

The 237 Best Movies on Video You've (probably) Never Seen

by

D. Scott Apel

Video Columnist, The San Jose Mercury News

THE PERMANENT PRESS

International Standard Book Number (ISBN): 1-886404-01-1

Library of Congress Catalog Card Number (LCC): 96-92879

First Edition: January, 1997

The Permanent Press
P.O. Box 700305
San Jose, CA 95170

Manufactured in the United States of America

DEDICATION

for
the beautiful wife

a beautiful dream...

"This is the sort of thing you'll really like,
if you really like this sort of thing."

—J.R. "Bob" Dobbs

CONTENTS

The Killer B *Challenge*

The astute, extremely observant (or incredibly anal-retentive) reader might notice that there are actually *238* titles listed in the index. This is not a mistake; it is, in fact, a challenge. One of these Killer B's is not a movie at all, but is in fact a fake. Your mission (should you decide to accept it) is to *spot the ringer.* Can you determine which is the *faux* film? (Here's a hint: if it were indeed a real movie, it would be the archetypal Killer B, embodying the most frequently repeated casting of the other 237 titles included in this book.)

This is not a contest—just a challenge. There are no prizes to be won, other than the personal satisfaction of knowing that you really know your Killer B's.

Good luck—and happy hunting.

Killer B's

The 237 Best Movies on Video You've (Probably) Never Seen

Introduction

We all go to the video store to rent entertainment. But all too often we end up renting crap.

The reason is simple. We want the latest releases and the biggest blockbusters—the movies we've read about, the ones we've heard about, the ones we never got to the theater to see. More often than not, these titles are missing from the shelves, already snapped up by earlier, luckier patrons. And we're left standing in a store full of films without any idea what else is worth renting.

It's a little like being blindfolded at a buffet: If we grab something at random, are we going to get paté or the dog's brunch?

The solution: *Killer B's: The 237 Best Movies on Video You've (Probably) Never Seen.*

Take a minute to skim the Title Index at the back of the book. Can you spot any movies that you loved, but no one you know has ever heard of? Do you see any films that you accidentally stumbled across and felt like you'd discovered? Recognize any titles that were recommended by word-of-mouth from a friend? Then maybe we're on the same wavelength.

Killer B's isn't "just another video guide." The overabundance of film and video guides is of little help when you're desperate for something decent to rent. How do you choose a single film worth watching from a book with 15 or 20 *thousand* entries, for instance? How much information can you really get from a two- or three-sentence review? And how can you trust *any* guide's opinion of a specific film when most of those "comprehensive" compendiums have *dozens* of contributors? Even armed with a movie guide, finding good entertainment is still a crapshoot: "Ya pays yer money and ya takes yer chances."

Killer B's is an attempt to put an end to the guesswork—and to the disappointment of leaving a video store empty-handed. To begin with, *every film in this book is recommended.* You don't have to wade through thousands of video guide mini-reviews to find a decent release—we've separated the wheat from the chaff for you. And where the "best of" books concentrate on "A" list movies that you're already aware of and have probably already seen, *Killer B's* makes full use of the video advantage: easy access to lesser-known films.

Killer B's is, in fact, the *direct opposite* of most video guides. To use those guides, you first find a film in a video store that looks promising, then you look it up in the guide to find out its rating. *Killer B's* works in reverse: It's our intention to suggest titles with the goal of inspiring you to *seek them out* in the video store. Once you've read *Killer B's,* you can walk into any video store in America forearmed—ready to recognize the gold among the dregs as you pan and scan the shelves. Let those other guides rehash the "A" lists endlessly. Let them compete to see which can collect the most titles. We'll concentrate instead on the delight of discovery and the joy of entertainment.

Just where do these 237 films come from? From one of the greatest but least recognized pleasures of home video: "buried treasures," or unknown little films that are just as entertaining as any big budget, high profile, famous film—and often even more so. These are the movies we delight in sharing with our friends, knowing they'd probably never discover them, or even consider renting them, if they weren't steered towards them.

Some of these films moved through theaters so fast they were almost subliminal: If you blinked, you missed them. Some played only at small art houses in large cities. Others skipped the theatrical circuit altogether and went straight to video.

They are the "sleepers": First-rate little films that never got the publicity, distribution or attention they needed for their audience to find them, or videos that were lost in the annual avalanche of tapes.

Hollywood puts out about 450 films a year: some great; most mediocre; a few, real turkeys. Since most of the titles in *Killer B's* haven't been widely seen, you might say this book contains the equivalent of about six months' worth of "new" movies. Obviously, you wouldn't go to the theater to see every movie released during a given six month period. The subject matter, genre or stars might just not appeal to you. The same holds true for this book: Not every film listed in *Killer B's* is suitable for every taste. But we've attempted to include descriptions detailed enough to allow you to decide whether to rent a particular picture. Death, taxes, and politicians lying aside, nothing is absolutely guaranteed. But if you find a review in this book that sounds appealing, it's a pretty good bet that you'll enjoy the movie. And if the review indicates that this particular film isn't your cup of tea, then consider the money you've saved by *not* renting it!

Don't be stung by bad videos—put *Killer B's* to work for you!

Killer B's

The Skeleton Key

Each review is formatted in the following manner:

1. Title

2. (subgenre)

(3. Year of theatrical release; 4. Video distributor; 5. MPAA rating; 6. Running time; 7. Misc.)

HEADING INFORMATION

8. Cast (Starring/Featuring)

9. Writer (and source material, where applicable)

9A. Music (where appropriate)

10. Director

BODY INFORMATION

11. Synopsis

12. Discussion

13. Rent this one for

14. You'll (probably) like this if you liked

15. Dissenting Opinion/Credentials

16. Vidbits

Killer B's

The Fine Print:

A Custom Key to the format, in full details

I. Heading information

1. Title: Listed in alphabetical order within each genre category. Initial words such as "A" and "The" are usually ignored. If a film is widely known by an alternate title, this is listed on the next line as *"AKA:"* ("also known as").

2. Subgenre: Few movies are a "pure type." Westerns, for example, can be action-oriented, or devoted to adult themes. Some Westerns are contemporary, rather than being set in the "Wild West." Others are essentially comedies dressed in Western chaps and boots.

Comedies, in particular, cover a wide range of territory: romantic, screwball, sophisticated, black comedy, and so on.

This entry attempts to quickly categorize those films which can't be stuffed into a single pigeonhole. Not all titles have a subgenre entry, but when one does, it denotes a specific spin on the genre type.

Another way to look at this category is not just as a subtheme, but as a clue to where a movie might be misfiled or alternately located in a video store (are you more likely to find *Escape From New York* in your store's "Action" section, or in its "Science Fiction" section, for instance? Is *Drugstore Cowboy* a comedy or a drama? And so on...)

3. Year of theatrical release: With only a few exceptions, all the films included in *Killer B's* were produced and released since 1980. Why? Several vague reasons. Video began to catch fire about then, for one. 1980 marks the beginning of the recent-memory, "post-modern" era, for another. Films began to take on a different sensibility around then; the beginning of the Lucas/Spielberg era. And the relatively new but rapidly expanding video (and cable TV) aftermarket made it easier for small film-makers to raise the money necessary to produce little films.

I'll be the first to admit that this cut-off date is arbitrary and based as much on intuition as on Hollywood business history. The question I asked myself was, "After how long do we take a flick off the 'popular recent release' list and move it to the 'Classics' shelf?" Which brings up another point; namely, that movies produced since 1980 will be easier to find on the video store shelves (theoretically, at any rate).

Ten percent of these Killer B's violate the 1980 cut-off date —and for nearly as many reasons as there are violations. Some border-straddling 1979 entries snuck in, for instance. No sense being too inflexible with the rules, particularly if they exclude a movie that would have otherwise been included. Some entries (like *Gun Crazy* and *The Big Clock*) are films that have gone long unseen but recently became available on video—the idea being that it even though it might be an old film, it's still a new video, and it deserves to be seen by a new generation of movie buffs.

Occasionally, a pre-'80 flick is included because a.) it fits the Killer B profile perfectly; and b.) it's timeless. *Bedazzled* (1967), for example, hasn't lost one iota of its charm or absurd humor over the past three decades.

4. Video distributor: In the volatile video industry, companies come and go with great irregularity. Who remembers Vestron Video, for instance—a company that ranked among the top ten distributors in the early 80's, then went belly-up? (Most of their stock was swallowed whole and re-released by LIVE Home Video.) Who remembers Magnetic Media, which distributed Scorsese's *Raging Bull*—a movie that *American Film* magazine readers voted as the "best film of the '80s"?

Mergers among video companies and mega-mergers among film studios have also changed the name of many companies over the years. Thus did RCA/Columbia "become" Columbia TriStar; thus did Thorn/EMI begat HBO Cannon which in turn begat HBO Video.

What complicates matters most for our purposes is that the majority of the films in *Killer B's* were *not* released or distributed by any of the long-term, stable distributors, but by smaller, less stable firms. If these little companies go out of business and sell off their titles, you could conceivably come across two (or more) editions of the same movie with two different distributor labels. Look for *Raging Bull* in an old video store, for instance, and you might uncover several strata of labels, from Magnetic Media to CBS/Fox Home Video (which has since metamorphosed into FoxVideo), to MGM/UA Home Video. The other side of this coin is that *Raging Bull* is popular and well-known—but there's no guarantee that the new owner of a minor title is ever going to re-release it.

I've attempted to be comprehensive here, listing all known labels a title has been distributed under (separated by commas), including the version I found on video store shelves as well as the latest information available on that title's distributor. I can't claim 100 percent accuracy, however—but that hardly matters.

For the purposes of scouting out and renting minor titles, knowing the distributor is not particularly vital. Either a store has a copy of the film, or it doesn't. Knowing the distributor becomes a vital piece of information only if you wish to track down a copy to purchase. Any video store can check a title's availability, but ordering tapes is outside the scope of this book.

5. MPAA Rating: MPAA, of course, is the "Motion Picture Association of America," which reviews and brands films with the familiar categories of G (General Audiences), PG (Parental Guidance Suggested), PG-13 (Some situations might not be appropriate for children under 13), R (No one under 18 admitted) and NC-17 (hubba hubba).

Some sources (a few newspapers and *Entertainment Weekly*) often list not just the rating but the reasons for the rating (e.g., strong language; violence; sexual situations; nudity; drug or alcohol abuse; adult themes; or some combination of these and other relevant details). I'm assuming this is done for parents or the feint-hearted, but the reviews in this book don't go into that much detail. The Synopsis should indicate anything objectionable and that you might wish to avoid. And I chose to do longer reviews than to take up space by including such "politically correct" data as the potentially objectionable aspects of a flick.

6. Running Time: Listed as "hours: minutes"; i.e., a film with a recorded running time of 101 minutes, or one hour and forty-one minutes, is written "1:41."

7. Miscellaneous: Here you will find any straggling data as needed. "Foreign language" is one example; this will tell you what language the film is in, and whether it is available in subtitled and/or dubbed versions. Assume a movie is in color unless it's marked "B&W" here. I must admit I'm not a minutiae buff, so don't look for fine distinctions between "color films with some B&W segments" (like *The Nasty Girl*) and "B&W films with some color segments" (like *Zelig*). Who needs to be that anal?

8. Cast: Simply a list of the actors, most often in order of importance (which won't always be a one-to-one correspondence with the order names are listed in the credits). "**Starring**" most often denotes the "names above the title," while supporting actors can be found on the following line, "**Featuring.**" This category is highly selective, mentioning for the most part only those names recognizable today, no matter what the relative importance of the actor's role in any particular flick. (Cameos, uncredited appearances, and bit players or extras who would go on to later fame can be found in "Vidbits.")

9. Written by: The scriptwriter. If the script is based on other material—a novel, say, or a short story—this information is listed parenthetically following the screenwriter's name. I've elected in most cases to ignore a "story by" credit if it's an original screenplay. And to avoid all the confusion that Writer's Guild litigation provokes—all the subtle differentiations among contributors, team credits and script doctors; all the subtle distinctions among the meaning of "and," "with" and "&"—I've adopted the convention of simply listing the writers' names in the order in which they appear on screen, separated by commas. Easy as A, B, C. See?

9A. Music by: Occasionally, the soundtrack of a film is a major addition to the emotional tone of the movie *(Sorcerer)*, or has been created by a well-known musician (like Tom Waits' score for *One From The Heart*), or has won a major award. In these cases, the responsible party is duly credited.

10. Director: The person who directed the movie. (Duh.)

A suggestion: If you like a listed film from a particular director, rent more by that artist. I've purposefully restrained from "stacking the deck" in favor of my favorites. There's only one Woody Allen title included, for example, although at least half a dozen of his movies qualify as Killer B's. But if you enjoy a film's style, quite often a director will have produced stylistically similar films. Bill Forsythe, Hal Hartley, Alan Rudolph, Henry Jaglom, John Sayles, Albert Brooks, Woody Allen, and many more have each developed a particular style that pervades their work. The inclusion of one or two titles by them in this book is an indication of my own favorite(s) from among their films, and can serve you as a pointer toward (or away from) their other works.

Note: When my research sources disagree about any of this data, I have used the videotape of the film itself as the final authority for information on credits, ratings, cast and copyright year. Even these aren't always 100 percent accurate, but if nothing else, they at least represent the "official line." (You want to drive yourself crazy? Look up the running time of a film in four or five different guidebooks. More often than not, you'll get four or five different times, each varying by a minute or two. Go figure.)

II. Body Information

The above categories all refer to objective data about the film (and video) itself. The following categories all relate to the critical analysis of the film.

11. Synopsis: The basic storyline or set-up, as opposed to a complete plot summary. I've tried to keep these summaries as objective as possible—"Just the facts, please, ma'am"—saving any discussion for the following category. And I promise not to give away anything that would spoil plot twists or surprises.

12. Discussion: This is the real heart of the book, and its real purpose. Here's where I attempt to convince you *precisely why* this movie is worth watching. Think of this section as a film review which accentuates the positive aspects (but which will warn you of serious flaws).

13. Rent this one for: The highlight of the film: the A-level feature which elevates this B movie to the realm of the Killer B's; the outstanding aspect (or aspects) that separate a minor movie from other mediocre or forgettable flicks. This could be a superb performance, an intriguing story, a fresh script, sumptuous photography, virtuoso directing, inventive filmmaking, an off-beat sensibility, a delightful score, genuinely affecting emotion—whatever. If this highlight isn't what you're looking for in a film —then *don't rent it.*

14. You'll (probably) like this if you liked: As an additional method of defining a film and assisting you in selecting something you'll almost certainly enjoy, I've listed similar movies where appropriate, and similar, but *better-known* movies when possible. Under *Truly, Madly, Deeply,* for example, you'll find the entry: "You'll probably like this if you liked: *Ghost.*" Further explanation is provided parenthetically if appropriate or necessary: "(other films by the same director)," for instance; or "(comic version)", meaning another movie with the same theme, but approached as a comedy instead of a drama (*Love At Large,* for example, can be viewed as a comic take on *Someone to Watch Over Me*). And of course the vice is versa.

I've also used other Killer B's as comparisons. You have the advantage in these cases of being able to read the full *Killer B* treatment to decide if *either* film might be to your liking.

Finally, these comparisons can (in most cases) be taken as "suggestions for further viewing" if you haven't seen the films.

What I'm aiming at with this category are movies with the same theme, or a similar plot, and, as often as possible, a similar *emotional tone or atmosphere.* You won't find *The Sting* and *Naked Gun* listed under *Breaking In,* for example; even though all three could be lumped together as "crime comedies," they are worlds apart in tone. *The Sting,* a light-hearted caper comedy, is nothing like the wild 'n crazy gag fest that is *Naked Gun.* Both are fine, fun films, but neither recommendation would prepare you for the gentle, wry character study with dramatic undercurrents that would describe *Breaking In.*

Unlike books devoted to this "similarity" theme, the suggestions here are not limited just to other films, but include some TV shows as well (many of which are also available on tape.) To avoid confusion, *movie titles* are italicized and "TV show titles" are in quotes.

15. Dissenting Opinion: I'm fully aware that I'm in dangerous territory here, choosing 237 unknown films and claiming they're all recommended. Some critics have loved some of the titles in this book. More often than not, however, most critics stuck two or three stars on the majority of them, then just ignored them. Once in a while, however, the artistic or aesthetic sensibilities of a particular reviewer are so deeply violated that he or she feels obliged to warn one away from the offending film.

I realize that my own choices are often quirky, and that I owe you, the reader (and potential viewer), as much information as possible to allow you to make an informed decision about the appropriateness of a particular film to your own sensibilities and entertainment desires. So when published critical opinion is vehemently opposed to a movie in *Killer B's,* I'll let you know who hated the flick, and why.

Where The Heart Is is a perfect example. The *Golden Movie Retriever* claims that it "flops in a big way," and the *Video Movie Guide*—which curiously lists it in the "drama" section, when it's unambiguously a comedy—gives it a lowest-rating "turkey."

In these controversial cases, my motto is, "One person's turkey is another's Thanksgiving." And my attempt in discussing these films is to point out what I believe these reviewers overlooked—or what quirks *they* succumbed to—to dislike the film. If other video guides are your bible, however, then temper my enthusiasm with their bile.

For the sake of limited space, the most frequently referred-to video guides are identified by their initials; a key can be found following this material. (page number?)

Credentials: The other portion of this category is entitled *Credentials,* and exists to indicate when the choice of a title as a super-sleeper is not just mine alone. For the most part, I've limited these credentials to listings of actual awards won by the film, Oscar nominations, or the results of large-scale voting by critics or film buffs (*The Thin Blue Line,* for example, was voted "The Best Documentary of the '80s" by a poll of 54 film critics performed by the now-defunct magazine, *American Film.*) Occasionally I've included a 4-star critical rating from one of the various video guides—sometimes to enhance the awards list; sometimes to contrast with the Dissenting Opinions. Taken together, these two subcategories indicate the wide range of ratings (and opinions) given a film by individual critics—as well as occasionally providing some amusing contradictions.

16. Vidbits: A catch-all category for trivia and details that just don't fit into the above structure, but which might be of interest if one watches and enjoys the movie.

Included here are details about actual shooting locations (versus the location in which a film is set); an actor's first or last appearance; cameo roles; and brief appearances. I *do* make the following distinctions, herewith defined: a "cameo" is an actor appearing *as him or herself* in a scene; an "appearance" is an actor *playing a role in a bit part.* Martha Plimpton has a *cameo* in *My Life's In Turnaround*—she plays herself, actress Martha Plimpton, who the main characters meet and try to convince to be in their film—but Bob Dylan makes an *appearance* in *Backtrack,* playing an unnamed artist (*not* Bob Dylan) in one scene. Clear?

The rest is pure miscellany. Did you know that both Phil Hartman of "Saturday Night Live" and Rita Wilson (*Sleepless in Seattle,* and the real-life Mrs. Tom Hanks) appeared in *Cheech and Chong's Next Movie*? Or that *Almost Hollywood* was shot on a budget of $100,000—about what a director of the Spielberg or Cameron strata spends before lunch on a single day of shooting? Do you care? Ah, well, this a handy way to put to some use all those thousands of factoids of irrelevant information squeezed into my brain cells from years of watching "Entertainment Tonight" and reading *Entertainment Weekly.*

III. Special Features of **Killer B's**

Flashback! above the title of a film indicates it was released prior to 1980. About ten percent of the entries are "Flashbacks!", included because they are essentially timeless treasures.

Double Feature! above the title combines two similar titles into a single review. Each feature film is counted as one movie of the 237; two single hours of TV programs (like *Police Squad!*), are considered a single "feature" entry. The films are lumped together because they are so similar that if you like one, you'll almost certainly like the other—but if you don't respond positively to one, don't even bother with the other.

Use it as a Cable Movie Channel Companion. *Killer B's* makes an excellent companion to the numerous cable movie channels—not necessarily the premium channels, like HBO and Showtime, as most of these films flew well below their blockbuster radar—but channels like AMC, TMC, Bravo and the Independent Film Channel.

Even though these channels occasionally air a title listed in *Killer B's,* I'd still strongly suggest renting the original video when you can, rather than settling for seeing the films on cable. Why? Because despite the self-congratulatory, highbrow disclaimers about "respecting the artist's vision," most cable channels still conform to PG-13 standards at best. A perfect example is watching *Midnight Run* on The Disney Channel. In the style of such classic comedies as *Slap Shot* and Richard Pryor's concert films, *Midnight Run*'s humor and characterizations rely heavily on the elevation of profanity to near poetic levels. Think you're gonna hear lines like, "I got two words for you: Shut the fuck up!" on The *Disney* Channel? Bravo, too, is guilty of censoring the profanity in films like *Drugstore Cowboy.* Even the anarchistic Comedy Central removes nudity—even when it's essential to the plot (as it is in *Just One of the Guys).*

Another irritating technique these channels are pioneering is zooming in on some innocuous area of the screen while nudity is occurring in the original full frame. Did director Nicolas Roeg really have in mind a "push-in" to a grainy close up of a lamp in the corner of the bedroom while Art Garfunkel and Theresa Russell make love in *Bad Timing?* Not only is this selective editing and forced perspective totally inappropriate, it violates the director's intention and framing of the scene.

So while cable film channels might offer more convenience than two trips to the video store, the cost is censorship and mutilated movies. The extra effort of locating and renting the video version is, in my view, more than compensated for by the opportunity to see a film in its uncut, uncensored form.

"Killer B's":
A Detailed Definition
(or, "Why is that *in this book?")*

So just what is a "Killer B"?

It's a B-movie that's every bit as first-rate as most first-run features—a small film of general interest to jaded video viewers.

We've already established certain defining characteristics: Killer B's are little-known films that never got the publicity, distribution or attention they needed to allow their audience to find them. Or they are videos that were lost in the shuffle of hundreds of cassette releases every year. They are "the sort of movie you feel impelled to tell friends about," as Shiela Benson put it in her 1985 *L.A. Times* review of *The Hit.*

Some of these films moved through theaters so fast that if you were sick that day, you missed them. Some played only at small art houses in large cities. Others skipped the theatrical circuit altogether, and went straight to video.

"Killer B's" are very similar to movies usually referred to as "buried treasures" or "sleepers." What is it, then, that differentiates a "Killer B" from these other types of little films?

My selection criteria were, for the most part, arbitrary.

First, I eliminated most movies that became popular enough to make any theatrical or video rental "top ten" list as being too well-known. I used a cut-off date of 1980, to limit the list and to keep the films contemporary. I rejected as candidates most cult films and sub-genres. (Read the next sections for details.)

Finally, there's *The Unwritten Rule*—one additional, important and unspoken criterion: *I had to like it.* If I didn't like a film, it's not in here. (See the "Don't Bother" list of titles I watched but which didn't make the cut, and particularly the "Top 10 Overrated Sleepers" list of movies which fit all the "Killer B" criteria *except* The Unwritten Rule.) Not all "blind dates" inspire a spark—but some create real chemistry.

So what did I look for in a "great" overlooked or minor film? *Excellence* in one or more aspects: exceptional performances, an intelligent script, lush photography, appropriate pace and direction. I looked for originality, wit, uniqueness, sincerity. I looked for overall engaging entertainment and for lasting impressions.

Most of all, however, I looked for *verisimilitude:* a big damn word meaning that it *seemed real.* I looked for genuinely affecting emotion, whether intended to inspire laughter, tears, awe or chills. I looked for an *experience*—for films that *affected* me.

You're holding 237 perfect examples of Killer B's.

Enjoy them!

Killer B's

Exclusions

What you won't *find in* Killer B's:

• No martial arts/kick-boxing/"Asian Trash Cinema"/chop-socky flickee. No Sonny Chiba or John Woo or Jackie Chan. While this genre has found a following in the U.S., whole books could be written about them (and probably have). They don't really fit the "Killer B" profile, anyway; they're mostly of cult interest rather than general interest. The same holds true with Japanese animation, or "animé." Those enraptured by these genres already know the films, and the publications devoted to them. And it's so difficult to tell the good Asian movies from the cheap Pacific Rim jobs.

• No "Women in Prison" or "Psycho Cycle Sluts" cheapies.

• No erotic thrillers (or anything starring Shannon Tweed or Shannon Whirry), although we do include a couple parodies.

• No slasher flicks. Period.

• No cult classics. (They wouldn't have become "classics" if you hadn't already seen them, now would they?) Many of the titles in this guide could easily *become* cult flicks, however, or (like *Zardoz*) fell just short of attaining cult status.

• No XXX-rated Adult fleshfests.

• No "Forgotten Favorites"—that is, movies which were seen by *everybody* when they were first released on tape, but which now languish on video store shelves. Just because you haven't watched the original *Lethal Weapon* or *Ghostbusters* or *Beverly Hills Cop* or *Raiders of the Lost Ark* in the last five years doesn't mean you've never seen them—or that you need to be reminded that they're still worth watching.

• No *trash.* No "so bad they're good" garbage. *Killer B's* is devoted to *good* movies—the best you've (probably) never seen.

(There are plenty of books, magazines and newsletters out there devoted to each of these special interest genres and *Killer B* exclusions. If you have an abiding interest in any of these genres, you know where to find both the flicks and the books.)

• Not many movies produced before 1980.

• No "Spoilers." I don't want to diminish the fun of discovery by giving away surprise endings or astonishing plot twists.

• No information on video prices. The cost of buying any tape varies from month to month and from year to year. Since this is a book about *renting* videos, I'm not even going to make an attempt to list a purchase price for the tapes listed herein.

• No laserdisc listings or availability information. This book concentrates on video rentals, rather than laserdisc purchases.

• No attempt to gauge the degree of difficulty of finding these titles. Even the smallest video store might have surprising titles.

Killer B's

Inclusions

What you will *find in* Killer B's:

• **Four-star films which are largely undiscovered**

Some played only in art theaters in larger cities. Others never got the publicity or distribution they deserved. Some never played in theaters at all, but went straight to video, or began as made-for-cable or made-for-TV films. Others got lost in the shuffle of hundreds of video releases every year. Still others have long been unavailable until their resurrection on cassette.

• **Three star movies which *become* four star videos**

Home viewing can actually improve the intended effect of certain films. While spectacle is certainly diminished, intimacy, for example, is enhanced. We might not be part of the mass audience experience, but, in the comfort of our own home, we allow ourselves to form a stronger and more personal connection with the characters. *Truly, Madly, Deeply* is a good example: What kind of stone-hearted fiend could go untouched watching a woman bawl her eyes out before an unflinching camera, when her life-sized face is right in front of you, right in your house?

Video also lends itself to repeated viewings, and therefore to second thoughts, which allows a deeper understanding of the subtleties of cinema. And subtleties can be found in the most unlikely places. You think Marty Scorsese invented the endless, Steadicam tracking shot? Check out *Gun Crazy,* produced in 1950—a Killer B which contains a scene where two people drive into town, park their car, rob a bank, and then drive off through town making their getaway. And it's filmed as *one single shot*—a shot that lasts *five minutes*. In a theater, if ya miss it, ya miss it. But on a VCR, if you intuit that something unusual is going on, you can rewind and validate your perception. And rewind again and marvel at the single shot. And rewind *again* and *time* the damn thing! And... Well, you get the point.

Finally, the lower cost of a video rental—on average, about a third of the cost of going to a theater—takes a lot of the "performance pressure" off borderline films. Call it a case of diminished expectations, or of standards which are relaxed in the relaxing environment of our own living room. But we all know that video invented an entire class of movies referred to as "wait for the tape" films. There are an awful lot of movies that we *know* aren't going to be worth seven bucks-plus, but which are entirely enjoyable for $2.50.

Killer B's

• Two star flicks with four-star parts

Who could claim that every one of these choices is a 4-star film? Not even me. Many among them can best be called "uneven"—but IMHO, they are films in which the highs outnumber the lows, and in which the highs are even worth *enduring* the lows. These are the movies that esteemed film critic Charles Champlin refers to as "brave imperfect tries."

My approach to analyzing films included in *Killer B's* is a bit different from most film critics' method of assigning a single overall grade to a movie. I feel that there are numerous movies which perhaps deserve two or three stars *overall,* but which contain elements that separate them from the majority of mediocre, forgettable films that merit these ratings. Is it fair to give a film three stars *overall* if the script—or the performances, or the cinematography—rates a solid "A"? If a film has a profound effect on our heart, if it provides a sublime emotional experience, do we downgrade it because it might not be "smart" enough? What kind of overall grade do we give to a flick with a brilliant script, but that's too low-budget to be a polished, Hollywood-style production?

How are we supposed to give an "overall" grade to a movie like *Used Cars,* for instance? Here's a movie that is insanely hilarious—for the first 65 minutes. But then it slips into formulaic mediocrity. Do we ignore those 65 brilliant minutes because that exceptional level of humor isn't sustained during the final 45 minutes? And how the hell can anyone justify giving a single overall grade to a movie like *Night On Earth,* which consists of *five* separate short stories, two of which are dull, but *one* of which is perhaps the funniest 20 minutes ever captured on film? My attitude is that any movie that excels in any category can be considered as a movie worth watching.

Many of the films in this book are movies with four-star segments or elements. But I believe that the pleasure obtained from these four-star parts more than compensates for the film's "failures"—and more than repays the time spent watching it.

You might consider *Killer B's* the video version of a yellow marker: I've highlighted the "good parts" of some otherwise flaccid films. But, man, those good parts are occasionally *great*—and well worth the price of a rental.

• "Turkeys" that deserve to be reconsidered

Exorcist II, for instance, was a universally reviled flick. Even the director, John Boorman, publicly renounced it. Why, for God's sake, does it deserve a second chance? (I've actually sat people down and forced them watch this one, talking them through it. And I've won a lot of converts. Intrigued? Look up the entry and discover why *no one* understood this movie.)

Killer B's

• Independent directors and filmmakers

They aren't mainstream, but rather "sidestream" directors: Henry Jaglom, John Sayles, Errol Morris, Alan Rudolph, Jim Jarmusch, Bill Forsythe, Hal Hartley. If you haven't been exposed to these guys, you're missing some of the most innovative and eccentric work being done in the movies.

On the other hand, be forewarned that many of these directors are "acquired tastes." I've never acquired a taste for small independent directors David Cronenberg (although his Stephen King adaptation *The Dead Zone* is in this book), or Mike Leigh, or Todd Haynes. Your tastes may vary.

• Contradictions

Every rule I've set up to find and choose these films has its exception. Nothing before 1980? Well...exactly 10 percent of the listed films were indeed produced before 1980. But they're still sleepers, and still worth watching.

Another general guideline I tried to adhere to was that any video that made it onto any of the many "top ten rental" lists (compiled by *Billboard, Variety, Video Store Magazine,* Blockbuster Video, or whatever source) was probably too well-known to qualify as a Killer B. And yet while most of these tapes never charted, some have been nominated for (or even won) Academy Awards, Golden Globes, foreign awards and film festival honors—any of which is probably a more accurate judge of quality than the "popularity contest" of rental lists. (Besides, neither rental lists nor box office receipts indicate what percentage of viewers actually *enjoyed* the film. And, unlike films, there are no "exit polls" for video rental returns.)

• A handful of foreign language films

Movie buffs and videophiles can be divided into two groups: Either they love foreign films or they avoid them like they'd avoid a postal worker purchasing a semiautomatic weapon. The first group doesn't need to be sold on the joys of world cinema. But if you belong to the second set—Trust me; these are all entirely accessible films. And there are only 13 of them—a mere five percent of the total number of entries.

• A variety of sources

A video in a store is a video in a store, and a good film is a good film, no matter what its origin. So you'll find a wide variety of sources for these films, including theatrical features, some made-for-cable or made-for-TV movies, some flicks which went direct-to-video (for various reasons)...and some surprises.

• 237 of the best movies you've (probably) never seen

Caveat Videor

("Let the watcher beware")

Taste.

It's probably the most loosely-defined word in the English language.

But just so there's no mistake, let me state definitively, once again, for the record:

Not every movie in this book is suitable for all tastes.

Just as *Killer B's* offers sleepers from a wide variety of sources—including major studios, independent productions, cable, made-for-video, unreleased and direct-to-video features—so does it cover a wide range of tastes.

Take the Comedy section. (Please.) Within its entries you'll find gentle romances and cynical black comedies, sophisticated satires and sophomoric silliness, deep themes handled brilliantly and scatological, no-brainer romps. Which categories you find funny is *totally* subjective.

Hence the numerous methods of presenting each movie: by plot, by highlights, by discussion of its merits—even by inclusion of reasons why other reviewers *didn't* like a given film. The only rule in this book is that if, after reading the description, a flick sounds appealing to you, you'll probably like it, and it will probably prove worth the extra effort to keep an eye out for it in video stores. But if a review in *Killer B's doesn't* sound interesting, you probably *won't* like it—so don't waste your time hunting the video down.

All this sounds obvious. It *is* obvious. And yet I'll *still* get letters from angry readers upset that they just *hated* some film I've listed. (I will politely refer them to this page. The assholes.)

The bottom line is that if you find just *four films* that you like and wouldn't have ordinarily taken a chance on renting—then you've paid yourself back for the purchase price of this book. To put it another way, if these reviews *warn you away* from four films you've thought of renting but decide you *wouldn't* like, then you've earned back the cost of the book just by avoiding rotten rentals.

Four out of 237 is *less than two percent* of the entries in *Killer B's*. Pretty good odds, I'd say.

Anyway, you've been warned...

Action/Adventure

Action/Adventure

Since I watch a lot of videos, I visit a lot of video stores. A few years ago I noticed another guy doing the same thing. Seems like I saw this guy at every store I entered. Not like he was hard to miss: He stood about 6-foot-4 and was always dressed in a T-shirt, camouflage fatigues and combat boots. And he was always in the "Action Movies" section.

Figuring he might be competition from a rival publication (maybe the video reviewer for *Guns and Ammo,* or *Soldier of Fortune*), one day I swallowed my fear and approached him.

"Didn't I see you the other day over at XYZ Video?" I mentioned gently.

"Yeah," he replied. "But I don't go there no more."

"And didn't I see you last week over at ABC Video?" I asked.

"Yeah," he said. "But I don't go there no more, either."

Maybe, I thought, *I don't want to know why.*

But I had to ask.

"So why don't you go to those stores anymore?"

He looked at me like I was the dense one.

"'Cause I watched every action movie they had," he explained with great patience. "So I hadda find a new store. Now I'm gonna watch every action movie they have in *this* store. Then I'll find *another* store."

This section is not for that man. This section is for people a bit less, uh...*dedicated*—and just a touch more normal.

By the way, there are, at last count, some 25,000 video stores in the United States.

Watch for this guy in a store near you.

Big Trouble in Little China

(comedy)

(1986; CBS/Fox; PG-13; 1:39)

Starring: Kurt Russell, Kim Cattrall, James Hong
Featuring: Dennis Dun, Victor Wong, Kate Burton, Suzee Pai
Written by: Gary Goldman, David Z. Weinstein, W.D. Richter
Music by: John Carpenter, Alan Howarth
Directed by: John Carpenter

Synopsis: "That's how it always begins," says Egg Shen (Wong). "Very small." Like witnessing the kidnapping of Wang's (Dun) Chinese fiancée. Or a trip into the back alleys of San Francisco's Chinatown. Or a stolen semi that belongs to macho man Jack Burton (Russell). Or a Chinese funeral that turns into a Tong war and ends in black magic. You know—small stuff. Wang wants his girl rescued from the clutches of 2,000-year-old black magician Lo Pan (Hong). Jack just wants his truck back. They break into Lo Pan's warehouse, they're captured, they escape. But now Jack, Wang and Egg have to go back in with reinforcements to rescue *two* women, and put an end to the threat of Lo Pan, the "Bodhisattva of the Underworld"—if they can. It'll take plenty of magic, lots of guns—and all the luck they can muster.
Discussion: Dismissed on release as a *Raiders* wannabe, a decade later, it couldn't look more different. Once Jack drives into that alley, we enter another world: a disorienting labyrinth of inscrutable Old World mystery. What we've got here is a grand-scale comic book adventure about Eastern magic butting heads with Western literalism. No wonder Russell mimics The Duke throughout the flick—although it has more in common with John Woo than John Wayne. Jack's a complex guy for a comic book hero: far braver than he realizes, but nowhere near as smart. Half the fun is watching this concrete-minded cement-head trying to understand that most of the action takes place on a mystical plane. "'China is here'?" Jack growls, in a deadpan rush. "What does that mean, 'China is here,' I don't even know what the hell that means." Wonderful, energetic performances, numerous quotable lines, superb effects and cartoonish martial arts all add up to a delightfully over-the-top action comedy.
Rent this one for: its wild, tongue-in-cheek, comic book fun.
Dissenting Opinion: • "...vacuous characters, limping fantasy" —*Sight and Sound* • "tiresome" —HFG • "heavy tongue-in-cheek attitude, but everything else about it is heavy, too"—MMG (1/2 star) • "sorry mess"—*People Magazine's Guide to Movies on Video*
You'll (probably) like this if you liked: *The Adventures of Buckaroo Banzai, The Golden Child, Escape From New York*

Black Moon Rising

(1986; New World, Starmaker Entertainment; R; 1:40)

Starring: Tommy Lee Jones, Linda Hamilton
Featuring: Richard Jaeckel, Robert Vaughn, Keenan Wynn
Written by: John Carpenter, Desmond Nakano, William Gray
Directed by: Harley Cokliss

Synopsis: Quint (Jones) is a hi-tech thief, free-lancing for the Attorney General to steal a cassette containing the Lucky Dollar Corp.'s crooked accounting records. With the Corp.'s goons hot on his tail, he hides the tape inside an experimental supercar at a truck stop, then follows it to L.A. Before he can retrieve the tape, however, the car is stolen by Nina (Hamilton) and her ring of carjackers. He chases her until she disappears into the underground parking garage of a twin-tower high rise office complex owned by the sinister Ryland (Vaughn), then teams up with Black Moon's inventors to recapture the car. They've only got three days before the car's potential investors pull out—and before Quint's government agents take him out for good. Can Quint get to Nina and turn her against mastermind Ryland? Can he get to the car and reclaim his tape before being caught by the Corp., the cops or the Feds? And can any of them escape Ryland's sinister surveillance and security forces?
Discussion: Is it *Mission Impossible* meets *It Takes A Thief*, or *Bullit* meets *Die Hard* ? It's got elements of all of them, with a plot that doesn't lag and action that doesn't disappoint. We're definitely in Carpenter territory: hi-tech toys, fast-paced action, a minimum of verbiage and enough humor to keep it from taking itself too seriously. The "driving" action includes some nicely choreographed car chases through the streets of L.A., and a final aerodynamic stunt that's still impressive. Even a decade later, the flick looks hi-tech (except for the bulky cell phones) which is no small achievement! (How much you wanna bet that Calvin Klein's ad agency saw Ryland's tape of Nina and came up with that "interviewing urchins" TV ad campaign?)
Rent this one for: the car chases, the stunts and the action.
You'll (probably) like this if you liked: *The Road Warrior*
Credentials: "...close to the quintessential Grade-B movie." —*People Magazine's Guide to Movies on Video*
Dissenting Opinion: • "...absurd, almost impenetrable" —HFG • "thoroughly lead-footed, low-tech affair...totally bald on thrills" —PVG • "...deserves to get a Big Moon Rising." —MMG (BOMB)
Vidbit: • Cokliss' prior directing experience included second unit direction on *The Empire Strikes Back.* • Don Opper (*Android)* appears as "Frenchie." • Jaeckel plays "Earl Windom"—any relation to *Twin Peaks'* villain "Windom Earle," you suppose?

Blind Fury

(martial arts/ comedy)

(1990; RCA/ Columbia, Columbia TriStar; R; 1:28)

Starring: Rutger Hauer, Terry O'Quinn, Brandon Call
Featuring: Noble Willingham, Randall "Tex" Cobb, Meg Foster
Written by: Charles Robert Carner
Directed by: Phillip Noyce

Synopsis: Blinded in Vietnam, Nick Parker (Hauer) is "adopted" by a village and taught to use his ears—and a sword. 20 years later, he arrives in Miami to look up his old Army buddy Frank Deveraux (O'Quinn). He finds that Frank has left his wife and son Billy (Call) and gone to Reno—where he's run up a huge gambling debt with casino owner and drug dealer MacCready (Willingham). Minutes later, MacCready's goons hit the house, attempting to kidnap the boy as insurance that chemist Frank will continue to manufacture designer drugs for the boss. Nick makes short work of the thugs and determines to take Billy under his wing and save him and his dad from the evil MacCready. They embark on a bus trip, slowly growing to know one another while regularly fending off attacks by MacCready's men. Can blind swordsman Nick rescue both father and son? We'll see...
Discussion: While a blind swordsman might seem as unworkable a concept as a Jamaican bobsled team, if handled with humor, both could make interesting films. *Cool Runnings* succeeded, and so does *Blind Fury.* It's an action flick with a sense of humor—the "blind man driving" scene is particularly funny—and it's nice to see the usually sullen Hauer laugh and smile. *Of course* the goons are evil idiots who deserve to die—which makes it all the more fun to watch Nick effortlessly outwit them. Eyes ain't brains! The script provides several clever methods of staging fights in an atmosphere conducive to Nick's strange talents (a darkened room is merely the most obvious, but...a *corn field?*). The action is nicely choreographed and directed, and the film is filled with fast and furious sword-flashing action—including a pair of final surprises which put Nick's odd abilities to the ultimate life-or-death test, and lead to some nicely satisfying violence and retribution. And it all works simply because, like Nick, the film refuses to take itself too seriously.
Rent this one for: it's unusual premise; its laugh-laced action.
You'll (probably) like this if you liked: *Scent of a Woman; Zatoichi, The Blind Swordsman*
Dissenting Opinion: • "...brash, lively (but failed) attempt... doesn't altogether work." —MMG (2.5 stars) • "Hauer works well...but...the movie doesn't." —GMR (2.5 bones)

Blue Thunder

(thriller)

(1983; RCA/Columbia; R; 1:50)

Starring: Roy Scheider, Daniel Stern, Malcolm McDowell
Featuring: Warren Oates, Candy Clark, Joe Santos
Written by: Dan O'Bannon, Don Jakoby
Directed by: John Badham

Synopsis: Sometimes it's a tough life, doing helicopter duty for the L.A. Police. It's tougher still when you keep having Vietnam flashbacks, like chopper pilot Frank Murphy (Scheider), and doubly tough when you're given a green partner like Lymongood (Stern). Frank is "volunteered" for special duty, test flying Blue Thunder, an armed, armored, turbocharged superchopper developed by the military for counter-terrorism. Something suspicious is going on, however: Murphy's old 'Nam nemesis Col. Cochrane (McDowell), now in charge of Thunder, sabotages the trial run. And when Frank has his computer whiz partner use the copter's sophisticated surveillance equipment to eavesdrop on a secret meeting between Cochrane and his cronies, they uncover an incredible conspiracy involving a political assassination and the true intended use of Thunder—knowledge which puts their own lives in mortal danger. Can Frank accomplish the impossible and turn their own technology against them?
Discussion: Tired of the same old car chases? Try a chopper chase instead. Tired of the same old car crashes? Try a couple of copter crashes. (I think you'll find them a refreshing change of pace.) Badham knows how to direct action (once he finally cuts to the chase), and here we get copters vs. copters; copters vs. cars; F-16's with heat-seeking missiles vs. Blue Thunder (and Frank's wits); and—just in case you *aren't* tired of car chases—a doozy of a chase that begins in a drive-in. There are in fact a *lot* of chases and a lot of destruction (but very little blood); some macho fun; adventure, suspense and wowing aerial action; and another wonderful performance from Scheider. All this, *and* you'll find out what JAFO means! What more could a guy ask?
Rent this one for: the incredible aerial dogfighting sequences.
You'll (probably) like this if you liked: *The Rookie, Firefox*
Dissenting Opinion: • "...slick but hollow..." —HFG • "...gets stupider (and crueler) as film goes on." —MMG (2 stars)
Vidbit: • Oates' last film. Dedication: "For Warren Oates, with love for all the joy you gave us." • Blue Thunder is adapted from the French Aerospatiale Gazelle copter. • Isn't that Dan Hedaya as the chopper tech? He's not listed in the credits. And who's the nude yoga lady, who is also uncredited?

El Mariachi

(Spanish with English subtitles or dubbed)
(1993; Columbia TriStar; R; 1:21)

Starring: Carlos Gallardo, Consuelo Gomez
Written and directed by: Robert Rodriguez

Synopsis: Young "El Mariachi" (Gallardo) aspires to be the fourth generation of mariachis in his family, so he roams from town to town, playing and gaining experience. Unfortunately, he wanders into a sleepy little Mexican town where the criminal Azul, toting his automatic weapons in a guitar case, has begun a vendetta against his ex-partner Moco. Word gets around to beware of a dangerous hitman, all dressed in black and carrying a guitar case—a good description of El Mariachi. Moco's men mistake him for Azul and chase him through town, killing one another in the process. Beautiful bartender Domino (Gomez) agrees to hide him in her room above the bar. Too bad Moco gave her the place so she'd give herself to him. The sticky situation grows even more complicated when the guitar cases are accidentally switched. Can a simple singer of romantic ballads clear up the confusion and save his skin—and Domino's?
Discussion: So it's in Spanish. So what! With action like this, who needs dialog? *El Mariachi* is not your basic "guns and guitars" saga. It's a wild ride, full of exciting stunts and furiously-paced chase scenes. The direction is flamboyantly assured, and the flick has a healthy helping of self-effacing humor as well (particularly in the bath scene). My one complaint is with the dead-serious ending, which rather undercuts the film's earlier, picaresque sense of humor. But this ending might also be the single element that reminds us we're watching an original: an independent film, rather than a Hollywood cookie-cutter with a guaranteed happy ending. And that in itself is refreshing enough to overlook a small personal complaint.
Rent this one for: its excellent action sequences.
You'll (probably) like this if you liked: *Desperado* (sequel), *Red Rock West, A Fistful of Dollars, For A Few Dollars More*
Credentials: 1994 Independent Spirit Award: Best First Feature
Vidbits: • Rodriguez also acted as cinematographer, editor and co-producer (with Gallardo). • Shot in two weeks for $7,000—although rumor has it that considerable money was invested by Columbia to clean up the 16mm print enough for theatrical release. • Rodriguez earned about $3K of production money as a human guinea pig in lab tests of a cholesterol-reducing drug. • Rodriguez also wrote a book about making the film, *Rebel Without A Crew* (1995; Plume)

The Emerald Forest

(drama)

(1985; New Line; R; 1:53)

Starring: Powers Boothe, Charley Boorman, Meg Foster
Written by: Rospo Pallenberg
Directed by: John Boorman

Synopsis: Bill Markham (Boothe) is an engineer overseeing the construction of a dam in the heart of the Amazon. One day his young son Tommy wanders into the jungle and is spirited away by natives. Ten years later, the dam is nearly completed; meanwhile, "Tommé" (Boorman) has grown up among the Indians, integrating into the tribe. Still searching, Bill is attacked by warriors but rescued by Tommé, who was told in a vision to travel to this spot. Tommé believes Bill is a spirit from his dreams become flesh, but he will not return with Bill: the tribe is his home now. The natives escort Bill to "the edge of the world," where deforestation begins, but make a distressing discovery when they return to their village—one which will require Tommé to infiltrate the civilized city and search for Bill and the assistance only his knowledge can provide. The fate and future of Tommé's tribe depends on their cross-cultural cooperation.
Discussion: "When I was a boy, the edge of the world was far," the old chief says, spying on the bulldozers; "but it comes closer every year." Boorman's paean to the disappearing rainforest and its people reveals a filmmaker's eye for the majesty of the jungle, an anthropologist's mind for the indigenous culture and rituals, and a dramatist's heart, instilling it with emotional intensity. All of Brazil's problems are visible here, from the native's point of view: death of the rainforest; culture clashes between modern technology and scared ancient ways; natural balance versus progress. Tommé stands as a bridge between worlds, from whom we could all learn a lesson in respect for the native ways, emphasizing a balance between man and nature. The ending is dramatically satisfying magical realism, but unfortunately not a realistic solution to real problems. Still, *Forest* is a beautiful, intelligent, dramatic and anthropologically accurate action film with a message even more vital now than it was a decade ago.
Rent this one for: The breathtaking cinematography.
You'll (probably) like this if you liked: *The Searchers, At Play in the Fields of the Lord; Dances With Wolves* (native culture)
Dissenting Opinion: • "...lack of emotional empathy...and contrived storyline weaken overall impact..." —MMG • EW: "D"
Vidbit: • Charley Boorman, who plays adult Tommé, is director Boorman's son. • "Based on real events and actual characters."

Escape From New York

(science fiction)

(1981; New Line; R; 1:39; Director's Special Edition: 1:46)

Starring: Kurt Russell, Lee Van Cleef, Ernest Borgnine
Featuring: Donald Pleasence, Isaac Hayes, Harry Dean Stanton, Adrienne Barbeau, Season Hubley
Written by: John Carpenter and Nick Castle
Directed by (and music by): John Carpenter

Synopsis: The year is 1997. Following a nearly apocalyptic war, Manhattan has become virtually uninhabitable, and the entire island has been walled off and turned into a maximum security prison. There are no guards and no rules—and once you're in, you're in for life, which usually isn't very long. So when Air Force One crashes inside the walls, and the President of the United States (Donald Pleasance) is taken hostage by the feral felons, the authorities decide their best bet for a rescue is to send in war hero and anti-social anti-hero Snake Pliskin (Russell), a walking attitude problem. And to ensure he figures a way to spring the President from this living hell, they inject him with an explosive device on a timer. If he doesn't get out in time for the authorities to deactivate the device, he dies too.

Discussion: If you can just suspend your sense of disbelief long enough to swallow the impossible premise, it's easy to enjoy this high camp parody of post-apocalypse action flicks like *The Road Warrior* and *Blade Runner* — a parody produced even as these films were just becoming popular. While the action is off-beat, intriguing and beautifully directed, the real reason this movie stands out is its dark humor—and most of that revolves around its ensemble of bizarre characters: the pants-wetting President; enthusiastic cab driver Borgnine ("Wait'll I tell the fellas who I had in my cab!"); Hayes as the self-styled Duke of New York ("I'm A-Number One!"); and Stanton, sullenly wonderful as the brains behind the ruling regime on this modern Devil's Island. Even Russell goons it up, playing his snarling anarchist Pliskin as an imitation Clint Eastwood—much as he played his character in Carpenter's action comedy *Big Trouble In Little China* as a parody of John Wayne.

Rent this one for: its comic-book-style, over-the-top action; for its black humor; for its rabidly anti-authoritarian attitude.

You'll (probably) like this if you liked: *Big Trouble In Little China, Mad Max, The Road Warrior*

Dissenting Opinion: "For a 'fun' film this is pretty bleak." —MMG (2 stars)

Vidbit: The 1994 "Director's Special Edition" adds about ten minutes of footage and a 25-minute interview with Carpenter.

Flashback!

The Great Train Robbery

(AKA: "The First Great Train Robbery")

(comedy)

(1979; MGM/UA; PG; 1:41)

Starring: Sean Connery, Donald Sutherland, Leslie-Anne Down
Music by: Jerry Goldsmith
Written and directed by: Michael Crichton (based on his novel)

Synopsis: To pay soldiers during England's war in the Crimea in 1855, £25,000 in gold was transferred monthly from London by train. It's a powerful lure for elegant outlaw Edward Pearce (Connery). But in 1855, no one had ever robbed a moving train. With the aid of his mistress (Down) and an eccentric safecracker (Sutherland), Pearce embarks on a quest for four keys to the safe, then boards the train to heist the gold. But the rules of this game are in continual flux. Will their criminal wits prove quick enough to improvise Midas-like solutions?
Discussion: This exhilarating (and extravagantly costumed) period caper comedy is, first, a masterwork of structure. "Freeing" the keys takes three distinct "chapters," with the final pull in the station a sequence of breath-holding suspense. The highlight of the film, of course, is the actual robbery, and Crichton wisely lavishes the time necessary to present it in all its glory—and hackle-raising complications. The fabulous photography of the archaic train (provided by the Railway Preservation Society of Ireland) steaming through the lush Irish countryside, though, is just background for the daredevil stuntwork—much performed by Connery himself. Smoke, speed and head-level bridges compose his dangerous terrain—and soot and soiled suitcoats threaten ruin for the robbery. The music adds immeasurably to the fun, with its blend of exuberance, suspense and railroad rhythms. Connery is as insouciant as ever: dashing and debonair, a droll rogue full of devilishly clever double entendres. Down proves a saucy seductress with a flair for mannered comedy. And Sutherland provides wonderfully goofy comic counterpoint. We get more than we have a right to expect in the photography by Geoffrey Unsworth (who died in post-production, and to whom the film is dedicated), with his Monet-like composition and coloring in several scenes. A timeless film—and pure gold.
Rent this one for: its rousing, exuberant adventure.
You'll (probably) like this if you liked: *The Sting*
Vidbit: • Based on an actual incident. • Read Crichton's 1975 novel for a detailed background on the criminal culture of the time, and his *Travels* for an essay about the making of the film.

High Risk

(comedy)

(1981; Video Treasures; R; 1:34)

Starring: James Brolin, Anthony Quinn, Lindsay Wagner
Featuring: James Coburn, Bruce Davison, Cleavon Little, Chick Vennera, Ernest Borgnine
Written and directed by: Stewart Raffill

Synopsis: Four unemployed buds (Brolin, Davison, Little and Vennera), pessimistic about the economy and their future in it, sneak into Colombia to rob the safe of rich drug lord Serrano (Coburn). Their best-laid plans begin to go awry the moment they reach the safe; even so, they score $5 million in cash and escape into the jungle, chased all the way. Two are captured by soldiers on the take, and they escape from prison with trippy hippie chick Oli (Wagner). The others are captured by a tribe of *banditos* (headed by Quinn) and promptly robbed. Eventually they all make their way back to the rendezvous point, their swag intact, only to be pinned down between the money-hungry bandits and Serrano's highly-armed guards, while they await a rescue that might never arrive...
Discussion: Non-stop action, breathtaking scenery, giddy excitement, hair-raising stunts, plot twists every few minutes, and even a final surprise in the last shot... What more could you ask of an adventure flick? How about a couple of sly performances, like Coburn as the sadistic coke king, and Quinn as the aging bandito leader? Or the serpentine plot, pitting the pair of suburban commandos in cat-and-mouse games against two ruthless gangs? How about a healthy dose of good-natured humor? "You got a cause?" gun dealer Borgnine asks Brolin while arming him for the raid. "Inflation," Brolin dead-pans. Or Quinn's unrepentant confession that "We used to be rebels. Now we're just thieves." ("You came all the way from the rich United States just to steal from *this* poor country?" he asks Brolin, incredulously.) Or the clever method of dealing with Serrano's Dobermans. Or the new meaning given to the words "jail break." Or... Well, you get the picture: Never a dull moment.
Rent this one for: its good-natured, fleet-footed fun.
You'll (probably) like this if you liked: *Romancing the Stone*
Dissenting Opinion: • 1.5 bones —GMR • "...a lot of it is just plain awful." —VMG (2.5) • "Preposterous movie...Ridiculous story, but good fun." —MMG (2.5) • 1.5 stars —SMV
Vidbits: • Raffill is best known as writer/director of "family" flicks like *The Adventures of the Wilderness Family* (76) and *Mac and Me* (88). • Davison currently co-stars in TV's "Star Trek: Voyager." • Beware the recent cheap, muddy EP mode version.

La Femme Nikita

(1991; Vidmark; R; 1:57)
(French; subtitled. Letterboxed)

Starring: Anne Parillaud, Jean-Hughes Anglade, Tcheky Karyo
Featuring: Jeanne Moreau, Jean Reno
Written and Directed by: Luc Besson

Synopsis: Nikita (Parillaud) is just another feral punk junkie, who kills a cop in a robbery gone wrong. Mystery man "Bob" (Karyo) springs her from jail and gives her a second chance—and a choice: learn to be a professional assassin in the service of her government, or die. She becomes a "prisoner of finishing school," learning the A-to-Z's of everything from firearms to etiquette. Her fierce independent spirit works against her—until she finds her saving grace in her unexplored femininity, under the tutelage of aging agent Amande (Moreau). After a crash course in living by her wits, she "graduates" to the outside world with a new identity. She finds a flat and a gentle boyfriend and begins to live. Then one day she receives a phone call using her code name: an assignment. And then another... Can she find guts enough to live both lives, and keep them separate—or will they both crash down around her? Or is there another alternative, one that no one could possibly imagine?
Discussion: Leave it to the French to invent the "existentialist action movie." But don't think this stylish post-modern *noir* is only for intellectuals. The emphasis is on atmosphere and thrills, and subtitles are almost unnecessary to follow the physical and emotional action. Nikita's first outside exercise is spectacular action; the Venice hotel scene is an original, full of intense suspense; and the high point of the film is the visit from "Victor the cleaner"—a sequence not recommended for the squeamish. (Harvey Keitel played this role in the American remake, and then parodied the same role in *Pulp Fiction*). Parillaud is a killer Nikita (pun intended), seamlessly transforming the character through her multiple incarnations as animalistic urchin, angry student, pro hitwoman and eventually, a fully-developed woman who finds herself into a moral hole so deep that not even the love of two men can rescue her. Ultimately it "goes all French," ending with a shrug rather than a bang. But aside from this small (American) complaint, it's a savvy, slick and superb piece of suspense; smart and sly, tense and original.
Rent this one for: the acting; the action.
You'll (probably) like this if you liked: *Point of No Return*
Dissenting Opinion: "...drifts into a pale imitation of James Bond." —SMV (3 stars)
Vidbit: Remade as *Point of No Return* (1993) with Bridget Fonda.

Flashback!

The Man in the Iron Mask

(literary classic)

(1977; CBS/Fox, LIVE; NR; 1:48)

Starring: Richard Chamberlain, Patrick McGoohan, Louis Jourdan, Jenny Agutter, Ralph Richardson
Written by: William Bast (based on the novel by Alexandre Dumas)
Directed by: Mike Newell

Synopsis: When Fouquet (McGoohan), the sinister Minister of Finance for France, discovers that his king, Louis XIV (Chamberlain), has a twin brother, Phillipe (also Chamberlain)—the first-born, and therefore rightful heir to the throne—he and Louis conspire to rid themselves of this threat to "their" throne. Louis decrees that not a drop of royal blood will be spilled—but that no one is ever to look upon the face of this "pretender" again, lest he be recognized. Fouquet has the baffled Phillipe taken to a remote fortress and his entire head encased in a mask of iron. Unknown to Fouquet and Louis, however, Minister Colbert (Richardson) and his loyal Musketeer D'Artagnan (Jourdan) are also aware of the twin's existence, and risk treason to release him from this cruel captivity and place him on his throne, that he might save France from the capricious tyrant Louis.

Discussion: A lavish, sumptuous and admirably faithful production (shot in many of the actual locations of the novel) of a classic tale of romance and revenge, and of intrigue in the court, with its elaborate rituals of etiquette, where the fate of a nation can hinge on the color of one's sash and covert negotiations take place even on the ballroom floor. The cast is top-notch, with Chamberlain believable both as the effete monarch, pampered and petulant, and as his own tormented twin, who must heroically sacrifice his life as Phillipe for the good of the State. Agutter, as the chaste maiden caught between them, adds the necessary element of High Romance, and Richardson is a quiet delight as the underestimated Colbert, whose grasp on political manipulation outwits even the most devious. McGoohan, as always, is perfect, playing the real power behind the throne, the hypocritically sycophantic Fouquet, smirking and imperturbable. A rousing adaptation of an epic adventure, where history is a chess match, and even a king can become a pawn.

Rent this one for: the superb adaptation of an adventure classic; the incredible cast; the sets and costumes.

You'll (probably) like this if you liked: *The Three Musketeers The Four Musketeers, Dangerous Liaisons*

Credentials: "...acted with panache by a sterling cast." —MMG

Midnight Run

(comedy)

(1988; MCA; R; 2:03)

Starring: Robert DeNiro, Charles Grodin
Featuring: Yaphet Kotto, Dennis Farina, John Ashton
Music by: Danny Elfman
Written by: George Gallo
Directed and produced by: Martin Brest

Synopsis: Jonathan Mardukas (Grodin) is a Mob accountant who embezzled $15 million from Vegas wiseguy Jimmy Serrano (Farina). Jack Walsh (DeNiro) is a bounty hunter promised $100K by Jon's bail bondsman to find and deliver him within five days—and before Serrano whacks him. It's an easy gig; a midnight run. Jack finds Mardukas easily, but Jon can't fly: he has a panic attack on the plane and they're thrown off. They board a train from New York to L.A.—but they're made. Seems Serrano's goons are hot on their tail—as well as FBI agents and rival bounty hunter Marvin (Ashton). Jack and Jon take a bus —and they're found again. Now they'll have to make it to L.A. any way they can: by borrowed car, by stolen car, by foot, by freight, by hook or by crook. Can they outrun and outwit their numerous pursuers and stay one step ahead—and alive?
Discussion: Like *48 HRS.* or *Beverly Hills Cop,* the relationship between the two central characters is central to the story. And they're mirror images of one another. Jack is rabidly sarcastic; Jon, the voice of serene reason. Jack is overtly obnoxious; Jon, covertly obnoxious, full of disdain for Jack's lack of responsibility in all areas of his life. Yet this "Odd Couple" opposition is only the surface of the mirror: beneath their opposing styles, they discover a shared integrity and history. On their cross country jaunt they bicker, question, confess and commiserate, and eventually develop a begrudging respect for one another—all the while engaged in a cat-and-mouse game of capture and attempted escape. Grodin holds his own against DeNiro (no easy feat) and the two have a real chemistry. It's a canny, deftly directed action flick with a sharp script, expert chase scenes, smart plot twists and delightful dialog—as well as Farina as a Mafia don with the most creative threats in cinema history.
Rent this one for: the performances, dialog and action scenes.
You'll (probably) like this if you liked: *Beverly Hills Cop* (Brest); *48 HRS. High Risk; Silver Streak, The Chase*
Vidbits: • Grodin told *Entertainment Weekly* (1/95) that *Midnight Run* was "the best movie I've done." • Brest cast Grodin against the wishes of the studio, who wanted Robin Williams.

Runaway Train

(1985; MGM/UA; R; 1:52)

Starring: Jon Voight, Eric Roberts, Rebecca de Mornay
Written by: Djordje Milicevic, Paul Zindel, Edward Bunker
(based on a screenplay by Akira Kurosawa)
Directed by: Andrei Konchalovsky

Synopsis: Hardcore convict "Manny" (Voight) escapes from a maximum security prison in Alaska, his young hero-worshipper Buck (Roberts) in tow. It's 30 below, however, and they're miles from anywhere—except a railroad yard. They hop a snow-covered freight train, but when the engineer has a heart attack, the cons are on their own. Throttle jammed wide open, brakes burned off, the train barrels through the icy wilderness. The cons find yard worker Sara (de Mornay) on board, but she only complicates efforts to save themselves. On a parallel track, the Warden (Kyle T. Heffner) relentlessly chases his strays, while railroad officials must decide whether to derail the train, spelling certain death for the passengers, or let it plow into a toxic chemical plant. Good, bad or ugly—they're all in this alone.
Discussion: Manny "believes in nothing. He's capable of anything," says the Warden, branding him "not a man. An animal." Manny's an animal who's read Nietzsche, though, growling that "whatever doesn't kill me makes me stronger." *Train* is full of furious action, beautiful photography, and surprisingly intelligent dialog for an action flick. Or *is* it just an action flick? Maybe it's an existentialist parable *disguised* as an action flick, reminding us we're all prisoners on that runaway train of Life, hurtling toward our inevitable destinies and in control of only a few ominous options. Or maybe it's a fast-paced Freudian fable, with Buck as Ego, trapped between the savage, self-serving demands of Manny-as-id and the faith in her fellow humans of superego Sara, who counts on a miracle to rescue them. Or maybe it's just a damn good action flick. As the film's philosophical railroad boss shrugs, "Some things can't be explained."
Rent this one for: The performances...and, of course, the breathtaking photography of the speeding train.
You'll (probably) like this if you liked: *Under Siege 2* (train mayhem); *Silver Streak, Back to the Future III* (comic versions).
Credentials: • 1985 Academy Award nominations: Best Actor (Voight); Best Supporting Actor (Roberts); Film Editing. • 1986 Golden Globe Award: Best Actor—Drama (Voight).
Dissenting Opinion: "Violent, foul-mouthed melodrama with no interest beyond the breathtaking photography of the speeding train. Its general pretentiousness, perhaps, is also something to experience." —HFG

The Stunt Man

(comedy)

(1980; CBS/Fox; R; 2:09)

Starring: Peter O'Toole, Steve Railsback, Barbara Hershey
Featuring: Chuck Bail, Alex Rocco, Allen Goorwitz, Sharon Farrell
Written by: Richard Rush, Lawrence B. Marcus
(based on the novel by Paul Brodeur)
Directed and produced by: Richard Rush

Synopsis: Escaping arrest, Cameron (Railsback) stumbles onto the location shoot of a WWI action flick. Megalomaniacal director Eli Cross (O'Toole) convinces him to hide from the law by replacing the star's stunt double—whom one of the two accidentally sent to his death. "New Burt" quickly integrates himself into the craziness of moviemaking, romancing actress Nina (Hershey), and playing a dangerous game of escalating stunts designed by Eli. Are they just engaged in macho posturing? Or is one completely out of his mind? Or are *both?* Is Nina Burt's girl, or part of Eli's plan? And can Burt survive Eli's ultimate stunt?
Discussion: "If God could do the tricks that we can do, He'd be a happy man!" proclaims Eli Cross in this homage to John Huston (who earlier played "Noah Cross" in *Chinatown*). Like Huston, director Eli engages in shameless manipulation, pushes everyone to the edge, and gets away with murder—here, literally. Eli's point of view is that reality depends on your point of view—as long as it's his. The film follows his lead, daring us to guess whether it's "real" real or "reel" real. There's plenty of comic action in the film-within-the-film, the occasional brilliant line, intense emotional revelations, levels of deception that add depth to everyone's story, and a number of aggressively "fooled-ya" stunt sequences to feed our need for illusion and belief.
Rent this one for: The skillful interweaving of movie reality and real reality; the performances; the suspense; the fun stunts.
You'll (probably) like this if you liked: *White Hunter, Black Heart* (Huston portrayals); *F/X, Hooper, Almost Hollywood*
Credentials: • 1980 Oscar nominations: Best Actor (O'Toole); Adapted Screenplay; Director. • 1981 Golden Globe: Best Score. • 1980 Montreal World Film Festival: Best Film. • 1980 National Board of Review Awards: 10 Best Films of Year. • 1980 National Society of Film Critics Award: Best Actor (O'Toole) • "Ambitious, demanding, and remarkably rewarding..." —SMV (★★★★)
Dissenting Opinion: "...portentous and mannered..." —Stanley Kaufmann, *New Republic*
Vidbit: • Filmed at the Del Coronado Hotel in San Diego. • It took Rush nine years to get this film going—and two more years after completion to get it released. • How tall is King Kong?

COMEDY

Comedy

There is nothing in this world as subjective as comedy. As Buck Henry says, "The scary thing is, no one *really knows* what's funny."* On the other hand, we *all* know what we like. Perhaps that accounts for the existence of the multitude of subgenres of comedy.

My own biases appear most prominently in this section, which leans heavily toward black comedies, romantic comedies, and wacky, anarchic, adolescent scatological fun-fests with no redeeming social value other than a good belly-laugh. (According to Norman Cousins, however, a sufficient quantity of belly-laughter is *indeed* a cure for cancer!)

Enjoy!

* Henry's statement is not entirely accurate. There is, in point of fact, *one thing* that is indisputably, universally and perpetually funny: *monkeys*.

Almost Hollywood

(1994; York; R; 1:40)

Starring: India Allen, Don Short, Rachel Dyer
Featuring: Greg Scott, Scott Apel, "Johnny Hollywood"
Written and directed by: Michael Weaver

Synopsis: Tony (Short) is at the top of the bottom of the movie business, cranking out cheesy, sleazy soft-core porn thrillers at "Straight To Video Productions." But his whole world begins to unravel when his investors have an "art attack" and bring in India Allen (Allen), a bitchy bimbo and fourth-rate video star who demands script approval, fires Tony's favorite director, Abdu (Apel), and appoints her airhead film-school boyfriend as her writer-director. Even worse, Tony's mistress and former star Kristen (Dyer) is discovered dead on the set. Tony's the obvious suspect, and he's such a bastard that everyone believes he did it. But did he? If not, then who did—and why? If there's any justice in the world, the real killer will be caught. But will India ever get her big break? Not if there's any justice in the world...
Discussion: You've seen plenty of them in video stores: tapes with titles like *Bedroom Eyes* and *Night Eyes,* usually starring some blonde named "Shannon" sporting lingerie and a pistol. Ever since *Basic Instinct,* these cut-rate, rip-off "erotic thrillers" have been the hottest form of direct-to-video films. Weaver has obviously worked on a few: he's got a gimlet eye for the details of the genre, combined with a true talent for lively dialog ("My artistic vision includes pubic hair!" *faux*-Pakistani director Abdu screams at a shy actress) and a born director's sense of cinematic magic (are the murders we're watching real, or part of the film-within-the-film?). The acting ranges from abysmal (Allen) to hilarious ("Johnny Hollywood" as agent Sid DeSilva). And keep an eye on the guy who plays "Abdu"—he might just be the new Peter Sellers! Cutting comedy and satirical suspense combine in this long-overdue skewering of the mini-industry, which simultaneously provides a fascinating insight into the mechanics—and the machinations—of low-budget filmmaking.
Rent this for: its satirical insight into low-budget productions.
You'll (probably) like this if you liked: *The Player, My Life's In Turnaround, Living in Oblivion, The Big Picture, Mistress*
Dissenting Opinion: • No listing; no review —VMG • Ditto —MMG • Ditto —GMR • Ditto —SMV
Vidbits: • India Allen was Playboy's "Playmate of the Year" sometime around 1935, I think. • Uncredited cameos: The lead singer of the band making the music video is Dean Cain, "Superman" in TV's "Lois and Clark." The other two band members are the film's producers, Dan Kaplow and Winter Horton.

Around the World in 80 Ways

(1986; Charter Entertainment; R; 1:30)

Starring: Philip Quast, Diana Davidson, Allan Penney, Kelly Dingwall, Gosia Dobrowolska, Rob Steele
Written by: Stephen MacLean, Paul Leadon
Directed by: Stephen MacLean

Synopsis: Wally Davis (Quast) is an entrepreneur in trouble. His Queensland tour company has been repossessed—a flashback to his parents' problem. Dad Roly (Penney) lost the family business to unscrupulous partner/neighbor Alec Moffat (Steele), then declined into "galloping senility," losing his sight and use of his legs. Mom Mavis (Davidson) embarks on an around-the-world trip (stuck next to Alec) before Wally can put the squeeze on her. But Roly's got a secret stash, and is determined to follow his wife before Moffat steals her, too. So Wally and his recording expert brother Eddie (Dingwall) stage an "audio tour" to separate dad from his cash, using props and costumes, cardboard cutouts and neighborhood locations, taking advantage of Roly's blurry, limited vision. They even bring along a nurse (Dobrowolska) Eddie's got a crush on, who treats Roly with health foods, vitamins and physical therapy. They "travel" to Hawaii, see Elvis in Vegas, and even wangle an audience with The Pope. Roly begins perking up, feeling younger. And seeing better...
Discussion: The irony is that Roly's *faux* tour turns out to be far more fun than Mavis' pre-packaged junket, where she's stuck next to the obnoxious Moffat, where they're herded like sheep to cheese factories—and where she even misses seeing "the bloody Pope." And of course Roly wreaks ironic revenge against the home wrecker by literally wrecking his home. Wally is a wizard, faking everything from airplane takeoffs to a Christmas blizzard using little more than sound effects and quicksilver character changes. Whole sections of the flick are laugh-out-loud funny: Wally's mumbling Elvis impersonation, for instance, and Roly's confession to the Pope (surrounded by a host of nuns made from inflatable sex dolls). There's a dose of juvenile humor (the nurse's name is "Ophelia Cox"—need we say more?) and the whole film is so thick with Aussie accents that it really needs to be subtitled. But aside from these minor errors in judgment, the flick is wacky, fast-paced and addled; exuberant and goofy; utterly original and full of clever inventiveness; in short, it's an off-kilter comedy that's the closest thing in tone and temperament to a Monty Python movie since they quit making them.
Rent this one for: its good dumb fun as a feel-good farce.
You'll (probably) like this if you liked: Monty Python
Dissenting Opinion: "...just not very funny." — VMG (2 stars)

Bagdad Café

(1988; Virgin Vision; PG; 1:31)

Starring: Marianne Sägebrecht, CCH Pounder, Jack Palance
Written by: Eleonore and Percy Adlon, Christopher Doherty
Directed by: Percy Adlon

Synopsis: An angry German tourist leaves his matronly wife and her suitcase on the side of a Nevada desert highway after an argument. Hours later, Jasmine (Sägebrecht) walks into the Bagdad Cafe, just after owner Brenda's (Pounder) husband has walked out on her. The slovenly, filthy and scattered condition of this truckstop motel—and of the lives of its denizens—disgusts Jasmine's orderly Aryan sensibilities. She cleans a bit. Then a bit more. Then a *lot* more. Brenda goes ballistic, but slowly grows to appreciate the effort—and the order. Meanwhile, Rudi Cox (Palance), silk-voiced, satin-bloused desert artist insists on painting Jasmine's portrait—repeatedly, and each time with a bit less clothing. Jasmine takes up hand-magic as a hobby and enchants the patrons. The place becomes a cabaret, a pit-stop Las Vegas. Business booms, until...
Discussion: But I can say no more. Much of the fun of this gentle entry lies in its unpredictability; we can never be sure where all this is going, where it will lead, or even what will happen next. How delightful to find a determinedly non-formulaic film! We can, however, be sure that whatever happens will be affectionately eccentric, and that plot points will hinge on character, not vice versa. *Cafe* is essentially a low-key comedy about culture clashes; of assimilation and changes. America is supposed to be a melting pot; maybe the desert heat speeds the process, as Brenda's anger boils off and Jasmine transforms from stodgy *hausfrau* to radiant angel—a Ruben-esque cherub. It *is* magic, as illustrated by Jasmine's hobby—but it's not illusion: it's the real magic of finding a niche, and the magic of humans connecting, no matter how unlikely the people, places or circumstances. It's about the magic of the ubiquitous boomerang: that what comes around, goes around.
Rent this one for: Palance; its unpredictable magic; its heart.
You'll (probably) like this if you liked: *City Slickers* (Palance); *Moscow on the Hudson, Coming To America* (befuddled "fish out of water"); *Mediterraneo* (cultural assimilation)
Credentials: • 1988 Academy Award nomination: Best Song ("Calling You"—still a haunting song even if it was co-opted for a phone commercial) • 1989 Cesar Award: Best Foreign Film
Vidbits: • Shot in Newberry Springs, Calif. • CCH Pounder went on to co-star on TV's *ER*.

Barbarians at the Gate

(1993; HBO; R; 1:47)

Starring: James Garner, Jonathan Pryce, Peter Riegert
Featuring: Joanna Cassidy, Fred Dalton Thompson, Leilani Ferrer
Written by: Larry Gelbart
(based on the book by Bryan Burrough and John Helyar)
Directed by: Glenn Jordan

Synopsis: It's 1988, and Ross Johnson (Garner) is Golden Boy: the high-powered CEO of RJR Nabisco, complete with Lear jet and trophy wife (Ferrer). He sprays money like urine, despite low stock prices, betting everything on a new "smokeless" cigarette. When they end up tasting "like shit," the only way to save his job is a leveraged buy-out (LBO): raising enough money to buy out the shareholders so he and his team can own and run the company. It has to happen quickly and quietly, or a feeding frenzy of potential buyers will be attracted to the undervalued company—people like Henry Kravis (Pryce), who virtually invented the LBO, and is pissed that Ross didn't come to him first, as he originally suggested this. Revenge, mismanagement, betrayal and abrasive egos turn a fierce and fearsome bidding war into a pissing contest, as the men try to grab the brass ring.
Discussion: Quite a story—one which proves fact is indeed stranger than fiction, at least when it comes to corporate greed in the excessive, extravagant '80s. In addition to a crash course in LBOs and the story of the biggest deal in history, we get a peek at the Lifestyles of the Rich and Executive: country estates and Monets, stretch limos and jet rides for the dog; cigars, suspenders and people who wield cell phones like six-shooters. The dialog is sparkling, often hilarious, and always delivered with deadly comic accuracy; the action fast and furious, jetting from boardrooms to backrooms to bedrooms to bathrooms (*lots* of bathrooms). Pryce is priceless as intense, humorless juggernaut Kravis, more concerned about his credibility as a player than the deal; Riegert specializes in playing Yuppie Scum; and Garner gives a gung-ho "good-old-boy" performance, sporting a colorful vocabulary and 3-D personality, with Hero Ross more worried about layoffs than leverages, while Villain Ross takes personal perks and corporate greed to new—unfair—levels. Altogether, it's an intelligent, adult comedy—with dramatic implications.
Rent this one for: Garner's performance; the witty script; a tale so unbelievable it had to be presented as satire and parody.
You'll (probably) like this if you liked: *The Hudsucker Proxy; Wall Street, All The President's Men* (serious)
Vidbits: • Originally a made-for-HBO movie. • Cameos (on TVs) by Dick Cavett and Tom Brokaw. • The final price: $25.7 billion.

Barcelona

(1994; Turner, New Line; R; 1:42)

Starring: Taylor Nichols, Chris Eigeman, Mira Sorvino
Written, produced and directed by: Whit Stilman

Synopsis: Barcelona, Spain, in the late '80s: Stuttering Chicago salesman Ted (Nichols), a 20-something with a "romantic illusion problem" receives a visit from career Navy man Fred (Eigeman), his cousin and sibling rival. Both are much more interested in their social lives (i.e., girls) than in their careers, however. Making the circuit of the hip, young "party & politics" scene, they meet girls, lose girls and obsess about girls (and, in off moments, about their careers). They find themselves in curiously parallel career and relationship crises. And then one day Fred's romantic hogwash backfires on him—politically, ironically and tragically. Can the American boys overcome cultural misconceptions, political ostracism and their own career confusions to win the girls of their dreams? Will they ever forget "The Incident" that occurred when they were ten, and stop sniping at one another? And will they *ever* understand why these foreigners won't just get over themselves and act like Americans?
Discussion: Call it *Annie Hall Abroad;* it's a relationship comedy about a pair of uptight, conservative American Yuppies thrown into a hip, sexually liberated environment. And it's a buddy flick, as the cousins bicker continually, as they've done since they were kids. It's a cross-cultural comedy as well, as the boys find themselves entirely out of their league debating politics with anti-American Europeans who discuss politics as facilely as Americans discuss celebrities. It's a fish-out-of-water flick: the American boys, for instance, attempt to be "retro" among the ultrahip Eurotrash who, ironically, haven't caught on yet that retro is more cutting edge than they are. Simultaneously, it's a sweet, off-kilter, coming-of-age comedy bursting with hilarious insights into cultural differences and confusions. (The Barcelonans constantly accuse the U.S. of being a land of crime, consumerism, vulgarity and fascism, so Fred must explain to the freedom-seeking girls that Ted isn't "a fascist of the marrying kind." But when the girls are given a chance to *live* here, well...) The dialog is smart, sharp and witty; comically arch, exaggeratedly overintellectual, and delivered with a deadpan sincerity which only enhances its laugh-out-loud content. It's an insightful satire with a good heart, gently poking fun at the troubles between genders no matter what their cultural background.
Rent this one for: its intelligent and hilarious dialog.
You'll (probably) like this if you liked: *Trust, Annie Hall, Metropolitan, My Life's In Turnaround* (doubling the guys' IQs)

Flashback!

Bedazzled

(1968; CBS/Fox; PG; 1:47)

Starring: Peter Cook, Dudley Moore, Eleanor Bron
Written by: Peter Cook
Music by: Dudley Moore
Directed by: Stanley Donen

Synopsis: Pity poor Stanley Moon (Moore). The shy short-order chef is alone, unloved, penniless and on the brink of suicide. Enter the debonair Mr. George Spiggot (Cook), who is in fact The Devil Himself, engaged in a gentlemen's bet with God to see who can collect a billion souls first. Stanley exchanges his for the traditional seven wishes, but Spiggot is dishonor-bound to take full advantage of any loopholes, which naturally turns the tables on Stanley in every one of his seven deadly scenarios.
Discussion: Long before Moore became a solo star in *10,* he was "Dud," the working-class half of the comedy team of Peter Cook and Dudley Moore. Which one was funnier? Submitted for your approval...The script for *Bedazzled,* by Peter Cook. This satirical update of the Faust legend is brilliant in its ability to wring every possible alternative from the seven wishes chestnut, and then counteract each increasingly precise set-up with an even more whimsical knock-down. Thick Stanley grows savvier each time a wish is effortlessly decimated—but what hope does he have of outwitting the Lord of Illusions? What really holds the film together is the friendship and mutual respect that develops between George and Stanley. They are in essence kindred spirits—both misunderstood souls. As they spend time together wandering around London, playing dirty tricks and talking philosophy and religion, George explains life and its trials from his point of view, and we gain some sympathy for the Devil. (He has problems, too. He can't get any good Sins to work for him, for one. "Must be the wages," he muses.) Satan has been portrayed in many ways, but Cook's version—an irrepressible, mischievous prankster, ordered to be obnoxious by a humorless God—is certainly the most sympathetic vision ever. Sly and subversive, intelligent and inventive, *Bedazzled* is a timeless comedy classic: deadpan, daring and demonically dazzling.
Rent this one for: its hysterically radical theology; for its wacky and inventive wish vignettes.
You'll (probably) like this if you liked: *The Witches of Eastwick, Monty Python and the Holy Grail, The Magic Christian*
Credentials: "...a great comedy." —PEF
Vidbits: Raquel Welch made her screen debut as "Lillian Lust," one of the Devil's Seven Deadly Sins assistants.

The Best of Times

(1986; Embassy Home Entertainment; PG-13; 1:44)

Starring: Robin Williams, Kurt Russell
Featuring: Pamela Reed, Holly Palance, M. Emmet Walsh, Donald Moffat, Kirk Cameron, R.G Armstorng
Written by: Ron Shelton
Directed by: Roger Spottiswoode

Synopsis: Every year for decades, the Taft, CA, high school football team is trounced by arch-rival Bakersfield—until 1972, when Taft produces ace quarterback Reno Hightower (Russell). With only seconds left in a scoreless game, Reno passes to Jack Dundee (Williams), and is crushed by the other team; his knees broken; any hope of a pro career ruined. Worst of all, Jack fumbles the pass—and the trauma has haunted him ever since. 13 years later, Jack's a wreck: a neurotic coward fixated on that dropped ball. Reno's no better off; he's lost his drive and now his wife Gigi (Reed). "If I'd just caught that ball my whole life would be different!" Jack wails. And inspiration strikes: Why not restage the game, re-run the play and *get it right this time?* Jack will do anything to get the town to go gung-ho over the game. But has he got guts enough to risk his marriage *and* multiplying his humiliation—and focus enough to catch that damn ball?
Discussion: It's not about football, really. It's about the war—or the game—between men and women. No screenwriter alive understands the jock mentality better than Shelton, and few understand women as well either. Does Jack catch the ball? Let me say this: *It just doesn't matter.* The game, the play, even the original fumble, are merely focal points: catalysts for the change these lovable lethargics desperately need. And that outcome could occur in either case. This sprightly, insightful and ultimately uplifting fable about how one neurotic's obsession can become a dream that inspires an entire town uses football as a metaphor for the redemption of spirit, love and life. Whether he grabs that ball or not, he grabs his own life by the balls—and by pursuing his own wacky dream changes the lives of everyone in Taft. And as a bonus, in the women's dressing room scene, we get an honest answer to the question, "What do men want?"
Rent this one for: its sparkling dialog; its witty insight into the ultimate sport: the game between men and women.
You'll (probably) like this if you liked: *Bull Durham, White Men Can't Jump, Tin Cup* (Shelton sports/relationship comedies); *Slap Shot, Semi-Tough*
Dissenting Opinion: • "...seemingly surefire film becomes too strident (and too exaggerated) to really score." —MMG (2.5 stars) • "Lots of rah-rah but no sis-boom-bah." —SMV (2 stars)

The Big Picture

(1989; RCA/Columbia; PG-13; 1:40)

Starring: Kevin Bacon, J.T. Walsh, Michael McKean
Featuring: Jennifer Jason Leigh, Teri Hatcher, Emily Longstreth
Written by: Michael Varhol, Christopher Guest, Michael McKean
Directed by: Christopher Guest

Synopsis: When student filmmaker Nick Chapman (Bacon) wins a prestigious film award, Hollywood doors swing open for him. What he doesn't know is that they're trap doors. Explaining his script for a sensitive feature film about intimacy and relationships to studio producer Alan Habel (Walsh), for instance, Habel suggests a rewrite with his favorite spin, "two women together." *Uh*-oh... Other trap doors include big-haired bimbo starlet Gretchen (Hatcher), who threatens Nick's relationship with long-time live-in Susan (Longstreth); and the chance to work with idols at the expense of friends who need a break, like his cameraman Emmet (McKean). And there are revolving doors, as well: when Habel goes through one and is ousted, Nick's project is put "in turnaround." Alone, broke and unemployable, Nick drops out of sight, only to discover that revolving doors can turn full circle—and that at the end of the day, you're never hotter in Tinseltown than when you're not available.
Discussion: "Flavor of the week! Getcher flavor of the week!" So goes the battle cry in a town that eats young talent for lunch and shits 'em out before dinner. Nick just wants to make movies. He *thinks* like a movie, and we get frequent mind's-eye views of his scenes and fantasies. But he's a victim of the seductive glamour of Hollywood, where image is everything, and making a deal is more important than making a film. This directorial debut of Guest (one of the industry's most underrated talents) is as much a tale of hubris ruining the important things in life as it is a pretension-shattering, gimlet-eyed satire of modern Hollywood, and it works both ways. The performances are a delight, too. Walsh, parodying his own humorless image, plays deadpan with aplomb; Martin Short (appearing uncredited) has never been weirder; and as for Hatcher, it's no wonder she became a sex symbol—the only question is why it took so long.
Rent this one for: Guest nibbling on the hand that feeds him.
You'll (probably) like this if you liked: *The Player, Almost Hollywood, My Life's In Turnaround, Living in Oblivion, Sweet Liberty* (Hollywood satires); *Spinal Tap* (written by and costarring Guest and McKean); *Dream On*
Vidbits: • Keep an eye out for "Special Appearances" by: Elliott Gould, Eddie Albert, Stephen Collins, June Lockhart, Roddy McDowall, Fran Drescher, John Cleese and Richard Belzer.

Cadillac Man

(1990; Orion; R; 1:35)

Starring: Robin Williams, Tim Robbins, Pamela Reed
Featuring: Fran Drescher, Zack Norman, Annabella Sciorra,Lori Petty
Written by: Ken Friedman
Directed by: Roger Donaldson

Synopsis: There's a word for people like Joey O'Brien (Williams): *sleaze.* But he's a super car salesman. He could sell a hearse to a funeral procession, then hit on the widow. *Sleaze.* Joey's got problems, though: 1.) He's got to sell a dozen cars in one day or he's history on the lot; 2.) He's having a go-nowhere affair with a whiny married woman (Drescher); 3.) He owes 20K to the local wiseguy; 4.) He's still in love with his ex-wife, Tina (Reed), who *knows* he's a sleaze. And on the day of the Big Sale, he gets The Big Problem: Secretary Donna's (Sciorra) whacked out hubby Larry (Robbins) shows up with an automatic weapon and takes the whole showroom hostage, bent on revenge against the salesman who slept with his wife. Surprise—it's not Joey! But guess who takes the rap, taking the heat off his boss? Can Joey pull off the sales job of his life, negotiating with cops and kook to make sure this "little domestic dispute" doesn't turn tragic?
Discussion: Joey's mission is to talk the guy down, using the same golden tongue that's earned him his problems in the first place. He's playing hostage negotiator and marriage counselor—with no cooperation from anybody, which doesn't help his escalating irritation. Even though this movie is filled with big stars just before they became big stars, maybe no one wanted to see Robin Williams as an irascible sleaze, or Tim Robbins as an innocent dimwit. Or maybe what kept audiences away in droves was the unlikely combination of screwball comedy and loud, nasty cynicism. But the film is full of delicious comic observations ("What kind of foundation for a relationship is that," Joey asks Larry, "calling your wife a 'lying bitch whore'?"), sharp dialog ("You didn't shoot a cop," Joey babbles to Larry. "You shot a *foot.* Maybe just a *shoe.*"), escalating absurdity (Joey's ex- and mother threatening Larry on the phone) and the world's rudest waitress (Lauren Tom), tougher than the NYPD and the Mafia put together. In this crucible, Joey finally learns the difference between bullshit and horseshit, sells both sides to avert disaster, and solves all his problems with his desperate gesture.
Rent this one for: the performances; the nasty, edgy humor.
You'll (probably) like this if you liked: *Dog Day Afternoon*
Dissenting Opinion: "Wildly uneven film tests the mettle of even the staunchest Williams fans...Infuriating at times, then occasionally redeemed by a great moment." —MMG (2.5 stars)

Captain Ron

(1992; Touchstone; PG-13; 1:40)

Starring: Kurt Russell, Martin Short
Featuring: Mary Kay Place, Meadow Sisto, Benjamin Salisbury
Written and directed by: Thom Eberhardt

Synopsis: Winter in Chicago. Yuck! The good news for Martin Harvey (Short): His uncle is dead and he's left Marty his boat. The one catch: To sell it, he's got to sail it from St. Potato Island in the Caribbean to Miami. The bad news is it's a barely seaworthy, ramshackle old ship. So he hires barely seaworthy Capt. Ron (Russell) to skipper the ship. Ron's a stoned-out, zoned out, gruff, eye patch-wearing, fast-talking, uh...*non-conformist.* He takes the Harvey family for a ride, big time, warning them about the Pirates of the Caribbean (who they end up shipping to their revolution) and sailing them to the wrong islands—like Cuba. When they find themselves in real trouble, can they use what Capt. Ron has taught them about spontaneity, resourcefulness and bravado to discover some real Family Values—like survival?
Discussion: Screw the meanings and "messages." Call it what you want—slapstick road movie set on the high seas; feel-good fish-out-of-water flick; dopey no-brainer—movies like *Captain Ron* were never meant for critics, they were meant for fun. The minimal message in this family flick can be summed up by bumper stickers ("Lighten up") or beer slogans ("Life's too short not to grab all the gusto you can"). What it's *really* about is having fun, and Ron gives this tight-ass family a crash course in partying heartily. It's not a film to be analyzed, it's a flick to be shared. And so, my favorite scenes: the sleeping eye patch gag; Ron and Ben playing Monopoly (Ron's relationship with the kids is unusual, but, as in *Uncle Buck,* exactly what they need); raunchy Ron with the camcorder; con man Ron's rapid recovery from a broken leg ("I've always been a fast healer. 'Course, I believe in Jesus..."). Let's not overrate *Ron.* It's no cure for cancer; it's a formula flick. But here the formula is applied to an unusual setting with original gags; it ends on a high note; and really, it doesn't need any justification to be just funny.
Rent this one for: Russell's energetic, lovable rogue; the inventive, goofy situations; the gorgeous Caribbean photography.
You'll (probably) like this if you liked: *Used Cars, Overboard* (Russell); *Uncle Buck, Neighbors, Planes, Trains and Automobiles*
Dissenting Opinion: • "...sinks like a stone." —GMR (1.5 bones) • "Dreadful timewaster..." —MMG (BOMB)
Vidbits: One of the few flicks in this book that made an appearance on the weekly top ten video rentals lists. But it was so roundly trashed critically, I felt it deserved a second chance.

The Chase

(1993; FoxVideo; PG-13; 1:28)

Starring: Charlie Sheen, Kristy Swanson
Featuring: Josh Mostel, Ray Wise, Henry Rollins, Claudia Christian
Written and directed by: Adam Rifkin

Synopsis: Jack Hammond (Sheen) is having a bad day. Falsely convicted of armed robbery, he escapes, until cops corner him in an L.A. quickie mart. To escape again, he kidnaps a Valley Girl and hijacks her BMW. Aaaaand the chase is on! Can things get worse? Oh, yeah. Jack's hostage is Natalie Voss (Swanson), daughter of übermillionaire Dalton Voss (Wise). They hit "The 5," heading for Mexico, the cops in hot pursuit. Voss commandeers the cops and calls Jack on the BMW's car phone. Threats turn to negotiation—and quickly degenerate into dysfunctional family psychodrama. Jack and Nat the Brat do therapy on the run. They trash her dad. They have some laughs and sympathize with each others' situation. Hounded by the law, the parents and the idiot media, will the two young falling-in-lovers manage to make it to Mexico without tragedy?
Discussion: Most modern movies have a car chase. This movie *is* a car chase—pure, but hardly simple. It's also a savage satire of The Media, from the "reality TV" crew in one cop car to the "Hardcore News" crews risking their lives for a peek inside the BMW, to the vapid, vacuous anchor teams providing live coverage of "Terror on the Freeway!" Everywhere anyone looks, TV cameras are pointing: at Jack, at the cops, at other TV people. And while the media circus clowns around, Jack and Nat are actually communicating. In the end, there is ironic justice in their using the media against itself and for their own survival. It ain't Shakespeare, but it's got a freeway-fast pace and action-packed direction, some wild stunts, and more car crashes than any flick since *The Blues Brothers*. More importantly, it's got sympathetic characters, some sparkling dialog, and a quicksilver performance from the usually laconic Sheen. Predictable fluff—but funny.
Rent this one for: the action, the dialog, and the satire.
You'll (probably) like this if you liked: *Smokey and the Bandit, Love and a .45, Sugarland Express, Cannonball Run*
Dissenting Opinion: • "Avoid this frivolous action-comedy... A predictable yarn." —VMG (2 stars) • "...which studio exec gave this the green light?" —MMG (1.5 stars)
Vidbits: • Sheen Executive Produced. • Stay tuned after the closing credits for a bonus scene: Sheen in full clown makeup reciting Duvall's "napalm/victory" speech from *Apocalypse Now*. • Red Hot Chili Peppers Flea and Anthony Kiedis appear as the monster truckers. • Shot not in L.A. but in Houston.

Cheech and Chong's Next Movie

(1980; MCA; R; 1:35)

Starring: Richard "Cheech" Marin, Thomas "Tommy" Chong
Featuring: Evelyn Guerrero, Edie McClurg, Rikki Marin
Written by: Thomas Chong, Cheech Marin
Directed by: Thomas Chong

Synopsis: A day in the life of a pair of slovenly stoners. They torment their prissy neighbor. They trick out their van to drive through the barrio. They apply for Welfare. Cheech ships Chong off to meet his redneck cousin Red (also Marin), who just blew into town with a satchel full of buds. Red and Tommy wander into a Hollywood massage parlor and fake a raid. They meet a rich girl who takes them home. They take her and her parents to a comedy club and start a riot. Tommy and Red score a car and get picked up by a UFO. Meanwhile, Cheech falls asleep waiting for his date to arrive, and has zoot suit dreams and album cover fantasies. That's *it,* man—just another typical wasted day.

Discussion: When people speak of C&C's film career, the single highlight mentioned is usually their first feature, *Up In Smoke.* From there it was all downhill. Except for this, their second feature, in which—by genius or accident—they managed to get everything right. (Probably by accident, as their every later effort sucked.) The result is a rambling odyssey through L.A., and a politically incorrect caricature of its ethnic stereotypes. It's got its share of gross jokes and bad taste (that's a given), but it's also got some great lines ("I been late for work five times this week, and it's only Tuesday"), and gags (like Tommy's stoned version of a magic trick in the club), and scenes (Cheech's song, "Mexican Americans," is a gem: punchlines set to music) and idiot anarchy. (When the UFO blasts a blue light into their car, Red puts his hand in it. "Hey, don't put your hand in there, man!" Tommy warns, inserting his own hand.) The surprise is that it's so funny. The better surprise is that it's *still* so funny.

Rent this one: because it takes a lot of clever to be this dumb.

You'll (probably) like this if you liked: *Up In Smoke, Caddyshack, Wayne's World,* "Beavis and Butt-Head"

Dissenting Opinion: • "Totally repulsive...gives a bad name to self-indulgence." —HFG • "...[the] comic duo go seriously awry in the crude, incoherent film..." —MMG (1.5 stars)

Vidbits: • C&C hired lots of friends from the L.A. comedy scene to appear in this flick—many of whom have gone on to fame in their own right. Look for Paul "Pee-Wee Herman" Reubens as the snotty hotel clerk, for instance, and SNL's Phil Hartman as the voice of "Chick Hazard, P.I." • Released in Great Britain under the title *High Encounters of the Ultimate Kind.*

Cinema Paradiso

(Italian, with English subtitles)
(1988; HBO; NR; 2:03)

Starring: Philippe Noiret, Jacques Perrin, Salvatore Cascio
Music by: Ennio Morricone
Written and directed by: Giuseppe Tornatore

Synopsis: Salvatore Di Vita (Perrin) hasn't been home to Sicily since he left 30 years earlier. But when news of Alfredo's death reaches him, the memories come back in a flood of sentiment. In their provincial village, the main form of entertainment was the single movie theater in town—"Cinema Paradiso"—and young "Toto" Di Vita (Cascio) had a special friendship with the projectionist, irascible old rascal Alfredo (Noiret). Persistent Toto eventually wore down the old man's resistance and became his apprentice in the trade of projecting dreams. Tragedy, joy, and will—both good and ill—conspired to promote Toto to main projectionist at the tender age of ten. As a teen, he began making his own films. He fell in love; he went to war; he left home and began his career. But he never forgot the gifts given him by Alfredo: love, wisdom—and a passion for the cinema. We share Toto's legacy as well: the final sentimental gift passed from the film-loving father-figure to his successful pseudo-son.
Discussion: "Life isn't like in the movies," Alfredo counsels a heartbroken Toto, victim of the sweet sorrow of love. "Life is much harder." Too true—and without the movies, how would we escape from vicious life, or vicariously live our fantasies? On a large scale, this film is nearly as superb a portrait of life in a post-War Sicilian village as Fellini's *Amarcord* was a picture of a pre-war parochial Italian community. The town is lousy with politics and practical jokes (many of which take place at the movies), and this little theater is as much their temple of entertainment as the Church is their spiritual center. On a small scale—and center stage—is the story of the life-long affection between Alfredo and his cinematic spiritual son, the fatherless Toto; a tale at turns insightful, funny, tender and tragic. Chances are that if you watch foreign films at all, you've already seen *Cinema,* as it was one of the most popular cinematic imports of all time. If for some personality quirk you *don't* watch foreign films, *Cinema Paradiso* makes an excellent starting point.
Rent this one for: its scope and sentiment, cinematic and real.
You'll (probably) like this if you liked: *Amarcord, Il Postino, The Last Picture Show; Radio Days, Visions of Light*
Credentials: • 1989 Oscar: Best Foreign Language Film. • 1989 Cannes Film Festival: Special Jury Prize. • *EW:* "A"

Clerks

(1994; Miramax; R; 1:31; B&W)

Starring: Brian O'Halloran, Jeff Anderson, Marilyn Ghigliotti, Lisa Spoonauer, Jason Mewes, Kevin Smith
Written and directed by: Kevin Smith

Synopsis: Dante (O'Halloran) isn't even supposed to *be* there today, but he shows up at the store to fill in for a friend. And he spends the day in Convenience Store Hell, forced to deal with nutjob customers, his ambitious, obnoxious girlfriend, his anti-ambitious best-bud Randal (Anderson), who works (yeah, right, "works") in the video store next door, and his idealized ex-girlfriend, who dumped him years ago but now wants to make up. And shoplifters and smokers (of all ages), his rooftop roller hockey league, his ex-g'friend's love monkey, his dead friend, and his basic life-in-a-senseless-funk-going-down-the-toilet attitude. Worst of all—he's not even supposed to *be* there today!
Discussion: It's a triumph of "BOB" ("Brains Over Budget"): When you've got no money to make a movie, you've got only one thing to depend on: talent. Smith has it in abundance. The dialog is archetypal, distilled Gen X: overeducated, undermotivated, overanalyzed, underachieving. It's a movie about slackers with no resources except a brain, a mouth and other sex organs, by a guy who knows them inside out. The film is built on its dialog, and it's outrageous, brilliant and hilarious. But...*37?*
Rent this one for: the hilarious, fast-paced and original script.
You'll (probably) like this if you liked: *My Life's In Turnaround, Trust, She's Gotta Have It*
Credentials: • 1994 Cannes Film Festival: International Critics Week Prize • 1994 Sundance Film Festival: Filmmaker's Trophy • Top 10 "Best Entertainment" films of 1995 —*Video Magazine* • Top 10 Films of 1995: *Time, Village Voice,* Chicago *Sun-Times.*
Dissenting Opinion: "...a couple of slackers...saying 'dude' a lot and telling occasionally amusing sissy-poo-poo-titty jokes... doesn't...make for exhilarating movie-going." —*Premiere* (4/96)
Vidbits: • According to Smith, *Clerks* cost exactly $27,575 to produce. He used credit cards to raise most of the production money, along with college tuition and the sale of his comic book collection. • Budget for his second film, *Mallrats*: $6 million. • Smith appears briefly in both films as the character "Silent Bob." • Smith also co-edited and co-produced, with Scott Mosier (who appears in three roles, notably the "Angry Hockey-Playing Customer"). • Shot in the same store Smith was working in at the time. • Laserdisc edition contains 25 additional minutes of footage, including seven scenes; one is an alternate ending in which Dante is killed during a stick-up of the store. • *37???*

Clockwise

(1986; Republic, HBO/Cannon; PG; 1:36)

Starring: John Cleese, Penelope Wilton, Alison Steadman
Featuring: Stephen Moore, Sharon Maiden
Written by: Michael Frayn
Directed by: Christopher Morahan

Synopsis: Brian Stimpson (Cleese) is the very model of the modern public school headmaster. Punctuality is his religion; the clock is his god. His entire existence is justified when he's elected Chairman of the national Headmaster's Conference and is invited to address the convention. But a missed train becomes the first toppled domino in a seemingly endless, escalating chain of events gone awry that pits his perseverance, patience and punctilious personality against the chaos of nature as he races against the clock to arrive in time to deliver his speech. And the clock is ticking...

Discussion: Chaos theory, the latest rage in scientific circles, gives us some insight into the nature of this splendid farce of escalating disasters: "Small perturbations in one's daily trajectory can have large consequences" (James Gleick, *Chaos*), for instance. And "Deep in the chaotic regime, slight changes in structure almost always cause vast changes in behavior" (Stuart Kauffman). Chaos theoreticians even have a label for Stimpson's problem: "Gambler's Ruin," roughly translated as "things run in streaks." In less enlightened times, we'd just call it Murphy's Law. But whatever name you give it, Cleese, master of exasperation, was tailor-made for this role as a pompous paragon of punctuality who's doomed to hang himself on the only loopholes left in every demoralizing detour. "It's not the despair," he admits to his traveling companion Laura (Maiden), when things look their bleakest. "I can stand the despair. It's the *hope!"* A delightful froth of random chance; of mistaken identities and mistaken motives; of being in the wrong place at the wrong time, and always with the wrong story; of the futility of going against the flow; of accidents and incidents and hints and allegations (sorry; thought I was Paul Simon for a moment); of mud and muddling through, stiff upper lip, then. Right!

Rent this one for: Cleese; its classic nature as a timeless farce.

You'll (probably) like this if you liked: *A Fish Called Wanda* (Cleese); *It's A Mad, Mad, Mad, Mad World, After Hours* (escalating disasters); *Noises Off* (Frayn); "Monty Python"; *Romance with a Double Bass* (Cleese)

Dissenting Opinion: "...a must for Cleese fans; others will be disappointed..." —MMG (2.5 stars)

Flashback!

The Clowns

(Italian, with English subtitles)
(1971; Hen's Tooth; G; 1:30)

Written, featuring and directed by: Federico Fellini

Synopsis: "Can the circus still entertain?" Fellini muses. "The world which it belonged to no longer exists." In an attempt to answer this question, he and a film crew set out on an oddball odyssey across Europe, visiting practitioners of the dying and discredited art of clowning, with its "terrifying comic violence." They recreate famous acts of history and view archival films. But everywhere they go, they find the old clowns retired, dying, and forgotten. Depressed and disappointed, The Maestro decides to stage a Clown Funeral—a literally hysterical affair.
Discussion: Clowns get a bad rap these days. I'm talking clowns like Krusty, Homey and Shakes, you bozos. But the modern clown is as much a degeneration of a centuries-old art form as an archetectural Golden Arch is from the Golden Mean. Fellini traces the roots of the original white-faced players and their surreal scenes in a fashion befitting the subject: film strips break; people bump into the camera; a dozen crewmembers pour out of the mini-car they drive to an interview, and so on. I have a photo on my office wall of Fellini, the left-hand half of his face made up as a clown, and that photo, I'm convinced, is the key to this film. Only someone half-genius, half clown, could ever have conceived of and staged the Clown Funeral—a comically somber procession which rapidly accelerates into the grandest, most elaborate, most exhilarating festival of anarchy ever set on film. Ecstatic and joyous, yet ending on an appropriately poignant note, this miniature masterpiece is a must-see for all Fellini aficionados, connoisseurs of comedy, and children of all ages. Mark Twain cautioned readers of "Huckleberry Finn" against looking for a "motive" or a "moral" in the story, and Signor Fellini issues his own version of this admonition to modern movie viewers in his answer to a reporter's question, "What message are you trying to give us here?" Any other interpretation pales in comparison. (A note to those who eschew foreign films: So it's in Italian? The acts are all pantomime, and slapstick is a universal language. Subtitles are unnecessary.)
Rent this one for: its genius in integrating tragedy and slapstick; as a loving and traditional tribute to a dead art form.
You'll (probably) like this if you liked: *Funny Bones, 8-1/2*
Vidbits: • Cameo by Anita Ekberg, star of Fellini's *La Dolce Vita.*
• Originally produced for Italian TV.

The Coca-Cola Kid

(1985; Vestron, LIVE; R; 1:34)

Starring: Eric Roberts, Greta Scacchi, Bill Kerr
Written by: Frank Moorhouse (based on his short stories)
Directed by: Dusan Makavejer

Synopsis: In the middle of the Australian outback, there is a tiny valley in which the people don't drink Coca-Cola. This is unacceptable to the management of a corporation that has saturated 155 nations and sells 260 million drinks every day. So his Atlanta masters dispatch Becker (Roberts)—a dynamic and brilliant, if unorthodox, troubleshooter—to solve this little mystery. He discovers the reason is T. George McDowell (Kerr), the man who owns Anderson Valley—and a man who brews and bottles his own soft drinks. Becker might finally have met his match in stubbornness and vision in this eccentric individualist, and develops a genuine affection for him, even as he engages in a battle of wits and wills with T. George—and with his own beautiful, ditzy secretary Terri (Scacchi), who's got her sights set on Becker—but for more reasons than the obvious...
Discussion: In South America, rival Coke and Pepsi distributors have been known to engage in lethal shooting matches warring over their territory. Even though this film doesn't carry the absurdity of cola wars to that extreme, the producers found it necessary to open with a disclaimer that "The Coca-Cola Company has not licensed, sponsored or approved of this film in any way." Hell, they should be *proud* of it! The movie is smart and charming, droll and delightful, and easily earns adjectives like offbeat, quirky and off-kilter. The performances are uniformly eccentric, nuanced and affectionate: Kerr is an admirable, if irascible, bastard; Roberts playing a culture-shocked good guy is a welcome stretch; and Scacchi makes an adorable wide-eyed ditz—her very presence is an aphrodisiac. The flick rambles a bit (like any good shaggy dog story), but even the side trips prove amusing. If this isn't enough, it's both witty and unpredictable, with a surprise in every scene. Add in a tender ending with a touch of poignance, and you've got a gentle gem. *The Coca-Cola Kid* is indeed "the real thing"—the pause that refreshes.
Rent this one for: its refreshing originality and quirky humor.
You'll (probably) like this if you liked: *Local Hero; The Efficiency Expert; Strictly Ballroom*
Dissenting Opinion: • "Flaccid drama..." —HFG • "...doesn't have enough bite to it." —VMG (3 stars)
Vidbits: Based on screenwriter Moorhouse's short stories, some of which appear in a collection entitled *The Americans, Baby*—the book Becker is reading in his hotel room.

Coneheads

(1993; Paramount; PG; 1:27)

Starring: Dan Aykroyd, Jane Curtain, Michael McKean
Featuring: Michelle Burke, Jason Alexander, Larainne Newman, Chris Farley, David Spade, Dave Thomas, Lisa Jane Persky
Written by: Dan Aykroyd, Tom Davis, Bonnie Turner, Terry Turner
Directed by: Steven Barron

Synopsis: Beldar Conehead (Aykroyd) and his mate, Primaat (Curtain), emissaries from the planet Remulak, start their enslavement of Earth by crashing their spaceship into New York Harbor. Beldar "phones home," but can't expect a rescue for "seven zerls"—a looooong time. Worse, Primaat is "with cone." When Beldar buys a Social Security Number to obtain work, the Immigration Service is on him like Velcro underwear. The Coneheads escape, and work their way up to the American middle-class dream: a suburban home, golf and weekend BBQs with the neighbors; a rebellious teenage daughter, Connie (Burke). But the INS agent from whom they escaped (McKean) is obsessed with nailing them. The rescue ship finally arrives; the bad news is that Connie has fallen in love with a "blunt skull" (Farley), and doesn't want to go "back" to a home she never knew. Maybe she's got the right idea: once back, they'll have to answer to the High Master (Thomas) about their failure to conquer Earth...
Discussion: It's not just a one-gag movie; actually, they never use the same gag twice. Running gags, however, concern the Coneheads' ability to "consume mass quantities" of *anything,* and disguising their skulls to escape detection. The flick also contains gently chiding satire of Middle American manners and mores, and a veritable parade of bit parts by standup comics (Sinbad, Ellen DeGeneres, Drew Carrey, Tom Arnold), and comedians from *Seinfeld* (Jason Alexander, Michael Richards), *SCTV* (Thomas), and *SNL* (Spade, Farley, Phil Hartman, Jan Hooks, Jon Lovitz Chris Rock, Adam Sandler, Julia Sweeney, Tim Meadows, Kevin Nealon, Garret Morris). Aykroyd, with his pop-eyed smile, stilted language, colorful descriptions and whiny, helium-sucking monotone hasn't been this funny since *Ghostbusters.* It's a fun, no-brainer, live cartoon. *Mebs!*
Rent this one for: sheer dumb fun; the parade of comedians.
You'll (probably) like this if you liked: "3rd Rock From the Sun," "Mork and Mindy," *Mom and Dad Save the World*
Dissenting Opinion: "Not much is really funny." —Ebert (1.5)
Vidbits: • Aykroyd's daughter Danielle made her screen debut as Baby Connie. • The Turners must have had a file full of left over jokes, which they used in their 1996 sitcom *3rd Rock From The Sun.* • The police sketch artist is Terry Turner.

Cousins

(romantic comedy)
(1989; Paramount; PG-13; 1:50)

Starring: Isabella Rossellini, Ted Danson, Sean Young
Featuring: Lloyd Bridges, William Petersen
Written by: Stephen Metcalfe
(based on the 1975 French film *Cousin, Cousine*)
Music by: Angelo Badalamente
Directed by: Joel Schumacher

Synopsis: When Larry's (Danson) uncle marries Maria's (Rossellini) aunt, they become cousins-in-law. And when they're left alone at the end of the wedding, they connect so quickly that their mismatched marriages stand out in rocky relief. What really brings them together is discovering that her husband Tom (Peterson) is having an affair with his wife Tish (Young). Turnabout is fair play—but it's just not in their repertoire. A *platonic* friendship would drive their spouses crazy, however—because they'd never believe it was platonic. Tom and Tish spat and feud and generally act like an old married couple, while Larry and Maria become fast friends—and catch all of the grief of an affair with none of the rewards. Until the day when... (Ah! No spoilers!) In this game of musical spouses, who will end up with whom—and who will end up heartbroken and alone?
Discussion: The original film was about a real affair, and scandalized even the "sexually sophisticated" French. The American massage pitches it to a platonic level—long enough at least for us (and them) to be sure they're really, *really* in love. Then... *vive la France!* It helps immeasurably that the personality roles are impeccably clear: Tish and Tom are bitch and bastard, in counterpoint to Larry and Maria's innocent sincerity and saint-like suffering for their moral convictions—and for daring to want to be happy! For the film to work, they must convince us that you don't have to be an infidel to commit an infidelity. It helps that they are a lovely couple: Danson, smart and charming; Rossellini, the image of childlike wonder, with her full moon face, crescent moon smile and sun-wide eyes. Watching them warm up to each other is the real treat of the flick: the smiles grow wider, the patter more flirtatious, the spaces between them slowly close... It's an undeniable charmer, placing the pair in the center of a whirlwind of energetic eccentrics, using fun to lead us gently into wonder, heartache—and a happy ending.
Rent this one for: being a wonderful "date movie."
You'll (probably) like this if you liked: *Four Weddings and a Funeral, Sleepless in Seattle, L.A. Story, Moonstruck*
Dissenting Opinion: "...too diffuse..." —SMV (2.5 stars)

Defending Your Life

(1991; Warner; PG; 1:52)

Starring: Albert Brooks, Meryl Streep
Featuring: Rip Torn, Lee Grant, Buck Henry
Written and directed by: Albert Brooks

Synopsis: Daniel Miller (Brooks) is a semi-successful ad man who's killed in a car crash before the opening credits. Where do you go from there? Judgment City, of course, where Dan wakes groggy, robed and regimented, just one of hundreds of incoming souls in this between-lives halfway house. Everyone spends five days here, while his life is put on trial; in a courtroom setting, selected scenes from one's life are reviewed to determine whether the soul "moves forward" or goes back for another life of earthly learning. Between sessions (where Dan is subjected to a series of humiliating scenes from his past), he meets Julia (Streep)—sweet, happy, and a virtual saint. They fall in love, and her influence changes his (after)life. Given one final chance, can Dan find the courage to evolve from *schlub* to *mensch*—or will these newly-minted soul-mates be separated forever?
Discussion: Judgment City is part Vegas, part L.A., part Disney World, part Universal Studios tour—and a little bit of heaven (you can eat as much as you want and never gain an ounce!): a fully thought-through purgatory, both practical and pleasant. The characters, too, are engaging: Dan, all too human, sweatily attempting to weasel his way out of his transgressions; Torn, as his lawyer, expansive, avuncular, with just a touch of condescending hubris. (A high point is hearing him explain why there are no children in JC.) The criteria for "moving forward" are a bit vague—one is "held back by fears"—but the essential question seems to be one of cowardice vs. courage: choosing to embrace life in spite of its tragedies, suffering and disappointments, or living timidly, in quiet denial and defeat. This film chooses to embrace life, and illustrates by example that while loving another is the biggest risk in life, it also yields the greatest rewards. Disguised as a romantic comedy, this philosophical fantasy will make you laugh, it will make you cry, and it might just leave you pondering questions both grave—and beyond. And isn't that what we really want from a film—or from a life?
Rent this one for: being a smart movie: smart dialog, smart ideas, smart philosophy—and its smartest part of all, reminding us that true wisdom resides in the heart, not in the "smart."
You'll (probably) like this if you liked: *L.A. Story, Joe vs. the Volcano, Truly Madly Deeply, Made in Heaven,*
Dissenting Opinion: "...overall is rather disappointing." —SMV (2.5 stars)

Delicatessen

(black comedy; French with English subtitles)
(1992; Paramount; R; 1:35)

Starring: Dominique Pinon, Marie-Laure Dougnac
Featuring: Jean Claude Dreyfus, Ticky Hidalgo
Written by: Gilles Adrien, Jean-Marie Jeunet, Marc Caro
Directed by: Jean-Marie Jeunet, Marc Caro

Synopsis: In a post-apocalyptic city, everything is scarce, especially meat. What's a career butcher to do? Play landlord to the eccentric residents of a decaying apartment house, for one. And advertise for handymen on a regular basis—handymen who have a disconcerting habit of disappearing the night before a new shipment of meat. Louison (Pinon) stumbles into this strange scenario, answering the ad, as the world has little use for an ex-circus clown. But the butcher's shy, myopic daughter Julie (Dougnac) takes a fancy to him. She pleads with her father to spare him from his fate as filet, but he's got mouths to feed. She has no choice but to contact an underground movement whose members despise "meat suckers" in an effort to save her beloved Louison. They are mostly idiots, however, and they invade the building just as all the tenants' personal hells are breaking loose. Can Louison and Julie—or anyone, for that matter—escape the butcher's block and the collapsing house?
Discussion: It's *Brazil* meets *Eating Raoul*—a lite black comedy which pretty much exhausts the thesaurus of synonyms for "bizarre." Atmosphere is everything, and it's a benignly nightmarish, happily hallucinatory ambiance, brimming with misshapen faces, odd lighting, wacky angles and insane sets, all too peculiar to be too threatening. The odd lot of freaks and weirdoes who inhabit the building are both grotesque and whimsical, as if drawn by Dr. Seuss on a bad acid trip. For the precious little French spoken in the film, it might as well be silent—except for the fanciful sound effects (the scene in which everyone in the building uses the rhythm of squeaking bedsprings as a metronome for their own activities is worthy of Keaton). If you've got an appetite for something visually brilliant, incredibly quirky, very original and exceedingly different—have a taste.
Rent this one for: its bizarre, eye-popping visuals.
You'll (probably) like this if you liked: *Eating Raoul* (theme); *City of Lost Children* (directors); *Brazil* (visuals); *Funny Bones*
Dissenting Opinion: "...will appeal enormously to some and offend others" —VMG (3.5 stars) **Credentials:** • *EW:* "A"
Vidbits: • "Presented" by Monty Python's Terry Gilliam. • Caro appears in the film as the Troglo with the black-rimmed glasses.

Diggstown

(sports comedy)

(1992; MGM/UA; R; 1:38)

Starring: James Woods, Louis Gossett, Jr., Bruce Dern
Featuring: Oliver Platt, Heather Graham, Randall "Tex" Cobb
Written by: Steven McKay
(based on the novel *The Diggstown Ringers* by Leonard Wise)
Directed by: Michael Ritchie

Synopsis: Diggstown was built on boxing—and stolen from its owners by rigged betting. But Gabe Caine (Woods) is using that knowledge to set up a sweet scam. First, the hook: Insult the crooked creep who runs the town. "Two things we never joke about here in Diggstown," John Gillon (Dern) warns Gabe after the slight; "our boxing and our betting." Next, the bait: An arrogant $100,000 bet that Caine's unknown fighter, "Honey" Ray Palmer (Gossett) can KO any ten men the town chooses—and can do it in 24 hours. With that comes the first hurdle: convincing Palmer to participate. There are a thousand behind-the-scenes details to manipulate (like buying off the boxers)—and, we discover, a deeper motivation than mere money, as well: a dedication to revenge against Gillon, who'll stop at nothing—including murder—to protect his financial interests in the town. Can Ray take 10 in 24? Or will the whole scheme go bust and cost them all their lives? Don't count them out yet...
Discussion: Call it *Raging Sting,* if you want—but it's definitely not your typical sports comedy. There are no goofy players, for instance—but there is an undercurrent of dead serious danger, with lives lost and more at stake as the aging Ray embarks on the fight of his life—literally. Casting two of Hollywood's top movie psychos against one another is a nice touch—even nicer to see Woods playing a good guy for once. *Diggstown*'s got an intriguing, evolving and ever-deepening story; smart lines; plenty of well-directed, fist-flailing action inside the ring (and out), and some gut-punching suspense. It's full of double-dealing, triple-crosses, and manipulation so deep it would boggle the minds of the *Mission Impossible* team—and it sports an ending that's satisfying on all levels: intellectually (the plot), emotionally (moral victory and poetic justice) and physically (just because you're beaten up doesn't mean you're beaten). It's a smart little flick that'll keep you on the edge of your ringside seat.
Rent this one for: the original, convoluted plot; the combination of serious suspense and good-natured "revenge" comedy.
You'll (probably) like this if you liked: *The Sting, Rocky*
Dissenting Opinion: "...script is contrived." —MMG (2.5 stars)
Vidbits: Gossett's then-wife Cyndi plays his character's wife.

Drugstore Cowboy

(black comedy/drama)
(1989; LIVE; R; 1:40)

Starring: Matt Dillon, Kelly Lynch, James Le Gros
Featuring: Heather Graham, William Burroughs, James Remar
Written by: Gus Van Sant, Jr., Daniel Yost
Directed by: Gus Van Sant, Jr.

Synopsis: Portland, Oregon, 1971: Bob Hughes (Dillon), 26, is a junkie. So's his wife, Diane (Lynch). They live to get loaded, on whatever's available. And the easiest way to make sure that good pharmaceuticals are available is to rob drug stores. Bob and Diane and their "crew"—Rick (Le Gros) and dopey amateur Nadine (Graham)—run a number of clever scams to slip their hands into a pharmacy's locked drawers. Then they shoot up and hang until it's time for the next score. When the heat from the cops gets too oppressive, they go on a road trip. And when things take a tragic turn, Bob finally decides to clean up his hand. Can he beat junk? At what cost? And if he can leave "the life"—does he really believe "the life" is going to just *let* him?
Discussion: It's a "shoot 'em up," but it ain't no Western. The real question is, Is this comedy or drama? Various guides and stores classify it differently. It is damn funny, though. Call it *The Three Stooges Do Dilaudid,* perhaps; it's black comedy filled with the darkest death-rattle laughter. "It's hard being a dope fiend," Bob explains in his opening narration—then proceeds to illustrate his one simple point. The film is a gritty, uncompromising vision of the junkie lifestyle, but it's detached and objective: not condemnation, condonation or glorification, simply explanation. The cast is perfection, especially Dillon's bleary-eyed Bob—slow, superstitious, but hardly stupid—and cult author Burroughs as the junkie priest; with his whiny nasal monotone drawl, he could pass for W.C. Fields' thinner twin, or Harry Dean Stanton's father. As befits the subject, the direction is iconoclastic, particularly in the fantasy sequences, and the score is eclectic, full of jazz, blues, and early '70s pop rock. It's rife with irony, right up to the final bittersweet scene—but its gallows humor is a tenuous bridge across an abyss of sadness and despair. Comedy or drama, it's still the cutting edge of hip.
Rent this one for: its dark humor; its gritty, insider knowledge.
You'll (probably) like this if you liked: *Heathers, Pulp Fiction, Bonnie and Clyde*
Vidbits: • Based on an unpublished autobiographical novel by Walla Walla prison inmate James Fogle. • Over the hospital PA is a call for "Dr. Howard"—a reference to The Three Stooges.

Earth Girls Are Easy

(musical comedy/ science fiction)

(1989; Vestron/LIVE; PG; 1:40)

Starring: Geena Davis, Jeff Goldblum, Julie Brown, Jim Carrey
Featuring: Damon Wayans, Charles Rocket, Michael McKean
Written by: Julie Brown, Charlie Coffey, Terrance McNally
Directed by: Julian Temple

Synopsis: "I'm sick of space!" fur-bearing alien Wiploc (Carrey) moans. *"I need a woman!"* Well, they *are* near Earth... So they pop over to San Fernando—"The Valley"—and plop right down into Val-Gal manicurist Valerie's (Davis) pool. She's ready for some new romance; fiancé Dr. Ted (Rocket) hasn't come across in—omigod!—*two weeks!* And she catches him with (gag me with a *spoon*!)—a *blonde!* But when bubblebrain stylist Candy (Brown) gives the trio of aliens a shave and a makeover, the gals discover—omi*god!*—they're *hunks!* Better: they're *dates*. Sure, the boys can party hearty. But Val's looking for Mr. Right, not Mr. Right Now. Can she find romantic happiness in the alien arms of a guy who can't even commit to one *planet? Shuh,* right!
Discussion: It's a musical! It's a comedy! It's a slapstick romantic sci-fi musical comedy for the MTV generation! But with Julie Brown songs like "I Like 'Em Big and Stupid" and "'Cause I'm a Blond," it's also a good-natured razzing of Lifestyles of Airheads, Beach Bimbos and the L.A. Brain-Burned. The trio of space-cases (Goldblum, Carrey, Wayans) are essentially the 3 Stooges de-evolutionized into monkeys, interested only in mimicking things or eating them; horny space sailors who learn to talk by watching TV ("Are we limp and hard to manage?") and are totally taken by Jerry Lewis in *The Nutty Professor.* There's a plot somewhere in there, but really, who cares? It's enough to watch them all cavort through this fluffy, goofy little romp—and to try to spot all the pop culture references in Val's sci-fi nightmare. All this and Davis half-naked half the time! *Awesome,* Dr. Dude!
Rent this one for: its goofy good humor; the music videos.
You'll (probably) like this if you liked: *Ace Ventura, Pet Detective,* "In Living Color" (Carrey); *The Coneheads, Mom And Dad Save The World, Clueless,* "Mork and Mindy," "3rd Rock"
Dissenting Opinion: • "Not enough substance to sustain a feature film..." —MMG (2.5 stars) • "Asinine...induces more headaches than giggles." —SMV (1 star)
Vidbits: • This was Geena Davis' first project after winning a Supporting Actress Oscar for *The Accidental Tourist.* • Co-writer McNally plays the doctor on the television soap opera. • Former L.A. billboard icon Angelyne appears in the gas station scene.

Eating Raoul

(black comedy)
(1982; CBS/Fox; R; 1:23)

Starring: Mary Woronov, Paul Bartel, Robert Beltran
Featuring: Buck Henry, Ed Begley, Jr., Edie McClurg
Written by: Richard Blackburn, Paul Bartel
Directed by: Paul Bartel

Synopsis: Paul and Mary Bland (Bartel and Woronov) don't fit into the "psychopathic environment" of Hollywood. They certainly don't fit into the Swingin' '70s. Paul's a retro kind of guy, a bow-tied wine snob; Mary's a lovely nurse continually accosted by horny morons. They live for their dream of opening a cozy little country restaurant. Just as they see that dream slipping away for lack of money, Paul accidentally kills a swinger attacking Mary. He's got a walletful of cash—just like all those sex-crazed maniacs who don't deserve to live, they reason... So they set up a mom & pop S&M business, catering to rich degenerates. Mary lures them in; Paul pops 'em with his frying pan and grabs the cash. Things are really cooking until charming Chicano Raoul (Beltran) stumbles across their scam and suggests a partnership: they get the cash; he gets the rest—including the bodies. But Raoul is an ambitious dude, and the body he really wants is live, hot—and Mary's. Only Paul stands in his way...
Discussion: "What a world!" Mary marvels about one of the wacky, kinky fantasies she's been forced to enact. What a world indeed, in which a warped and wicked satire on the Swinging Singles scene is even needed. What a world that could pull off a black comedy about murdering perverts, featuring blind nuns, sex shops and the amazing things you can do with a cheap piece of meat. What a world in which this low budget pre-cult comedy continues to be rediscovered and recommended. (If it doesn't have a large following, at least it has a long shelf-life.) And what a world where the creator of the "Bland enchilada" discovers that you can indeed keep a good man down.
Rent this one for: its whimsical, deadpan black humor.
You'll (probably) like this if you liked: *Delicatessen, Heathers, Rocky Horror Picture Show, Parents*
Credentials: "...funny but never obnoxious." —SMV (★★★★)
Dissenting Opinion: "Insufficient humor to offset the tastelessness" —HFG
Vidbits: • Shot for under $1 million. • Co-writer Blackburn plays their real estate agent. • Beltran co-stars in "Star Trek: Voyager." • Beltran, Bartel and Woronov would appear again together in *Scenes from the Class Struggle in Beverly Hills.*

Ed Wood

(1994; Touchstone; R; 2:04; B&W)

Starring: Johnny Depp, Martin Landau, Sarah Jessica Parker
Featuring: Bill Murray, Patricia Arquette, Jeffrey Jones, Lisa Marie
Written by: Scott Alexander, Larry Karaszewsk
(based on the book *Nightmare of Ecstasy,* by Rudolph Grey)
Music by: Howard Shore
Directed by: Tim Burton

Synopsis: Edward D. Wood, Jr., (Depp) loves everything about the movies, and is determined to make his mark in the industry. It matters little that he has no talent whatsoever. Through fast-talking and sheer persistence, he gets his big break, writing, directing and starring in a sexploitation cheapie which he turns into a sensitive portrayal of a cross-dresser (a subject close to his cashmere-covered heart). Fate brings him together with frail, aging film legend Bela Lugosi (Landau), and together they set out to revive Bela's career and create one for Ed. Assisted by a stock company of outcasts, mutants and assorted weirdoes, they create a legacy of the most inept horror movies ever made.
Discussion: Depp's lovable, loopy Wood is more used car salesman than artist; all ambition and enthusiasm, but devoid of even an atom of talent. He's a tireless and effective cheerleader, though, and when we see him watch every take with wide-eyed wonder, we understand that what drives him drives *every* artist —as Wood himself realizes when he meets Orson Welles and discovers that they share similar problems as "filmmakers." The center of gravity of the film, however, is the genuinely affectionate friendship that develops between Wood and Lugosi—the latter washed-up, desiccated, addicted to morphine, yet still attempting to retain some dignity. *Ed Wood* succeeds both as "biopic" parody and as a fond, ultimately touching tribute from a visionary filmmaker to a pair of casualties of their own vision.
Rent this one for: Landau's Oscar-winning performance; the detail-perfect recreations of Woods' cheesy sets and makeup.
You'll (probably) like this if you liked: *Plan 9 From Outer Space, Night of the Ghouls* (or *any* Ed Wood flick); "MST3K"
Credentials: • 1994 Oscars: Supporting Actor (Landau); Make-up • Top 10 "Best Entertainment" films of 1995—*Video Magazine* • "Top Ten Films of 1994" list —Gene Siskel
Vidbits: • If you like *Ed Wood,* rent *Look Back In Angora* (Rhino), the "real"—but just as wacky—biography of Wood. • In 1980, Wood was voted "Worst Director of All Time," finally bringing him the fame which eluded him in his lifetime. • The budget for *Ed Wood* was nearly 100 times the combined budgets of all Wood's actual films. • Theatrical gross of *Ed Wood:* $5.9 million.

Double Feature!

Elephant Parts

(made-for-video; 1981; Pacific Arts; NR; 1:00)

Television Parts Home Companion

(made-for-TV; 1984; Pacific Arts; :40)

Starring: Michael Nesmith
Featuring: Bill Martin, Bill Dear, Lark Alcott, Robert Akerman, Katherine McDaniel, Paddy Morrissey
Written by: Michael Nesmith, Bill Martin, William Dear, Jack Handy, Michael Kaplan, John Levenstein
Directed by: EP: William Dear; *TP:* William Dear, Alan Myerson

Synopsis: Sick and tired of endless reruns of "Saturday Night Live," "Kids in the Hall" and "Monty Python"? Former "Monkee" Michael Nesmith had the solution a decade ago: a variety show on acid, featuring surreal skits and absurdist satire, punctuated by music videos both straight and satirical.
Discussion: The genial and energetic Nesmith makes a jovial host, and everyone involved appears to be having a great time. The feeling is infectious. Whether it's a commercial for "Neighborhood Nuclear Superiority" ("At NNS, we know people are just *no damn good*") or a concept bit like "5 Second Theatre," there are more wacky ideas and quirky chuckles on each tape than in most recent seasons of "SNL." Surrounding these bizarre bits are music videos from Nesmith (who virtually invented the form) ranging in tone from the fond, nostalgic tribute of "I'll Remember You" to the benign magic of "Eldorado to the Moon" to "Rio," the most evocative, inventive and fall-down funny musical number since Donald Duck and his pals sang "Three Caballeros." Time has not diluted the best of these whimsical skits or the wit, imagery and emotion of the songs.
Rent these for: their amiable blend of zany comedy and unconventional (and often touching) music videos.
You'll (probably) like this if you liked: "Monty Python's Flying Circus," "Saturday Night Live," "The Kids in the Hall," "The Monkees"; Weird Al Yankovich (*UHF*)
Dissenting Opinion: "Viewers were mystified." —*The Complete Directory to Prime Time Network TV Shows* by Brooks & Marsh.
Vidbits: • Not only did Nesmith host, co-write and produce these tapes, but he also released them on his own video label, (the now defunct) Pacific Arts Home Video. • Nesmith used essentially the same format for his short-lived TV series "Television Parts," which ran on NBC during the summer of 1985. • Also available: *Dr. Duck's Super Secret All-Purpose Sauce*—more of the same, but who needs a triple feature?

The Englishman Who Went Up A Hill But Came Down A Mountain

(romantic comedy)

(1995; Miramax; PG; 1:36)

Starring: Hugh Grant, Tara Fitzgerald, Colm Meaney
Featuring: Kenneth Griffith, Ian McNeice, Ian Hart
Written and directed by: Christopher Monger

Synopsis: One Sunday in 1917, two English cartographers (Grant, McNeice) pull into a tiny town near Cardiff to measure "the first mountain in Wales." The town is proud of their mountain; it defines their very Welshness. Imagine their shock, dismay and outrage when the Brits inform them that a mountain must be over 1,000 feet to qualify for the definition—and that their Ffynnon Garw is only 984 feet...merely a hill. Bone-weary of losing family, friends and fellows to The War, they cannot tolerate the loss of their mountain, their identity. And so the entire town conspires to detain the Brits while laboring mightily to add another 20 feet of soil to "top off" their mountain.
Discussion: For years, I endured praise for *Local Hero,* because I couldn't put my finger on what exactly was wrong with it. Now when someone mentions that overrated rental, I hand them a copy of this: the movie *Local Hero should* have been. Apparently a shaggy dog story of epic proportions, it is in fact a pixieish, picaresque true tall tale, setting quirky characters against some of the most enchanting landscapes on earth. While the subplot, concerning the romance between the affable Anson (Grant, in his usual shy, stuttering, self-effacing screen persona) and Betty (Fitzgerald), the spunky maid with the delightful over-bite, is sweet, the real emotion is generated by the town's almost religious mission to exalt, literally, their would-be mountain, pulling together in a fight against time, storms and limited resources. Their task is not without its redemptive rewards—but also not without its bittersweet sacrifices. A joyous, uplifting, triumphal, endearingly wry smiler; and, yes, even *precious* (in its best sense), right down to a delightful surprise at the end, lest we believe that this is indeed just another shaggy dog tale.
Rent this one for: the eccentric story and uplifting ending.
You'll (probably) like this if you liked: *Local Hero, Sirens*
Dissenting Opinion: • "Woe be the one-joke movie when the joke isn't much of a grabber..." —MMG (2.5 stars) • "...never moves beyond the hopelessly lethargic...a glorified travelogue... [a] snoozer." —*Entertainment Weekly* #310 (1/19/96)
Vidbits: • Based on a real Welsh legend. • Grant and Fitzgerald starred together as husband and wife a year earlier, in *Sirens.*

Experience Preferred But Not Essential

(coming-of-age comedy)
(1982; MGM/UA; PG; 1:17)

Starring: Elizabeth Edmonds, Sue Wallace, Ron Bain
Written by: June Roberts
Directed by: Peter Duffell

Synopsis: July, 1962: Mousy Annie (Edmonds) arrives at the Grand Hotel on the coast of Wales, to spend her college summer break as one of the live-in staff. It doesn't look promising, however: they stick her in the leaky attic with roommate Mavis (Wallace), and *everybody's* having a bad day. Only Mike (Bain), the Scottish cook, is cordial—almost aggressively friendly. Annie discovers she's in the middle of a small-town atmosphere: each of the staff has his or her own romances, prejudices, quirks, frailties—and secrets. It's difficult to keep secrets, though, when everyone's affairs are endlessly discussed and dissected. Annie soaks it all in with bewildered bemusement. She gets an earful, and an education—mostly about the war between the sexes. And over the course of the summer, she blossoms from naive waif to confident woman—with a little help from her friends.
Discussion: "I'm the only one I know here who doesn't have a past," Annie laments. She needn't worry—she catches on quite quickly, and has every opportunity to get an education in life in this hotel full of genuine eccentrics, all placed in affectionately eccentric situations. (There's Ivan the naked sleepwalker and his nightly "floor show," for instance—although no one remembers to warn Annie about him in advance.) The wildly different women eventually take Annie under their collective mother-hen wing and remake her from weed to wildflower, and her tentative trials at gaining "a past" build her confidence and transform her from mouse to tiger. Edmonds has Paul McCartney's soulful eyes and is perfect in the part; her summer fling, Mike, is a delightful flirt; affectionate and attentive. Three parts *Gregory's Girl,* one part "Fawlty Towers," this low-key, gentle and tender tale of one young woman's wondrous summer removes the bitter from bittersweet to become a wee charmer.
Rent this one for: its quiet charm.
You'll (probably) like this if you liked: *Gregory's Girl*
Credentials: "★★★★" —VMG
Vidbits: Originally produced for British TV, as one of a series of low-budget films produced by David Puttnam (*Chariots of Fire*) under the blanket title *First Love.*

The Experts

(1989; Paramount; PG-13; 1:34)

Starring: John Travolta, Ayre Gross, Kelly Preston
Featuring: Charles Martin Smith, James Keach, Brian Doyle-Murray
Written by: Nick Thiel, Steven Greene, Eric Alter
Music by: Marvin Hamlisch
Directed by: Dave Thomas

Synopsis: Somewhere in the heart of the Soviet Union is an exact replica of a small town in Nebraska, used as a training ground for KGB spies. It's got one minor flaw, however: it was build in the mid-'50s and has never been updated since. The residents have no clue about sushi, jogging and Walkmen, or of MTV, CDs and VCRs. Against the better judgment of "Mr. Jones" (Doyle-Murray), "Mr. Smith" (Smith) intends to give the town the late-80s facelift it desperately needs. He scours New York City until he find his "experts": Travis (Travolta) and Wendell (Gross), an adult "Bill & Ted" who dream of opening a nightclub someday. Smith offers them the chance, in "Nebraska." To them, this retroville is part "Happy Days" and part "Twilight Zone." But they transform the "Polynesian Lounge" into the ultrahip "So So Ho" club, recruit staff from the yokels—and find the girls of their dreams. But if they ever wise up and discover the truth about the town, they'll be terminated—unless they can appeal to the American in everyone and lead a revolution for freedom.
Discussion: Travolta's career slump hit rock bottom with this film, which was considered too stinkeriffic to release theatrically, and went virtually straight to video. Newsflash: It ain't that bad. It's a cute, sweet, funny culture clash comedy, with Travolta and Gross as likable lunkheads and an entire town in the "fish out of water" role. As the innocently good-natured Travis, Travolta is half Vinnie Barbarino, half Tony Manero, and the flick is worth renting just to watch his incredibly hot dance number with future (and current) wife Preston (whom he met while making the movie). Is it dated because the Evil Empire fell since its release? Or was it prescient, understanding that no poor repressed culture could possibly withstand an onslaught of materialistic American products and entertainment? Well... let's not go overboard. Chekov it ain't. But good dumb fun it is.
Rent this one for: an undiscovered Travolta performance.
You'll (probably) like this if you liked: *Dumb and Dumber, Saturday Night Fever, Moon Over Parador, Back to the Future*
Dissenting Opinion: • "Fatally bland...bleak in all respects." —MMG (2 stars) • "★★"—VMG
Vidbits: • Nebraska? Russia? Nope—shot in Vancouver, B.C., Canada. • Produced in '87 but sat unreleased for two years.

Freaked

(1993; FoxVideo; R; 1:18)

Starring: Alex Winter, Randy Quaid, Megan Ward
Featuring: Keanu Reeves, Michael Stoyanov, Brooke Shields, Mr. T., Bobcat Goldthwait, Calvert DeForest
Written by: Alex Winter, Tim Burns, Tom Stern
Directed by: Alex Winter & Tom Stern

Synopsis: Snotty child star Ricky Coogan (Winter) is all grown-up now—a greedy 20-something with a bad attitude. He accepts $5 million play "goodwill ambassador" to the South American country of Santa Flan for the EES ("Everything Except Shoes") Corp., which manufactures Zygrot 24, a toxic fertilizer used in that third-world flyspeck. He and his pal Ernie (Stoyanov) pick up cute protester Julie (Ward) and take a side trip to see the "Freek Show" run by the warped Elijah C. Skuggs (Quaid). They discover to their horror that Skuggs *creates* his "freeks" using (get ready for a real surprise) *Zygrot 24!* He combines Julie and Ernie into a single half-man, half-woman masochistic monster, and turns Ricky into half a gruesome gremlin. They're forced to sleep in a barn with the other freeks and are regularly trotted out for stage shows. Can they escape and regain their normal form—or has Elijah got an even worse fate in store for them?
Discussion: "The public does not want to see depraved, disgusting, violent filth," Ricky informs Elijah—and judging by how the public avoided this flick, he might be right. But some of us can handle—even *enjoy*—a film in which every frame is a bad acid trip, or Pee-Wee's Playhouse in Hell; a bizarro black comedy which brims like a backed-up toilet with tasteless, outrageous, gross-out, rude, crude, sophomoric humor and shockingly funny Stooge-style violence. The flick is indeed a freak show: a festival of irreverence, a cartoon with a bad attitude (an "atti-toon"?) and a sideshow of horrid puns, stolen gags (Monty Python's "power-puking," for one), wild special effects (including claymation, puppeteering and makeup), cult figures and inside jokes. It's original, strange, nasty, hip and *definitely* a cult item. Recommended—but only to the fringiest of our fringe readers.
Rent this one for: its bad attitude, cartoonish humor and FX.
You'll (probably) like this if you liked: *Repo Man, Airplane!, Gremlins, Shakes the Clown,* 3 Stooges, "Beavis and Butt-head"
Dissenting Opinion: "...hammers home every joke." —MMG (2)
Vidbits: • "Dawg Boy" is played by an uncredited Keanu Reeves ("Ted" to Winters' "Bill" in the "Bill and Ted" flicks). • The airplane pilot introduces himself as "Capt. Benway"; "Dr. Benway" is a recurring character in William Burroughs' fiction.

Get Crazy

(1983; Embassy, Sultan; R; 1:38)

Starring: Malcolm McDowell, Daniel Stern, Allen Goorwitz
Featuring: Gail Edwards, Ed Begley, Jr., Mary Woronov, Paul Bartel
Written by: Danny Opatoshu, Henry Rosenbaum, David Taylor
Directed by: Allan Arkush

Synopsis: It's gonna be the Mother of All Concerts: New Year's Eve, 1982, at Max Wolfe's (Goorwitz) Saturn Theater. All the greats will be there: King Blues (Bill Henderson); punk group Nada; rock legend Reggie Wanker (McDowell); even reclusive folksinger Auden (Lou Reed)—if he ever finishes writing his latest song, "We're Late For The Show." If things aren't crazy enough, they're about to get crazier: Ruthless millionaire Colin Beverly (Begley) is determined to erect an 80-story office complex on the site of the Saturn—and since Max refuses to sell it, Colin will simply blow it up, at the stroke of midnight. The concert will be a blast—maybe the last one any of the revelers ever hear!
Discussion: *Woodstock* meets *Airplane!* in this miles-over-the-top comedy which does for concert rock what *Spinal Tap* did for heavy metal. It's difficult to exaggerate a scene as extravagant as a rock concert, but this exuberant, lightning-paced gagfest manages it in virtually every shot. The writers know the Fillmore inside out (the scene in Men's Room alone is enough to prove that), but a multitude of details—like the Olympic-style balcony-diving competition—also show they haven't missed a single detail of the experience. The parodies of performers are wickedly on-target as well, especially McDowell as a barely-exaggerated Jagger and Bill Henderson as BB King. The center of gravity (or levity) is Stern as a first-time stage manager, forced to deal with a million mini-crises (like manic Fire Marshall Robert Picardo) while trying to launch a backstage romance with Edwards; every time he looks at her we see what he sees in his lusty libido. Add in the cult comedy duo Bartel and Woronov, the inspired casting of rock legends Fabian and Bobby Sherman as Beverly's echo-ready yes-men, ex-Turtle Howard Kaylan as superhippie Capt. Cloud, and *a little something special* in the backstage water supply, and you've got the makings of a great concert—and a great, zany "car-tune" comedy.
Rent this one for: its wacky, fast-paced comedy.
You'll (probably) like this if you liked: *Phantom of the Paradise, Airplane!, The Blues Brothers, This Is Spinal Tap!*
Dissenting Opinion: "...sloppy send-up...For rock music fans only." —SMV (1.5) • "...hit-and-miss..." —PVG (2.5)
Vidbits: • Clint Howard appears as an usher. • Ken Kesey's bus "Further" makes a cameo appearance.

The Gods Must Be Crazy

(slapstick)

(1981; CBS/Fox; PG; 1:49)

Starring: N!Xau, Marius Weyers, Sandra Prinsloo
Written, produced and directed by: Jamie Uys

Synopsis: The Bushmen of Africa's Kalahari Desert are a simple, gentle people, completely unaware of the "civilized" world. So when a Coca-Cola bottle carelessly tossed from a plane lands in their midst, they consider it a gift from the gods. Every day brings new uses for this "thing"—but with the gift also comes new feelings: possession, jealousy, anger. They decide it's an *evil* thing, and Xi (N!Xau) takes it upon himself to walk to the edge of the world and throw it off. Meanwhile, a band of guerrillas on the run from government troops is headed his way, as is naturalist Andrew (Weyers), who becomes tongue-tied around pretty women like Kate (Prinsloo), the new schoolmarm he's escorting to a nearby village. When all three paths inevitably converge, they're all in for the biggest culture clash of their lives.
Discussion: It starts like a godzillion National Geographic documentaries—and carries on its anthropological tone and terminology even as it begins deconstructing the life of the working class in the Big City. But it soon becomes the sort of documentary Mack Sennett might make for The Discovery Channel. It's filled with slapstick comedy, speeded up photography and charming, sympathetic characters; even the terrorists are portrayed more as dumb bunglers than serious dangers. The plot might be thin, but this is character-driven comedy about a gentle clash of cultures. It's a cute, wacky, funny, sweet little pixie-witted picture with a madcap romance worthy of any screwball movie as a subplot. And it's at its most insightful, sympathetic and humorous when dealing with the perceptions and interpretations of the indigenous people. Referring to the flick as racist in any sense misses the point: it isn't satirizing natives, blacks, whites or even terrorists—it's a slapstick slap in the face of civilization in general and human foibles in particular. After all, if the gods made us in their image, the gods are *definitely* crazy.
Rent this one for: its slapstick satire and silliness.
You'll (probably) like this if you liked: *Bananas*
Credentials: "★★★★★" —VMG • "innocent and charming" (GMR)
Dissenting Opinion: • "...hackneyed...sledgehammer direction ...technically inadequate" —*Variety* • "...throwback farce...blacks behaving...stupidly...One for the Race Relations Board" —HFG
Vidbits: • Uys also shot and edited the film. • Released in the U.S. in 1984, it became the biggest foreign film hit to that date.

Gregory's Girl

(romance/coming-of-age comedy)

(1981; Embassy Home Entertainment; NR; 1:31)

Starring: Gordon John Sinclair, Dee Hepburn, Clare Grogan
Written and directed by: Bill Forsyth

Synopsis: Gregory (Sinclair) is a gawky, gangly, but good-natured 16-year-old Scottish lad. He's sprouted so fast that he's no longer coordinated enough for his "football" team (that's soccer to us), and is replaced by...a *girl.* He should hate Dorothy (Hepburn)—so of course he develops a desperate crush on her. He swoons, he sighs, he stares at her from afar; he discusses her with his mates and with his little sister (Grogan), whose practical advice about affairs of the heart belies her tender age of ten. When Gregory finally lands a date with Dorothy, things don't go quite as he expected; it seems that girls have their own wily ways, and Gregory is set up like a soccer ball for their own emotional goals. Well, if you can't be with the one you love...

Discussion: "Hard work, being in love, eh?" Gregory's sister Susan sympathizes. Indeed. Hard work being a teenager at all, particularly an ambling, shambling romantic who wears his heart on the sleeve of his football jersey. "It's a tricky time for me," Gregory explains to his coach. Double indeed. It's difficult to be nonchalant when every detail of life is important, when nothing ever seems to go right, and when the quest for confidence is constantly undermined—often by your own body! Not much "happens" in this quiet little film—unless, of course, you count every awkward gesture, every tentative expression and every line of dialog. The bittersweet curse of unrequited love—so familiar to us all, and yet still so painful, after all these years!—has rarely been presented as affectionately as in this gem. Simply put, *Gregory's Girl* is the very definition of the word *charming.*

Rent this one for: the charm; the lyrical lilt of the language.
You'll (probably) like this if you liked: *Comfort and Joy, Local Hero, Housekeeping* (other Forsyth movies); *Experience Preferred...., Lucas, Angus, My Life As A Dog*
Dissenting Opinion: • "...perhaps a bit overrated." —MMG • "...handicapped by impenetrable accents" —HFG (which nonetheless distinguished it with two stars, when *none* is its norm!)
Vidbits: What in heaven's name is the deal with the kid in the penguin suit? Did a Monty Python member sneak on the set?

Hear My Song

(1991; Paramount; R; 1:44)

Starring: Adrian Dunbar, Tara Fitzgerald, Ned Beatty
Featuring: David McCallum, Shirley Anne Field
Written by: Adrian Dunbar, Peter Chelsom
Directed by: Peter Chelsom

Synopsis: "Mr. X: Is he or isn't he?" That's the question on every Liverpudlian's lips when rakish entrepreneur Mickey (Dunbar) claims to have booked legendary tenor Josef Locke into his failing nightclub. Jo—whose singing "makes women weep"—fled England to avoid jail for tax evasion 25 years earlier. So it's no surprise to find that Mr. X "isn't"—although the discovery holds grave consequences for Mickey—like the loss of his lady love, Nancy (Fitzgerald). There's only one thing for Mickey to do: Go to Ireland, find the *real* Jo Locke (Beatty), and bring him back for one final concert. Even if he's successful in his quest, will this win back Nancy? And if Locke appears in public, can he escape the tax man who's waited a quarter of a century to catch him?
Discussion: Chelsom must have show biz in his blood: he's a born entertainer and understands them as well. Here, it's music hall singers; in *Funny Bones,* it's vaudevillians. *Song* can almost be seen as a trial run for *Bones:* both concern performing and long lost loves; both contain wild slapstick humor and a Keystone view of Kops. This charming, picaresque and laugh-out-loud funny fable is filled with charismatic characters, delightful dialog ("I'd rather be in jail than in love again," spits one old sod), and a pair of rocky romances inspiring the exigencies of the plot. Locke and Mickey find themselves in parallel predicaments, which bring them together as they assist one another in reuniting with the women who'd love to love them—if the boys hadn't betrayed them so badly. We care about these people and their plights; we root for them. A little history, a little legend, intermingled with wit and heart—if that isn't the essence of a great film (and of being Irish!) I don't know what is at all, at all.
Rent this one for: its charm and humor; the acting and script.
You'll (probably) like this if you liked: *Funny Bones, The Englishman Who Went Up A Hill..., Local Hero*
Credentials: • "...the very soul of a great small film." —Roger Ebert (3.5 stars) • "...charming, hilarious..." —GMR (3.5 bones) • "...joyful, exuberant...funny, uplifting and magnificently presented. A near-perfect entertainment." —SMV (3.5) • *EW:* "A"
Vidbits: • Beatty was nominated for a best supporting actor Golden Globe. • Locke's singing voice was provided by Vernon Midgley. • According to the credits, Locke "is now living in County Kildare, Ireland." May the wind always be at his back.

Heathers

(black comedy/ cult)

(1989; Starmaker; R; 1:45)

Starring: Winona Ryder, Christian Slater
Featuring: Kim Walker, Shannen Doherty, Lisanne Falk
Written by: Daniel Waters
Directed by: Michael Lehmann

Synopsis: At Westerburg High, Heathers rule! The ruling clique consists of three Heathers (Falk, Walker & Doherty) and Veronica Sawyer (Ryder). And cruelty, thy name is Heather! Veronica admits to outrageously cool new kid J.D. (Slater) that "I don't really like my friends," and after a vicious bitchfest with the head Heather (and consummating her friendship with J.D.), they decide to teach #1 a lesson. Veronica just wants to make her puke. J.D. fills her cup with industrial strength cleaner and croaks her. Luckily, Ronnie can fake anyone's handwriting—like Heather's, on a suicide note. And when some jocks start spreading rumors about spreading Veronica, the deadly duo decides to throw a scare into them, too. Unbeknownst to Veronica, J.D. decides live ammo would scare them even more...
Discussion: "My teen angst bullshit has a body count," Veronica confides to her diary after a second fatal "joke." "Are we going to Prom or to Hell?" Teen suicides? Guns in school? This is funny? Duh! It's so *very!* Lehmann's feature debut is a pitch black comedy, filled with sparklingly witty dialog, deliciously edgy action and energetic acting. Ryder runs the gamut from mopey teen to action heroine, and Slater does a sly turn, half James Dean ("J.D."), half Jack Nicholson. Along the way, the psychology of high school social status is viciously vilified. The one problem with this flick is that it turns too serious in the last half hour, as J.D. morphs into a psychostalker and the movie degenerates into an action thriller. While it does redeem itself once Veronica steps outside the school, it would have been much more darkly courageous to imply that J.D. was on the right track all the time. Even so, *Heathers* lives up to its mini-cult rep as a "killer comedy." Call it *A Nightmare on Clueless St.*
Rent this one for: its pitch black comedy.
You'll (probably) like this if you liked: *Clueless, Lord Love A Duck, Harold and Maude, The Ruling Class*
Dissenting Opinion: "Somewhat smug satire...uneven script ...goes far astray." —MMG (2.5 stars)
Vidbits: "Veronica Sawyer" and "Betty Finn" were named after two other famous pairs of friends, Betty and Veronica from the "Archie" comics, and Tom Sawyer and Huck Finn.

Hexed

(1993; Columbia TriStar; R; 1:33)

Starring: Ayre Gross, Claudia Christian, Adrienne Shelly
Featuring: R. Lee Ermey, Norman Fell
Written and directed by: Alan Spencer

Synopsis: Gorgeous supermodel Hexina (Christian) is paying a secret visit to Dallas, staying at the Holiday Palace. Too bad that Matthew (Gross)—compulsive fibber and still a desk clerk at 30—has been spreading rumors that he's dated her. Capitalizing on a confusion in communication, Matthew ends up taking her out, and finds out that she is indeed to die for: first she jumps his bones, then she jumps him with a knife. Too bad the man Matthew is posing as has been blackmailing Hexina. Once their identities are straightened out, he agrees to help her deal with the blackmailer; too bad her idea of "dealing with" is so, um, *confrontational.* She's the psychobitch from hell; he's just a geek. Who'll win a showdown between a hoaxer and a hexer?
Discussion: He's a loser, baby, so why don't you kill him? Of all the movies in this book, this one is perhaps the toughest to defend. But I watched it twice and laughed both times. *Hexed* has a kind of innocent charm, much like Spencer's TV series, "Sledge Hammer." Both emphasize over-the-top comedy and goofy humor about inherently violent events. While "Sledge" was a spoof of Dirty Harry flicks, *Hexed* is half Hitchcockian "wrong man" send-up and half long-overdue skewering of the *Fatal Attraction/Basic Instinct femme fatale* flicks. Gross's role as dejected schlub is quirky, and more than one-dimensional; he's a compulsive storyteller who can't even convince himself of his own fantasies. Christian is energetically insane; only Shelly is underused. (Is Hal Hartley the only director who knows how to use her special skills?) There's nothing new here (Hexina punches a mime! How daring!) but its lack of pretension is quite refreshing. *Citizen Kane* it ain't; 90 minutes of adolescent amusement, it is.
Rent this one for: the one *Basic Instinct* parody that works.
You'll (probably) like this if you liked: *Fatal Instinct,* "Sledge Hammer"
Dissenting Opinion: • "Inane, charmless" —GMR (1.5 bones) • "...doesn't quite know the difference between being outrageous and being absolutely tasteless." —VMG (2 stars) • "Very hit-and-miss—and at worst, terrible." —MMG (2 stars)
Vidbits: Christian's body double for nude scenes was Shelley Michelle (listed in the credits, in an unusual move), who also doubled for Julia Roberts in *Pretty Woman.* • Christian is a regular player on TV's *Babylon 9* and appeared as a victim of the alien in *The Hidden.*

Flashback!

Inserts

(drama)

(1975; Key Video; Rated X; 1:33)

Starring: Richard Dreyfuss, Bob Hoskins, Jessica Harper
Featuring: Veronica Cartwright, Stephen Davies
Written and directed by: John Byrum

Synopsis: In the days of silent films, he was The Boy Wonder (Dreyfuss). But now it's 1931, and he's a "ghost story," cranking out stag flicks in a corner of his crumbling Hollywood mansion between swigs from the cognac bottle. This day's shooting starts out badly and quickly goes downhill. His lusty leading lady Harlene (Cartwright) shoots up before the shoot, for instance; then his mobster financier "Big Mac" (Hoskins) shows up with his silver screen wannabe moll, Miss Cake (Harper), to meddle in the production. When Harlene ODs, Mac and twitish male lead "Rex the Wonder Dog" take her corpse out to dispose of it, leaving The Boy Wonder alone with Cathy Cake—young, attractive, and willing to do anything to break into the business. *Anything.* Will The Boy Wonder finish his fuck flick—or will it finish him?
Discussion: Beloved film star Richard Dreyfuss in an X-rated movie? Call it *Mr. Holland's Onus.* It's a somber comedy, and a genuine curiosity, perverse even by today's standards: an odd combination of slapstick, histrionics, nudity and pathos. The scattershot approach misses often, but when it hits, it's morbid magic. On one level, it's The Hollywood Story (use and abuse everyone, including yourself), along with The Hollywood Moral (intelligence and talent don't stand a chance against bad taste, big bucks and blind ambition). The film is staged like a play, with a heavy reliance on dialog (much raunchy), and the second act—mostly about Hoskins' obnoxious "Big Mac" and Rex—drags and grates. But the third act is electric, as The Boy Wonder engages in an intense, escalating game of truth-or-dare with a woman nowhere near as naive as she seems. As they explore the overlap between real life and reel life, the question becomes Who's tutoring whom? Give all the actors points for risking their reps on this strange, uneven, unique experiment.
Rent this one for: the ensemble acting; its experimentation.
You'll (probably) like this if you liked: *Living in Oblivion*
Dissenting Opinion: • "...pretentious, long-winded...Affected, windbaggish performances kill it." —GMR (1 bone) • "Dreary..." —VMG ("Turkey") • "Pretentious, unending nonsense...Dreadful." —MMG (BOMB)
Vidbits: Dreyfuss co-produced; Harper was Music Consultant.

Flashback!

I Wanna Hold Your Hand

(1978; Warner; PG; 1:44)

Starring: Nancy Allen, Bobby DiCicco, Wendie Jo Sperber, Marc McClure, Susan K. Newman, Theresa Saldana, Eddie Deezen
Written by: Robert Zemeckis, Bob Gale
Directed by: Robert Zemeckis

Synopsis: New York City, February 8, 1964: The Beatles invade America! Meanwhile, in New Jersey, Grace (Saldana) hits on a scheme to sneak into Their hotel with fellow Beatlemaniacs Pam (Allen) and Rosie (Sperber). Dang if it doesn't work! Separated, they prowl around the hotel attempting to enter Their room while avoiding security goons. Pam makes it in and plays Goldilocks with Their stuff; Rosie steals an elevator and hooks up with Beatlegeek "Ringo" Klaus (Deesen); Grace follows the Fab Four to Ed Sullivan's studio, but has to raise $50 to bribe a guard before she can get in. And so on. By hook or by crook (or by luck), each girl scores show tickets—but each also runs into an obstacle that might prevent her from attending. Will their resourcefulness desert them at the crucial moment? All they need is...not love, but *luck*. Yeah, yeah, yeah!
Discussion: A good-natured, loud, slapstick teen comedy, both frantic and frenetic. Leave it to Zemeckis and Gale to pull off interweaving four stories, and to make a Beatles movie in which The Boys "appear" as feet, voices, the backs of heads, and performing on studio monitors (while the faces on stage remain cleverly hidden behind those monitors). Z&G have always had an eye for culture clash, like *Back to the Future's* clever contrast of the placid '50s with the crazy '80s; here, they focus on the moment in which Elvis gave way to England—and also manage to capture the hysteria that was Beatlemania (in a flick which curiously ends with a high-speed drive and a fortuitous bolt of lightning...) It's fab, it's gear—*and* it features 17 Beatles tunes!
Rent this one for: The manic, high-energy performances.
You'll (probably) like this if you liked: *A Hard Day's Night, The Rutles, Back To The Future*
Vidbits: • "...one of the biggest money-losers of 1978..." —VMG • Saldana inadvertently became famous a few years later as the victim of a stalker attack. • "Cindy the Hooker" is played by Kristine DeBell, who in '76 played the title role in an X-rated version of *Alice in Wonderland,* and who, in '79, would co-star with Bill Murray in *Meatballs.* • Inside joke: Will Jordan, playing Ed Sullivan, makes reference to an upcoming guest, "young impressionist Will Jordan, who does an impression of me." • Cameo: DJ Murray the K appears as himself.

Flashback!

J-Men Forever

(1979; Vestron; PG; 1:13; B&W)

Written by and featuring: Peter Bergman, Philip Proctor
Edited by: Gail Werbin
Directed by: Richard Patterson

Synopsis: *J-Men* is the story of the Secret World War, or how that villainous ultrahipster, The Lightning Bug, attempted to squash the brown-shoed squares and make their ballroom ballads go ballistic using his secret weapon, degenerate rock and roll music. Superheroes like The Caped Madman and Rocket Jock join government agents like Mr. Armhole and Sleeve Coat in an attempt to stop this invasion of "senseless, sensuous" non-stop rock around the clock, doc! What's next—hash gas?
Discussion: Any serious student of comedy will testify that the '70s produced only three comic highlights: "Saturday Night Live" and Steve Martin—which were pretty much on the same wavelength—and The Firesign Theatre, who were riding a wavelength from some far off, far out, drug-addled dimension (or is that "dementia"?). Remember *What's Up, Tiger Lily?,* where Woody Allen took an obscure Japanese spy flick, then rewrote and redubbed the sound track to make it a comedy? In *J-Men,* Proctor and Bergman, two-fourths of The Firesign, went The Woodman one better, slicing and dicing numerous old Republic Studio serials from the '40s and re-editing selected scenes to create an entirely new movie. (P&B themselves appear in new transitional scenes, also shot in glorious black and white.) Although turning screen icons like Capt. Marvel into goofy new heroes (in this case, the over-eager Caped Madman) is droll, their cleverest invention by far is that costume-swapping, mask-fetishist fiend, The Lightning Bug—a shrewd device through which they were free to combine footage of *any* serial villain into a single sinister scoundrel. ("Pack my costumes!" The Bug orders. "*All* of them?" an underling whines.) If you've ever been a Firesign fan, I'm "overwhelmingly overconfident" you'll dig this pun-filled lampoon of '40s flicks and '50s right-wing nightmares.
Rent this one for: the merry marriage of archaic imagery and wacky wordplay, yielding a surreally silly cinematic curiosity.
You'll (probably) like this if you liked: *What's Up, Tiger Lily?, Firesign Theatre's Hot Shorts, Dead Men Don't Wear Plaid,* "MST3K"
Dissenting Opinion: "...way too long for this type of treatment" —VMG (2 stars)
Vidbits: One bit features the screen debut of Leonard Nimoy, in the last Republic serial produced, *Radar Men From The Moon.*

Joe Versus The Volcano

(1990; Warner; PG; 1:46)

Starring: Tom Hanks, Meg Ryan
Featuring: Lloyd Bridges, Robert Stack, Abe Vigoda, Ossie Davis
Written and directed by: John Patrick Shanley

Synopsis: "Once upon a time there was a guy named Joe," the opening titles tell us. And his life sucks like a high-powered Hoover. Joe (Hanks) works in a dingy, dismal factory ("Home of the Rectal Probe"); he's always sick; and one day a doctor informs him that he's got a "brain cloud," and only six months to live. Enter eccentric millionaire Samuel Graynamore (Bridges) with an odd proposition: sail his yacht to the South Pacific isle of Waponi Woo, and jump into a volcano to appease the fire gods before it blows and sinks the island—the only source of a mineral Graynamore needs to run his business. "Live like a king; die like a man!" Graynamore enthuses. Joe's reaction: Yeah, OK. He heads for L.A. with a quartet of giant, buoyant steamer trunks full of travel accessories, where he's met at the docks by Graynamore's plucky daughter, Patricia (Ryan). She may be skipper of the ship, but she's as soul-sick as he is, they discover as they establish a rapport. Once they reach Waponi Woo, what will be their fate? Will Joe really jump into the fire? Can he and Pat rely on miracles, or have they used up their share? Do they have even half a chance at living happily ever after?
Discussion: It begins as all fables begin, and ends as all fables end. And it's one strange fable. On the surface, *Joe* is a wacky, comic book comedy; a twisted vision of adventure, full of warped characters and funhouse imagery; a series of silly incidents and a sweet romantic fantasy. Everyone is obviously having fun (particularly Ryan, who plays three very different women). Much of the humor in the performances comes from the matter-of-fact underreactions to peak emotional events, epitomized by the deadpan Vigoda and by Joe's eventual confession of love to Pat. And the flick is indeed "fabulous," in the dictionary definition of "barely credible; astonishing."

Maybe this is where it lost the audience, in its extravagantly embellished, enormously exaggerated fantastic elements. (Look what happened to Gilliam's *Baron Munchausen.*) But *Joe* is *not* a fantasy, and it's not a fable. Technically, it's a *romance,* in several senses of the word—the most common of which is exhibited in the fond relationship which develops between Joe and Pat.

But the film is also a "romance" like *Don Quixote:* an heroic (and satirical) tale of extraordinary events. It's a romance novel for men—and it's the only one. Consider the pattern: Joe is clearly suffering from a mid-life crisis. ("I'm losing my sole," he says, looking at his shoe, oblivious to his own perfect pun.) He's sick all the time, but it's *ennui,* a spiritual illness—the only cure for which is to do the things that will challenge his existence and inject his gray life with the joy of living. So he tells off his boss and quits his job, leaving behind his gray desk, his gray office, his gray suit. He grapples with his own Mortality. He embarks on an Adventure (offered by "Mr. Gray-no-more"). He discovers his ability to Love. He experiences an epiphany of pure, perfect Connection with the Universe, in all its awe and mystery. He wrestles with Destiny and takes control of his Fate. He faces his greatest Fears. He performs a Selfless Act of Sacrifice requiring enormous Courage. He becomes a Hero. What more could he ask from Life than to be given the chance to follow this ageless, mythic roadmap to masculine mastery? In mundane terms, he performs all the actions and endures all the experiences that make a man a Man. The film is in effect an allegorical blueprint of masculine development and mid-life fulfillment, presented in satiric symbology. And if this isn't a template that parallels the exaggerated romantic fantasies of women's romance novels, then what is?

Joe is an Epic Adventure taken with its tongue placed firmly in its cheek. Its a combination of High Romance, Middle-age redemption, low comedy, and deep philosophy; a painless, joyous, liberating way to get the essential message that life is a precious gift. It's a hyperbolic yarn spun by a mythic Fool which, in one brief scene—Joe's "lost at sea" prayer—manages to transcend the merely surreal and even "magical realism" to achieve an achingly poignant epiphany of "magical surrealism."

Shanley, in his directorial debut, proves his playwright's ear for a phrase and poet's soul for understanding what it means to be a man in the late 20th century. Bly and Keen and their ilk all explain; Shanley illustrates. The price he paid for his insights was that this gem was ignored. Don't make that mistake.

Rent this one for: its surreal, cerebral celebration of existence.

You'll (probably) like this if you liked: *Groundhog Day, Defending Your Life, L.A. Story* (male mid-life crisis fantasies); *Sleepless in Seattle* (Hanks/Ryan romantic comedy); *Big*

Dissenting Opinion: "...pointless...a shaggy dog story that doesn't pay off." —MMG (2.5 stars)

Vidbits: The company's distinctive lightning-slash logo appears in numerous destructive guises throughout the film, including the path to the factory, a crack in the wall of Joe's apartment, the lightning bolt that sinks the yacht, the torch-lit procession up the mountain to the volcano, and the lava flow. • Among the minor players: Nathan Lane, Amanda Plummer, Dan Hedaya and Carol Kane. • "Joseph Banks" was Capt. Cook's chief botanist during his 18th century South Pacific expeditions.

Just One of the Guys

(1985; RCA/Columbia; PG-13; 1:40)

Starring: Joyce Hyser, Clayton Rohner, Billy Jacoby
Featuring: Kenneth Tigar, Sherilyn Fenn, Toni Hudson, Ayre Gross
Written by: Dennis Feldman, Jeff Franklin
Directed by: Lisa Gottlieb

Synopsis: Terry (Hyser) is a gorgeous high school queen, but she's no airhead: she's determined to win a writing contest and land a summer internship at a newspaper to start her career as a serious journalist. Disadvantage: She's female, and everybody treats her like "a decoration." Advantage: Her parents are gone for two weeks...just enough time to transfer to a rival high—disguised as a guy. She'll take a walk on the wild side then write up the experience as her entry. She's got a lot to learn (her horny little bro (Jacoby) teaches her how to walk and scratch, for instance), but she's got a lot to teach as well, especially to Rick (Rohner). A lonely bookworm on the outside, inside he's got a James Brown mojo just aching to bust loose. Terry remakes him in her image, as a cool guy. Then the triple whammy: She falls for Rick, who thinks she's a guy; the school slut (Fenn), thinking she's a he tries to get into "his" pants; and Terry's male chauvinist boyfriend finds out she's posing as a guy. Can Terry mend her gender-bending ways and engender a tender ending?
Discussion: It's difficult to apply the adjective "innocent" to a sex farce, but I think it applies here. Never smirky or smarmy, it's filled with spirited performances from likable actors. Hyser is engaging (and a knockout in her female incarnation), obviously digging the disguise, and we share in her vivacious enthusiasm. There are a lot of just funny lines, many from Jacoby as the unrepentant, unrestrained teenage Hormone That Walks Like A Man. And of course everyone learns A Valuable Lesson, but the lessons are both honest and bittersweet. Why not watch this free on TV? Because the resolution involves a graphic exposure of Terry's anatomy—and even cable channels always edit it out.
Rent this one for: being a funny, ebulliently-acted, good-natured sex farce with its heart in the right place (even if some other major organs aren't)—an antidote to crap like "Porky's."
You'll (probably) like this if you liked: *Clueless, Fast Times At Ridgemont High; Tootsie, Victor/Victoria*
Dissenting Opinion: "1.5 stars" —SMV
Vidbits: Hyser might not make many screen appearances (*Wedding Band, Greed,* a season of "L.A. Law"), but her personal life is incredibly active. She was Bruce Springsteen's girlfriend for five years, spent a year with Timothy Hutton, and lived with Warren Beatty. If I weren't married, I'd send her *my* address.

L.A. Story

(romantic comedy/fantasy)
(1991; LIVE; PG-13; 1:38)

Starring: Steve Martin, Victoria Tennant, Sarah Jessica Parker
Written by: Steve Martin
Directed by: Mick Jackson

Synopsis: "I was deeply unhappy," Harrison K. Telemacher (Martin) tells us; "but I didn't know it because I was so *happy* all the time." This is no paradox in the "intellectual-free zone" of La-La-Land. And why *shouldn't* he be happy? He's the "Wacky Weatherman" on TV (looks like that Ph.D. in Arts and Humanities didn't do him much good), and life is one endless brunch, full of sunshine and air kisses. Except for the occasional earthquake, a shallow, bitchy, cheating girlfriend, and an absolute total lack of depth. Until he meets Sarah (Tennant), a wistful, quirky journalist from London. He also meets two other characters who make a major difference in his life: ditzy boy-toy SanDeE (Parker), and a huge "freeway condition" sign that takes a shine to him and lights up his life with advice and predictions ("The weather will change your life. Twice.") Fate, wind (and the sign) conspire to bring Harris and Sarah together, but they pull apart. They get together again—and circumstances pull them apart... He realizes he can't live without her. But it would take a miracle to bring them back together. Nice day...Think it'll rain?
Discussion: Love is magic. But can romance and magic exist in L.A.? Where else *could* it exist but in the land of make believe? One of several recent midlife crisis-romantic comedy-fantasies (see below), this film is simultaneously wacky and wondrous; funny and touching. It's a West Coast *Annie Hall* for the '90s (and, like *Annie Hall,* takes on even more poignant dimensions knowing that Martin and Tennant were married at the time and have since divorced. Sorry, Steve; I know precisely how you feel.) Lovely touches include Martinesque insights into brain-dead L.A. lifestyles (driving next door; restaurants that do credit checks); a parade of appearances (including Patrick Ste-wart, Chevy Chase, George Plimpton and Woody Harrelson); an abundance of Shakespearean references (watch for Rick Moranis in an uncredited role as a gravedigger); and a score featuring several Enya songs: the perfect ethereal accompaniment for this sweet romance. See it with someone you love—or would like to.
Rent this one for: its status as the perfect modern date movie.
You'll (probably) like this if you liked: *Defending Your Life, Groundhog Day, Joe vs. the Volcano*
Vidbits: Burbank Ave. near Sepulveda Dam doubled as freeway.

Love At Large

(mystery/romance)
(1989; Orion; R; 1:30)

Starring: Tom Berenger, Elizabeth Perkins
Featuring: Anne Archer, Ann Magnuson, Annette O'Toole, Kate Capshaw, Ted Levine, Neil Young
Written and directed by: Alan Rudolph

Synopsis: Harry Dobbs (Berenger), cheap P.I., is in over his head. His girlfriend Doris (Magnuson) has thrown him out, and his new client, Miss Dolen (Archer), is one high-toned broad—uh, high-class chick—*awwww!* Anyway, she hires Harry to follow Rick (Young), who she suspects is cheating on her. Lucky Harry ends up tailing the wrong guy: family man King (Levine), who's cheating on his wife. *Both* his wives, actually; his city wife (O'Toole) *and* his country wife (Capshaw). Imagine Harry's irritation when he discovers *he's* being followed by another P.I., hired by *Doris! Awwww!* Stella (Perkins) is half tough and half bluff, given to studying books about the psychology of love. An accident throws them together, and when Doris finds out, she fires Stella. Traveling home on the same plane, Harry confronts Stella and they engage in half a battle of wits—and a discussion of romance. Well, if two professional detectives can't unravel the mysteries of the heart—their clients' or their own—who can?
Discussion: "There ain't no cure for love," Leonard Cohen moans from the soundtrack. There ain't no explaining it either. It's a mystery—which is why it's such a delightful and insightful conceit, actually putting a couple of detectives on the case. Berenger is immediately likable as the gravel-voiced dick who is honest and dedicated, if none too bright; and Perkins is perky as the smart but wounded Stella, more in search of herself and a man she can trust than a client. They're all people trapped out of time: Harry wants to be Philip Marlowe; the quirky Miss Dolen wants to be a '40s chanteuse, "glad and dizzy" all the time; even Stella yearns to return to a more romantic—and romantically simpler—era. Why else would they have become detectives if they weren't closet romantics? But even if they can solve a case, can anyone solve a bad case of love? Smart, sweet, and charming—a great date movie. Track it down.
Rent this one for: the clever conceit of using a detective as a metaphor for the search for love; for the performances.
You'll (probably) like this if you liked: *Choose Me, Trouble in Mind* (w/d by Rudolph); *Someone to Watch over Me* (serious)
Credentials: "3.5 stars" —SMV
Dissenting Opinion: "A challenge to Rudolph cultists everywhere...[a] coy mess..." —MMG (2 stars)

Double Feature!

Lucas

(1985; FoxVideo; PG-13; 1:39)

Starring: Corey Haim, Kerri Green, Charlie Sheen
Featuring: Courtney Thorne-Smith, Winona Ryder, Jeremy Piven
Written and directed by: David Seltzer

Synopsis: Lucas (Haim) is a precocious, "intellectually accelerated" runt who tumbles heavily one summer for the new girl in town, magnificent Maggie (Green). They pal around during the summer, but Lucas dreads returning to school. Problem is, he's 14, and she's 16—which puts them worlds apart in the strict high school social structure. Sure enough, she falls for football player Cappie (Sheen)—even though both Maggie and Cappie would do almost anything not to hurt sensitive Lucas' feelings. Depressed and dejected, Lucas determines that the one way to win Maggie back is to become a football hero himself. He risks both injury and ridicule to take the field—but he's used to both. And maybe the old adage is true: Whatever doesn't kill you makes you stronger. *If* it doesn't kill you, that is...

Angus

(1995; Turner; PG-13; 1:27)

Starring: Charlie Talbert, George C. Scott, Ariana Richards
Featuring: Chris Owen, Kathy Bates, James Van Der Beek
Written by: Jill Gordon (based on a short story by Chris Crutcher)
Directed by: Patrick Read Johnson

Synopsis: How could they *not* have been mortal enemies from birth? Angus (Talbert), the Fat Kid, and Rick (Van Der Beek), the Aryan Adonis Football Hero? Angus, however portly, is good at science—but miserable at socialization. No wonder: His mom (Bates) is a truck driver, and his growling grandpa (Scott) is a semi-somnambulant septuagenarian with a fiancée 30 years his junior. It's no surprise when the delicious Melissa (Richards) is named Queen of the Winter Ball—but Angus named King? Obviously, this is a mistake; or worse, a joke; or worst of all, a set-up for the ultimate humiliation at the hands of Rick. But even armed with foreknowledge, will Angus have the guts to show up and turn it into a showdown? And if Fate has finally thrown Angus together with Melissa—the object of his distant desire—can he find courage enough to seize the moment?

Discussion: We could almost retitle *Angus* as *Lucas '95,* which is why I've combined them. *Angus* isn't as articulate as *Lucas,* but the title characters share an outsider's understanding and a hard-won wisdom of the heart—and about the hard facts of life of adolescence. And while they both worship unobtainable women from afar, all either really wants is just his "moment."

Of the pair, *Lucas* is superior in virtually all respects. The emotions and situations are genuine, the dialog is smart, the central trio are as sensitive as teens can be. Sheen is a gem as the nice-guy gridiron hero; witty, charming, and self-assured. He's Lucas' friend and protector, and as frustrated as Lucas gets seeing Maggie falling for him, he's denied a "bad guy" to hate in response. And he knows depressingly well that friendship is just a consolation prize for failure to inspire love.

Lucas is in essence an oxymoron: a formula flick without clichés; a teen comedy which does not rely on stereotypes but instead features believable characters. The film is unpredictable yet realistic, full of original situations—and quite amusing. (Highlights include Cappie and Maggie's laundry room connection, laden with innocent innuendo; the choral practice, where the camera pans to catch every character watching their object of affection in a droll round-robin; and Ryder as the frumpy rejected girl—as if!) And as if all that isn't enough, *Lucas* ends —against all odds—on a sweet, uplifting and triumphal note.

Angus suffers problems similar to Lucas, but without the benefit of a Cappie; his nemesis is the stereotypical evil jock. But Angus has some secret weapons working for him. First is his chemistry project, a metaphor for his situation: an attempt to illustrate that "If you put a small, abnormal element in a large homogeneous system, the system will reject the deviation rather than mutate." But, he discovers, it doesn't have to be that way, "if the element is brave." When he applies Chaos Theory to social systems, he proves that "There is no 'normal'." And he's got the wise words of his growling grandpa, the redoubtable George C.: "As for what anybody else thinks...Screw 'em!"

Angus has much to recommend it: delightful dialog, a mousy best friend (Owen) who looks like a living Muppet, more than one touch of poignance, and a genuinely original and surprising handling of Angus' first nervous encounter with Melissa.

If they are both formula films, they're first-rate expressions of that formula—and movies with some wit, depth and tenderness, too. Besides, it's a formula that never fails to fascinate—and which every high school generation must learn anew.

Rent these for: the bittersweet insight into the awkward social lives of sensitive teens; the original situations; the humor.
You'll (probably) like these if you liked: *Say Anything...*
Credentials *(Lucas)*: • "...one of the year's best films." —Roger Ebert (★★★★) • "...a real sleeper..." —MMG (3 stars)
Dissenting Opinion *(Angus)*: "obvious and superficial" —MMG
Vidbits *(Lucas)*: Ryder's screen debut; Seltzer's directorial debut; (Angus): Scott's silent chess partner is director Irvin Kershner.

Matinee

(1993; MCA; PG; 1:39)

Starring: John Goodman, Cathy Moriarty, Simon Fenton
Featuring: Omri Katz, Lisa Jakub, Kellie Martin, Jesse White
Written by: Charlie Haas
Directed by: Joe Dante

Synopsis: Key West, Florida, 1962: The local movie house gears up for a special preview screening of *Mant* ("Half man! Half ant! All terror!"), producer Lawrence Woolsey's (Goodman) latest low-budget schlock shocker. Just Larry's luck that he shows up at the wrong moment in history to debut a thriller, as the entire country is on red alert, caught up in the Cuban Missile Crisis. Residents of Key West, only about a hundred miles from Cuba, expect atomic warheads to start raining down on them any minute—hardly the atmosphere in which people want to escape to the movies to be scared; they're frightened enough by reality. But Woolsey persists with his premiere, and teenaged Gene (Fenton) sets out to befriend the man behind his favorite flicks. No one counts on Murphy's Law, rather than martial law, being enforced during the packed premiere of the flick—or on the life-and-death disasters that mass hysteria can create on its own.
Discussion: Right from the opening, a trailer for *Mant,* with its portentous tone, screaming females and cheesy effects, we know we're watching a movie that knows its Grade Z sci-fi. Only later do we discover that *Matinee* knows our heart as well. Bomb-age Barnum Woolsey, master of the ass-grabbing gimmick ("Filmed in Atomo-vision and Rumble Rama!"), might be full of hustle and bluster, but he's basically an OK Joe, and passes on his surprisingly insightful understanding of mass psychology to his young charge. Ice queen Cathy Moriarty is perfectly cast as Woolsey's jaded lady, and the film is filled with amusingly quirky characters and intertwining subplots. By continually overlapping reality and fantasy, it cleverly questions where one leaves off and the other begins—and the role that belief plays in the distinction. A sweet black comedy about teen traumas, the proper use of fear, nuclear madness—and giant ants.
Rent this one for: the scenes from the parody film-within-the-film, *Mant;* for delivering far more than you're led to expect.
You'll (probably) like this if you liked: *The Atomic Café, Mystery Science Theatre 3000*
Vidbits: • Goodman's character was based (not so) loosely on '50s horror movie producer William Castle. • Kevin McCarthy, star of the '50s classic *Invasion of the Body Snatchers,* appears in *Mant,* along with character actor William Schallert. And yes, that is director John Sayles in the role of the tall rabble-rouser.

The Milagro Beanfield War

(1988; MCA; R; 1:58)

Starring: Ruben Blades, Richard Bradford, Sonia Braga, Chick Vennera, John Heard, Carlos Riquelme
Featuring: Daniel Stern, Julie Carmen, Christopher Walken, Freddy Fender, Melanie Griffith, M. Emmet Walsh, James Gammon, Freddie Fender, Robert Carricart
Written by: David S. Ward, John Nichols (based on Nichols' novel)
Directed by: Robert Redford

Synopsis: Joe Mondragon's (Vennera) dusty beanfield is dying of thirst. Suddenly, water begins flowing into it. Too bad it's just a leak: the water belongs to the Divine Land Development Co., the conglomerate that's tearing down most of Milagro to erect the biggest condo/golf course/recreation area in all of New Mexico. Joe's tiny plot of inherited property is the only piece they don't own—yet. The accidental irrigation polarizes the town—and the state government, which wants Joe stopped, but without any publicity which would focus attention on the shady development deal. They *certainly* don't want Joe turned into a folk hero. So they send in boogeyman Montana (Walken), who masterminds a series of dirty tricks which only aggravate the situation; as it escalates and everyone grows edgier, the shopkeeper does brisk business in bullets. It'll take a big sacrifice to solve this, Coyote Angel (Carricart) advises. But what sacrifice is big enough? A road grader? A pig? The field? A neighbor?
Discussion: "I know a lost cause when I see one," reluctant activist Bloom (Heard) informs quixotic homegal Ruby (Braga). But "Milagro" is Spanish for "miracle," and that's exactly what the lethargic residents require. If the development deal proceeds, skyrocketing taxes will force the poverty-stricken local folk to sell out and move, spelling death for their quirky little community. Stubborn Joe's got *huevos,* however—and his aged neighbor Amarante (Riquelme, in the film's best performance), who walks between two worlds, has the spirit of Coyote Angel on their side. Picaresque, whimsical, brimming with truly magical magical realism, this amusing fable is filled with gorgeous photography, and there's a twinkle in the eye of every frame. It provides both smiles and out-loud laughs in abundance, excellent ensemble acting, sweet insight into human nature and its foibles, and some delightfully cliché-breaking defusing of tense situations.
Rent this one for: the performances; its picaresque magic.
You'll (probably) like this if you liked: "Northern Exposure"
Credentials: • Academy Award: Best Score • "...should delight everyone but hard-core cynics." —SMV (3.5 stars)

Moving

(1988; Warner; R; 1:29)

Starring: Richard Pryor, Beverly Todd, Randy Quaid
Featuring: Dana Carvey, Dave Thomas, Stacey Dash, Gordon Jump
Written by: Andy Breckman
Directed by: Alan Metter

Synopsis: Arlo Pear (Pryor) is living the Suburban Dream—or Nightmare. He's harassed by his insane neighbor (Quaid); he's got a 17-year-old daughter (Dash) who can't wait to split; and he has to find out from his replacement that after 15 years he's been "downsized." He's a damn good engineer, but the only job he can find is in Idaho. It's a dream job, but...*Idaho?* He uproots his firmly-rooted family from New Jersey—or tries. His daughter nearly destroys the house so it can't be sold. The movers disappear with their stuff. The clean-cut driver hired to deliver his new Saab (Carvey) has multiple personalities. The beautiful house they bought in Boise is—but that would be telling. His new neighbor is—a surprise. The same kind of surprise you'd get walking into your office the first day on the job and finding a "60 Minutes" crew waiting for you... Arlo's got a very long fuse—but how much stress can one man take before he goes ballistic?
Discussion: "Is life just a big joke to you?" a bartender growls at the drunken, defeated Arlo as he laughs at his piles of problems. "Life is not a big joke," Arlo explains. "It's a series of 8 or 9,000 little jokes, all lined up in a row." The joy of this film is as an antidote to "The Cosby Show"; if Cliff Huxtable ever had these problems, he'd burst a vein. The real joy is Pryor, exhibiting a last flash of brilliance among lesser works, showcasing the characters that made him famous, like the set-upon optimist desperately trying to hold it together but eventually erupting like an obscene geyser. Solid, silly and cynical—a revenge fantasy for anyone who's ever been oppressed. (But "predictable"? Hardly. The movers alone are the most off-the-wall, flamboyant thieves in ages. They even steal scenes from Pryor!)
Rent this one for: the original situations; Pryor's performance.
You'll (probably) like this if you liked: *National Lampoon's Vacation, Clockwise,* W.C. Fields' *Man on the Flying Trapeze*
Dissenting Opinion: • "Predictable calamities...Not apt to move you." —GMR (1 bone) • "Chalk this up as another disappointment from Richard Pryor." —VMG (2 stars) • "Wallows in the predictable." —MMG (1.5 stars) • "1 star" —SMV
Vidbits: • Rodney Dangerfield appears in an uncredited role as the bank loan manager. • Writer Breckman spent two years on Letterman's "Late Night" writing staff, and three seasons writing for "Saturday Night Live."

My Favorite Year

(1982; MGM/UA; PG; 1:32)

Starring: Mark Linn-Baker, Peter O'Toole, Jessica Harper
Featuring: Joseph Bologna, Lainie Kazan, Bill Macy, Lou Jacobi
Written by: Norman Steinberg, Dennis Palumbo
Directed by: Richard Benjamin

Synopsis: 1954: TV was live and comedy was king. Benjy Stone (Linn-Baker), freshman writer on *Comedy Cavalcade,* starring "King" Kaiser (Bologna), is thrilled to hear the show's special guest will be Alan Swann (O'Toole), the greatest movie idol of all time—and Benjy's personal hero. Being assigned to baby-sit Swann is Benjy's big dream—but it might become his biggest nightmare: Swann, it seems, has degenerated from swashbuckling screen legend to washed-up drunk. The two embark on a series of misadventures, Swann dispensing romantic advice to aid Benjy in his frustrating chase of K.C. (Harper); Benjy desperately attempting to be Swann's short leash. Will he succeed in delivering Swann to the live show in a lively condition? Either way, it will be a turning point in his life.

Discussion: Allegedly based on Mel Brooks' (Benjy) experiences working with guest star Errol Flynn (Swann) on Sid Caesar's ("King") *Your Show of Shows*—but knowing this is not a requirement for full enjoyment of this brilliant film. The first half is comedy, pure and simple: wacky characters; punch line dialog; timing so precise you could use it to set an atomic clock. The second is tempered with moments of drama, tenderness and affection, adding depth and dimension to the characters. Everyone is wonderful, but O'Toole steals the show: he's a stick-figure acrobat adept at effortless physical slapstick, and plays the elegant legend as half-gentleman, half devil; a genteel dipsomaniac, ethereal, unflappable and humble; world-weary and amused by the world swirling around him. It's about heroes and humans; about an idol with feat of clay but the heart of a lion; about our innate need for larger-than-life figures to admire. And it's a wonder; a pure delight, from first to final frame.

Rent this one for: O'Toole (key scenes: Swann in the Women's Room; at dinner with Benjy's relatives; his pre-show panic)

You'll (probably) like this if you liked: *The Dick Van Dyke Show, Ten From Your Show of Shows* (video), *Noises Off*

Credentials: • 1982 Oscar nomination: Best Actor (O'Toole) • "...a real treasure" —VMG (4.5) • One of the "Ten Most Underrated Movies of the '80s" —*Premiere Guide to Movies on Video*

Vidbits: • Swann's film clips are taken from O'Toole's features *Lord Jim* and *The Great Catherine.* • Turned into a Broadway musical a decade later. • Benjamin's directorial debut.

My Life's In Turnaround

(1994; Arrow Video; R; 1:24)

Starring: Eric Schaeffer, Donal Lardner Ward, Lisa Gerstein
Featuring: Dana Wheeler Nicholson, Martha Plimpton, Phoebe Cates, Casey Siemaszko
Written and directed by: Eric Schaeffer, Donal Lardner Ward

Synopsis: Splick (Schaeffer) is a New York cabby who doesn't just get rejected by beautiful women—he gets spit on by them. His buddy Jason (Ward) is a playwright spit on by critics. After a decade of failure, they determine to "break the fuckin' chain" and make a movie. "We're filmmakers now!" they rejoice—although they can't be bothered with details, like who's going to write, produce, direct or star in their film. Or even what it will be about. They stumble through meetings without a script, a star —or a clue. Then who should jump into Splick's cab but Phoebe Cates! He chats her up and gets her on board. Then they meet Martha Plimpton! And they get *girlfriends,* too—well, kind of, anyway. But nothing ever runs smoothly. Will they ever make a film, or will they lose everything—including their girlfriends, their stars and their friendship—in their hapless gambit?
Discussion: Low-budget, independent movies about guys trying to make a low-budget, independent movie are becoming a cottage industry (see below), but this one is much more: it's a buddy flick up, with a romantic comedy back—and a very funny, original film (subtitled: "Based on a true story"). It's really about two American dreamers; lovable losers on a quest for success. How funny you find this flick will depend entirely on how funny you find Schaeffer and Ward. I love 'em: they're a Gen-X Abbott and Costello on speed, with machine gun delivery and a gift for wacky dialog and description. Besides, how can you *not* like guys who invented the "self high-five," or who do a "we have girlfriends now" dance? They're sweet, nice and funny —and they've made one smart movie about two dumb guys.
Rent this one for: its endearingly dopey characters and dialog.
You'll (probably) like this if you liked: *Almost Hollywood, ...And God Spoke, Living In Oblivion* (low-budget moviemaking); *Dumb and Dumber, Wayne's World, Clerks;* "New York Daze"
Dissenting Opinion: "Tired...Someone should have put *this* in turnaround" —MMG (1.5 stars)
Vidbits: • Schaeffer actually was a NY cabby, and actually met many of the cameo performers by picking them up on calls. • The three principals later starred in their own Fox sitcom, "Too Something/New York Daze". • First feature from Schaeffer, who went on to write, direct and star in the romantic comedy, *If Lucy Fell* (1996). • Director John Sayles plays the angry backer.

Neighbors

(black comedy)

(1981; Goodtimes/Kids Klassics; R; 1:34)

Starring: Dan Aykroyd, John Belushi, Cathy Moriarty
Featuring: Kathryn Walker, Lauren-Marie Taylor, Tim Kazurinsky
Written by: Larry Gelbart (based on the novel by Tom Berger)
Music by: Bill Conti
Directed by: John G. Avildsen

Synopsis: Earl Keese (Belushi) and wife Enid (Walker) live a dull, boring, meaningless suburban existence—until that fateful day that Captain Vic (Aykroyd) and Ramona (Moriarty) move into the house next door. Vic and Ramona are...well...*different.* Completely bonkers. Vic is a catalog of insanity: obnoxious, boorish, flamboyant; a habitual liar with no inhibitions or regard for social conventions. Ramona is the horniest woman ever born (played by one of the sexiest). Enid finds them a breath of fresh air, but Earl's too polite and repressed to do anything other than grin and bear their outrageous behavior. The harder he tries to maintain some sense of propriety or restore some order, the more they all blame him for being a fuddy-duddy. Curiously, the more they taunt and abuse him, the more they muck with his mind *with no apparent motive,* the closer he grows to them. (Kidnap victims often come to identify with their captors, don't they?) Earl begins to depend on Vic's random spontaneity—so what's he going to do when Vic and Ramona decide to move?
Discussion: Funny as hell and 100% unpredictable, this celebration of rampant insanity is basically one big cartoon, complete with the goofiest incidental music ever—a cartoon soundtrack featuring an eerie theramin, a moaning trombone, and minor variations on the "Twilight Zone" and Loony Tunes themes. The action all takes place within about 24 hours—but it's certainly the strangest day in Earl's life; one which subverts everything he ever thought he knew and shatters every illusion of "normality" he's ever believed in. The dialog is hilarious; the relationships, as odd as the music; the action, a bad acid trip.
Rent this one for: its cartoon looniness and unrepentant insanity; for the inspired decision to cast the boys against type.
You'll (probably) like this if you liked: *The Blues Brothers* (Aykroyd and Belushi); Warner Bros. cartoons; *Animal House* (Belushi); *Moving;* "Saturday Night Live" (the early years)
Dissenting Opinion: • "Appallingly unfunny and tiresome... Pointless" —MMG (BOMB) • "One-joke premise wears thin before too long...the performances start to grate."—SMV (2.5) • EW: "F"
Vidbits: Belushi's final film.

Newscrew

(1987; Vestron; R; 1:34)

Starring: Tom Berenger, Kurt Russell, Joanna Cassidy, Teri Garr
Featuring: Jeff Daniels, Meg Foster, Jeff Goldblum, Ayre Gross, Michael McKean, Harry Dean Stanton, Daniel Stern, Donald Sutherland, J.T. Walsh, M. Emmet Walsh
Written and directed by: Abdu D'Jabuti

Synopsis: A mobile TV news unit (cameraman, soundman and "on the spot" reporter) is assigned to cover a small, independent film crew shooting a documentary about the location filming of a major motion picture occurring in their city. The feature film in production tells the story of small, independent film company producing a documentary about a day in the life of a three-person mobile TV news crew. Mistaken identities multiply like infinite reflections in a funhouse mirror, and wackiness ensues.
Discussion: It's a bargain-basement version of *Mad, Mad World* —and a lost comedy classic. The ingenious conceit of pairing off character actors, Bizarro-style, works brilliantly—once we sort them out. Is Otto (Stanton) the real news director and Otto (Sutherland) the actor *portraying* the news director—or is it vice versa? Why is anchorman Bob (Berenger) doing a Kurt Russell impression, while anchorman-actor Bob (Russell) doing a dead-on Tom Berenger impersonation? What's in Eve's (Cassidy) errant briefcase that makes Eve (Garr) crazy? And can *anyone* tell Jeff Daniels and Daniel Stern apart? ("Jeff Danielstern"?) The scene in which the acting station manager (Walsh) confronts the actor *acting* as acting station manager (Walsh), erases any line between fantasy and reality, rocketing everyone (including the viewer) through the loony looking-glass into a warped Wonderland, where reality is whatever you can get away with.
Rent this one for: the cast; its clever mistaken-identity farce.
You'll (probably) like this if you liked: *Noises Off, A Night At The Opera, Caddyshack, The Producers, Almost Hollywood*
Dissenting Opinion: • "...nothing new; we just get screwed..." —MMG (BOMB) • "...unfathomable, pretentious, mind-numbingly dumb..." —GMR (*Woof!*) • ...newscrew yourself..." —VMG (turkey) • "...straight-to-tape tripe might force us to reconsider bookburning...." —SMV • "...one of the ten most wretched 'films' I've ever been forced to endure..." —Roger Ebert • *EW:* "F-"
Vidbits: • Watch for cameos by cult figures like Paul Bartel and Mary Woronov (the roach coach owners), Edie McClurg (the message-mixing secretary) and Robin Williams (in an uncredited appearance) as J.R. Dobbs. • The "voice" of the station belongs to Orson Welles. • Legend has it that three editors suffered nervous breakdowns trying to keep the scrambled plot straight.

Night On Earth

(1991; New Line; R; 2:05)

Starring: Winona Ryder, Gena Rowlands, Giancarlo Esposito, Armin Mueller-Stahl, Rosie Perez, Roberto Benigni
Music by: Tom Waits
Written and directed by: Jim Jarmusch

Synopsis: The central conceit of this uneven entry is five taxi trips taken simultaneously in five different nighttime time zones around the world. The first vignette, set in L.A., is a wry dialog between a tough casting agent (Rowlands) with an eye for talent and a tougher young cabbie (Ryder) with her own life agenda. Number Two, set in New York, is a loud, raucous comedy about the difficulty of understanding anything different, whether it's another culture, another person or another gender. The third, and shortest, segment, set in Paris, explores the question of who's really blind: a bitter but insightful sightless woman, or the driver who can't see past his own prejudices. Number Four alone justifies the entire price of a rental: a Rome cabbie's (Benigni) nonstop, mile-a-minute confession about his sexual perversions to a priest with his own problems. Oddly, this "comedy" ends in a tale of tragedy set in Helsinki, when a driver sobers up a group of drunken buddies with his own sob story.
Discussion: An ambitious, admirable and essentially successful experiment. (Who else works in the short story form on film? Besides Altman.) The high points outnumber the lows, and these highs fly higher than the lows ever go. Add the advantage of a roadmap (below) and the fast-scan button, and this is a fabulous film. My suggestions: Skip the bookends and watch the three central segments. The New York story features characters so unique they *must* be real, and Rosie Perez's baby voice and potty mouth allows her the ultimate last word when she "curses him out." My major complaint with this film is the final segment. If only Jarmusch had added *a single shot* to the end—the driver arriving home to be greeted by his little daughter—the entire segment would have been put into a sweet ironic perspective. As it stands, I felt cheated, having had so much fun, only to be abandoned at the end by the side of Jarmusch's sobering road. End a great comedy on a note of despair? What *was* he thinking?
Rent this one for: Roberto Benigni's segment in Rome, which just might be the funniest 20 minutes ever committed to film.
You'll (probably) like this if you liked: *Stranger Than Paradise, Down By Law, Short Cuts*
Dissenting Opinion: "...only [Jarmusch] fans will find it completely satisfying." —VMG (3 stars)

Penn & Teller Get Killed

(1989; Warner; R; 1:31)

Starring: Penn Jillette, Teller, Caitlin Clarke
Featuring: David Patrick Kelly
Written by: Penn Jillette, Teller
Directed by: Arthur Penn

Synopsis: "I wish someone were trying to kill me," boasts Penn Jillette, the bad boy of magic, on TV. "Wouldn't that be great? It'd give focus to your life. Excitement!" You gotta be very careful what you wish for, because you might get it: before they can say "hocus pocus," nuts are coming out of the woodwork with knives and guns. Some of them are elaborate practical jokes staged by Penn's own partner (Teller) and his alleged friends, like manager Carlotta (Clarke). But when a sniper really wings him, things get seriously weird. "Maybe now you'll think twice about saying stupid shit on TV," a bystander laughs. Penn enters a paranoid *film noir* life, until his police protector catches the guy (Kelly), a Penn & Teller wannabe/stalker. But in the end, the most elaborate practical joke of all goes horribly awry, and Penn and Teller get killed. Yeah, I know I promised in the Introduction that I wouldn't reveal any spoilers. But come *on,* people—didn't you read the *title* of the goddamn movie? Jesus! *Just what the* hell *did you* expect, *you cretinous pinheads???* (My Penn parody.)
Discussion: Comedy is timing, and so is magic. So is it really a surprise that these guys do both well, and even introduce themselves as "comedians, and the best magicians in the world"? If Hunter Thompson did magic, he'd be Penn Jillette; a screaming, in-your-face charlatan, growling his "shock appeal" material at the audience, with a rabidly bad attitude; shrugging off Teller's messy death with "Ya win some; ya lose some." Teller is the bastard offspring of Harpo and Houdini; a skilled escape artist whose cherubic grin hides a devilish trickster. The one thing they hate is nice, sweet, *safe* magic. So let them take you to the edge, laughing—and then push you over. Laughing. And then bring you back, where we all share a laugh. Now, you see it!
Rent this one for: its magical manipulation of reality; the fun.
You'll (probably) like this if you liked: "Cruel Tricks For Dear Friends"; *The Sting; The Escape Artist, House of Games* (serious)
Dissenting Opinion: • "...cult possibilities: others beware." —MMG (2) • "...flounders while marking time"—SMV(2) • *EW:* D+
Vidbits: • Brief appearances by Jon Cryer (Frat Boy) and playwright Christopher Durang (Jesus Freak). • Penn & Teller "make a cottage industry out of revealing how [stage magician David] Copperfield does his tricks. Copperfield has stated publicly, 'They should die!'"—*Spy* (5-6/95) • Bonus: Teller talks!

Double Feature!

Police Squad! Help Wanted! and More! Police Squad!

(television series)

(1982; Paramount; NR; 1:15 each)

Starring: Leslie Nielsen, Alan North
Featuring: Ed Williams, William Duell, Peter Lupus
Created by: Jerry Zucker, David Zucker, Jim Abrahams

Synopsis: In the opening credits of every episode, a portentous announcer proclaims we're watching "Police Squad! In Color!", a jab at the old QM Productions intros. Each episode introduces a special guest star (Florence Henderson, William Shatner), who's promptly murdered. We meet Sgt. Frank Drebin (Nielsen), "Detective Lieutenant, Police Squad—a special detail of the Police Department" and his boss, Captain Ed Hawkin (North). ("Hawkin and Drebin"—sounds like some sort of head-cold expectoration). Their cases cover all the bases—murder, kidnapping, extortion—but their suspects are anything but the usual. Running gags in each episode include an announced title that doesn't match the on-screen title; end-credit *faux* freeze-frames (which allow criminals to escape, or a monkey to trash the set); and recurring characters like Mr. Olsen, the mildly perverted lab man, and Johnny, the shoeshine guy who knows "the word on the street," and—for a price—will pass on the straight scoop to Drebin (or Dr. Joyce Brothers, or Tommy Lasorda...).
Discussion: Long before the *Naked Gun* movies, this series did a fly-over on the TV-watching public. Only six episodes of this wacky police spoof were ever produced, but they're so packed with gags they're worth watching repeatedly. Nothing is left unwacked (look out every window, for instance). They take the Mel Brooks approach to humor: if one gag doesn't strike you funny, just wait a second. There are sight gags (the "Club Flamingo" nightclub sports a sign which features a tuxedoed gent clubbing a flamingo); verbal gags ("Cigarette?" Drebin offers, shaking one from the pack. "Yes, I know," is the standard reply); non sequiturs, bad jokes, worse puns and the most zany insanity ever to hit the TV screen—every line of which is delivered in Nielsen's dopey, dead-serious deadpan, which makes it all work.
Rent this one for: more verbal and visual gags per square frame than any other film or TV show was ever able to pack in.
You'll (probably) like this if you liked: The *Naked Gun* films (essentially feature versions of this show); *Airplane!* (the ZAZ team); *Hot Shots!* and *Hot Shots! Part Deux* (Jim Abrahams); *Who Framed Roger Rabbit?, Blazing Saddles, Young Frankenstein*

Flashback!

The President's Analyst

(1967; Paramount; NR; 1:40)

Starring: James Coburn, Godfrey Cambridge, Severn Darden
Featuring: Joan Delaney, William Daniels, Pat Harrington
Written and directed by: Theodore J. Flicker

Synopsis: New York psychiatrist Dr. Sidney Schaefer (Coburn) is the best in his field: smart, sharp, savvy and hip. He's so good he's drafted to be the personal shrink to the President of the United States; someone the big guy can talk to, to take the edge off his supercharged life. His head brimming with secret information, Sidney believes he's a valuable commodity on the world spy market. He begins seeing spies everywhere, goes a little bit ultraparanoid and "disappears" himself, discovering that just because you're paranoid doesn't mean they *aren't* after you. And, man, are they after him! Virtually every country on the globe is intent on capturing Sidney. Some just want to kill him. Most want to debrief him, *then* kill him. Who can he trust in this deadly game of double-dealing and triple-crosses—and if he's nuts, why should *they* trust *him?* And when he uncovers the most sinister secret plot of all, can his handful of operative-patients put an end to the comically psychotic conspiracy?
Discussion: If this movie was remade today, the villain would probably be The Cable Company. (I can say no more...) 30 years ago, in between the Warren Commission and Watergate, this brilliant film was a comic cross-section of contemporary culture; a spoof of spies (Bond), acid-head hippies ('67 was the Summer of Love) and suburban insanity (the Quantrills). Today it's a time capsule—yet still an oddly prescient movie (the President losing sleep over Libya in *1967?*), predicting the national mood-swing while simultaneously skewering it savagely. Whatever its politics, it's still an enormously funny film for Luddites of any era, and a sure cure for paranoia. Coburn is a delight as the reluctant hero whose only defensive weapons are his insight into human nature and his wall-to-wall smile. The video version is disappointing, suffering from the twin indignities of bad editing and the removal of Barry McGuire's original songs; in this one case, it's one to look for on TV to see the original version.
Rent this one for: it's time capsule satire; Coburn's acting.
You'll (probably) like this if you liked: *Our Man Flint*
Credentials: • "...superbly written, brilliantly executed...Vastly entertaining." —GMR (3.5 bones) • *EW:* "A-"
Vidbits: • Flicker and partner Danny Arnold would go on to develop TV's *Barney Miller.* • As Sidney leaves the White House with the Quantrills, that's Flicker (with a goatee) behind them.

Queens Logic

(slice-o'-life)
(1991; LIVE; R; 1:54)

Starring: Joe Mantegna, Linda Fiorentino, Kevin Bacon, John Malcovich, Chloe Webb, Ken Olin, Tom Waits, Jamie Lee Curtis
Written by: Tony Spiridakis
Directed by: Steve Rash

Synopsis: The five guys grew up in Queens, were roommates in the '70s and have been friends ever since. So when struggling artist Ray (Olin) pops the question to hairdresser Patti (Webb), they reunite to attend the wedding—and the bachelor party. There are complications, though. Ray's ebullient brother Al (Mantegna), for instance, is in deep dutch with his wife Carla (Fiorentino), who leaves him. And Ray has a case of glacier feet, and isn't planning to show up for his own wedding. Carla and Patti hang and chill and discuss how men are animals (duh); the guys hang and talk and try to pick up chicks. Uhh...*women.* Yeah, dat's right... If they're successful, they risk ruining any return to their relationships—or is this just what they need to make them realize what they already have and don't appreciate?
Discussion: It's the war between the sexes, Queens style—equal parts buddy-bonding and female frustration. (You know: "Men are from Mars...and they can *stay* there!") There are no bad guys, just a bunch of friends who don't always communicate—and often dance on each others' nerve endings. It's an ethnic romance about people who lust for a lust for life (because lust is its own reward). In a uniformly superb ensemble cast, Mantegna is first among equals; his loud, expansive Al polarizes everyone around him to diagnose him either as exuberant extrovert or obnoxious asshole. Fiorentino is fabulous as his frustrated, finally fed-up keeper, and Malcovich brings a unique, complicated character to life in a realistic manner. The flick is full of sharp, smart-ass dialog, and almost top-heavy with musical hits, featuring everything from Marvin Gaye and Van Morrison to Benny Goodman. What exactly is "Queens Logic"? It's the logic of a clear-eyed heart, and it makes men kings. This gentle gem is at once affectionate, forgiving and wise, even as its population staggers, off-kilter and chagrined, towards their only vaguely realized goals of reconciliation and maturation.
Rent this one for: its energetic, affectionate characterizations.
You'll (probably) like this if you liked: *Diner, The Big Chill*
Dissenting Opinion: • "...rambling, uneven, but amiable..." —VMG (3 stars) • "...so-so script..." —MMG (2.5 stars)
Vidbits: Screenwriter Spiridakis also plays "Vinny."

Flashback!

Real Life

(1979; Paramount; R; 1:39)

Starring: Albert Brooks, Charles Grodin, Frances Lee McCain
Written by: Albert Brooks, Monica Johnson, Harry Shearer
Directed by: Albert Brooks

Synopsis: In 1973, PBS aired "An American Family," a unique series in which a real family's life was filmed and shown on TV. "The motion picture you are about to see," states an introductory note to *Real Life*, "is the next step. It documents not only the life of a real family, but of the real people who came to film that family, and the effect they had on each other." Thus begins a year-long invasion of the lives of Phoenix veterinarian Warren Yeager (Grodin) and his wife Janette (McCain) by comedian-turned-filmmaker Albert Brooks (Brooks). Murphy's Martial Law is declared immediately: Brooks accompanies Mrs. Y to the gynecologist (who's "had a bad experience with the '60 Minutes' people"). Janette comes on to Albert, who makes only token efforts to dissuade her. Janette's grandmother dies, and Warren loses his patient (a horse) and his mind. "That was just the beginning of what was to be a bad time in the Yeager's lives," Brooks narrates. And even a battery of psychologists aren't enough to keep Brooks' own ego in check. But despite disintegrating lives, personalities and projects, he's determined to give his first film a memorable, *Gone with the Wind*-style finale...
Discussion: Quantum physics revealed the principle of "observer interference," but no one ever took it quite as far as Brooks. In his first feature, a parody of the seminal PBS series, he illustrates how that documentary might have turned out had it been overseen by an excessively ambitious, passive-aggressively manipulative megalomaniac; a whining, wheedling weasel too egocentric to have the camera pointed anywhere but at himself. Brooks proves a constant frustration to the shrinks assigned as observers, as well; informed that his filming has triggered "drastic emotional changes" in the family, his response is, "And that's bad?" Upfront he states, "We're making a movie about *reality*"—but fortunately for us, it's Brooks' neurotically warped version of reality that ends up on film: a reality that even Brooks eventually has to admit "sucks." Lucky for us!
Rent this one for: Brooks' warped, self-mocking humor.
You'll (probably) like this if you liked: *Lost In America, Defending Your Life* (Brooks); *Zelig, The Rutles* (mockumentaries)
Credential: "...the funniest movie ever made." —Conan O'Brien
Vidbits: Cameos: Director James L. Brooks (no relation) as the Driving Evaluator; Harry Shearer as Pete the cameraman.

The Ref

(1994; Touchstone; R; 1:37)

Starring: Denis Leary, Judy Davis, Kevin Spacey
Featuring: Robert J. Steinmiller, Jr., Christine Baranski
Written by: Richard LaGravenese, Marie Weiss
Directed by: Ted Demme

Synopsis: It's Christmas Eve in Connecticut; even so, acrimonious couple Lloyd (Spacey) and Caroline (Davis) are at the marriage counselor. On their way home, they're hijacked by bad-luck burglar Gus (Leary), on the run after a botched robbery. He forces them to take him to their house, where he plans to lay low and wait for his partner to pick him up. Complication: They're expecting the whole damn family for Christmas dinner. Hostile Gus fits right into their non-stop argument, and all three start savagely analyzing each others' failed lives and personal shortcomings. Masquerading as their therapist, Gus tries desperately to deal with the nuclear-strength dysfunction of their nuclear (and extended) family. Can he escape without hurting anyone—or even without losing his fuckin' mind?
Discussion: You've heard of "psychodrama." Welcome to "psychodramedy." This savage psycho-satire is a Christmas card drawn jointly by Currier & Ives and Hieronymous Bosch; a venomous, vituperative comedy with sharply filed fangs. Spacey and Davis are the dynamic duo of dysfunction, who couldn't get along if their lives depended on it—literally. He's a smug, priggish mama's boy who's given up on life; she's a "nasty, selfish woman" (much like Lloyd's mother!) unconscious of her own artsy-fartsy pretentions to "good taste." Even pitted against such accomplished character actors, rasty-nasty Leary holds his own, brusque and bitter against their button-pushing, bickering and backbiting. The irony is that *everyone* hates his own miserable life and envies everyone else's—and the one with the worst life among them might be the only one with his head screwed on straight enough to give the others a healthy dose of "reality therapy." This stimulating, refreshing farce is so strong on dialog, character and in-your-face comic animosity (and so limited in locations) that it could easily succeed as a stage play.
Rent this one for: its sharp dialog and vicious wit.
You'll (probably) like this if you liked: *Cadillac Man, Faithful, Trapped in Paradise*
Credentials: "Top 10 Films of '94" list —B. Williamson, *Playboy*
Dissenting Opinion: • "It's supposed to be a black comedy, but it's just bleak at times." —VMG (3 stars) • "...gets unexpectedly serious—then silly and illogical." —MMG (2.5 stars)
Vidbits: Ted Demme is director Jonathan Demme's nephew.

Repo Man

(cult/punk/black comedy)
(1984; MCA; R; 1:33)

Starring: Harry Dean Stanton, Emilio Estevez, Tracey Walter
Featuring: Olivia Barash, Susan Barnes, Fox Harris, Vonetta McGee
Written and directed by: Alex Cox

Synopsis: Otto (Estevez) is a *punk,* man. And his life *sucks,* man! He can't even hold a normal job. So when cynical car repossessor Bud (Stanton) offers to mentor him in the trade and teach him to be a "repo man," Otto finds a home for his 'tude among the angry, hostile, bitter guys. On a pickup run, he picks up Leila (Barash), who works for a citizen's group chasing a lobotomized weapons scientist who's stolen a couple of dead, radioactive aliens and is driving around L.A. with them in the trunk of his car. There's a $20K reward for whoever confiscates the car, so everyone is after it, including Otto and Bud, their co-workers, rival repo men, the cops, Leila's people, government agents and even some punks on a robbery spree. And everyone will do anything to stop everyone else. Only mechanic Miller (Walter) seems to understand The Big Picture—but he's an acid burnout nutcase! The trouble is, *he might just be right...*
Discussion: It's a movie about synchronicity—"this lattice of coincidence that lays on top of everything," Miller "explains." It's the first punk movie, and might be the first post-modern quantum physics film, as paths crisscross in an intricate interweave of meaning (and lack thereof). It's an original: an intense action movie on acid, full of razor-sharp cynicism, comedy as dark and edgy as death, and brilliant dialog. ("Ordinary fucking people," Stanton spits. "I hate 'em.") *Everyone* in this movie is nuts; there's no center of sanity to anchor us—so just go along for the weird, warped, wild ride. *Of course* it makes no sense, even while seeming to—just like most dreams. A cult classic.
Rent this one for: the cleverly engineered synchronicities; deadpan Stanton's best performance ever; its unique punkitude.
You'll (probably) like this if you liked: *Heathers, Twin Peaks*
Credentials: • "★★★★" —SMV • "...takes chances, dares to be unconventional, is funny, and works." —Roger Ebert (3 stars)
Dissenting Opinion: "...a little...goes a long way." —MMG (2.5) • "...trash...It stinks from here to Pasadena."—Rex Reed, NY *Post*
Vidbits: • Bus destination: "Edge City." • Hospital PA calls for "Dr. Benway," a William Burroughs character. • Executive Producer: Ex-Monkee Michael Nesmith • Many of the characters are named after beers (Bud, Miller). • Credits scroll from the top of the screen to the bottom, a reversal of the typical direction.

Rustler's Rhapsody

(Western)

(1985; Paramount; PG; 1:29)

Starring: Tom Berenger, G.W. Bailey, Andy Griffith
Featuring: Marilu Henner, Sela Ward, Patrick Wayne, Fernando Rey
Written and directed by: Hugh Wilson

Synopsis: Legend has it that between 1938 and '47, Hollywood churned out 52 low-budget Westerns starring Rex O'Herlihan, "The Singing Cowboy" (Berenger). But what would one of those old B-movie "horse operas" look like if it was made in today's self-conscious, post-modern world? Rex finds out when he rides into Oakwood Estates and realizes that the town is virtually identical to every frontier town he's ever been in, complete with stereotypical characters like "Miss Tracey" (Henner), a virginal hooker with a heart of gold; a power-mad cattle baron, "Colonel Ticonderoga" (Griffith), who really runs the town; and "Peter" (Bailey), the eccentric but friendly town drunk. Rex is a bit confused about why he's reliving the same "sheepherders versus cattle baron" plot for the 53rd time—and he's getting a bit tired of it as well. His presence threatens The Colonel, who enlists the aid of the villainous railroad builders to kill him. And just about the time Rex gets a handle on this "self-awareness" thing, people start throwing him curves. Peter trades in his drunk suit for a "sidekick" outfit, for instance. And The Colonel devises a giddily twisted plan to pit Good Guy Rex against the single foe he's never faced and can never defeat: *another Good Guy.*
Discussion: It's *Blazing Saddles* for intellectuals: an absurdly aware romp that asks the insidiously simple, comically quirky question, "What would happen if a character in a movie suddenly became aware that he is *a character in a movie?"* The real wonder of this Western is that it works on many levels. On the surface, it's a fun-filled, affectionate tribute to a long-gone genre; a gentle lampoon of childhood idylls about cowboy idols like Roy Rogers, Gene Autrey and Hopalong Cassidy. Wilson knows these flicks inside out, and hasn't missed fondly mocking even the most minor detail. His Rex O'Herlihan is an archetype among stereotypes, complete with all the external accouterments of the perfect Singing Cowboy (flashy, color-coordinated costumes, hand-tooled boots, extravagant guitars), as well as all the psychological characteristics that qualify him as a Good Guy: humility, respect for a lady's virtue, and a pledge never to shoot a bad guy anywhere but in the hand. As wild parody, it's stocked with strange takes on standard cardboard characters: the sheepherders are Hassidic Jews, for example, and Griffith

does a truly eccentric turn as the closet queen Colonel. Wayne alone almost steals the film in an engagingly enthusiastic performance as the "other good guy," Bob Barker. (His every line is a gem, especially those concerning his own background, and his requirements for being a Good Guy.) But *Rustler's Rhapsody* is more than just smart slapstick, insightful foolery and poignant nostalgia. Rex's blossoming into consciousness has devastating effects. He's cursed with foresight, for one; merely remembering his repetitious ride gives him a thorough education in Western conventions. And almost like a communicable disease, Rex's self-awareness seems to infect everyone—and critical awareness changes everything, liberating them all from endless repetitions of their habitual patterns of "oater" action. Even Rex grows increasingly edgy, first at the oddity of his newfound knowledge, and eventually in realizing that something is about to happen *that has never happened before.* It's this seemingly simple detail that makes this a demonstrably brilliant film. The perfect explanatory analogy lies in *The Good, The Bad and the Ugly.* For 100 years, books and films and TV Westerns had only two forms of shoot-out: the all-out melee (think "Gunfight at the O.K. Corral"), or the one-on-one, face-to-face quick-draw confrontation. Then Sergio Leone came along and added a new dimension to Westerns with his famous "three-way gunfight." This was something *new.* Something *no one had ever thought of before.* A *shift in the archetype* we all thought we knew so well! Wilson accomplishes the same thing here by asking an obvious question, impeccable in its logic and childlike in its simplicity: What happens if you match a Good Guy against another Good Guy? In the morally unambiguous universe of "B" Westerns, Good always triumphs over Evil. But how can Good triumph over Good? The complications and implications are both mind-bending and hilarious. Wilson accomplished something new—something no one ever thought of before. There is of course the danger that overanalysis can strip the film of its fun—but fun is just the surface of this surprisingly insightful flick. I absolutely adore this sweet, unique and memorable gem, and would forgive Hugh Wilson a hundred *Police Academy* entries for creating it.
Rent this one for: its ingenious insight into, and its fond, affectionate tribute to, 1940s "B" Westerns.
You'll (probably) like this if you liked: *Support Your Local Sheriff, Back to the Future Part III, Blazing Saddles;* any "B" Western from the '40s; *Draw, Cat Ballou, The Marx Bros. Go West; The Purple Rose of Cairo; Young Frankenstein*
Dissenting Opinion: • "...fails to corral enough laughs to sustain its feature length." —PVG • "If the old cowboy movies were as dull as this film, they never would have survived." —MMG (2 stars) • "...the laughs are few and far between." —SMV (2 stars)

Flashback!

The Rutles:
"All You Need Is Cash"
(musical/parody)

(1978; Pacific Arts, Rhino; NR; 1:10)

Starring: Eric Idle, Neil Innes, John Halsey, Rikki Fataar
Featuring: Dan Aykroyd, John Belushi, Gilda Radner, Bill Murray
Conceived and written by: Eric Idle
Music and lyrics by: Neil Innes
Directed by: Eric Idle, Gary Weis

Synopsis: Take the most complex pop-culture phenomenon you can think of. Then take every detail and parody it perfectly. If you picked The Beatles, you needn't carry this exercise any further; just rent this "mockumentary," which tells the story of "The Rutles"—Dirk (Idle), Stig (Fataar), Barry (Halsey) and Nasty (Innes), a.k.a. the "pre-fab four," in delicious, delightful detail. From their songs ("Let's Be Natural," "Love Life"), and their albums ("Tragical History Tour," "Let It Rot") to their movies ("A Hard Day's Rut," "Ouch!", "Yellow Submarine Sandwich"), this is a brilliant, hilarious and deadly accurate lampoon of every memorable interview, newsreel, photo, quote, scandal, trend, marriage, album cover, book, TV appearance, guitar lick, synthesizer squeal, musical sting, costume and hairstyle.
Discussion: This has *got* to be an actual documentary imported from some alternate dimension. How else could anyone have had the time, the cleverness, the keen powers of observation and the funds not only to write this one-to-one, note-for-note, frame-for-frame correspondence to an entire career, but to duplicate all the original styles (film, video, newsreels, TV, orchestrations, album covers), and still manage to capture the innocent essence of the originals? Even the impersonations are perfect. It's a magical history tour that will "flog your memory" with fun.
Rent this one for: its spot-on, dead-perfect, yet still affectionate satire of the Beatles' entire career; for the soundtrack.
You'll (probably) like this if you liked: *Spinal Tap*; *The Beatles Anthology, The Compleat Beatles* (real Beatles docs); *A Hard Day's Night, Help!* (Beatles films); *Zelig* (fake bio)
Vidbits: • Originally made for TV, and Executive Produced by SNL's Lorne Michaels. • In addition to bit parts by the original SNL crew and George Harrison as an interviewer, also appearing in cameos (as themselves) are Mick and Bianca Jagger and Paul Simon. • The soundtrack CD is also available. And in late '96, in response to the Beatles Anthology, The Rutles released a CD "Archaeology," containing new and unreleased tracks.

Scenes from the Class Struggle in Beverly Hills

(1989; Virgin Vision; R; 1:43)

Starring: Jaqueline Bisset, Ray Sharkey, Mary Woronov, Robert Beltran, Ed Begley, Jr., Wallace Shawn, Paul Bartel, Paul Mazursky, Arnetia Walker, Rebecca Schaeffer
Written by: Bruce Wagner (story by Bartel and Wagner)
Directed by: Paul Bartel

Synopsis: Rich bitch and newly-minted widow Clare (Bissett) plays hostess for a weekend in her Beverly Hills mansion to a fumigating neighbor, Liz (Woronov), Liz's clinging ex- (Shawn), Liz's pretentious playwright brother (Begley) and his new black bride (Walker), Dr. Mo (Bartel), a fey "thinologist"—and the ghost of her husband (Mazursky), who wasn't invited. At the other end of the social spectrum, Clare's "houseman," Juan (Beltran) is in a jam: he's got to raise $5K in three days or face the Asian Mafia. Liz's horny houseman Frank (Sharkey) suggests a contest involving their employers: "You go for my divorcée; I go for your widow. Whoever wets his wick wins." If Juan wins, he gets the money from Frank. If Frank wins, he gets...Juan. Meanwhile, the women are devising schemes of their own—and everyone in the house begins switching partners with every whim. Can there be any winners? Or did the Stones have it right when they sang, "You can't always get what you want. But if you try sometimes, you might just find you get what you need"?
Discussion: "This is for sure some twisted shit," Juan shrugs, taking the bet. So is this tricky little film—a comedy of manners, most of them bad. It begins as a wickedly witty, saber-toothed skewering of the pretentious rich and their scheming servants; a nasty, cynical, lewd, raucous, raunchy sex farce, complete with random pairings, mistaken identities, secret pasts and mixed-up midnight rendezvous. But is it in fact a sex farce or a morality play? By the end of the weekend, we see moments of bittersweet intimacy beneath the smarmy surface of their sitcom lives; moments of honor, honesty and innocence. Sex and death are intimately intertwined here—just ask the mad Mayan maid.
Rent this one for: the barbed repartee; its repentant nature.
You'll (probably) like this if you liked: *Serial, Down and Out in Beverly Hills, A Midsummer Night's Sex Comedy*
Dissenting Opinion: "...inane, veering uncomfortably between drama and farce" —MMG (1.5 stars)
Vidbits: • Essentially a remake of Renoir's *Rules of the Game.* • Reunites the starring trio of *Eating Raoul.* • Novelist Wagner (*I'm Losing You*) is the ex-husband of Rebecca De Mornay.

Shakes the Clown

(cult)

(1992; Columbia TriStar; R; 1:23)

Starring: "Bobcat" Goldthwait, Julie Brown
Featuring: Blake Clark, Adam Sandler, Tom Kenney, Sydney Lassick, Paul Dooley, Tim Kazurinsky, Florence Henderson
Written and directed by: "Bobcat" Goldthwait

Synopsis: Shakes (Goldthwait) could have been a contender. Instead, he got a one-way ticket to Palukaville. It's tough enough being a professional clown in a city full of clowns, but Shakes is also an alcoholic. No—he's a drunk and a half. And he cheats on his girl, Judy (Brown), a pro bowler and waitress at The Twisted Balloon, a "clown bar." He's even lost out on his dream job, hosting a kid's show, to Binky, an obnoxious, hot-tempered, vindictive, evil clown. Shakes' drinking causes him to screw up so often that his boss, Mr. Cheese (Dooley) finally fires him. Shakes, with a snootful, threatens to kill him. So when a coked-up Binky actually does the job, who better to pin it on than Shakes? Can he get his act together and clear his name?
Discussion: There's never been a movie quite like this: weird, warped and wicked. Even though at times it is slow, repetitive and dead serious, even though it's not entirely successful, it's worth watching for the jokes that work ("I'm gonna fire you so fast that you'll be out of a job immediately")—and for its basic twistedness. The opening sequence is a killer, and the social structure of Palukaville is a funhouse mirror of real life: rodeo clowns hate the circus clowns, and *everybody* hates the mimes. Maybe, like the recent SNL spin-off, *Stuart Saves His Family,* this isn't really a comedy after all. Maybe beneath that facade of greasepaint is a grotesque metaphor about alcoholism, a parable of a mid-life crisis, a statement about the Human Condition, in which any attempt at dignity is a joke, and our own weaknesses make fools and clowns of us all.... *Nahhhhh!*
Rent this one for: its daring experiment; the scenes that work.
You'll (probably) like this if you liked: *Stuart Saves His Family, The Rocky Horror Picture Show, Cheech & Chong's Next Movie, Quick Change,* "In Living Color's" Homey the Clown
Credentials: "The *Citizen Kane* of alcoholic clown movies." —*Boston Globe*
Dissenting Opinion: • "Bizarre, uneven...satire's strained..." —SMV (2.5) • "Excruciating would-be-comic mish-mash...Aimless, crude and headache-inducing..."—MMG (BOMB) • *EW:* "D-"
Vidbits: • Robin Williams makes an uncredited appearace as "Mime Jerry," a mime instructor. • Yep, that is indeed Florence Henderson in the opening scene. Mrs. Brady, how could you?!

Slacker

(experimental)
(1991; Orion; R; 1:37)

Starring: Nobody you (probably) ever heard of
Written, produced and directed by: Richard Linklater

Synopsis: A young guy (Linklater) steps off a bus and grabs a cab. He gabs away to the bored cabbie about alternate realities. He sees a woman hit by a car and goes for help. The camera follows the culprit, who is arrested and taken away. Outside his house, we follow two passersby, one engaged in a passionate rap about government conspiracies...
Discussion: ...and so on, as we're passed from hand to hand and character to character, crisscrossing Austin and eavesdropping on the lives of its underground subculture: talentless musicians, pretentious coffeehouse and barroom intellectuals, conspiracy theorists, bums, TV freaks, even some "ordinary" people. The flick is a comic time capsule for Generation X; a living definition of the title character. Even the structure mirrors that lifestyle: the short attention span; the unsettling randomness of life and the future; people who never really connect, but merely intersect. The dialogs (more often monologs) mirror their sound-bite philosophies: passive and cynical; soured on the future; all talk, no action; spouting '70s media references with insider irony. As in life, some of the characters we encounter are fascinating, others irritating; some are sane, others in; but all are involved in a desperate attempt to make themselves *real* by finding someone with whom to share their beliefs—or, at very least, to just *listen* to them. If this film was a scientific experiment, it would be a "latitudinal study": a cross-section, or slice of life, of a culture at a given moment. More appropriately, it might be an old-fashioned physics experiment, where we're the detached observer. Quantum physics has proven that there's no such animal, but as passive movie viewers, we *can't* get involved. We're *prevented* from getting involved. We're *powerless* to get involved. Just by watching the film, we become *slackers.* Like *Stranger Than Paradise* and *Clerks, Slackers* is a triumph of smart dialog and unique structure over the limitations of a frayed-shoestring budget. Talk might be cheap, but this is comic commentary worth its weight in Scooby Treats.
Rent this one for: the experimental structure; the comic raps.
You'll (probably) like this if you liked: *Clerks, Mallrats, Stranger Than Paradise, My Life's In Turnaround*
Vidbits: • Features 97 roles, none over 5 minutes. • Linklater's first feature, produced on a budget of $23,000.

The Snapper

(1993; Buena Vista; R; 1:30)

Starring: Colm Meaney, Tina Kellegher, Ruth McCabe
Written by: Roddy Doyle
Directed by: Stephen Frears

Synopsis: "Who was it?" daddy Dessi Curley (Meaney) demands when his 20-year-old unmarried daughter Sharon (Kellegher) announces she's got a bun in the oven. Preggers! Jay-sus! She's determined to keep the "snapper," she doesn't care to be married, and she won't reveal the identity of the "Da"—not even to her mates. A scandal, it is! All of Barrytown engages in endless speculation. But Georgie Burgess has been overheard in the pubs bragging about what a "great little ride" Sharon was, and when word gets back to Dessi, all hell breaks loose. Georgie is, after all, a neighbor, and married—and has a daughter Sharon's age! Georgie goes middle-aged crazy, abandoning his family to be with Sharon—but she wants no part of him. The block is polarized into two competing camps: She's a slut, or he's a bastard. No wonder she didn't want the father known. Or *was* it really a Spanish sailor? Can her frazzled dad hold the family together through this crisis without having a conniption?
Discussion: *Father Knows Best?* No, more like *Da Knows Fook-All.* But it is an affectionate father-daughter story, effervescent and sparkling, bubbling with witty dialog and lively delivery. Poor, set-upon Dessi, trying to hold things together while attempting to cope with a house full of kids, defend Sharon's honor, and be a responsible surrogate father, when all the rules have changed since his day—and all the while surrounded by smart, strong-willed women. And on the verge of becoming a grandfather himself! "A man needs a pint after all that," he sighs. Amen. Meaney is the pivot of the film and has never been better, displaying a real flair for comedy while running the gamut of emotions as the well-meaning but confused Dessi. The film is enormously entertaining, and its humor springs from all the appropriate sources: character, situation and life itself. It's a sweet treat, full of tart-tongued lines, the humor of truth and a huge helping of heart. Add in a virtual thesaurus of slang ("she's up a pole") and lyrical accents thick enough to walk a spoon on ("Fook the naaaaay-bers!"), and you've got a winner.
Rent this one for: the true humor and affectionate relations.
You'll (probably) like this if you liked: *The Commitments, Parenthood, Father of the Bride II*
Credentials: "This is a gem!" —VMG (4.5 stars)
Vidbits: • Originally produced for the BBC. • Part of Doyle's "Barrytown Trilogy," as was the film *The Commitments.*

S.O.B.

(1981; CBS/Fox; R; 2:01)

Starring: Richard Mulligan, William Holden, Julie Andrews
Featuring: Robert Preston, Robert Webber, Shelly Winters, Robert Vaughn, Larry Hagman, Robert Loggia, Marisa Berenson, Stuart Margolin, Loretta Swit, Craig Stevens, Larry Storch, Rosanna Arquette
Music by: Henry Mancini
Written and directed by: Blake Edwards

Synopsis: Felix Farmer (Mulligan) is a big time movie producer whose latest big-budget blockbuster bombs—big time. Felix tries suicide, but botches that, too. The studio wants to recut the film, but Felix has an iron clad contract: They'll change his film only over his dead body. But then Felix has a multi-million dollar inspiration: Why not shoot some new, nude scenes and re-release the sweet fable as an X-rated, Freudian phallic fantasy? He gambles every penny he possesses that the public will pay to see his wife, America's squeaky-clean G-rated darling, Sally Miles (Andrews), in the buff. His obstacles are legion: Can he talk her into doing a nude scene? And can he keep the studio spies, saboteurs and lawyers at bay long enough to finish the film? He's determined to take his best shot to steal the show—but being under the gun, the studio has to take a few shots as well. Will the movie prove the killer film Felix believes it can be? Or will it die at the box office, shot down by sinister interests?
Discussion: *Geez* (he wrote, shaking his head). That Blake Edwards. Half genius (*The Great Race*); half retard (*Skin Deep*). What do you do with a guy who has a deep understanding of comedy—but only about half the time? Most distressing of all: his *audiences.* A year after ignoring this masterpiece, critics and the public awarded rave reviews to the mediocre *Victor/Victoria.* Sure, it was a funny flick. But *S.O.B.* remains by far the funnier—and more intelligent and insightful—of the two. (And I say this despite the rude, crude and juvenile humor of *S.O.B.*)

Legend has it that *S.O.B.* is based on Edwards' experiences making *Darling Lili* in 1969 with his wife, Andrews. Things must have gone horribly awry, for him to hold a grudge for over a decade! *S.O.B.* is his revenge: an hilariously savage satire of the creative individual at odds with The Industry; a valentine with a death threat scrawled on the back. It's *Sullivan's Travels* meets *Fatal Instinct*—and the very idea of a scene in which an actress exposes her "boobies" (Andrews' word, not mine) being considered "shocking" seems quaint—almost innocent—today, following Sharon Stone's exposure in that latter flick.

S.O.B. is chock-full of character actors, all in fine form, all performing gloriously, flamboyantly over the top. Few do physical comedy like rubberman Mulligan; Webber is hysterical (in both senses of the word); and Preston steals every shot he's in as the tart-tongued, devil-may-care Dr. Feelgood, world-weary and full of cynical wisdom (essentially the same personality he played in *Victor/Victoria*). As a trio tied together by their camaraderie with Felix and their sense of integrity (an endangered species in Hollywood), Holden, Preston and Webber perform in fine fettle as "The Three Muscatels" in the final few minutes of the film, recreating in fiction a legendary event in Hollywood history involving W.C. Fields and his cronies and the about-to-be-buried body of actor John Barrymore. Here, the ensemble goes a step further in fiction than their kindred forebears did in fact, and their farewell tribute is at once original, hilarious, heartbreakingly poignant, and totally appropriate.

Be warned, however: A major plot twist occurs about three-quarters of the way through the film (one which I can't reveal, because of our "no spoilers" rule). This twist is so unexpected, so shocking, so sobering, so downright appalling—and is such a personal violation of the viewer (precisely what Edwards intended, no doubt)—that you may very well be tempted to turn off the tape and give up on the film. (When I first saw this movie, after this event I was actually ashamed of ever having laughed at Felix's predicament.) You might well be convinced at this point (as I was) that you will never again laugh at this "comedy." Well, guess what? The last half-hour of the flick shifts into comic high gear, becoming twice as fall-down funny twice as fast as anything that came before it. Edwards accomplishes *two* brilliant transitions, manipulating our expectations and emotions, as *S.O.B.* transforms from light comedy to sobering tragedy to pitch black slapstick at its finest. It is in effect a reverse roller coaster ride, rocketing us from an acceptable elevation of levity to distressing depths, then recovering at the speed of lightness to attain the highest dark comic heights.

Rent this one for: its daring structure; its sharp dialog; its savage satire of the Hollywood studio system; Robert Preston.

You'll (probably) like this if you liked: *Sullivan's Travels, The Player, The Big Picture, Almost Hollywood, Postcards From The Edge* (Hollywood spoofs); *Sunset Boulevard* (serious treatment); *W. C. Fields and Me; Dumb and Dumber*

Dissenting Opinion: • "Tasteless, vulgar and unfunny..." —HFG • "...wildly uneven..." —MMG (2.5) • "...failed attempt at satire...Self-indulgent."—VMG (3) • "...a film of undisguised hatred...sour insults...ugly characters..."—*People Magazine*

Vidbits: • Holden's last film; he died later in '81. • The "S.O.B." of the title stands for Hollywood's "Standard Operational Bull-shit." • Andrews wore a pair of prosthetic breasts for her brief "boobie" scene. (Sorry, guys.)

Someone To Love

(romantic comedy)

(1987; Paramount; R; 1:50)

Starring: Henry Jaglom, Michael Emil, Orson Welles
Featuring: Sally Kellerman, Andrea Marcovicci, Oja Kodar, Stephen Bishop, Ronee Blakley, Kathryn Harrold
Written and directed by: Henry Jaglom

Synopsis: When his brother Mickey (Emil) comes to Santa Monica to check out a property he's bought—an historic old theater about to be razed to make way for a shopping center—Danny (Jaglom) decides to throw him a party. He's got a full agenda, though: to document the dying theater, to introduce Mickey to some women, and to gather all his single friends who are alone on Valentine's Day together for a filmed discussion of why they can't seem to make romantic relationships work. Things really pick up when Orson Welles shows up to pass on some wisdom.
Discussion: One of the Big Metaphors of the Me Decade said, "Your life is a movie; write your own script." Henry Jaglom took this to heart, and deeply. His is a truly original filmmaking style: part documentary, partially scripted; films in which fictional characters improvise dialog and real people often use scripted lines. Even if it doesn't always work, the effect does blur the line between life and art in interesting ways. Here—much like at a real party—the interview responses run the gamut from the infuriatingly banal ("I think we're all wonderful mirrors for each other") to the insightful ("I feel like I'm being X-rayed") to the witty ("Who do I have to fuck to get out of this movie?"). If you can endure the "second act," in which these clips are intercut with eavesdrops on various pick-up attempts, you get the Big Payoff: Orson Welles as a one-man Greek Chorus, the ultimate Voice of Authority, holding court from the back of the theater, pontificating real answers to tough questions about happiness, love and loneliness in provocative monologs. Orson, in his final performance, is a brilliant, wise, laughing, happy Buddha. What a lovely valentine to us, courtesy of Henry Jaglom.
Rent this one for: being a brave, quirky experiment; for Orson.
You'll (probably) like this if you liked: *My Dinner With Andre, When Harry Met Sally..., Annie Hall; Always* (1984), *New Year's Day, Eating* (Jaglom)
Dissenting Opinion: • "Wallows in all there is to detest about the Los Angeles art scene" —VMG (2 stars) • "...alternately boring and interesting."—MMG (2.5 stars) • "Silly, self-indulgent pretentious nonsense." —Emil as Mickey, in the film itself.
Vidbits: • Welles' final film. • Oja Kodar was Welles' mistress during his final years (for more of her, see *F For Fake*).

Something Wild

(black comedy)
(1986; HBO; R; 1:53)

Starring: Jeff Daniels, Melanie Griffith, Ray Liotta
Written by: E. Max Frye
Directed by: Jonathan Demme

Synopsis: Free spirit Lulu (Griffith), adrip with costume jewelry, spots businessman Charlie (Daniels) jumping a lunch check and pegs him as a "closet rebel." She offers to drive him back to work, but instead takes him for the ride of his life, including a stop at the motel room of endless pleasures. He's hooked, and enlists for the rest of her road trip. They end up in her home town in rural Pennsylvania, where she makes an amazing transformation into virginal Audrey and passes him off as her respectable husband at her high school reunion. The fun and games turn deadly, though, the second Ray (Liotta) enters the room. Guess who had a past with Audrey? Guess who taught her to be wild, but doesn't have fun in mind? And guess who's intent on keeping her, no matter who he has to kill? Guess again...
Discussion: "She's got some strange notions about life," Audrey's mom sighs to Charlie. So does this flick—along with one serious flaw: it never decided whether it was a cutting edge comedy or a cutthroat suspense entry. Taken in its entirety, though, it's a smooth slide from one to the other, and it does clarify itself at the end. In one sense, it's an ironic modern morality play: Psycho Ray is the only one among them telling the truth; the only one clear and open about his desires and his past. Even though he plays judge and jury over their "harmless" lies, when it comes time to pay for their crimes, the deep difference becomes evident: Only Charlie is man enough to take responsibility for their fates. A romance with a twist, some provocative questions about truth and liberation, and a harrowing, ultraviolent final fight make this well worth watching.
Rent this one for: its unusual, original plot; the acting.
You'll (probably) like this if you liked: *The Ruling Class, Love and a .45, The Chase, Bonnie & Clyde, Pulp Fiction, Trust*
Dissenting Opinion: • "Unremarkable melodrama with trendy musical trappings"—HFG • "...end result isn't satisfying"—MMG
Vidbits: • Features brief appearances by film directors John Sayles (motorcycle cop) and John Waters (used car guy). • The two old ladies in the secondhand shop are Demme's and musician David Byrne's mothers. • Daniels, on the phone, says "Tell Scott I love him." Aw, shucks! It's probably only because he's mentioned in this book four times!

Flashback!

Start The Revolution Without Me

(1970; Warner; PG; 1:31)

Starring: Gene Wilder, Donald Sutherland, Hugh Griffith
Featuring: Billie Whitelaw, Victor Spinetti, Ewa Aulin, Orson Welles
Written by: Fred Freeman, Lawrence J. Cohen
Directed by: Bud Yorkin

Synopsis: A Corsican Count rushes his pregnant wife through the French countryside, trying to make it to Paris before she delivers. Too late, they land in a little village, where the only doctor is already attending to the birth of the peasant innkeeper's wife. They both have twin sons, and in the confusion, the infants are mixed, one from each pair going to each parent. 30 years later, escalating enmity between peasants and aristocrats under the rule of Louis XVI (Griffith) is ready to ignite, and a pair of dopey, cowardly peasant twins (Sutherland and Wilder), are drafted into a rebel band. Meanwhile, the other pair of mismatched twins has been raised in the luxury of nobility. The King sends for the Corsican Brothers (guess who) to assist him in saving France from the sinister schemes of Queen Marie (Whitelaw) and her co-conspirator, the evil Duke d'Escargot (Spinetti). Arriving in Paris disguised as peasants, each set of twins is quickly mistaken for the other, and chaos ensues. Can the country boys talk some sense into Louis before the peasants revolt? Can they thwart the coup and prevent the throne from being overthrown? Don't bet your history books on it...
Discussion: Wilder is wilder than ever as the wild-eyed, leather-clad sadistic twin ("I'll join you in the chapel later," he informs his wife. "Bring the rawhide and the honey.") Sutherland, as a lacy, lisping fop, does his best to keep up ("One day I shall be King!" Wilder cries. "And I," Sutherland sighs, "shall be Queen.") Add in a virginal love interest/political pawn (Aulin) a sex-crazed Queen, a sweet old doddering codger of a King, ready to meet the peasants' demands if it will avert a revolution, an increasingly complicated series of alliances and betrayals, conspiracies and confessions, a portentous narrator with an endless supply of overextended metaphors, *and* an appearance by Orson Welles, and you've got a fast-paced lampoon of the "intrigue in the palace" genre of action epics, circa...*1789!*
Rent this one for: its view of history as slapstick farce; Wilder.
You'll (probably) like this if you liked: *History of the World, Pt. I, Tom Jones, Monty Python and the Holy Grail, The Man in the Iron Mask* (serious); *The Producers* (Wilder)
Vidbits: • Executive Producer: Norman "All In The Family" Lear.
• Lest we forget, the movie takes place in...*1789!* Yes...*1789!*

Stranger Than Paradise

(1984; Key Video, CBS/Fox; R; 1:30; B&W)

Starring: John Lurie, Eszter Balint, Richard Edson
Music by: John Lurie
Written and directed by: Jim Jarmusch

Synopsis: Willy's (Lurie) cousin Eva (Balint) is flying in from Budapest, and New Yorker Willy is appointed by Aunt Lotte to look after her for a few days. Man, she's gonna disrupt his whole routine! Mostly, he hangs out. Just...hangs out. Sometimes alone, sometimes with his near-identical twin buddy Eddie (Edson). They smoke. They play solitaire. They go to the track. They all try to be nice to one another, without really knowing how. Eva leaves. A year later, Willy and Eddie take a road trip to Cleveland. Eva's living there with Aunt Lotte, and the three of them...hang out. They decide to take a drive to Florida. So they do. Several twists of fate play ironic tricks on them.
Discussion: Portraying boredom is a tricky thing to do without actually *being* boring, but Jarmusch, in his first feature film, managed to pull it off by elevating ennui into deadest-pan comedy. These people are the original and ultimate "slackers," with no future, no hope, no direction—and no interest in any of the above, or much of anything else. They don't communicate so much as posture, and it's not just their silences that are awkward—every detail of their existence is awkward. The film consists of a series of single scenes punctuated by blackouts; it sometimes feels as though we're burgling a peek into someone else's family photo album, or watching surveillance tapes rather than a movie. The stark black and white photography defines their existence and magnifies the squalor of New York and the wretched industrial countrysides they drive through. Willy prides himself on having cut his Old World ties, but from the look of the landscape, he appears, ironically, to be living in his own worst nightmare of the Eastern Block. Their listless existence becomes hypnotic: in some scenes, just waiting for one of them to move is quirkily comical. Looked at from this perspective, the film is a strange celebration of the absurdity and surreal strangeness of plain old everyday boring normality.
Rent this one for: its deadpan humor; its efficient use of a tiny budget to tell a human story in a unique manner and tone.
You'll (probably) like this if you liked: *Down By Law, Mystery Train* (Jarmusch)*; Slacker, Trust, Patti Rocks*
Credentials: • "★★★★" —SMV • #21 on *Premiere* magazine's poll of 24 critics' "Best Movies of the '80s" list.
Vidbits: End credits thank Paul Bartel *(Eating Raoul)* for "special help." Also thanked among a long list: director Wim Wenders.

Strictly Ballroom

(romantic comedy)
(1992; Touchstone; R; 1:44)

Starring: Paul Mercurio, Tara Morice, Bill Hunter
Written by: Baz Luhrmann, Craig Pearce, Andrew Bovell
Directed by: Baz Luhrmann

Synopsis: "Boxed in" during a ballroom dancing competition, top contender Scott Hastings (Mercurio) shocks judges and audience alike by breaking into his own unconventional, nontraditional and *flashy* steps! When warned away from this dangerous trajectory, a horrid truth is loosed: Scott is "sick of dancing somebody else's steps" and is determined to pursue his own path. His partner drops him, but drab Fran (Morice), a clumsy beginner, understands his dream and becomes his apprentice, his partner—maybe even his girl? Everyone is dead-set against their pairing, attempting to link Scott with another pro to win the coveted Pan Pacific Grand Prix—a feat even his dancer parents never accomplished. At the eleventh hour, however, the star-crossed dancers find assistance from unexpected sources—as well as a dark secret that will affect their destiny as dancers.
Discussion: Them Aussies sure make some weird, wacky—and wonderful—films. This one is a mutant hybrid of *That's Dancing* and *This Is Spinal Tap;* a terpsichorean satire with a singular style, an enormous heart and an extravagant sense of humor. The competitions, for example, are surreal spectacles of psychedelic lighting and costumes even Elton John would reject as garish. Much of the film consists of sly skewerings of the typical "illicit lovers" romance plot and the "rebel without applause" genre; the surprise lies not so much in clichés that are tweaked, flipped and twisted, but in how endearing the characters are, and how attached to them we become. Their coach tells them a dancer needs looks, charm and confidence; this film has all three. Often hilarious, occasionally exhilarating, touchingly romantic and deeply sweet, *Ballroom* is a delightful reminder that you can find liberation and redemption in *any* form of artistic expression, if you just have the courage to follow your heart—and even if you dance to the beat of a different drummer.
Rent this one for: its wild humor; its heart; the performances.
You'll (probably) like this if you liked: *This Is Spinal Tap!, That's Dancing!, The Cutting Edge, Funny Bones*
Credentials: Australian Film Institute Awards, 1992: Best Film, Writing, Director, Editing, Costume Design, Supporting Actor (Barry Otto) and Actress (Pat Thomsen). • *EW:* "A"
Vidbits: • Lurhmann's film debut. • Mercurio is a ballet dancer.

Flashback!

Sullivan's Travels

(1941; MCA; NR; 1:30; B&W)

Starring: Joel McCrea, Veronica Lake
Featuring: William Demerest, Robert Warrick, Franklin Pangborn
Written and directed by: Preston Sturges

Synopsis: John L. "Sully" Sullivan is a movie director with a mission: to produce an important film, a movie about human suffering, an epic about misery and trouble. "What do you know about trouble?" a skeptical studio executive questions the rich, college-educated, over-inflated director teetering on the edge of pretentiousness. Sully realizes the guy is right, and determines to hit the open road as a hobo, vowing not to return "until I know what trouble is." Thus begins an oddball odyssey of epic proportions, encompassing raucous comedy and grim misery; real people, both generous and evil; the hopeless depths of despair and the secret of salvation, Hollywood style.

Discussion: "If you want to tell people the truth," Shaw once wrote, "you'd better make it funny, or they'll kill you." Sturges could have used that epigram as his motto for this movie. Any description of this brilliant film requires superlatives: it's a gem, a masterpiece, a treasure; a work of deep insight into the Human Condition, of genius and compassion, of truth told only as a comedy can. The wisecracking dialog is sharp enough to cut diamonds, yet completely absent when it would only slow what pictures can make clearer faster. Never pretentious or didactic, yet as true a view of humanity (and Hollywood) as ever set on film, and as fresh as the day it was made. It doesn't "stink with messages" about the redemptive medicine of laughter, but they're there. "There's a lot to be said for making people laugh," Sully says, marveling at his own (and Sturges') special wisdom. Amen, brother—wherever thou art. Lighten *your* burden a little.

Rent this one for: every single frame.

You'll (probably) like this if you liked: *Funny Bones, S.O.B., Sunset Boulevard,* any other Sturges film

Credentials: • "★★★★" —HFG • "A brilliant fantasy in two keys —slapstick farce and the tragedy of human misery." —James Agee • "Pure genius...the most witty and knowing spoof of Hollywood ever realized." —VMG (★★★★★) • "Landmark Hollywood satire...grows more pertinent with each passing year." —MMG (★★★★) • *EW:* "A+"

Vidbits: • Veronica Lake was pregnant during filming, which necessitated some fancy camera and costume work. • Could this film have been the inspiration for Woody Allen's movie-house epiphany in *Hannah and her Sisters*?

Double Feature!

Swimming To Cambodia

(1987; Lorimar, Warner, Evergreen; NR; 1:27)

Monster in a Box

(1992; New Line, Columbia TriStar; PG-13; 1:28)

(humorous monologs)

Written by and starring: Spalding Gray
Music (both) by: Laurie Anderson
Directed by: Jonathan Demme *(Swimming)*;
Nick Broomfield *(Monster)*

Synopsis: "It was the first day off in a long time..." Spalding Gray begins, relating his experiences working in Thailand as a minor performer in the film *The Killing Fields*. This "wandering bachelor mendicant poet" proceeds to enact, from his chair behind his table on stage, his many stories: about Thailand and New York, nuclear war, his girlfriend Renée, his "perfect moment" almost drowning off the most beautiful beach in the world, and the fall of Cambodia. Politics plays little part in *Monster*, however; the beast of the title is the 1,900 page novel that Gray will use any excuse not to finish. The book is about a Puritan who can't take a vacation. The monolog is about living in L.A., panic (his), alien abduction (not his), death (hopefully not his), traveling to Nicaragua and Moscow, dying on stage in a production of *Our Town*—and taking a much needed vacation.
Discussion: I confess: I resisted Gray for years, turning a deaf ear to the urging of my most intelligent friends. A "monologist"? A "performance artist"? How *tres* pretentious! If he was any good, he'd be a standup comic. Guess what: Gray is as funny as most comedians, and as smart as any of them. He's an affable actor and a spellbinding speaker with a gift for description; his style is expressive, energetic, engaging and at times almost hypnotic. Although well-practiced on stage, he comes off fresh and spontaneous. With his endearing lisp and New England accent ("a bob-wyah fence"), his tall tales are part memoir, part description, part insight, part explanation, a little political history and a large part confession of his own fears, foibles and human idiosyncrasies. Often hilarious, occasionally poignant and always compelling, this pair of similar films can easily become two acts of an evening's double bill. If you like one, you'll like both. But if you can't warm up to either, forget the other.
Rent this one for: Gray's spellbinding style of storytelling.
You'll (probably) like this if you liked: *My Dinner With Andre*
Credentials: • "...intellectually stimulating..." —SMV (3.5 stars)
• "A new wave Mark Twain..." Minneapolis *Star & Tribune*

Tampopo

(Japanese with English subtitles)
(1986; Republic; NR; 1:54)

Starring: Tsutomu Yamazuki, Nobuko Miyamoto
Written and directed by: Juzo Itami

Synopsis: A lone stranger in a cowboy hat saunters into a bar for some grub. One of the locals is giving the widowed owner a hard time, and our hero calls him out. There's no quickdraw gunplay involved, however—this is no spaghetti Western, it's a *noodle* Western. The location is modern Japan; the bar is a soup bar run by mousy Tampopo (Miyamoto); the would-be cowboy is Goro (Yamazuki), a tough truck driver. He loses the fight, and Tampopo ("Dandelion") takes him in and nurses him. In return, Goro agrees to become her soup guru, tutoring her in how to make and serve the perfect bowl of broth. Training, timing, temperature, technique—all mean little without the right recipe, so they embark on a quest for the perfect formula, begging, borrowing, buying and (when necessary in this cut-throat business) even stealing the necessary information. In between episodes of their quest, we're presented with vignettes about food, which illustrate that it's more than just sustenance, but can also be part of a glorious gustatory orgy of eroticism.
Discussion: On one hand, it's a spoof of spaghetti Westerns—which were originally rip-offs of samurai films, so we've come full circle. On the other hand, it's an exuberant, one-of-a-kind comedy about the depths of obsession. Goro and Tampopo deconstruct, to our endless amusement, every detail of recipe, service, setting, style, taste and presentation, assembling a virtual "Magnificent Seven" of soup specialists along the way. They remake the soup, the store, and even the chef, in delightful detail. And on the *other* other hand, *Tampopo* is a celebration of the erotic element of edibles, envisioning lively new uses for crawfish, whipped cream and honey, oysters and egg yolks. (Serving suggestion: Take a date to dinner then screen this film. Your date will be dessert.) It's a four-star film that's every bit as satisfying as a four-star meal; food for nourishing the spirit, which, with a single touching image at the end, makes perfectly plain the source of this inseparable food/sex connection.
Rent this one for: its unique, erotic and delicious comedy.
You'll (probably) like this if you liked: *Like Water For Chocolate, Babette's Feast* (the magical and erotic power of food)
Credentials: Made 23 major critics' "Top 10 Films of 1987" list, including the NY *Times*, *Time* magazine and the Washington *Post.* • "You will love this movie." —Siskel & Ebert • *EW:* "A-"

There Goes The Neighborhood

(1992; Paramount; PG-13; 1:29)

Starring: Jeff Daniels, Catherine O'Hara
Featuring: Chazz Palminteri, Hector Elizondo, Judith Ivey, Dabney Coleman, Rhea Perlman, Harris Yulin
Written and directed by: Bill Phillips

Synopsis: "Not all therapists are into money," psychologist Willis Embry (Daniels) explains to his prisoner therapy group. Not until a dying con tells him about $8.5 million of casino-skimmed cash buried beneath the foundation of a local home. Too bad the other group members also hear the deathbed confession. And escape. And try to take Willis out of the run for the money by blowing up his apartment. Willis gets lucky, however: he survives—and the criminals get the wrong address, descending on the house next door. But nothing comes easy for Willis; the owner of the real house Jessie (O'Hara), has just tossed her husband out and is feeling *very* antagonistic towards *all* men—particularly nutcases who try to tear up her basement. The parallel excavations proceed apace, narrowly escaping detection by nosy neighbors, a sex-addict realtor and warring spouses. And romances begin to blossom among unlikely couples. But what happens when the cons discover they've got the wrong house—and stage an all-out assault on the treasure?
Discussion: Remake *It's A Mad, Mad, Mad, Mad World* on a basement budget and you might end up with this flick. It's a total second-banana-fest—but they're a first-rate bunch of second bananas. Yulin's Marvin deserves to be singled out as the most relaxed psychopath ever—the bastard offspring of Brando's "Godfather" and Frankenstein's monster. Everyone is given solidly comic lines and performs with the gusto of great enjoyment. The script is a surprise; a sharp satire of psychobabble and suburban silliness, in which every scheme, action and sentence is analyzed as though every one among them was a therapist—or had at least logged enough hours on the couch to bandy the terminology about with abandon. Full of unexpected plot twists, unlikely alliances and love in the least likely places, there's not a serious thing about his flick. It's just good, frothy fun, and there's not a damn thing wrong with that.
Rent this one for: the dialog; the performers; for its frothy fun.
You'll (probably) like this if you liked: *A Fish Called Wanda, It's A Mad, Mad, Mad, Mad World, Moving*
Dissenting Opinion: • "Feeble..." —MMG (1.5 stars) • *EW:* "D+"
Vidbits: Filled with *third* bananas, too, including Morgan Sheppard (*Max Headroom*), Robin Duke (*SCTV*) and Mary Gross (*SNL*).

Trust

(black comedy)
(1991; Republic; R; 1:47)

Starring: Adrienne Shelly, Martin Donovan
Featuring: Merrit Nelson, Edie Falco, John MacKay, Karen Sillas
Written and directed by: Hal Hartley

Synopsis: Maria (Shelly) has dropped out of high school; she's pregnant; and, during a heated argument about these events with her father, she slaps him—and he drops dead. Matthew (Donovan) is an electronics whiz with a mad-on for the entire world. He has an abusive father (McKay), an intolerance for mediocrity—and a hand grenade in his coat pocket, "just in case." Exiled from their suburban homes, they meet seeking shelter in an abandoned house. He takes her home and she discovers his father is a monster. She takes him home to protect her from her mother (Nelson), who blames Maria for her father's fatal heart attack. He gets a job fixing TVs ("the opiate of the masses"). She begins reading his books and discovers she actually has a brain. They understand one another intuitively and begin to trust each other, tentatively. They complement one another. But do they have a hope in hell of overcoming their own neuroses—or will their psychopathic families conspire to ensure that they, too, will never transcend the level of failure and misery *that they certainly deserve?*

Discussion: The tone is Chekov meets Woody Allen; the dialog is David Mamet writing "Dragnet." Hartley's most perfectly-realized film is net-free, high wire emotional slapstick: outrageously eccentric situations in which one false move—a single misplaced breath or eye-blink—will send every single character tumbling into an abyss of the worst imaginable tragedy. And this juxtaposition of the imminently tragic and the insanely mundane creates an intense, edgy energy which pulses through every single scene.

In one sense, it's the story of two emotionally crippled kids from far-beyond-dysfunctional families, suffering from guilt and responsibility forced on them by circumstances and perverse parenting, desperately attempting to make some sense of the insanity that surrounds them, and still harboring a hope for happiness—the only basis for which, they realize, lies in their tentative sense of trust. Their situations are so extravagantly, absurdly horrid that they inspire compassion rather than mere sympathy.

Hardly sounds like a comedy! And yet the inspired, stylized dialog, the arch and purposefully stilted delivery, the mannered, awkward pauses, and the singular situations themselves combine to generate hilarity as the only defense against impending hysteria. The depths of dysfunction their parents are willing—*eager*—to stoop to is shockingly comic. (Matthew's dad's cleanliness fetish would seem a silly idiosyncrasy, for example, but for the fact that it leads to abusive behavior, and Maria's mother's twisted ploy to destroy her relationship with Matthew is one of the most insidious schemes in cinema history.)

Hartley has a special talent for casting as well. Shelly is an adorable waif, and—with her ever-so-slightly caricaturish features—is a virtual marionette of an angelic woman/child. She's appeared in other films, but never shines as brightly as in a Hartley feature (see *The Unbelievable Truth,* below). Donovan's Matthew is sallow, sullen and determinedly deadpan; a passive-aggressive Spock seething beneath the reserved surface, and "dangerous," Maria's mother sneers, "because he's sincere."

The crux of the story is how they temper each other in this crucible of crazy crises. And while Matthew's final fate might be ambiguous, there is no mistaking Maria's blossoming psychological strength: her steely stance in the final shot is the very image of indefatigable determination, producing an ending that is both optimistic and ennobling.

Emotionally spellbinding; unrelentingly intelligent; rich with psychological intricacies; startlingly original; and accompanied by a bizarre yet totally appropriate score, *Trust* is absolutely one-of-a-kind: a brilliant, insightful, outrageous and thoroughly unique film.

Rent this one for: its dangerous comedy.

You'll (probably) like this if you liked: *The Unbelievable Truth, Amateur, Funny Bones*

Credentials: • Best Screenplay Award, Sundance Film Festival • "Well acted, wonderfully written and directed, and completely absorbing." —SMV (3.5 stars) • "...a film poet unfettered by rules." —*Playboy* (5/95) • *EW:* "A-"

Dissenting Opinion (sort of)**:** "The work of [Hartley] is, no doubt, an acquired taste. [His] films...with their elliptical narratives, dislocated characters, and airtight deadpan humor, often feel like elaborate inside jokes....*Trust* remains easily the strongest and most accessible of the lot..." —*Premiere* (1/96)

The Unbelievable Truth

(black comedy)
(1990; Vidmark; R; 1:40)

Starring: Adrienne Shelly, Robert Burke
Featuring: Christopher Cooke, Julia Mueller
Written and directed by: Hal Hartley

Synopsis: Audrey (Shelly) isn't worried about college, or even showing up for high school. The world is coming to an end, after all, probably by nuclear war. Her dad, Vic (Cooke), hopes she's just going through a phase. Meanwhile, Josh (Burke), just released from prison after 15 years, returns to the little New York town in which he grew up, and finds work as a mechanic in Vic's auto shop. Everybody knows the legend of Josh—but everybody's version is different. Rape, murder, multiple murder, mass murder—all they know is he's bad news, and he's back. Audrey is intrigued, fascinated, and smitten by this handsome, mysterious, sinister stranger. Vic bullies, bribes and negotiates to keep them apart, but the attraction persists. Bit by bit, the truth about Josh's past is revealed. Ultimately, it's truth that is undeniable, inescapable—and thoroughly believable.
Discussion: There's no doubt that Hal Hartley's films are an acquired taste, or that his sense of humor is more intellectual than visceral. His dry, stilted dialog is executed with an arch, deliberate delivery which gives everyone a certain quirk: an awkward detachment, making them sound more like people reading the written word than conversing. But this calculated constraint serves to accentuate the absurdity of our poor human attempts to grapple with deeply philosophical issues, like faith and trust: the dialog *sounds* like syllogisms of formal logic. And the ending is a philosophical spin on a French bedroom farce, with the principals all lurking around looking for "truth" instead of a tryst. The result is a caustic, contemplative comedy about people trying to be rational rather than human—and usually losing the battle. Hartley specializes in "dangerous comedies"; absurd situations which could turn tragic with a single wrong gesture. And his actors work wonders within these limits: Burke is a young Christopher Walken, and beautiful, baby-voiced Shelly, a gamin marionette. If Hartley's first morsel doesn't whet your appetite, don't quit before trying main course, *Trust.*
Rent this one for: its deadpan, philosophical comedy.
You'll (probably) like this if you liked: *Trust, Amateur* (Hartley films); *Stranger Than Paradise*
Credentials: "A little gem of a movie." —SMV (3 stars)
Vidbits: Reportedly shot in 11 days.

Used Cars

(1980; Goodtimes, Columbia TriStar; R; 1:51)

Starring: Kurt Russell, Jack Warden, Deborah Harmon
Featuring: Gerrit Graham, Frank McRae, Joe Flaherty, Michael McKean, David L. Lander, Wendie Jo Sperber
Written by: Robert Zemeckis, Bob Gale
Directed by: Robert Zemeckis

Synopsis: Rudy Russo (Russell) has a Dream: to give up his low-life as a sleazy, greedy used car salesman, buy an election, and become a sleazy, greedy State Senator. The only thing that stands between him and his American Dream is money. That, and being stuck in the middle of a vendetta between competing car dealers who are also twin brothers (Warden). When ruthless Roy L. Fuchs has his twin Luke "taken for a ride," Rudy knows he's up Crap Creek without a paycheck—or the cash Luke was about to loan him. And when Luke's estranged daughter (Harmon) walks on to the lot, and Rudy finds himself falling for her, he risks losing every shallow, cynical ideal he holds dear to his plastic heart if she should ever discover his role in her dad's disappearance—and what he's done with her inheritance.
Discussion: How can you not love any film in which the first word uttered is "Fuck"? But how can I recommend a flick that begins as the most aggressively anarchic comedy since the Marx Bros. made movies, then slows into a dumb love story, and eventually shifts into reverse, as a formulaic, feel-good, cliché-ridden car chase flick? Here's how: *Don't watch it all the way to the end.* You'll only be disappointed. You *know* the good guys are gonna win—and after watching V8-motormouth Rudy in action, baiting and skating and cynically scheming, you do *not* want to see him morally redeemed in the name of love. Watch it instead as 65 minutes of manic anarchy and obscene cynicism. The high points of the movie are the pirate commercials; after the "Marshall Lucky" sequence (a rabid masterpiece of commercial lampooning), just *turn the damn thing off!* And be thankful we got even *that* much brilliance stuffed into one film!
Rent this one for: its first 65 minutes, which revel without remorse in sleaze, obscenity, anarchy and subversive satire.
You'll (probably) like this if you liked: *Caddyshack, Repo Man, Slap Shot, Midnight Run, Richard Pryor Live, The Blues Bros*
Dissenting Opinion: • "...revels in bad taste, but does it...good-naturedly..." —MMG (3 stars) • "...nasty...veers into the grotesque too often..." —SMV (2.5 stars)
Vidbits: • The naked girl in the football game pirate commercial is Cheryl Rixon, former Penthouse Pet of the Year. • Executive Producers: Steven Spielberg and director John Milius.

Vibes

(adventure/fantasy/romantic comedy)
(1988; Columbia TriStar; PG; 1:39)

Starring: Cyndi Lauper, Jeff Goldblum, Peter Falk
Written by: Lowell Ganz, Babaloo Mandel
Directed by: Ken Kwapis

Synopsis: Nick (Goldblum) is a psychometrist; he touches objects and psychically "sees" their history. Sylvia Pickle (Lauper) is a lovelorn medium with "friends in the spirit world." Both have their impressive talents abused by friends and lovers alike. So they both jump at the chance to go on a humanitarian mission to Ecuador to find Harry Bustafusco's (Falk) missing son. It's a surprise to them (but not to us) to find out there is no son—just a partner lost on a search for the Inca Room of Gold, high in the Andes. They're not alone on their quest, either: a second, ruthless, group is hot on their heels, shadowing them to the Lost City. There's more than gold at the end of their perilous quest, however: there is also death, temptation, revenge—and a weird pyramid containing the most concentrated source of psychic energy on the planet. Who'll gain access to the power first—and to what end? And will Sylvia *ever* find a decent guy?
Discussion: Just look at the string of hits written by Ganz and Mandel: *Nightshift* (82), *Splash* (84), *Parenthood* (89), *City Slickers* (91), *Vibes* (88). *"Vibes"?* It's a goofy spoof of romantic adventure flicks, and while it might not congeal into a great film, there's plenty of fun along the way. Lauper is the very definition of a ditz: a cheeky chick; brazen, brassy and sassy, yet still sensitive and sympathetic; a naturally wacky broad playing wacky broad comedy with a brash flair. Falk, as the single-minded con man, is brimming with eager ebullience. The screwball psychics are an engaging pair of opposites—and consider this: in '88, pop phenom Lauper got top billing; eight years later, Goldblum has starred in the two biggest moneymakers in cinema history (*Jurassic Park, Independence Day*), and Cyndi *is* a bit of cinema history. What a world, eh? Boisterous good fun.
Rent this one for: the punchline dialog; the flip performances.
You'll (probably) like this if you liked: *Romancing the Stone*
Dissenting Opinion: • "Unfortunate misfire..." —MMG (2 stars) • "Flat..." —GMR (1 bone) • "...sad misfire..." —VMG (2 stars)
Vidbits: • Lauper's first and only starring role, although she'd reappear in the 1993 Michael J. Fox comedy, *Life With Mikey.* • Psychic "Ingo Swelvio" is a parody of psychic Ingo Swann, although they'd probably never admit that in court. • Cult fave Steve Buscemi appears briefly at the track as Sylvia's boyfriend.

Where The Heart Is

(1990; Touchstone; R; 1:51)

Starring: Dabney Coleman, Uma Thurman, Joanna Cassidy
Featuring: Suzy Amis, Crispin Glover, Christopher Plummer
Written by: John Boorman, Telsche Boorman
Directed by: John Boorman

Synopsis: Stewart McBain (Coleman) gets no respect. He's elevated demolition to an art form—he could flatten Manhattan. But he gets no respect from the City of New York, which declares a monstrous little building in midst of his biggest downtown development as an historical monument, halting all construction—and if Stewart can't build, he goes broke. He gets no respect from his trio of artistic, far-past adolescent kids, either. So he "hardens his heart" and exiles them to live in the landmark monstrosity. "You can't just spoil us then stop spoiling us when it suits you!" wails ditzy daughter Daphne (Thurman). But Stewart is convinced that kicking the kids out of the nest is the only way to teach them to survive the harsh realities of the world. To do so, they're forced to take in an eclectic assortment of borders, including Lionel (Glover), an eccentric fashion designer; "Shitty" (Plummer), an aged, homeless magician; a smug young stockbroker in love with daughter Chloe (Amis); and an off-center psychic. When Stewart's stock collapses due to the city's ban on building, he loses everything. He and his loyal (if slightly scatter-brained) wife, Jean (Cassidy), are forced to move in with the kids they had earlier evicted. Only that horrible house stands between Stewart's success and a total meltdown of the McBains. It'd be a shame if anything happened to it...
Discussion: Right from the opening note we know we're in for something special: a sentimental orchestration accompanies the image of a hand, painting a New York skyline scene. And when the rock score rises and drowns out the classical track, and the scene becomes real, and the building *collapses*...we might wonder what the hell is happening. But it's merely the first of a series of slight-of-hand maneuvers that make this movie magic.

It's safe to say there's never been a film quite like *Heart;* it's a very European-style comedy about a very American family. Although it's billed as a comedy, there are few huge belly-laughs. But Paul Mazursky's films are labeled "comedies," and their main virtue is their ability to keep you thinking for days afterward. Fellini's *Amarcord* is classified as comedy, too—but only because there is no genre label to describe a film filled with love, sweetness and fond familial infighting. Like these pictures, *Heart* is a different animal entirely. (One clue to its unconventionality: there are no villains!) The film's strength lies not in its plot, but in its portrayal of the people whose company we are privileged to share. No character is mere caricature; each is a full-fledged, fully-fleshed individual—and each struggling, suffering person is treated with infinite affection and amusement.

Coleman's quirky character humor has always eluded the big screen, even while being brilliantly showcased in TV series' like "Buffalo Bill" and "The Slap Maxwell Story." This is the best film role (and performance) of his career; one which captures his irascible intensity and frustrated fury—but which then piles on enough suffering to soften him into a sympathetic survivor. Cassidy dares to turn her back on the smart, tough women roles in which she excels (think *Blade Runner, Under Fire, Who Framed Roger Rabbit?*) to play a sheltered, giggling, thinking-impaired *hausfrau,* a victim of the "empty nest" syndrome—a role which she pulls off brilliantly. An almost unrecognizable Plummer is charming and funny beneath his whiskers and hoarse howling; and Glover is at his comically eccentric peak. The one among them, however, who turns in a perfect performance is Thurman as the innocent little sister: effervescent and vivacious, naive and naughty, desperate to please, simultaneously gangly and ethereal—her Daphne is, in a word, adorable.

The tapestry of interweaving themes is almost too rich to discuss quickly. The film is rife with irony, for instance, from conservative Stewart's incongruous attitude that what makes America great is not preservation, but tearing down the old to make way for the new, to the final irony that in order to prevent their family from becoming outcasts, they must become outlaws—for the family to survive, the landmark must perish. (A nice touch, that; pitting Family Values against Political Correctness. "Only the rich can afford principles," Stewart's son proclaims, indicating that *lack* of money is the root of all evil...) Two of Boorman's recurring themes—dancing and magic—appear here in their most refined form. And a whole page could be devoted to the subtle Shakespearean references in the film, from Chloe's painting of "The Tempest" with Stewart as Prospero, to McBain raging against the rain like Lear, to the round-robin of romantic relationships, a feature of many of the Comedies.

Add to all of the above one of the most delightful soundtracks of the past decade—an eclectic collection of everything from Rimsky-Korsakov to The Cowboy Junkies—and some breathtakingly beautiful, wholly original artwork—a unique and stunning form of *trompe l'oeil* integrating body-painted humans hidden into murals ranging in style from Magritte to Rousseau (courtesy of artist Timna Woollard)—and you've got a film that is visually brilliant, original and unique.

Unfortunately, neither the soundtrack nor Chloe's art-filled calendar were ever made available as spin-off merchandise. The reason is undoubtedly because the movie was such a wretched box office flop. Which brings up a baffling question: Given all the above elements, why was *Where The Heart Is* so universally reviled by critics? (See "Dissenting Opinion" below for a smattering of the damage.) Have critics become so hard-hearted that they can't sense genuine affection radiating off the screen? Have audiences become so action-oriented that a gentle, character-based comedy, filled with love and laughter, just isn't marketable? Have we all become so accustomed to "Hollywood style" cinema that the French farce influence of a film like this falls flat? Do we choose bullets and blood over art and affection? Answers are beyond the scope of a minuscule essay like this—but I can, however, suggest a few reasons why the film failed on video: The box art is instantly forgettable and gives no indication of what's in the movie; the tape got no promotion, but was unceremoniously dumped onto video (probably following the logic that since it flopped in its theatrical release, why throw good promotional money after bad); and, since the title begins with "W," it's virtually the last tape anyone combing video store shelves comes across—and then it's usually stuck on a shelf only slightly higher than floor level.

"You can't take out insurance against failure in art!" a businessman warns Chloe—sentiments which could well echo John and his co-screenwriter, daughter Telsche, Boorman's own fears about their bold experiment. But then consider their answer, as spoken by Chloe when her murals are destroyed along with the Dutch House: "At least we finished it. *We* know it's beautiful."

You'll have to decide whether or not *Where The Heart Is* is beautiful in your eyes. There's no doubt in mine. Beyond the obvious, it's beautiful because its message is not "life imitates art" or "art imitates life," but that they are one and the same. It's beautiful because it celebrates the triumph of art and affection over material concerns. It's beautiful because it suggests that dedication to one's vision can elevate the mundane to the elegantly ecstatic, and because it reminds us, as too few films do, of the wisdom of bliss and the magic of the moment; to appreciate the fleeting—and that the heart is truly where home is.

Rent this one for: the performances; the art; the heart.

You'll (probably) like this if you liked: *Amarcord, Funny Bones, Strictly Ballroom*

Dissenting Opinion: • "Mindless drivel" —VMG ("turkey") *(VMG lists this under "Drama." Hello?)* • "Disappointing farce...[a] hodgepodge that's too outlandish to be taken seriously." —MMG (2 stars) *("taken* seriously*?" It's a* comedy*!)* • "Dated comedy is a major misfire..." —SMV (1.5 stars) *(Your* Mama*!)*

Vidbits: • This flick reunites Coleman and Cassidy, who starred together in the sitcom "Buffalo Bill."

Worth Winning

(romantic comedy)

(1989; CBS/Fox; PG-13; 1:43)

Starring: Mark Harmon, Madeleine Stowe, Lesley Ann Warren
Featuring: Maria Holvoe, Mark Blum, Andrea Martin, David Brenner
Written by: Josann McGibbon, Sara Parriott
(based on the novel by Dan Lewandowski)
Directed by: Will MacKenzie

Synopsis: Taylor Worth (Harmon) is a happy bachelor with a six-figure income and a glamorous job. He's a nice guy as well. It's not that commitment is an *issue*... His married male friends, however, think he should suffer like they do, and propose a high-stakes wager: Taylor has three months to become engaged to three women of their choice. Their goal: entrapment. Eleanor (Warren) is a dissatisfied wife ripe for an affair; Erin (Holvoe), a sweetly empty-headed blonde goddess. But Veronica (Stowe), a feisty, fiercely independent classical pianist, is different. There's a real spark there—probably ignited by their personalities grating. Has Taylor finally met his match? And will he lose his big chance at romantic happiness because of a stupid bet?
Discussion: What could easily have degenerated into a *Porky's* style frat-boy smirk-fest, degrading both sexes, is here kept on a higher, lighter plane. Even when the predictable inevitably occurs (farces featuring affair-juggling *have* been around for a few hundred years, after all, and have a specific structure) and the whole stupid scheme threatens to blow up in Taylor's face, it teaches him an understated, undervalued lesson: that nice guys don't always finish last. Sometimes they can actually win the Grand Prize—but only if they remain *nice guys*. The dialog is amusing, and the invention of "Mouse Olympics" unexpectedly endearing. But the success of the movie rests squarely on Harmon's charm—on his winning grin, his shrugging chagrin, his laid-back delivery. Even the potentially pretentious convention of his addressing us directly works, allowing us to feel like confidants rather than voyeurs—but only if you let yourself succumb to Harmon's charm. Is this a romance for the ages? Probably not. But sweet? Romantic? Pleasant love-fluff about honesty and second chances? It's all this—*and* worth watching.
Rent this one for: being a farce with its heart in the right place; for Harmon's affable charm. (If you're immune, skip it.)
You'll (probably) like this if you liked: *Sleepless in Seattle, The Cutting Edge,*
Dissenting Opinion: • "...dead-in-the-water..." —GMR (1.5 bones) • "turkey" —VMG • "Occasionally obnoxious (and predictable)" —MMG (1.5 stars) • *EW:* "D"

Zelig

(mocumentary)

(1983; Warner; PG; 1:29; B&W)

Starring: Woody Allen, Mia Farrow
Music by: Dick Hyman
Written and directed by: Woody Allen

Synopsis: "He was *the* phenomenon of the '20s," Susan Sontag informs us. "It is ironic to see how quickly he has faded from memory," adds Saul Bellow. "He" was Leonard Zelig (Allen), AKA "The Chameleon Man"—an odd little dweeb so desperate for acceptance that his entire body morphed to match whatever company he found himself in. From black jazz musician to Chinese opium addict to American Indian—Zelig transformed into them all. Held for psychiatric observation, Dr. Fletcher (Farrow) attempts to uncover the roots of his unique "identity disorder." Meanwhile, the Jazz Age public makes him a tabloid sensation, complete with wacky dance crazes and toys. Zelig is exploited by ambitious but uncaring relatives, until Dr. Fletcher obtains custody and attempts a cure. Their relationship deepens, but relapse and scandal seem Leonard's destiny. Can he be cured? Can he and his compassionate shrink ever find happiness? Or will things get even weirder than we could ever imagine?
Discussion: Like Zelig himself, this film is many things. It's a technical triumph predating *Gump's* digital history by a decade, integrating Zelig into film footage with everyone from Babe Ruth to Hitler. It's a pixel-perfect recreation of an early "talkie," and an hilarious parody of documentaries. It's a grab bag of comedy, from slapstick to brilliantly intellectual—like a Marx Brothers movie with Woody playing all three parts. It's a feature-length shaggy dog story—and it's a gentle parable about accepting ourselves as we are, not as everyone would have us. Bravo! A+!
Rent this one for: the unique story and images; the humor.
You'll (probably) like this if you liked: *Forrest Gump*; *The Rutles, Take the Money and Run; Dead Men Don't Wear Plaid*
Credentials: • Academy Award nominations: Cinematography (Gordon Willis); Costume Design. • "★★★★★" —VMG • "★★★★" —SMV • One of "Ten Best of Genre" —*People Magazine's Guide to Movies on Video* • #22 on *Premiere* magazine's poll of 24 critics' "Best Movies of the '80s" list • "*Citizen Kane* miraculously transformed into side-splitting comedy." —NY *Times*
Vidbits: • Cameos include interview clips with Susan Sontag, Saul Bellow and Irving Howe. • Mae Questal, the voice of Betty Boop, sings "Chameleon Days." • Mia Farrow's sister Stephanie plays Dr. Fletcher's sister Meryl.

Docutainment

Docutainment

The media seem intent these days on coining new words to pigeonhole "new" ideas. Movies like *Rain Man* that combine comedy and drama are "dramedies." Fictional recreations of real events are "docudramas." "Lite news" shows like "Entertainment Tonight" are "infotainment." The newest CD-ROM games are tagged "edutainment." And of course there are those irritating, ubiquitous late-night "infomercials."

Maybe our endless quest for novelty is to blame. Maybe it's the desire to appear unique. Or maybe it's just another example of the degradation of the English language.

Whatever the reason, it's about time video got in on the fun. And so we herewith unveil the latest buzzword: *docutainment*, short for "entertaining documentaries."

Let's define "docutainment" as "theatrically-released feature films designed more to entertain than to educate." You won't find any dreadful high school-style 16mm educational entries on this list, nor any PBS science or nature series; no "Cosmos," "Connections" or Cousteau. They all have their place—that place just happens to be education. But as *entertainment,* any one the documentaries in this section is an adequate Saturday night substitute for the latest Hollywood blockbuster.

A perfect example is *Woodstock,* the most commercially successful documentary to date (and a film far too well-known and popular ever to grace these humble pages...) *Woodstock* is a film where wall-to-wall music and sly social commentary combined to document a unique, landmark event in counter-culture history. Simultaneously, it's a tremendously entertaining feature film. But while *Woodstock* might be the best example, there are a handful of similar, lesser-known fact-based films that can prove every bit as entertaining as a work of fiction.

Is truth stranger than fiction? Regardless of the answer, it can at least, on occasion, be every bit as entertaining.

The Atomic Café

(black comedy)
(1982; Thorn/EMI; NR; 1:28)

Written, produced and directed by:
Kevin Rafferty, Jayne Loader, Pirece Rafferty

Synopsis: This collection of newsreel footage and clips from propaganda film presents the history of atomic weapons in the U.S., from the day of their creation into the Cold War, focusing mainly on the myths and madness they inspired in the '50s.
Discussion: In the opening interview, Paul Tibbets, pilot of the *Enola Gay,* describes his bomb run on Hiroshima as "a perfectly ordinary and routine thing"—until he saw the damage. This single sound bite summarizes the entire film, which portrays the atomic innocence and subsequent education of an entire society. With no narration other than the soundtracks of the clips, the days of the A-bomb and H-bomb, of Civil Defense sirens and home bomb shelters, are preserved in a time capsule as frightening, embarrassing and hilarious as any home movie. In one sense, this movie is a real-life horror film. When military experts explain to foot soldiers before an "atomic maneuver" that there's no need to worry about radiation, then send them heading toward a mushroom cloud just seconds after detonation, the sight is as horrifying as it is surreal. Yet *Café* is as funny as it is chilling: we chuckle nervously at ourselves for being so naive about atomic weapons and radiation, and for buying official defenses like the ludicrous "duck and cover." In a beautifully choreographed finale, previous clips are recombined to illustrate the Final Nightmare: an Atomic Attack on America, from alert to event. Dad's wise advice to his nuclear family in their post-holocaust bunker: "Nothing to do now but wait for orders from the authorities and relax." With its twisted humor and almost nostalgic tone, *Café* is a fascinating, discomfiting document about the nuclear madness of the 1950s—the innocence and guilt; the facts, the follies, and the outright lies.
Rent this one for: being the blackest of black comedies.
You'll (probably) like this if you liked: *Dr. Strangelove, Matinee*
Credentials: "...one of the finest feature-length documentaries of the decade." —SMV (★★★★)
Dissenting Opinion: • "...has little to offer" —VMG (2 stars) • "...argues its point a little longer than necessary." —MMG (3)
Vidbits: • Co-producer Jayne Loader is the author of *Between Pictures,* a satirical novel about Hollywood. • Among many singled out for thanks in the credits: Yuppie leader Abbie Hoffman.

Buster Keaton:
A Hard Act To Follow

(comedy)

(1987; HBO; NR; three vols, :52 each; B&W)

Starring: Buster Keaton
Written and produced by: Kevin Brownlow, David Gill
Music: Carl Davis
Narrated by: Lindsay Anderson

Synopsis: This masterful three-part biography of silent film star Buster Keaton covers the entire career of "The Great Stone Face," from his birth in 1895 to his heyday in the '20s, through his ignoble demise in the '30s, his problems with alcoholism and romance, to his eventual "rediscovery" in recent years. Through interview clips with Keaton and his contemporaries, friends and family—and a plethora of clips from his own films—the originality and ingenuity of this "game little guy" are beautifully illustrated. Special emphasis is placed on the enormous amount of thought, preparation and risk that went into his impeccably timed physical comedy, and the numerous physical indignities he suffered in performing his hazardous stunts (including a broken neck).

Discussion: You can keep your Chaplin, your Langdon, your Sennett. There was only one genius making silent comedies: Buster Keaton. Writer, producer, director, star; impassive slapstick performer; part clown, part gymnast, part acrobat, part Houdini, he was as serious about his work as he was frivolous on screen, and as ambitious and perfectionist about his films as he was eccentric in their presentation. This PBS-produced "American Masters" special is both amusing and amazing, containing excellent research and even key scenes from Keaton's classics like *The General* (unbelievably unappreciated by critics and the public alike at the time of its release) and *Sherlock, Jr.* This is timeless comedy, captured for the ages.

Rent this one for: being fascinating, brilliant and hilarious; as a bittersweet biography of an extraordinary performer; for the collection of classic comedy clips.

You'll (probably) like this if you liked: *The General* (or any Keaton film, for that matter); *Chaplin, Unknown Chaplin*

Credentials: "...truly superb...★★★★★" —VMG

The Day After Trinity

(history)

(1980; Pyramid Video; NR; 1:28)

Written by: David Peoples, Janet Peoples, Jon Else
Directed and produced by: Jon Else

Synopsis: The story of the development of the first atomic bomb, placed in the context of a biography of J. Robert Oppenheimer, director of the Manhattan Project. This skillful blend of still photos, newsreel and archival footage, and contemporary reminiscences illustrates how the man and the "gadget" were intimately connected, and how both were used and abused.
Discussion: What would you name as the defining date of the 20th century? November 22, 1963? July 20, 1969? How about July 16, 1945—the day the first atom bomb was detonated, an event which forever changed the way we look at war and peace? *Trinity* is not just another documentary about building The Bomb, but instead an insightful biography of "Oppie," the gentle and eloquent physicist credited with its creation. This fascinating, sobering inquiry is not afraid to address questions such as why The Bomb was ever built—or used—in the first place. The answers lie within the climate of the times, but are still debated today. And while many of us know the story of those heady days of patriotism and paranoia which surrounded the single most concentrated and expensive scientific experiment in history, it is the introduction of Oppenheimer that gives the story its additional dimensions, both human and mythic. Mythic comparisons are inevitable; in his own quoting of Hindu scripture ("Now I am become Death, the destroyer of worlds"), or if seen as a present-day Pandora. Most appropriate, perhaps, is Oppenheimer as a modern Faust, whose "deal with the Devil" elevated him to a position as "philosopher-king," the savior of the nation—and to his fall from grace, as post-war politics led to ostracism by the scientific community and betrayal by the very country he'd helped save. The final interview with Oppenheimer reveals a broken, betrayed man, bitter because of his inability to control the powers he'd unleashed—and all the more bitter because so few others even tried.
Rent this one for: condensing a global nightmare into a human story; for bringing a human dimension to history.
You'll (probably) like this if you liked: *Fat Man and Little Boy, The Atomic Café, Fail-Safe, Dr. Strangelove*
Credentials: "★★★★" — Roger Ebert
Vidbits: The Peoples also wrote the script for Terry Gilliam's *12 Monkeys*. • Else was videographer on James Burke's PBS series.

Flashback!

F For Fake

(1973; Public Media/Home Vision; NR; 1:39)

Written and directed by and starring: Orson Welles
Featuring: Oja Kodar, Howard Hughes, Clifford Irving, Elmyr de Hory

Synopsis: "I'm a charlatan," Orson admits in his introduction. "And this is a film about trickery. About fraud. About...*lies.*" It's all that, and much more. There are four principal players in this story "rotten with coincidence." First is Elmyr de Hory, the world's greatest art forger, who paints in the style of every modern master (we watch him paint a passable Matisse), and claims to have works hanging in every major gallery in the world. The second character is Clifford Irving, who wrote a book about Elmyr entitled "Fake"—and who would later become famous for attempting his own hoax, obtaining an enormous advance for a book based on an alleged interview with billionaire recluse Howard Hughes. The third character is Welles himself, a man who began his career with a spectacular hoax (the "War of the Worlds" radio broadcast) and who then headed for Hollywood to film a thinly-veiled biography of an eccentric millionaire—not William Randolph Hearst, but *Howard Hughes.*
Discussion: If it sounds as though the film comes full circle, be aware that the above is only the first of numerous wheels-within-wheels revolving within the pinwheel of Welles' penultimate film. This mind-boggling movie is a trip through the looking glass of truth and lies, which chase each other's tails to the point that they become indistinguishable. (Consider the story of the man who paid for a forgery with a bouncing check, or Welles' attempt to distinguish between real fakes and *fake* fakes, and you might see how these strange loops of deception spiral deeper, ever deeper.) It's a very personal document as well: a meditation on Art, and on the art of larceny. As Pablo Picasso (who becomes the fourth major character in the film) said, "Art is a lie—a lie that makes us realize the truth." Welles would never confess to "committing masterpieces," but at least he left us this final magic trick: a Chinese puzzle box for the intellect.
Rent this one for: its heady mixture of fact, fantasy and forgery, told in the inimitable style of a born raconteur.
You'll (probably) like this if you liked: *The Sting; House of Games* (con theme); *Melvin and Howard* (Hughes legend); *Someone To Love* (Welles & Kodar)
Dissenting Opinion: • "an irritating effusion" —HFG • "...a curio only a Welles completist could love." —*Entertainment Weekly* (8/9/95)
Vidbits: Cameos by Joseph Cotton and Laurence Harvey.

For All Mankind

(space program/history)
(1989; National Geographic Video; NR; 1:30)

Directed by: Al Reinert
Edited by: Susan Korda
Original music by: Brian Eno

Synopsis: Producer/director Reinert raided NASA's massive film vaults and sifted through literally thousands of hours of footage taken during all nine manned missions to the moon, choosing the best shots from each and combining them into a single, seamless composite trip to the moon—the best and most beautiful of all trips. The result is a vicarious voyage: a distilled description combining visual majesty, otherworldly wonder and quiet excitement. The soundtrack enhances the format of the film, allowing anonymous astronauts to give their descriptions without interruption, enhancement or explanation, accompanying a mesmerizing flow of perfect pictures of the earth, the moon, the ships, and our destiny and eventual destination, the stars.

Discussion: Reinert obviously understands the phrase "a sense of wonder"—and no documentary on the space program has ever illustrated the awesome appeal of space travel better than *For All Mankind.* The subtle structure of the film ensures that no distractions come between the ethereality of the actual experience and the viewer's gentle perception of it, leaving us with the visceral impression that we are ourselves on board, experiencing the awe and exhilaration firsthand. *For All Mankind* is about as close to "being there" as any of us are likely to get—and watching this breathtaking film reminds us what a damn tragedy that really is.

Rent this one for: its transcendentally beautiful imagery.

You'll (probably) like this if you liked: *Apollo 13, The Right Stuff* (space films); *Koyaanisqatsi* (beautiful imagery)

Credentials: *EW:* "A-"

Vidbits: • Oscar nomination: Best Documentary. • Reinert would later collaborate on the script of *Apollo 13.* • Dedicated "to the men and women who have given their lives in the exploration of space."

Flashback!

Gates of Heaven

(1978; RCA/Columbia; NR; 1:25)

Directed, produced and edited by: Errol Morris

Synopsis: "This is gonna be my project of life," says Floyd McClure, a gentle paraplegic who picks out a property in Los Altos, California (part of what's now referred to as "Silicon Valley"), and establishes a pet cemetery to honor his dog. Told entirely through interviews, those involved relate the history of their venture; when it fails, the dead pets must be exhumed and relocated to the Bubbling Wells Pet Memorial Park, north of San Francisco in Napa Valley's wine country. The owner/operators, the Harberts family, tell us their stories and relate their (often conflicting) philosophies and plans for business and for life.

Discussion: It's two documentaries in one, and both are totally engrossing. On the surface, its the story of two pet cemeteries, and a touching tale of peoples' love of their pets—a love which is often taken to extremes and sometimes carried overboard. Merely by presenting a sequence of pet headstones, for instance, Morris draws a fine line of quiet irony, forcing us to ask, Is this dignity or depravity?

The Harberts, as an example, operate their own chapel and incorporated religion, the first tenant of which is that their Supreme Being is not "species-centric," and doesn't differentiate among living beings or limit his compassion just to humans. (I'm reminded of a news story I heard on the radio long before I ever saw this film: Land speculators in Japan were attempting to buy a Buddhist pet cemetery—which was, they believed, an almost criminal waste of real estate on that tiny island—in order to turn it into a high-rise. But the Buddhist caretaker was determined to fight for the spiritual rights of his deceased charges, stating with perfect Zen wisdom that "Even a fishhead can become a god." As Pee-Wee would say, "I love that story!")

Watched more closely, however, we begin to glean that this apparently simple film is barely about pets at all, but uses pets as a metaphor—as an excuse to deliver a philosophical (and psychological) treatise on human relationships, familial relations, on business and pleasure, on hopes and fears, dreams and reality, change, grief, and—above all—love. The pivotal interview that ties the two topics together and illustrates this point is with an old woman who begins talking about her pets but inevitably ends up venomously denouncing her good-for-nothing, no-account, deadbeat, white trash grandson, who she raised from birth as if she was his own mother; who loaned him money to buy a car and who now never visits or drives her anywhere; who... But you'll get the picture.

Once beyond the surface story of the pet cemetery, the film becomes a study of the three male members of the Harberts family. Despite their radically different personalities (daddy Cal is the tough patriarch; older son Phil is a Type-A "motivation expert"; younger son Danny, a forlorn hippie who never made it with his music) all three exude the desperate stench of failure, and generally give the impression that each is grasping at any small straw of success, trying to make his own loopy view of life apply to successful business management. Beneath their thin demeanor of calm sincerity, the camera captures the subtle undercurrents of panic and despair. They know this is their last chance at the American Dream, and they know in their bones they'd better damn well take it seriously. They all look lonely, unloved and unhappy. They are obviously no ones' pets.

With the apparent effortlessness of a seasoned storyteller and the misdirection of a master magician, Morris mesmerizes us and manipulates our emotions so insidiously that we're run through the full range of feelings before we even realize that we've been caught with our guard down. With just the subtlest of switches, the film can break us up one moment and break our hearts in the next. More than just another movie, *Heaven* is an emotional experience: it is humanly impossible not to be touched, amused and disturbed by this quirky, subversive, poignant, understated and overlooked little gem.

Rent this one for: its touching goofiness; its subtle poignance.

You'll (probably) like this if you liked: *Vernon, Florida* (another quirky Morris documentary); *Shoah, My Dinner with Andre; Roger and Me* (comic version)

Credentials: • "...one of the most affecting portraits of winning and losing in America that's ever been put on film." —SMV (3.5) • "...one of the top ten films of all time.—★★★★" —Roger Ebert

Vidbits: • Maltin's guide claims the pet cemetary is in "Southern California"; it's actually in *Northern* California—another indication that the multitude of editors just don't seem to watch some of the films they review all that carefully. • German director Werner Herzog once vowed that if Errol Morris ever actually finished a film, he would eat his shoe. Morris finished this film and Herzog lived up to his promise, boiling and consuming his desert boots at the UC Theatre in Berkeley. The event was documented by independent filmmaker Les Blank *(Burden of Dreams)* in a 20-minute 1990 short entitled *Werner Herzog Eats His Shoe,* which is available on tape from Facets Video. • One of my own many cats, Ashbless, is buried at Bubbling Wells. I accidentally ran him over with my car, but he forgave me and reincarnated as my cat Addison. Well, that's *his* story, anyway.

Flashback!

Gizmo!

(comedy)

(1977; Warner; G; 1:16; B&W)

Written, produced and directed by: Howard Smith
Narrator: Milt Moss

Synopsis: America has always been fascinated by machinery and by the myth of the lone inventor with vision changing the world. *Gizmo!* illustrates, however, that for every Edison there are dozens of dimbulbs. A parade of goofy gadgets, culled from old black and white newsreels, includes a host of ingenious machines destined for (and deserving of) oblivion. Bizarre musical instruments; quirky improvements for autos; rockets attached to anything that moved; and labor-saving devices which would make Rube Goldberg proud are prominently featured. Flying devices are legion, and the flapping, rolling, steaming—and inevitable crashing—of these comical contraptions were lovingly documented for posterity in the feeble hope that history was being made. Forgotten novelty acts are included as well: escape artists, human flies, wing-walkers. Physical abuse is a constant theme here, as brave entertainers break a multitude of objects with their hands, chests or heads.
Discussion: In his PBS series "Connections," James Burke explained the fascinating links between basic discoveries and successful modern products. *Gizmo!* might be entitled "Disconnections," and features the flip-side of the coin: the flops, failures and dead-end devices that cranks and crackpots have tinkered together over the decades. If invention is trial and error, *Gizmo!* is a whimsical tribute to the latter; a paean to misguided gearheads whose eccentric visions surpassed their common sense, even though they projected the best intentions into their wacky inventions. And yet some double-visionaries really *were* ahead of their time and technology, as illustrated by final footage of the graceful takeoff and flight of a skier wearing a hang-glider. Who'da thunk it? The nuts. (P.S. If you find the narrative smirky and the music gawdawful, just turn down the sound and enjoy the glimpse into an era almost as odd as ours.)
Rent this one for: the sheer jaw-dropping oddity of its clips; for the comic closing commentary, a masterpiece of doublespeak.
You'll (probably) like this if you liked: *The Absent-Minded Professor; Tucker: A Man and His Dream; Zelig*
Credentials: "Hilarious..." —SMV (★★★★)
Dissenting Opinion: "...can't quite sustain feature length" —MMG (2.5 stars)

Roger & Me

(comedy)

(1989; Warner; R; 1:31)

Written, produced, directed by and starring: Michael Moore

Synopsis: When General Motors announces it will close 11 plants in Flint, Michigan—the birthplace of GM—resulting in some 33,000 layoffs, journalist and home-town boy Michael Moore decides to find out why. He embarks on a quixotic quest to ask the honcho responsible, GM Chairman Roger Smith. And while tracking the elusive Roger, Moore checks out the effect of his decision on the Flint economy. It is, in a word, devastating. Houses empty and decay as people flee. The rats outnumber the residents. A parade passes dozens of boarded-up store fronts. Moore follows a Deputy around town as he evicts people from their homes. He documents numerous sad schemes to revive the town's economy. Does he succeed in collaring Roger? Well... let's just say that in some cases the journey *is* the destination.
Discussion: Mike Moore doesn't look like a genius, or a threat. But beneath that slovenly, goofy guise lurks the cynical spirit of an avenging angel. Moore's genius is using that image: posing as a lisping simpleton too stupid to understand Orwellian Corporate Newspeak—or when to *go away.* If he were snide or snotty or confrontational, he'd lose us in a second. But he never attacks or accuses; he just baits and waits. Eventually, inevitably, his subjects hoist themselves by their own petards. The film is a masterpiece of bitter, savage, flamboyant irony: Moore merely casts a cold, quiet eye on actual events and lets them speak for themselves. They speak volumes; they speak loud and clear—and they speak heartbreakingly hilarious truth.
Rent this one for: its bitter truths about current corporate America; for being a classic revenge fantasy come comically true.
You'll (probably) like this if you liked: "TV Nation," *The Atomic Café, Falling Down*
Credentials: "A must-see." —SMV (★★★★)
Dissenting Opinion: "Smarmy and smug; one of the most overrated films of recent years." —*The Book of Video Lists*
Vidbits: • Moore's first feature allegedly cost only $250,000, but became one of the highest-grossing non-fiction films of all time. • Spawned both a 23-minute sequel (*Pets or Meat: The Return to Flint,* 1992) and the TV series, "TV Nation." • According to the Harper's Index, only half the U.S. companies that "downsized" in the last decade have shown increased profits. • The Flint Plasma Center is open Mondays, Tuesdays, Wednesday, Thursdays and Fridays. Saturday and Sunday, they're closed.

The Thin Blue Line

(mystery/ drama)
(1988; HBO; NR; 1:36)

Written by: (No writer listed)
Music by: Philip Glass
Directed by: Errol Morris

Synopsis: At 12:30 AM on the night of November 29, 1976, Dallas police officer Robert Wood was shot to death—apparently without provocation—by the driver of a car he had pulled over. The driver, however, swore that his hitchhiker, one Randall Dale Adams, did the deed. Adams was subsequently arrested, tried, found guilty, and sentenced to the death penalty for the crime. But was he actually guilty?
Discussion: Director Errol Morris didn't believe so when he set out to make this dispassionate and objective review of the case and the facts. In doing so, he created a new movie form—investigative cinema—as well as a new role for himself: the director as detective. Using little more than interviews he filmed with everyone involved and dramatic recreations of different people's versions of the crime, Morris presents a spellbinding story of justice gone horribly—and obviously—awry. Although the tone of the film is slow, sober and somber, as befits the subject matter, this mesmerizing movie plays more like a murder mystery than a dry documentary. Furthermore, this little film prompted a reopening of the case, which established the innocence of Randall Adams and resulted in his release from prison: a factual finale rivaling the best of Hollywood's fictional happy endings. Long before "reality TV" programs like "America's Most Wanted" and "Cops" became the latest craze, Morris was single-handedly creating the genre—as well as its best entry yet.
Rent this one for: the riveting story, both on screen and off; for its fascinating use of film as a medium for social change.
You'll (probably) like this if you liked: *Fatal Vision; In Cold Blood, Executioner's Song* (true crime); "America's Most Wanted"
Credentials: • A 1989 poll of 54 film critics by (the now defunct) *American Film* magazine rated this "The Best Documentary of the '80s." • #23 on *Premiere* magazine's poll of 24 critics' "Best Movies of the '80s" list. • "Remarkable, perhaps even landmark documentary..." —MMG (★★★★)
Vidbits: • The title refers to the police force, a "thin blue line" between polite society and savage anarchy (or so the police say). • Following the film's release, the case was reopened and Adams was exonerated. Apparently, freedom wasn't enough: he later sued Morris to regain the rights to his own life story.

Visions of Light
The Art of Cinematography
(movie history)
(1992; FoxVideo; NR; 1:34)

Written by: Todd McCarthy
Directed by: Arnold Glassman, Stuart Samuels, Todd McCarthy

Synopsis: *Citizen Kane. The Godfather. Gone With The Wind.* All three stand at the apex of American filmmaking as an artistic endeavor. The scripts, the stars and the directors all left indelible marks on these motion pictures, and are the elements most often credited with the success of any film. But one major factor which contributed to the success of these films, and which can literally make or break any movie, is all too often overlooked: the cinematography. This oversight is finally rectified with *Visions of Light, The Art of Cinematography,* which explores the profession of cinematographer through interviews with masters of the craft, and illustrates their artistry with luminous images from over 125 memorable motion pictures.
Discussion: This fascinating film, produced in conjunction with the American Film Institute, chronologically chronicles a century of movie making as seen through the lens of the camera, rather than through the script's meaning, the star's interpretations, the director's ego, or—as is all too common these days—the producer's pocketbook. Along the way, the film pays visual tribute to such legendary artisans as Gregg Toland, famous for his use of "deep focus" in *Citizen Kane;* Gordon Willis, who reveals the techniques he used to light Marlon Brando in *The Godfather;* and Vittorio Storaro, who discusses the challenges of shooting *Apocalypse Now.* The films featured include everything from Edison experiments and *Birth of a Nation* to such contemporary classics as *Raging Bull, Lawrence of Arabia, Easy Rider, Taxi Driver, The French Connection, Annie Hall, Jaws, Blue Velvet* and *Chinatown;* in a suitably appropriate tribute to the subject, the clips are letterboxed whenever necessary. This film is a treasure chest for both film *and* photography buffs: a captivating look behind the scenes at many immortal movies, presented in a manner which allows us to view these familiar images through new eyes.
Rent this one for: The moving moving pictures; an enhanced education in film; for a new perspective on favorite old images.
You'll (probably) like this if you liked: *Hearts of Darkness: A Filmmaker's Apocalypse; George Stevens: A Filmmaker's Journey* (movie-making documentaries).
Credentials: *EW:* "A"

DRAMA

DRAMA

Biography and history. Unknowns and Oscars. Big stars in little films. Labors of love. Love, romance, relationships. Families in crisis. Insight and intelligence. Fantasy and reality. Dedication and obsession. Psychology, philosophy and spirituality. Attention-arresting performances and cinematic style. Obstacles, revenge and deception. Life, death and beyond. Hard hearts and poignance.

You'll find every one of these within this section—as well as inspiration to think, and, above all, to feel.

Atlantic City

(1981; Paramount; R; 1:44)

Starring: Burt Lancaster, Susan Sarandon
Written by: John Guare
Directed by: Louis Malle

Synopsis: Sally (Sarandon) is a poor waitress, and none too pleased when her sleazy hippie husband Dave (Robert Joy) and his pregnant lover (who's also Sally's sister) show up at her Atlantic City oyster bar. Dave ropes her aging neighbor, Lou Pasco (Lancaster), once a small-time mobster, into helping him deliver some coke he's stolen. But the deal goes sour for Dave—and Lou's left holding the bag. He uses the opportunity (and the drug money) to charm Sally into believing he'd be a good sugar-daddy. But when the goons who got Dave come after Sally, can Lou live up to his own mental legend and protect her?
Discussion: Ever get the feeling they're tearing down your past? Lou Pasco does. He lives in delusions not of grandeur, but of a grand past, glorying in his alleged glory days. Demolition and construction, in an unceasing cycle, is the theme of this special film; demolition and construction of both landmarks and lives, the literal merely mirroring the inner rhythms of the restless characters. Lancaster's Lou is dapper but trapped in the past; to him, Sally is "a regular Princess Grace," attempting to deal her way into a Monte Carlo casino. Her hunger for wisdom and his chance for rejuvenation lead them into a May/December romance as tender and curious as it is bittersweet. It starts out slowly, but picks up momentum exponentially, both in action and character development. And, in a final irony, everybody gets exactly what they wanted—whether they knew what they wanted or not. Nah, they just don't make 'em like this anymore.
Rent this one for: The performances; the story; the lemons.
You'll (probably) like this if you liked: *A Perfect World*
Credentials: • 1981 Academy Award nominations: Best Picture, Actor, Actress, Director, Original Screenplay. • 1981 British Academy Awards: Best Actor, Best Director. • 1981 National Society of Film Critics Awards: Best Film. • A 1989 poll of 54 film critics by *American Film* magazine rated this the #5 "Best American Film of the '80s." • #20 on *Premiere* magazine's poll of 24 critics' "Best Movies of the '80s" list. • "A stunning, brilliantly acted film." —SMV (★★★★) • "★★★★★" —VMG • "★★★★" —MMG • "...one of the few authentic masterworks of the decade." *—People Magazine Guide to Movies on Video*
Vidbits: • Originally shot in 1977, but sat unreleased until '81. • Wallace ("Wally") Shawn makes a brief appearance as a waiter, and Robert Goulet does a cameo, dedicating the hospital wing.

Barnum

(U.S. history/ biography)
(1986; Academy Entertainment; NR; 1:34)

Starring: Burt Lancaster, Hanna Schygulla
Written by: Michael Norell
Directed by: Lee Philips

Synopsis: Against the backdrop of a circus rehearsal, legendary showman P.T. Barnum (Lancaster) recounts the story of his life, which encompassed virtually the entire 19th century (1810-1891). From lowly shopkeeper driven by imagination—"the elixir of life"—to world-renowned impresario, he guides us on a wild ride through the peaks and valleys of his triumphant (and occasionally disastrous) career, including stage and traveling shows, museums, the discovery and promotion of diminutive dramatist "Tom Thumb" (who became America's first "superstar" and helped Barnum conquer European audiences), his role as impresario to Swedish soprano Jenny Lind (Schygulla), a variety of temporary careers, and the invention of the circus, which he humbly dubbed "The Greatest Show on Earth."
Discussion: Although he protests throughout the film that he never said (nor believed) "There's a sucker born every minute," we still regard Barnum as the consummate hustler: equal parts showman and sham, hypnotic huckster and lovable humbug; arrogant, charismatic, inspirational—and a true American original. As such, his self-told tale must be taken with a lick of salt, and 94 minutes is barely enough time to scratch the surface (his wife of some 40 years barely has a speaking part in the film). But as a "coffee-table video" of the historical highlights of an incredible career, the film contains some fascinating material, particularly in the segments detailing the 20-year association between Barnum and Tom Thumb, and peaking in the "mighty mite's" touching audience with Queen Victoria. Even the potentially pretentious conceit of allowing Barnum to directly address the audience is surprisingly justified by his closing remarks: More than a hundred years after his death, he still inspires awe and wonder—and can still draw an audience.
Rent this one for: Lancaster, who imbues the energetic entrepreneur with the evangelical fervor of an Elmer Gantry; for the recreations of Barnum's exhibits and museum curiosities.
You'll (probably) like this if you liked: *The Greatest Show on Earth, Tucker: A Man and His Dream*
Credentials: • *EW:* "A"
Dissenting Opinion: "...a bit uneven..." —SMV (2.5 stars)
Vidbits: Originally a made-for-TV movie.

Chan Is Missing

(mystery)

(1982; New Yorker; NR; 1:20; B&W)

Starring: Wood Moy, Marc Hayashi
Written by: Terrel Seltzer, Wayne Wang
Directed by: Wayne Wang

Synopsis: Jo (Moy) and his nephew Steve (Hayashi) are cab drivers in San Francisco. They plan to buy their own independent license, and entrust the $4,000 fee to Jo's old friend Chan Hung—who promptly vanishes without a trace. Jo and Steve search the highs and lows of Chinatown to find him. They interview friends and family but come up with very few clues: a car accident, a flagwaving incident, a mysterious letter from the mainland, a gun beneath the front seat of Chan's cab—and so on. Did Chan abscond with their savings? Is he hiding from a political faction? Did he commit a murder? Or did he simply give up on American culture and move back to China? Jo discovers there are no simple answers when dealing with a complex man.
Discussion: "You don't look like anybody's conception of Charlie Chan," one of Jo's friends jokes to the would-be detective. He's right—about Jo and about this film, a cultural documentary disguised as a detective story. The search for Chan is an excuse for a detailed tour of Chinatown—not a scenic tour, but a psychological tour, exposing us to the various factions and subcultures of a community virtually transparent to Anglo-America. Polanski used L.A.'s Chinatown as a metaphor for chaos in *Chinatown;* Wang takes this literally, crafting a metaphorical mystery less about the disappearance of an individual than about the disappearance of cultural identity, and the struggle that Chinese immigrants have in holding on to their heritage once in America. "Chan" becomes a symbol of that old-world culture and identity, which slips away into assimilation the longer one lives here. Don't expect any pat answers to the plot problem in this "appropriately Chinese" mystery, where "what's not there seemed to have just as much meaning as what *is* there," and in which "nothing is what it seems to be." What you *can* expect, however, is a fascinating, often amusing glimpse into an unexplored subculture in a movie where the low budget is compensated for by a high level of filmmaking skill.
Rent this one for: its fascinating insight into Asian-America.
You'll (probably) like this if you liked: *Eat A Bowl of Tea* (Wang), *Eat Drink Man Woman, Dim Sum, Living on Tokyo Time*
Vidbits: The first American feature film produced by an exclusivley Asian-American cast and crew.

The Cutting Edge

(romantic comedy)

(1992; MGM/UA; PG; 1:42)

Starring: D.B. Sweeney, Moira Kelly
Featuring: Terry O'Quinn, Roy Dotrice
Written by: Tony Gilroy
Directed by: Paul Michael Glaser

Synopsis: They're both Olympic losers, big time: Doug Dorsey (Sweeney), hockey's finest amateur, gets boarded and loses enough peripheral vision that he can never go pro; Kate Moseley (Kelly) gets dropped by her partner in figure skating finals. Two years later, he's playing in a bar league, and she's just fired her eighth partner. He's angry; she's bitchy; but they are each others' last chance at Olympic glory. And they're at each others' throats from their first words. But neither will give in or give up, so the butt-heads continue to butt heads, each too buttheaded to bury the hatchet. Little by little they let down their defenses and start to know—even respect—one another. But neither will ever admit to falling for the other; both are too proud and headstrong, and bickering over every detail becomes their version of foreplay. Will their personal peccadilloes endanger their professional performances? And have they really got a shot at an Olympic gold medal—or will they shoot each other first?

Discussion: Call it *Flashdance* meets *Slap Shot*. And while it is undeniably formulaic, within that comfortably familiar formula there are some undeniable highlights. First among them is the barbed banter between the skaters. Their dueling tongues are as razor-sharp as the blades on their skates (and wouldn't be half as pointed without the note-perfect performances). Another is the dynamic direction, an MTV-style music video approach to figure skating, which exhibits the beauty, grace and fluidity of the sport better than television can. Finally, and peripherally, there is some fascinating background into the worlds of figure skating and Olympic competition, illustrating the grueling effort and obsessive dedication necessary to become an Olympic contender. But the heart of this unpretentious flick is the rocky romance, and the requisite time is given to let it blossom believably over the course of the movie. As a team, they're a reversal of the Astaire/Rogers secret: she gives him class; he gives her sex appeal. And naturally, it develops into "a fine romance."

Rent this one for: the skate-sharp dialog; the MTV direction.

You'll (probably) like this if you liked: *When Harry Met Sally, Flashdance*

Vidbits: Olympic skater Jojo Starbuck plays an interviewer.

Dark Eyes

(romance)

(Italian with English subtitles; AKA Black Eyes*)*

(1987; CBS/Fox; NR; 1:58)

Starring: Marcello Mastroianni, Elena Sofonova
Featuring: Silvana Mangano, Marthe Keller
Written by: Nikita Mikalkov, Alexander Adabascian
(based on several short stories by Anton Chekov)
Directed by: Nikita Mikalkov

Synopsis: On board a ship in the early part of the century, aging Romano (Mastroianni) relates his sad tale to a newlywed man: 40 years earlier, he married rich and lived a life of leisure and luxury in Italy. On a trip to a spa a decade ago, he met a lovely young Russian woman, Anna (Sofonova). They fell in love—but she left him. She married for money, ensuring the security of her poor family, and was afraid that the love she felt might ruin her situation. Lovestruck Romano followed her to Russia; she was shocked, then overjoyed, to see him. They decided she'd leave her husband and he'd leave his wife. All very simple—they thought. On his return to Rome, however, Romano discovered that the family business had collapsed and they were penniless. Now he faced the most difficult decision of his life: abandon his family for love, or abandon his love in loyalty to his family. Either choice leads only to heartbreak...
Discussion: Everyone has a story of lost love; this one is as romantic as any and as bittersweet as most. As Romano relates his tale, we have the added advantage of visual embellishments: elegant sets, lush locations and glowing photography. A born raconteur, Romano unravels his narrative slowly; indeed, he takes joy in the recounting, as though he had related the story regularly; as though his very identity is defined by his tragedy. This showcase for Mastroianni's masterful acting runs him through the entire range of feelings, tempering them with touches of all-too-human humor in his frequent befuddlement and buffoonery. A star-crossed romance with an O.Henry ending, *Dark Eyes* is one of those rare films that leaves us speculating beyond the ending, on the alternate endings—and choices—that might have been: Of all the words of mice or men...
Rent this one for: Mastroianni's consummate performance; the gorgeous photography and scenery; the engaging story.
You'll (probably) like this if you liked: Fellini's *8-1/2*
Credentials: • 1987 Academy Award nomination: Best Actor. • 1987 Cannes Film Festival: Best Actor
Vidbits: The title comes from the Russian ballad in the score.

The Escape Artist

(1982; LIVE, Vestron; PG; 1:36)

Starring: Griffin O'Neal, Raul Julia, Joan Hackett, "Gabriel Dell"
Featuring: Teri Garr, Desiderio (Desi) Arnez, M. Emmet Walsh, Jackie Coogan, Huntz Hall, Harry Anderson
Written by: Melissa Mathison & Stephen Zito (based on the novel by David Wagoner)
Directed by: Caleb Deschanel

Synopsis: Danny Masters (O'Neal), pre-teen son of the world's second-greatest escape artist, runs away from home to join his aunt and uncle (Dell and Hackett) in their stage magic act, playing in the same town where Danny's father became a crook and was shot dead trying to escape jail—or so goes the official story. Danny, however, is compelled to discover the truth. He double-crosses paths with the mayor's spoiled (and possibly psychotic) son Stu (Julia), ending up with a wallet stuffed with graft money that everyone concerned will do anything to get back. Danny uses this as leverage to form an uneasy alliance with Stu, who helps him gain access to the mayor's (Arnez) safe and uncover evidence of his corruption as revenge. The final portion of their plan leads Danny to attempt his greatest stunt: escaping the fate of his father.
Discussion: No one knows better than screenwriter Mathison (*E.T.*) the special magic that childhood can hold. But magic can be fantasy or chicanery—as well as white or black. The sly message of this gentle, enchanting fable of two sons is the magic influence their fathers have upon them, for better or worse. And although many of the characters and plotlines in this film lead nowhere, perhaps they're just intentional misdirection, hm?
Rent this one for: Julia's eccentric, lively performance; lovely little touches, especially in the casting; the dreamlike direction.
You'll (probably) like this if you liked: *E.T., Indian in the Cupboard* (same screenwriter); *Paradise; The NeverEnding Story.*
Dissenting Opinion: • "Confusing, rambling..." —VMG (2) • "A good movie is trying to escape from this one"—SMV(2.5)
Vidbits: • Deschanel is best known as a cinematographer (*The Black Stallion; The Right Stuff*); this was his first directorial effort. • Technical Advisor for magic: Ricky Jay. • Yes, Griffin O'Neal is Ryan's son and Tatum's brother. • Co-Executive Producer: Francis Ford Coppola—who'd probably just as soon forget this film, as only a few years later Griffin O'Neal would be at the helm of the speedboat accident which took the life of Coppola's son. • Why do the credits insist that "Uncle Burke" is played by former "Dead End Kid/Bowery Boy" Gabriel Dell, when it's obviously Harry Dean Stanton? Go figure.

Flirting

(coming-of-age tale)
(1990; Vidmark; R; 1:40)

Starring: Noah Taylor, Thandie Newton, Nicole Kidman
Written and directed by: John Duigan

Synopsis: Rural Australia, 1965: Sent off to a strict boarding school in so he wouldn't become a delinquent, introverted runt Danny Embling (Taylor) develops an eye for the new student at the girl's school across the lake. His first awkward encounters with the British-educated Ugandan Thandiwe (Newton) reveal that they've got much in common, including high intelligence, a sense of independence and a crippling sense of isolation. A loose love letter makes them the laughing stock of both schools—but they receive assistance from a most unlikely source. Just as their affection begins to bloom, however, a family crisis calls Thandiwe away—and the young couple decides to take one last romantic risk, defying the prison-like oppression of their schools to consummate their affection. What lies in store for them: bittersweet liaison, tender tragedy—or a little of both?
Discussion: This virtually unknown Australian entry is at once a smart, sweet and sympathetic coming of age story and a spot-on portrayal of youthful romance and first love: the awful, awkward pain of yearning, the tender tentativeness, the exciting exploration, the desperate immediacy, the giddy affinity—and the horror of separation. The teenage couple, separated by social forces both large and small, are a modern Romeo and Juliet; but while they might be sophisticated beyond their years, they are no wiser than Shakespeare's star-crossed lovers. Even though she receives only third billing in this film, Kidman nearly steals the show as the bitch-goddess/ice queen who rules her school—and she was lucky enough to get to perform in a film which allows her character to be more than the snobbish brat she seems. One of the movie's many delights is that with a number of characters, as with Kidman's, just when you think you've got them pegged, they surprise you with hidden depth and complexity. Add in a healthy dose of humor, and you've got the very definition of a "Killer B": an unseen four-star film that more than deserves to find an appreciative audience.
Rent this one for: its affectionate understanding and portrayal of young love.
You'll (probably) like this if you liked: *Gregory's Girl*
Credentials: Australian Film Institute Award winner.
Vidbits: Duigan's prequel, *The Year My Voice Broke,* also starring Taylor, is also available on video.

Funny Bones

(comedy)

(1995; Hollywood; R; 2:08)

Starring: Oliver Platt, Lee Evans, George Carl, Freddie Davies
Featuring: Jerry Lewis, Leslie Caron, Oliver Reed, Ian McNeice
Written by: Peter Chelsom, Peter Flannery
Directed by: Peter Chelsom

Synopsis: Tommy Fawkes (Platt), 35, is the son of "America's Funnyman," "Mr. Originality," George Fawkes (Lewis). But as a comic, Tommy's a total bomb. He wants it badly enough, but he just hasn't inherited his father's "funny bones." After a humiliating flop in his Vegas debut, he heads for Blackpool, England, a seaside resort that boasts of being the birthplace of British vaudeville—and the place where young Tommy collected his most cherished childhood memories. He hires an agent to parade local "talent" before him, in the hopes of discovering and buying the performance rights to a unique and hilarious physical comedy act. On a parallel track, young Jack Parker (Evans), Blackpool's certified city maniac and son of England's most obscure comedy team, is trying to get his own act into a club—but no club will hire him since...*the accident.* In flashback, we see the terrible tragedy that befell him as a young circus clown-in-training. (Jack's also on the lam from dishonest cops and a group of Frenchmen who... Oh, it's just too complicated.) Tommy sees one act that floats his boat: Jack's. But when he sees Jack's dad and uncle, the legendary "Parker Brothers," perform, he witnesses more than he bargained for. As clues and memories and confessions fall into place, Tommy realizes his attraction to their acts indicates that this collection of funny bones is taking the shape of a skeleton in his family's closet...
Discussion: "I never saw anything funny that wasn't terrible, that didn't cause pain," Tom Parker confesses to George Fawkes. One theory of comedy says that it springs from pain—and what could be more painful than a crisis of sanity, or a spiritual crisis? And by applying this philosophical logic, couldn't the greatest pain then yield the greatest humor? To put it another way, *comedy is a serious business. Funny Bones* knows this and interweaves high drama and low comedy with seamless skill.

The performances, first off, are first rate. The pudgy, intense Platt seems dangerously close to breaking into a ranting tantrum even when playing panic, and Jerry Lewis has never done better work (which you can interpret any way you wish). The real standouts are the Brits, however. Carl and Davis as "The Parker Brothers" are wonderfully funny, and Evans is a true buffoon: a rubber-faced alien; a 'toon in loony goon's clothing. As for the slapstick routines in the film, I am reminded of reading *The World According to Garp* nearly 20 years ago. Garp himself is described as a brilliant writer, and John Irving takes a courageous gamble to clinch this description by including a story "written" by him. If the story is brilliant, we'd have proof of Irving's claims. But if the story was anything less than amazing, the character (and therefore the entire novel) would have lost all credibility instantly. In *Funny Bones,* if the comedy routines did not live up their legendary status, the entire film would flop for lack of credibility. Luckily for us, they *do* prove the claims of the characters, and are laugh-out-loud funny.

The complex plot is strewn with red herrings, like the mysterious giant wax eggs, containing a mysteriouser rejuvenating powder sought by the mysterioust Reed character—a bit of magical realism that merely garnishes the central stories. Plot twists that seem immanent and inevitable never occur, and the slowly unfolding story of the two families, connected by more than just karmic comedy, tells tales of trust and betrayal, lust and larceny, professional success and personal tragedy. And the incredibly original ending is simultaneously a bittersweet story of salvation and dangerous, cutting-edge comedy. Like the films of Hal Hartley (*Trust, The Unbelievable Truth*), *Funny Bones* dances on a razor-thin tightrope between comedy and tragedy, where even the slightest gesture could nudge the entire film right off the rope. It's a hilariously liberating film: you'll laugh; you'll cry—and you'll laugh *while* you cry.

This book is filled with "probablies," but let me state this unequivocally: *Funny Bones* is unique; an original; a work of cinematic and philosophic brilliance; an hilariously serious film about the spiritually redemptive power of comedy. I urge you most strongly to see this singular cinematic insight if you're funny, or suspect you're funny—or wonder why you aren't.

Rent this one for: being a serious film about the spiritually redemptive power of slapstick comedy.

You'll (probably) like this if you liked: *Fellini's The Clowns, Buster Keaton: A Hard Act To Follow, S.O.B., Shakes the Clown*

Credentials: Listed as one of six 1995 video releases "most deserving of a second chance" in *Entertainment Weekly's* "1995 Year-End Special" video roundup.

Dissenting Opinion: • "Extraordinarily strange movie [that] never adds up—or figures out what it wants to be..."—MMG (2.5 stars) • "...overchewed bit of whimsy..." —Owen Glieberman, *Entertainment Weekly* (C+) • "...entertaining and absorbing for what it is. But what it isn't could have really been something." —Roger Ebert, Chicago *Sun-Times* (3 stars)

Gas Food Lodging

(coming-of-age story)
(1991; Columbia TriStar; R; 1:41)

Starring: Fairuza Balk, Brooke Adams, Ione Skye
Featuring: James Brolin, Donovan Leitch, Chris Mulkey
Written and directed by: Allison Anders
(based on the novel *Don't Look and It Won't Hurt* by Richard Peck)

Synopsis: Three women living alone in a tiny trailer can get on each others' nerves—and these three do, constantly. "I knew what was missing from my life," adolescent Shade (Balk) cognites while watching a romantic movie: "a *man*." Not for *her*, however; for her waitress mom, Nora (Adams), so they could do "all the dumb normal stuff that regular families do." But men are tough to come by in the dusty truckstop town of Laramie, New Mexico. And problems abound. There are so many *kinds* of guys. Shade knows—her older sister Trudi (Skye) has slept with them all. And could mom like *any* man since their dad (Brolin) walked out on them years ago? Can any of the three overcome their trouble with trust and find romantic happiness, or will hope and disappointment be their only lifetime companions?
Discussion: "What does woman want?" Freud asked a century ago. Good question. Maybe the same thing most men want: to love and be loved, with some assurance that it will last. In other words, the impossible. Anders' directorial debut illustrates the three phases of women's relationship to men: young Shade is brimming with mystery, hope and romance; beautiful Trudi is trapped between yearning and cynicism, destined to be a victim of circumstance; Nora has few illusions left, just disenchantment. Despite their experiences, all three are in equal measure tough and vulnerable, hurt yet hopeful, defensive and sensitive—and this film displays a tender clemency and vast compassion for their plight. Is it a "chick movie"? Oh, yeah. But it's also a *human* movie, one which deserves to be appreciated by woman and the men who want to understand what they want. Bittersweet and innocent, wistful and hopeful, world-wise and sympathetic, *Gas Food Lodging* is a sweetly somber film which excels in conveying that aching yearning for connection that so often yields only disappointment—and is so seldom satisfied.
Rent this one for: its sensitive insight into romance.
You'll (probably) like this if you liked: *Paradise*
Dissenting Opinion: "Overrated by some..." —MMG (2.5 stars)
Vidbits: • Ione Skye and Donovan Leitch are real-life sister and brother. • The letter informing Nora of Trudi's absences from school comes from principal "Allison Anders." • Rockhound Cecil is played by J Mascis, responsible for the soundtrack music.

Grand Canyon

(1991; FoxVideo; R; 2:14)

Starring: Danny Glover, Kevin Kline, Mary McDonnell
Featuring: Steve Martin, Mary-Lousie Parker, Alfre Woodard
Written by: Lawrence Kasdan, Meg Kasdan
Directed by: Lawrence Kasdan

Synopsis: When his car breaks down in the 'hood one night, successful LA lawyer Mack (Kline) is rescued from gang violence by streetwise tow truck driver Simon (Glover). They strike up a conversation, then a friendship. On a parallel track, Mack's wife, Claire (McDonnell), finds an abandoned baby, which brings out her suppressed motherly instincts. Back in the ghetto, Simon's got his own problems, like a widowed sister with a young son who is fast becoming a gangbanger. Their lives and others interweave as they all seek some sort of sense in a world gone mad.
Discussion: *What's it all about?* That's the Big Question of this film. It's about being middle-aged, and Kasdan's metaphor is the Grand Canyon. It's about fear, desperation, insecurity, lack of control; about earthquakes, heart attacks, abandoned babies, drive-by shootings, and cut fingers; about how your entire life can change, for better or for worse, in an instant, in an act. It's about peering into the existential Abyss, and trying to find something that will imbue life's trials and (apparently) random accidents with some order and meaning. It's also about the other side of fate's coin: the poignant moments of epiphany, the magic of connecting, the miracles. It's about taking action, even when you can't be sure that trying to make things better won't muck them up even more. Full of adult characters, dialog and concerns, this is one of the few movies to capture the chaos and angst of mid-life. These grand questions posed on a grand scale require a Grand Canyon to symbolize them. The real question (if you're middle-aged) is: Are you brave enough to see this film?
Rent this one for: its brave, insightful, intelligent ruminations on the search for meaning in mid-life.
You'll (probably) like this if you liked: *The Big Chill* (written & directed by Kasdan); *Short Cuts, Do The Right Thing, Hannah and Her Sisters, Husbands and Wives, Unforgiven*
Credentials: • 1991 Oscar nomination: Original Screenplay. • 1991 National Board of Review Awards: 10 Best Films of Year. • "No motion picture is flawless, but this...comes pretty close." —VMG (4.5 stars)
Dissenting Opinion: "...mushy, superficial and unconvincing." —MMG (2.5 stars)
Vidbits: Kasdan appears in the screening room as Davis' producer. The Davis character was loosely based on Joel Silver.

Heavenly Creatures

(mystery/coming-of-age/true crime)
(1994; Miramax; R; 1:39)

Starring: Sarah Pierce, Diana Kent, Clive Merrison
"Introducing": Melanie Lynskey ("Pauline"), Kate Winslet ("Juliet")
Written by: Francis Walsh, Peter Jackson
Directed by: Peter Jackson

Synopsis: A text prolog informs us that in Christchurch, New Zealand, "during 1953 and 1954, Pauline Yvonne Parker kept diaries recording her friendship with Juliet Marion Hulme. This is their story." Pauline is sullen and snide; a dumpy, frumpy, scowling toad of a 14-year-old. Then Juliet—bright, beautiful, worldly-wise; sunny, smarmy and superior—is transferred to her school. Unlikely friends, yes; but they have much in common: high intelligence, ages spent in hospitals, an outsider attitude, contempt for convention. And both yearn for escape: Juliet to a world of art and beauty; "Paul" from this dull, mundane existence. They become inseparable friends, creating their own world of romantic fantasy. "We have decided how sad it is for other people," Paul writes, "that they cannot appreciate our genius." But their life together turns sour when their parents question their "unwholesome" relationship. Threatened with separation, their world collapses. Paul believes her Mum is the main obstacle in their path. But if she were out of the picture...
Discussion: It's the obsessive intensity of the girls' friendship that worries the parents; the girls' motivation also hinges on family dynamics, but ironically so. Juliet's parents are too intellectual to care for her or about her, or to attend her fears of abandonment, while Pauline, the product of a family that actually loves her despite her rudeness, insolence and rabid teen angst, is convinced that any parental discipline is cruel and unusual punishment. In a final irony, the girls' brutal move ensures that they will never have the one thing they both desire most. A fabulous combination of flawless acting, a harrowing and insightful script, and direction that is jaw-droppingly original whenever the girls' real and fantasy worlds overlap.
Rent this one for: its excellently acted, intriguing true story.
You'll (probably) like this if you liked: *The Good Son, The Bad Seed, A Cry in the Dark, Dreamchild*
Credentials: • "★★★★★" —VMG • Listed as the #5 best video release of 1995 in *Entertainment Weekly's* "Year-End Special."
Vidbits: Hulme has a successful career as mystery writer "Anne Perry." • Oscar nomination: Original Screenplay. • Jackson appears as the bum Juliet kisses outside the movie theater.

James Joyce's Women

(literary/performance)
(1983; MCA; R; 1:34)

Starring: Fionnula Flanagan, Timothy E. O'Grady, Chris O'Neill
Written and produced by: Fionnula Flanagan
(adapted from her one-woman stage show)
Directed by: Michel Pearce

Synopsis: Fionnula Flanagan portrays six women influential to author James Joyce in this adaptation of her stage production. Framed as a recreation of a rare interview with Nora Barnacle (Flanagan), Joyce's wife (and previously his mistress for 27 years), the people and characters she discusses come to life in key scenes from his life and work. Among these are Sylvia Beach, an American expatriate in Paris in the '20s who explains the curious history of how she published his novel *Ulysses* as she introduces Joyce (O'Neill) to an audience at her bookstore; one of the gossiping washerwomen from *Finnegans Wake;* and Molly Bloom, one of the central characters of *Ulysses.*
Discussion: The 20th century had no greater writer than James Joyce. From the stream of consciousness technique he pioneered in *Ulysses* to the ocean of the unconscious disguised as the crypto-illogical pun-fest *Finnegans Wake,* Joyce's daring experiments with language and exacting grasp of our inner lives remains exceptional and unsurpassed. Nora Barnacle—earthly, sharp-tongued and fiercely proud of her essential simplicity and "cynical frankness of conduct"—was his muse, his mistress, his manifest anima, and often the inspiration for his finest female characters. In addition to intimate biographical details of their relationship, this adaptation of Flanagan's one-woman stage show features some exceptional scenery, recreating real and fictional scenes. The film's *raison d'être,* however, is Flanagan's tour de force performance as Nora and five other women who populated Joyce's inner and outer worlds. And the high points of the these are her interpretations of Molly Bloom's soliloquies. Molly's internal monologues are here given a voice, a face, and a depth of emotion—particularly the book's life-affirming finale, a graphic masturbation sequence ending with the repetitive *yes.*
Rent this one for: Flanagan's brilliant acting—and Joyce's brilliant writing.
You'll (probably) like this if you liked: *Ulysses, My Dinner with André*
Dissenting Opinion: "God preserve us from writers." —Nora
Vidbits: Flanagan's original stage production was directed by Burgess Meredith.

Like Water For Chocolate

(romance/comedy/magical realism)
(Spanish with English subtitles; also available dubbed)
(1992; Touchstone; R; 1:45)

Starring: Lumi Cavazos, Marco Leonardi, Regina Torme
Written by: Laura Esquivel (based on her novel)
Directed by: Alfonso Arau

Synopsis: Tita (Cavazos) was born on the kitchen table—literally. Fed and tutored by the family cook, Tita grows up in the kitchen, learning the secrets of food and mastering the culinary arts. At 20, she feels the first stirrings of love. But as the youngest of three daughters, she is tradition-bound to serve her mother Elena (Torme) until her death, destined never to marry, and her hopes are dashed by her stern mother. Pedro (Leonardi) resolves to marry Tita's sister, if that's the only way he can be near his beloved. When Tita's tears fall into the batter for the engagement party cake, it has a devastating effect on the party: every guest is overtaken with weeping melancholy over lost loves. Slowly, Tita begins to realize and develop her kitchen alchemy, projecting her deepest feelings into food and transforming the lives of everyone near her—for better or worse.
Discussion: Thus begins this multi-generational family saga of strong-willed women frustrated by love; of sisters at war and at peace; of fate teasing people with hope and dashing their hopeful plans; of tragedy and joy and love that transcends death; of birth and life and death and the threads that tie them all together: food and love. The film is suffused with a gorgeous saffron glow, as if filmed through honey, and the passion—such as lust that can literally ignite fires—reaches right off the screen. The travails of the lovers are many, long-lasting and heartrending, but above all the film is a celebration of food for the soul: food as a metaphor for passion, sublimation, redemption and salvation. The movie's kitchen *bruja,* reveling in romance, even reveals the secret ingredient in any recipe, whether it's a dish, a meal, a marriage or an entire life: make them all *con mucho amor.* After viewing this movie, you might never look at food (or bareback riding) the same way again. *Salute!*
Rent this one for: its charming, original and magic story; for the gorgeous photography; for its unabashed romanticism.
You'll (probably) like this if you liked: *Tampopo, Babette's Feast* (the magic and eroticism of food); *Romeo and Juliet*
Credentials: Roger Ebert's "10 Best of Year" list, 1992.
Vidbits: Arau and Esquival are husband and wife.

A Midnight Clear

(war drama/parable)

(1992; Columbia TriStar; R; 1:47)

Starring: Ethan Hawke, Kevin Dillon, Arye Gross, Gary Sinise
Featuring: Peter Berg, Frank Whaley, John C. McGinley, Curt Lowens
Written and directed by: Keith Gordon
(based on William Wharton's novel)

Synopsis: The time: December, 1944. The place: The Ardennes Forest separating France and Germany. The surviving half of a 12-man intelligence squad is ordered to occupy an abandoned chateau and watch for German activity. What they find is a small squad Germans who "seem to believe in turning off the war every once in a while," notably for a temporary truce to celebrate Christmas—and to surrender. The catch: If it looks like they gave up too easily, their Vaterland families might suffer the consequences of their cowardice. They suggest staging a mock skirmish then all heading back to American lines. "I think we got a chance to make something good come out of this," the American instigator urges his companions, "if we just use our heads." But all that's required for a tragic accident is a single head that's not screwed on quite right...
Discussion: "The horror of war" is a cliché, but few films have conveyed the more subtle horrors of war as well as this original entry. The movie starts with a scream—a scream which echoes silently throughout the entire somber story as a pervasive sense of anguish and anxiety, of isolation and despair. The imagery enhances these emotions; surrounding us is dark, foreboding forest or stark white snow; our only respite, the dim flicker of a fireplace. Although punctuated by graphic violence, these few scenes contrast well with the playful segments in which the Germans toy with the confused soldiers in an attempt to set up a tentative truce. "War is hell" is a cliché as well, but this movie makes the metaphor literal, transforming the odd encounter from an anti-war statement into a religious allegory. From the Christmas setting to anointing a sacrificed companion (a failed divinity student) to pouring his blood into the grail of a canteen as part of a plan to finesse their way from behind enemy lines, the latter third of this somber and sobering film is rife with Christian symbolism. In this vision of war, there are no heroes—and few survivors. Aspects of *Midnight* might begin in cliché, but the finished film is as far from cliché as is possible.
Rent this one for: its eloquent and philosophical message; its breathtaking photography; its original and sobering story.
You'll (probably) like this if you liked: *Birdy, Paths of Glory*
Vidbits: Sites in Utah filled in for the Ardennes Forest.

The Music of Chance

(1993; Columbia TriStar; R; 1:38)

Starring: James Spader, Mandy Patinkin
Featuring: Joel Grey, Charles Durning, M. Emmet Walsh
Samantha Mathis, Christopher Penn
Written by: Philip Haas, Belinda Haas
(based on the novel by Paul Auster)
Directed by: Philip Haas

Synopsis: Two drifters—quiet, repressed Nashe (Patinkin) and obnoxious loudmouth Pozzi (Spader)—meet by chance and team up to compete in a high-stakes poker game against a pair of eccentric lottery-winning millionaires (Durning and Grey). Against all odds, they lose everything; all they have left to bet is their own sweat and toil. They lose—and find themselves literal prisoners, tasked with building a wall of 10,000 stones across a meadow to work off their debt. Living in a trailer in the meadow, they endure the taunts of task-master Calvin (Walsh), a dim-witted little dictator. Tensions mount between Pozzi and Walsh, and a violent confrontation seems immanent. Before it can happen, however, Pozzi disappears. Has he escaped, or has he been killed? Nashe is forced to decide which fate is more risky—attempting his own escape, or staying, which could prove fatal.
Discussion: "Mystery," wrote L. Ron Hubbard, "is the level of always pretending there's always something to know earlier than the mystery." So it is with this ambiguous allegory. The characters have suggestive names (like the odd couple Flowers and Stone), mysterious motives and ambiguous goals. But there is nothing more fascinating than a mystery—especially one that lends itself to our own individual interpretations. And that's the key to this film: it inspires interpretation. It forces us to think about important and nebulous concepts like, Who defines our freedom and our barriers? Does integrity end when discomfort—or danger—begins? Where does control end and Fate begin? Just what *is* "luck"? And so on. Yes, it's a mystery—but that's the point: it's a philosophical mystery, a cryptic parable that serves as a mirror for the mystery of our own existence. Auster is an engaging storyteller, and this faithful adaptation does an admirable job of turning his narrative fluidity into pictures—with the added advantage that the rewritten ending of the film is far superior to the novel's finale. (How's *that* for a switch?)
Rent this one for: the performances (including Spader like you've never seen him); the thought-provoking mystery.
You'll (probably) like this if you liked: "The Prisoner," *Un Chien Andalou, Last Year at Marienbad*
Vidbits: The driver of the pickup in the final shot is Auster.

My Dinner With Andre

(1981; Pacific Arts, New Yorker, Ingram; NR; 1:50)

Starring: Andre Gregory, Wallace Shawn
Written by: Andre Gregory, Wallace Shawn
Directed by: Louis Malle

Synopsis: Playwright/actor Wallace Shawn meets old friend and theatre colleague Andre Gregory for dinner at an elegant restaurant. Wally has heard some disturbing rumors about Andre's odd mental state. But once he gets around to asking what he's been up to the past few years, Andre opens up and relates tales of his travels to the corners of the globe—and of his own heart, mind and soul—in search of elusive enlightenment. Wally listens with rapt attention, until he must make a stand for rationality, attempting to refute Andre's mysticism with a more practical, pragmatic view of life and the modern world.
Discussion: And that's about it: Two hours of food-for-thought conversation, in a screenplay which "wrote itself" as the edited cream of excerpts from dozens of hours of dialog between the principals. In this timeless treasure, they discourse passionately on every topic from art to life and death to eating sand in the Sahara. But it's not like we're eavesdropping; it's more like we're Wally, hearing of experiences we're never likely to have with a friend we'd be lucky to find. Gregory is a captivating raconteur: opinionated but self-effacing; energetic without being overbearing; recounting with humor his deadly serious philosophical search. What's his quest all about? Even he isn't certain. "It has something to do with living," he says. "To know what's it's like to be truly alive." Joseph Campbell, late in life, summarized his wisdom by saying "The meaning of life is the experience of being alive." Gregory illustrates this principle—as well as the difficulty of distilling experience into words, and of wresting meaning from experience. In the end, as Wally rides home, exhilarated, we realize that his conversation with Andre has had the requisite effect: He's observing; he's thinking; he's feeling. He's *living*.
Rent this one for: the stimulating intellectual conversation.
You'll (probably) like this if you liked: *Swimming To Cambodia; Mindwalk* (intellectual discussions)
Credentials: • #14 on *Premiere*'s list of 24 critics' "Best Movies of the '80s." • "A dazzling cerebral comedy of ideas." —LA *Times* • "One of the most daring films ever made... ★★★★★" —VMG
Dissenting Opinion: "..moments of insight, drama and hilarity —but not enough to sustain a feature-length film." —MMG (2.5)
Vidbits: A little known fact: the verb "discuss" once also meant "eat." This usage is now considered rare—much as a film of this intellectual depth is considered rare.

The Nasty Girl

(German with English subtitles)
(1990; HBO; PG-13; 1:33)

Starring: Lena Stolze, Monika Baumgartner, Michael Gahr
Written and directed by: Michael Verhoeven

Synopsis: Sonya (Stolze)—third generation resident of Pfilzing, Bavaria, and a good Catholic girl—wins a National essay contest, inspiring her to enter another. The subject: "My Home Town During the Third Reich." She'll write about how her town resisted the Nazis, and how the Church retained its integrity. She talks to older residents. She combs the Church archives and town records. But all she encounters are closed mouths, closed minds and closed files. Something is being hushed up, and she intends to unearth the truth, despite insults, threats and actual attacks on her family. Her determination grows into obsession over the years, alienating everyone around her as she struggles against the conspiracy of collective denial and convenient amnesia. What is it that's being covered up? And will the light of truth also bring tragedy? For whom?
Discussion: What starts as a lighthearted biography turns by degrees into an intriguing mystery and finally a nightmare for all involved. More questions than answers arise: Is Sonya a scholar or simply insolent? Is her motive the truth or revenge? How long does it take to forget a single shameful skeleton in the collective closet? Is it better to "let sleeping dogs lie"? Where does social responsibility end and personal integrity begin? Is social acceptance a goal or the final temptation? And how much punishment and public fickleness can even an indomitable spirit endure? Real life does not always provide neat plot resolutions and happy endings, but the unexpected, unsettling end of her *kampf* comes as a major shock—and, upon reflection, a totally appropriate one. On the "happy" side, the film's peculiar structure is unique and engaging: using luminous black and white photography to indicate memory is an enchanting device, as is the frequent use of slides instead of sets to indicate the surreal nature of Sonya's investigation/crusade. Finally, Stolz is adorable, aging from pigtailed schoolgirl to middle-aged mom: effervescent, with a devilish intelligence in her eyes and smile.
Rent this one for: its central questions; the artistic direction.
You'll (probably) like this if you liked: "The Prisoner" ("individual vs. society" theme); *All The President's Men*
Credentials: • Academy Award nomination 1990: Best Foreign Language Film • "★★★★★" —VMG
Vidbits: Based in part on the true story of Anna Rosmus.

The New Age

(black comedy/ satire)
(1994; Warner; R; 1:52)

Starring: Peter Weller, Judy Davis
Featuring: Adam West, Corbin Bernsen, Samuel L. Jackson
Written and directed by: Michael Tolkin

Synopsis: It's a bad day for Peter (Weller) to quit his 300K/year job at a Hollywood ad agency: his commercial artist wife Katherine (Davis) just lost her biggest client. Businesses are crashing all over. So's their marriage. In desperate financial straits, they discover their destiny: They'll open a fashion boutique! But when they do, they're deserted by their fashionable "friends," who don't want to see their problems. On the verge of losing the store, the house and their sanity, they cling desperately to each other. Only as a last possible resort does this become a *spiritual* crisis, one of life or death...or a third, horrid option: *true inner change*. Their self-defined transformation ritual of gives new meaning to the phrase "till death do us part."
Discussion: Some people are born with a silver spoon in their mouths; some are destined to die that way. Nothing New Age helps Peter and Kat: not yoga, retreats, gurus, visualization or even Tibetan bowls. Spirituality is expensive! They need a New, Improved Age. But ain't it always the way? Just when you think you've hit rock bottom...somebody takes away the rock. The real question is whether this is an obscenely funny, deeply dark, sardonic skewering of the New Age scene portrayed as a fall from grace of two worthy victims—or whether it's a dead serious drama about two people attempting to establish some connection but limited in their communication to the only language they know—New Age clichés. Is it a mordant mocking of the shallow ultra-hip—people who'd opt for suicide before they'd accept a lower standard of living—attempting to find depth, or is it a complex portrait of the pain and frustration of enduring a spiritual crisis, no matter what your socioeconomic level, while surrounded by the self-righteous? Live with the question.
Rent this one for: The complex emotions and motives (and gallows humor) of the brilliant script; the performances.
You'll (probably) like this if you liked: *The Player, The Rapture* (written/directed by Tolkin); *The Object of Beauty*
Credentials: "Ten Best of 1994" list —Roger Ebert
Dissenting Opinion: • "...dry, overlong whining contest...Much ado about nothing" —VMG (2.5 stars) • "Deadening deadpan satire, which its studio could only barely release..." —MMG (1.5)
Vidbits: • Co-Executive Produced by director Oliver Stone.

One From The Heart

(musical/avant garde/romantic comedy)
(1982; Columbia TriStar; PG; 1:38)

Starring: Frederic Forrest, Teri Garr, Nastassia Kinski, Raul Julia
Featuring: Lainie Kazan, Harry Dean Stanton, Allen Goorwitz
Written by: Francis Ford Coppola, Armyan Bernstein
Music by: Tom Waits (with Crystal Gayle)
Directed by: Francis Coppola (no "Ford" in the credits!)

Synopsis: It's the 4th of July in Vegas, and Frannie (Garr) and Hank's (Forrest) relationship is on the rocks. She splits and is picked up by Ray (Julia), a slick lounge singer; Hank is picked up by free-spirited circus acrobat Leila (Kinski). Ray wants Frannie to run away with him, and Leila invites Hank to do the same. But Hank realizes he loves Frannie, and makes a desperate attempt to reclaim her. Will any of them have a happy ending?
Discussion: Simple story; complicated film. 15 years after the hoopla over Coppola's experimental techniques, it's still a visual knockout—and still flawed. Or was it experimental in *all* aspects? Did Coppola *purposefully* turn typical film priorities on their head, daring to put plot at the bottom and use actors as set dressing, while emphasizing the extraordinary ordinarily background elements like music, technique, sets, lighting and editing? Dean Tavoularis' technical tour-de-force of creating Vegas on a sound stage (including crowded intersections, sunrise and rain, and an entire airport, with jet taking off overhead!) is a wonder to watch. So what if the film is a triumph of style over substance? The key word is still "triumph." Don't reject it for what it isn't—embrace it for what it *is:* a fearless experiment in cinematic magic. A stage full of pawns; neon, sleaze and emptiness—Coppola really *did* capture the soul of Vegas!
Rent this one for: its visual brilliance; the ecstasy of style.
You'll (probably) like this if you liked: *Flashdance*
Credentials: • Oscar nomination: Original Song/Score • The editors of *Video* chose this as one of their "favorite tapes of '83."
Dissenting Opinion: • "Giddy heights of visual imagination and technical brilliance are lavished on a wafer-thin story." —*Variety* • "...practically plotless...pretty images do not a film make." —MMG (2 stars) • "...misguided, unmagical...a full-fledged fiasco...inane screenplay..."; One of "Ten Worst of Genre" —*People Magazine's Guide* • "...a major disappointment." —Ebert
Vidbits: • Cost $27M to produce, but earned only $4M, forcing Coppola (by most accounts) to sell his studio. • Rebecca DeMornay is an extra in the restaurant scene. • The old couple in the motel elevator are Coppola's parents, Italia and Carmine.

Paradise

(1991; Touchstone; PG-13; 1:52)

Starring: Don Johnson, Melanie Griffith, Elijah Wood
Featuring: Thora Birch
Written and directed by: Mary Agnes Donoghue
(based on the French film *Le Grand Chemin*)

Synopsis: School's out for summer, and 10-year-old Willard's (Wood) mom, pregnant and abandoned, ships him off for "a vacation" to the rural South Carolina home of her oldest friends, the Reeds. He's barely there before he meets precocious tomboy Billie (Birch), who shows him the sights: the river, the fire tower, the local witch, her older sister naked. What could be an idyllic summer turns sour, however, as Willard discovers he's walked into the middle of a tense situation. Ben (Johnson) and Lily's (Griffith) marriage is on the rocks, due to a recent tragedy. But will Willard's presence accentuate the wedge between them, or can it act as a catalyst for their reconciliation?
Discussion: "One thing you can't hide," John Lennon sang, "is when you're crippled inside." But many of us spend much of our lives and emotional energies attempting to do just that. Ben and Lily are two such people; as much the victims of tragedy as their lost child. The performances are the highlights of this effectively affecting adult drama, and its leisurely pace allows the time to show subtleties of character as well as the minute gradations of their changes. The kids come across cute, when there was a real risk of bad casting creating brats. But Johnson and Griffith (husband and wife at the time of filming) both shine as the quiet, low-key couple with real electricity in their glances and coursing beneath the surface of their strained relationship. The anguish they act out is honest; their tenderness impressive, and their attic catharsis blends brilliant monolog pieces into heart-wrenching confessions. There are many deep themes woven into this bittersweet film: adult problems seen through a child's eyes, with all the attendant pain and confusion; the tenuous grip we have on one another; the agony of missing fathers, of families in crisis, of facing fears; and the difficulty—and sheer magic—of simply *connecting* with another human being. Curiously, critics decry that there aren't enough films like this—and then ignored this perfect example.
Rent this one for: the nicely nuanced performances.
You'll (probably) like this if you liked: *My Life As A Dog*
Dissenting Opinion: "Corny..." —SMV (2.5 stars)
Vidbits: Then-married Johnson & Griffith also starred together in the mediocre 1993 remake of *Born Yesterday*—as well as appearing together 20 years earlier in *The Harrad Experiment.* (73)

Patti Rocks

(1988; Virgin Vision; R; 1:26)

Starring: Chris Mulkey, John Jenkins, Karen Landry
Written by: David Burton Morris, Mulkey, Jenkins & Landry
Directed by: David Burton Morris

Synopsis: "I was jammin' this chick in LaCrosse," Billy (Mulkey) confesses to his old buddy Eddie (Jenkins), "and I knocked her up." He's in deep doody—especially if his wife finds out. Billy talks the reluctant Eddie into riding down with him to talk her into having an abortion. On their road trip they joke and drink and talk about sex and chicks and other gonadal stuff. Patti Rocks (Landry), the "beef" Billy "chopped," is none too happy to have the boys invade her place at midnight. Billy can't explain why he doesn't want her to keep the baby—but that's why he brought Eddie. Patti turns out to be an unlikely lover for Billy: she's savvy, insightful, sensitive—and has her act together. She and Eddie talk: about Billy, about men and women, about Eddie's divorce, which wounded him deeply. And then things really take a turn for the weird...

Discussion: The slender premise serves as an excuse for the characters to engage in dialogs about love, sex, friendship, sex, divorce, sex, loneliness, sex and other vital topics. While slight on plot, the characters are key, and they define the tone of the film: half macho misogyny, half sensitive questioning. Mulkey's Billy is some piece of work, and could best be described as any number of body parts, none of them above the waist. He's a sleazy weasel, a low-class, potty-mouthed slob; he's dumb and angry, rude, crude and lewd; a jock and a jerk. And it takes the entire film to find out whether or not there's anything beneath his obnoxious bravado. Patti is a pleasant surprise: a strong, smart, adult woman completely comfortable in her sexuality. And poor Eddie is caught between the two worlds. The emotions are naked and exposed; the dialog down and dirty. It's a raw, raucous, raunchy drama with a razor-sharp edge of angry comedy: original, edgy and unpredictable; a high class, low budget film that relies on character and dialog and does not disappoint.

Rent this one for: its originality; its edgy and sensitive dialog.

You'll (probably) like this if you liked: *Stranger Than Paradise, Someone To Love, She's Gotta Have It*

Dissenting Opinion: "...doesn't play nearly as well as it should." —MMG (2 stars)

Vidbits: • The same characters and players were featured in Victoria Wozniak's 1975 film, *Loose Ends* (unavailable on video). *Patti Rocks* picks up their story a dozen years later. • Credits include a "Skunk Wrangler" and a "Spiritual Advisor."

A Perfect World

(suspense/crime thriller)
(1993; Warner; PG-13; 2:18)

Starring: Kevin Costner, Clint Eastwood, T.J. Lowther, Laura Dern
Written by: John Lee Hancock
Directed by: Clint Eastwood

Synopsis: Philip (Lowther), age 8, becomes a hostage by accident after Butch Haynes (Costner) and his psycho cellmate break jail. But tough Texas Ranger "Red" Garnett (Eastwood) is hot on their trail, his manhunt hampered by a trailerful of hangers-on, including pre-feminist criminologist Sally Gerber (Dern) and an FBI sharpshooter. Butch and the kid sundance across Texas, forming an unlikely alliance on the lam.
Discussion: It's November, 1963—just weeks before JFK is due in Dallas, a cue that history is in the making. This time, however, it's personal history, and as the film unfolds we realize it's repeating itself. Butch knows that little Philip, raised by a strict, abandoned mother, needs a father figure—a strong male presence to teach him how to be a man: How to pee on trees, shoot guns and be self-sufficient. Butch understands the kid. Hell, 20 years ago, he *was* this kid. And maybe he can help Philip turn out differently. But he's *kidnapped* the kid—so underlying every second of their relationship is a sense of menace. How can we trust him? Turns out that the Geritol-swilling, no-nonsense Garnett was, in a weird twist of fate, a sort of similar surrogate father for Haynes years earlier, altering the courses of both their fates. History does in fact begin repeating itself as Philip learns his lessons—maybe too well—and his own future trajectory hangs in the balance. The men's fates are settled; they're merely playing out their predestined drama. And while the law is concerned with Philip's life, Butch seems to be the only one concerned with the boy's psychological salvation. This tale of unexpected relationships, of the needs and responsibilities of fathers and sons, is complex, subtle and often disturbing; long but never dull, full of moments of pathos, compassion, humor, anger and long stretches of breath-clenching suspense. In a perfect world, it would have won several Oscars. Don't miss it.
Rent this one for: its depth of characterization; its smart, adult themes; the performances, notably Costner and Lowther.
You'll (probably) like this if you liked: *Kalifornia, Badlands*
Dissenting Opinion: "Something new in screen entertainment: A manhunt movie with no urgency, and no suspense." —MMG (2 stars)

Proof

(1991; New Line; R; 1:30)

Starring: Hugo Weaving, Genevieve Picot, Russell Crowe
Written and directed by: Jocelyn Moorhouse

Synopsis: Martin (Weaving) is blind—and bitter. He trusts no one, convinced that everyone lies to him, "because they can." His method of performing a "reality check" is taking photos, which he later has described to him by sighted people. An accident hooks him up with Andy (Crowe), a jaunty young dishwasher who has a way with words that Martin appreciates —simple, direct, honest. They begin palling around, have some adventures, and Martin begins enjoying himself—and trusting Andy. But Martin's housekeeper, Celia (Picot) becomes jealous of their relationship and turns Martin's own quest for evidence against him, embarking in a complicated game of manipulation in which any hope of his trust hangs in a precarious balance.
Discussion: "Seeing is believing"—unless you're blind. Martin was born sightless, and apparently trustless as well. He is certainly correct in refusing to trust Celia, who lusts after him even while tormenting him. The intricate, tangled web they weave, locked in this cruel battle of wills, is the hinge of the film, and could be analyzed at book length: for her, it's a love/hate relationship; for him, she's the pitiful one—and as long as he refuses to indulge her, she can't pity, but only hate, him. At heart, she doesn't want his body, but his *trust,* and will stop at nothing to rid herself of any competition for this prize. Weaving is sour, dour and marvelously cynical, and Crowe is charming— think "young Mel Gibson"—as the irrepressible, admittedly irresponsible Andy, ironically responsible for the film's lightest moments, as well as its deepest. And Picot creates a unique and memorable character in Celia, a person more vulnerable and truly crippled than Martin could ever be. Moorhouse's directorial debut is a one-of-a-kind film, and a very powerful picture; with Martin's emotional life and death at stake, it's as suspenseful, harrowing and riveting as any mystery. The feint of heart might wish to look away—or close their eyes.
Rent this one for: its daring metaphor of emotional blindness portrayed as literal blindness; its intense drama.
You'll (probably) like this if you liked: *Scent of a Woman, Trust*
Credentials: • Swept the 1991 Australian Film Institute Awards
• "Electrifying...don't miss it!" —Andrew Sarris, NY *Observer*
• "Magnificent and utterly original..." —SMV (★★★★) • *EW:* "A"
Vidbits: Often classified as a "comedy," but only by people who have obviously never seen it.

The Rapture

(supernatural)

(1991; Columbia TriStar; R; 1:40)

Starring: Mimi Rogers, David Duchovny
Featuring: Patrick Bauchau, Will Patton, Kimberly Cullum
Written and directed by: Michael Tolkin

Synopsis: There's got to be more to life than being a phone company operator by day and a swinger by night. At least that's what Sharon (Rogers) suspects. She needs a new direction in her life, to fill the void inside her. Suicide is an acceptable alternative—until she dreams of The Pearl, and accepts Jesus Christ into her heart. "There is a God, and I'm going to meet him," she determines. "I want my salvation." Her conversion costs her her old life, but brings her into a circle of evangelical Christians awaiting the immanent Apocalypse of the Book of Revelations. She marries Randy (Duchovny) and raises her daughter Mary (Cullum) to believe these are the Final Days. But bad things happen to good people; when God takes Randy early, visions invite the girls into the desert to await His call. They go, and wait. And wait... Obviously she's nuts. *But what if she's right?*
Discussion: It's a safe bet to say you've never seen a movie like this before: one which Biblical predictions come literally true. And yet they remain as metaphors for a meditation on faith in a faithless age. Is Sharon experiencing religious conversion or a nervous breakdown? Is she "doing God" instead of drugs? Is it faith or fanaticism? And the ultimate chilling question: What if, in spite of all logic, the Fundamentalists are correct, and the Day of Reckoning is indeed at hand? The plot of *The Rapture* is so astonishingly original that we can never predict or even guess the twists it takes; the film itself is slow but mesmerizingly tense, glowing with luminous photography and suffused with an ethereal spirit, ending in a hallucinatory nightmare of black magical realism. Traces of Abraham and Job can be detected, and Mary's "Sermon on the Mount" is a terrifying masterpiece of logic at odds with religion—an awe-striking high point of the drama. The heart of this film, however, is the ultimate question of faith: How can one love a God who'd murder his own son?
Rent this one for: its astonishing originality.
You'll (probably) like this if you liked: *The New Age* (Tolkin on spirituality); *Resurrection, The X-Files, Paperhouse*
Dissenting Opinion: • "Not for every taste..." —MMG (3 stars) • "Robotic acting and a sci-fi fantasy ending derail what might have been a challenging film." —SMV (2 stars)
Vidbits: Tolkin's directorial debut

Resurrection

(supernatural/drama)
(1980; MCA; PG; 1:43)

Starring: Ellen Burstyn, Sam Shepard, Eva LeGallienne
Featuring: Roberts Blossom, Clifford David, Richard Farnsworth
Written by: Lewis John Carlino
Music by: Maurice Jarre
Directed by: Daniel Petrie

Synopsis: A car crash flatlines Edna McCauley (Burstyn), who enters a tunnel of light filled with peace, music and departed friends, when—BANG! She's back in her body, flat on her back in a hospital bed, crippled from the waist down. Her sullen father takes her back to the family farm in Kansas to recuperate. When she stops a young hemophiliac's bleeding, her grandma (LeGallienne) thinks she might have returned from the Other Side with the gift of healing. Through pain and faith she heals herself and walks again. She becomes a local legend, and even attracts a young suitor Cal (Shepard), who begins to question why she never mentions Scripture... To some, her miracles are wondrous gifts. But others are threatened. Can her love overcome the closed minds and closed hearts of the loveless around her, or will her great good attract even greater obstacles?
Discussion: Slow-paced, low-key, quiet and somber, gentle and tender, smart and insightful, the film never degenerates into New Age drivel, but instead stays on track as a psychological drama of emotional catharsis, more character- than gimmick-driven. It's stocked with first-rate performances; Burstyn in particular is tasked with displaying a range of emotion from grief to compassion, from hungry lust to angelic ecstasy—all the while convincing us that despite her empathic powers, she's just as human as any of us. If every actor could claim a film like this in his or her portfolio, that actor could enter the tunnel of light fully fulfilled. *Resurrection* packs an emotional wallop from its earliest scenes right through to its knockout ending, a heart-rending moment that will leave you with a transcendent glow.
Rent this one for: Burstyn's performance; the deep emotion.
You'll (probably) like this if you liked: *The Dead Zone*
Credentials: • 1980 Oscar nominations: Best Actress (Burstyn), Supporting Actress (LeGallienne) • 1980 National Board of Review Awards: 10 Best Films of Year; Best Supporting Actress (LeGallienne) • "...wonderful and underrated" —MMG (3.5 stars)
Dissenting Opinion: • "Curious modern parable with nowhere to go; even religious reactionaries may find it rather boring." —HFG • "...strains credibility..." —SMV (3 stars)

The Right Stuff

(1983; Warner; PG; 3:12)

Starring: Sam Shepard, Scott Glenn, Ed Harris, Dennis Quaid, Fred Ward, Pamela Reed, Barbara Hershey
Featuring: David Clennon, Kim Stanley, Mary Jo Deschanel, Veronica Cartwright, Scott Wilson, Jeff Goldblum, Harry Shearer, Donald Moffat, Royal Dano
Written and directed by: Philip Kaufmann
(based on the book by Tom Wolfe)

Synopsis: 1947: Test pilot Chuck Yeager (Shepard) punches a hole in the sound barrier for the first time in history. Before long, the sky is filled with sonic booms from ultracompetitive flyboys anxious to "push the envelope"—including Yeager, who beats them all for speed. "What's next?" he wonders. October 4, 1957: Sputnik orbits earth. The free world is shocked—and threatened. Government officials order the military to take the high ground of space before the Commies establish a foothold. The government begins scouting for "astronauts," but finds itself at odds with civilian test pilots like Yeager—which is just fine by him; he's sure they don't want pilots, just "Spam in a can." There are, however, plenty of unflappable flyguys eager to volunteer. Following rigorous physical and psychological testing of the candidates, NASA announces The Seven—and we follow them through their demanding training, as well as frustrations caused by bureaucrats, engineers and Yuri Gagarin. Every one of the seven gets his shot at space, and we follow the first three dramatic missions (Shepard, Grissom and Glenn) and the final flight of the Mercury Program (Cooper)—all while Yeager continues his solitary career, still the best of the last of his breed, and one of the very few Americans who possesses The Right Stuff.
Discussion: An undertaking as epic as our first steps off the planet certainly deserves an epic film. This is it. And yet it's more than just a slice of history; it's history put into perspective. On one hand, it's the story of the "changing of the guard," from rugged individualist, "lone cowboy" heroes like Yeager (who rigs a makeshift door handle for his jet plane from a broomstick minutes before a flight) to the Government-approved, high-profile, hi-tech triumph of teamwork over individual accomplishment. In this sense, it's an elegy to the passing of the jet torch from one type of rocket jockey to the next generation, and it's a wonderfully touching film. If Kaufmann were to recut the movie to include *only* Yeager's story—his flying triumphs; his tender, unspoken understanding with his wife (Hershey); his wistful reactions to the accomplishments of the astronauts—he'd still have a fabulous feature, full of excitement and emotion.

But the story of this historical transition composes only about a third of the film. The rest is devoted to the seven astronauts. We go behind the scenes, behind the headlines, behind the hype, discovering that their story is rarely the PR dream *Life* magazine had us believe—but it's all the more fascinating for being so fully human. The three hour-plus length of the film allows time to establish many of the seven as real personalities: Shepard, the joker; Glenn, the smarmy Boy Scout; "Gordo" Cooper, the hot dog hotshot, and so on. And we get some insight into the lives of the wives—and of the wives' nightmares: Never provided with "lessons in bravery," they're forced to share their anxiety with the world, gracefully, all the while waiting with baited breath to discover whether they'll ever see their men again. The ensemble acting is uniformly superb.

It's a very funny film as well. Jeff Goldblum and Harry Shearer wander through the second act like Rosencrantz and Guildenstern, providing comic relief, for example. The Cape Canaveral antics of the men are a source of great amusement, as are the wretched tests—and only a serious film could pull off (so to speak) a sperm-sample scene as rasty as this one, or spend five minutes illustrating how Shepard almost scrubbed his historic first flight by "soiling himself."

Since it's history, there are few surprises and little suspense—yet it's never dull. As the human side of an epic adventure, there is great emotion, drama, humor and even a touch of tragedy. *The Right Stuff* is a majestic, triumphal, often exhilarating film—and as expansive a saga of the bright side of America as *The Godfather* trilogy is of our dark national shadow.

Rent this one for: its epic scope, the performances.

You'll (probably) like this if you liked: *Apollo 13, For All Mankind* (U.S. space program history)

Credentials: • 1983 Academy Awards: Film Editing, Sound, Original Score. Nominations: Best Picture, Supporting Actor (Shepard), Art Direction/Set Direction, Cinematography • A 1989 poll of 54 film critics by (the now defunct) *American Film* magazine rated this the #12 "Best American Film of the '80s." • "★★★★★" —VMG • #13 on *Premiere* magazine's poll of 24 critics' "Best Movies of the '80s" list. • "...a great film." —Roger Ebert

Dissenting Opinion: • "...simplistic attitudes, stupid mysticism, and cheap shots at the public, the press, and government officials...a big, small-minded movie." —*People Magazine's Guide to Movies on Video* • "...too brash and inhuman to provide much entertainment." —HFG

Vidbits: • Ed Harris rejoined the Hollywood space program (and earned an Oscar nomination) in 1995, playing flight director Gene Kranz in *Apollo 13.* • Pilot Chuck Yeager appears briefly as a bartender, first seen shaking hands with Hershey in the bar.

Running On Empty

(1988; Warner; PG-13; 1:56)

Starring: Christine Lahti, River Phoenix, Judd Hirsh
Featuring: Martha Plimpton, Steven Hill, Ed Crawley
Written by: Naomi Foner
Directed by: Sidney Lumet

Synopsis: Holding a family together is never easy—but it's nearly impossible when you're radicals on the run. When Arthur (Hirsh) and Annie (Lahti) engaged in anti-Vietnam activist activities, they had no idea their actions would force them to live underground in America for 20 years: taking menial jobs; relocating regularly; living by their wits to stay one step ahead of the Feds. Their two boys never knew any life other than this regular uprooting and assuming of new identities. And their parents never let themselves consider that son Danny (Phoenix) would grow up, fall in love, and want a life of his own—which could jeopardize their hard-won freedom. Artie and Annie have nothing but their family—so how can Danny leave them, even if staying means sacrificing his own future as a piano prodigy?
Discussion: "You can run, but you can't hide," Satchel Paige is famous for saying. Artie and Annie discover a variation: You can indeed hide, for a while. But you can't run forever, especially from your own past. *Empty* is a family drama with a difference, involving us in the complicated lives of complex characters, including a budding romance between intelligent teens and the multiple ironies plaguing three generations of their family's dashed dreams. It's an intense, intelligent and deeply moving film about heart-wrenching crises, tough decisions and major sacrifices—and a film which cuts to the heart of what it means to be a family. Phoenix is exceptional as the sensitive, shy, vulnerable and confused teen who falls for tomboy Plimpton. The harmonious interplay of a smart script (convincing in its fascinating details of their lifestyle), understated direction, and A-level performances brilliantly accomplishes the difficult task of making the people in this outrageous situation seem not just sympathetic, but realistic and believable.
Rent this one for: the intense emotion and superb acting.
You'll (probably) like this if you liked: *Ordinary People*
Credentials: • 1988 Academy Award nominations: Original Screenplay; Supporting Actor (Phoenix) • 1989 Golden Globe Award: Best Screenplay • 1988 L.A. Film Critics Association Award: Best Actress (Lahti) • 1988 National Board of Review Award: Best Supporting Actor (Phoenix) • "...one of the best films of 1988." —Roger Ebert (★★★★)
Dissenting Opinion: "Misconceived tale..." —SMV (2 stars)

Say Anything...

(romance/coming-of-age)

(1989; CBS/Fox, FoxVideo; PG-13; 1:43)

Starring: John Cusack, Ione Skye, John Mahoney
Featuring: Lili Taylor, Joan Cusack
Written and directed by: Cameron Crowe

Synopsis: It's graduation day at their Seattle high school. Diane (Skye) has won a major Fellowship to study in England; Lloyd might have a career in kickboxing, and babbles when he's nervous—which is most of the time. But he's smitten with her, and asks her to a party. Surprise: She agrees. Double surprise: She has a great time—and she really likes him. They go out. A lot. Maybe they even fall in love; they don't know. Her father (Mahoney) raises objections, but he's her father, after all—and he's got his own problems, like an IRS investigation into his business. Pressure forces Diane to break up with Lloyd. Pressure squared and cubed: Lloyd's heart is breaking; Dad's world is rapidly collapsing. Will everything fall apart, or can someone pull the pieces together—and maybe even find happiness?
Discussion: Everyone has a special talent; Lloyd's is being with Diane. He knows it; he just has to convince her. Cusack's Lloyd is an original: sensitive, spontaneous, seriously silly; an attentive gentleman; a motor-mouthed marvel, desperately intense, doggedly persistent and an unrepentant romantic. Skye's Diane is vulnerable and trusting; innocent, and naive enough to believe she really can "say anything" to her doting dad. While it's Lloyd's movie, it's also a father/daughter tale about trust and betrayal—and about breaking away, as Diane graduates painfully from girl to adult. And it's a falling-in-love flick with amusingly accurate insight into the flurry of confusing feelings accompanying a heart's first tentative test drive. It's a teen romance about serious responsibility, treated with adult respect and intelligence. And it's an old-fashioned love story (and great date movie): smart, sweet and subtle; warm, witty and wise.
Rent this one for: its refreshing intelligence and performances.
You'll (probably) like this if you liked: *Singles, L.A. Story*
Credentials: "...one of the best films of 1989. ★★★★" —Ebert
Dissenting Opinion: "Do you really *need* to see another teen dating-angst movie?" —SMV (2 stars)
Vidbits: • Lois Chiles appears as Diane's mother; Joan Cusack, John's real-life sister, plays his sister; both appear uncredited. • Keep a close eye out for Eric Stolz, Chynna Phillips, Jeremy Piven, Bebe Neuwirth (as Lloyd's career counselor) and pro kickboxer Don "The Dragon" Wilson (Lloyd's sparring partner).

Searching for Bobby Fischer

(1993; Paramount; PG; 1:51)

Starring: Joe Mantegna, Ben Kingsley, Max Pomeranc
Featuring: Joan Allen, Lawrence Fishburne, David Paymer
Written and directed by: Steven Zaillian
(based on the book by Fred Waitzkin)

Synopsis: Josh (Pomeranc) is seven—time for baseball, thinks his sportswriter dad Fred (Mantegna). But Josh is fascinated by chess—and he's a natural. Dad takes him to Bruce Pandolfini (Kingsley), once Bobby Fischer's coach, now tending a rundown chess club. Pandolfini watches Josh play and sees the intuitive sense that made Fischer a world champion. He disciplines, tutors and mentors Josh with stern intensity—but Josh has more fun playing speed chess in the park with Vinnie (Fishburne), a jive-talking, street-smart player who teaches him the wild side of the sport, like how to "psyche out" his opponents. Josh begins winning tournaments, and everything is great—until a New Kid appears on the circuit. He's arrogant, ruthless, obnoxious—and a virtual chess machine. In the midst of a crisis of confidence, can Josh beat him—and if so, at what cost to his delicate spirit?
Discussion: Based on the real-life story of Josh Waitzkin, it's ultimately not about a kid at all. It's about the problems we all have dealing with adult concerns, facing pressure by adult self-interests, and our own fears of failure. It's about how we all make wrong moves in playing the game—not chess, but life. Josh is the focal point of this Jungian quaternity of personified personality functions: victory-oriented Dad is the sensation function; Vinnie, the feeling/emotional; Bruce, the thinking/intellectual; Mom, the intuitive—the only one among them with insight enough to recognize Josh's decency is not weakness, but *innocence,* to be protected at any cost. And Josh eventually proves his intuitive artistry by integrating the strengths of each of his quartet of teachers and transcending the limitations of all. Pomeranc is determinedly unprecocious; one small part of what makes Josh such a charmer. Atmospheric photography and Oscar-caliber performances by all enhance this intelligent, sensitive and spirit-affirming film, at once warm, witty and wise.
Rent this one for: the performances, script and photography.
You'll (probably) like this if you liked: *Little Man Tate*
Credentials: '93 Oscar nomination: Cinematography. • "...the kind of film that people are always saying they're dying for. And then nobody sees it." —Kenneth Turan, *LA Times* • *EW:* "A"
Vidbits: After the film is a short interview with the real Josh, now grown up—and still playing chess. • Josh's real-life sister Katya appears as the girl rated 82nd at the final tournament.

Secret Honor

(monolog/performance/revisionist history)
(1985; Vestron, LIVE; NR; 1:30)

Starring: Philip Baker Hall
Written by: Donald Freed, Arnold M. Stone
(adapted from their stage play)
Directed by: Robert Altman

Synopsis: Midnight in Richard Nixon's San Clemente residence, sometime after his resignation. The disgraced ex-president (Hall) dictates his memoirs into a recorder, becoming increasingly drunk, angry and irrational in the process. On his desk is a loaded revolver. Hysterical, on the edge of insanity, he stalks through his study, spewing his vitriolic vision of his political career. Slowly, one fragmented phrase at a time, a picture begins to emerge of "the most terrible secrets of all," as he reveals "the reasons behind the reasons" behind his resignation.
Discussion: Subtitled "A Political Myth," the film begins with a disclaimer, explaining it is a "fictional meditation...not a work of history," and "a work of fiction, using as a fictional character a real person." Hall, in a one-man show, gives a tour de force performance, growling and grimacing, ranting and raving, sputtering and spouting stings of obscenities that would make a Tourette's syndrome victim blush. His rage is aimed at any and all targets, from the "goddam Kennedys" and "that hypocrite" Ike all the way back to George "that fucking liar" Washington. Hall has first-class material to work with as well: The movie is a masterpiece of dramatic unfolding, creating a portrait of a poor Quaker boy whose lust for power and bulldog persistence led him into a morally impossible paradox, the only solution to which was "secret honor—public shame." He often claimed that only Dick Nixon could destroy Dick Nixon—and reveals how he orchestrated his own downfall rather than continue as the blood-stained puppet of a logical, believable and incredible conspiracy involving The Mob and his Bohemian Grove billionaire puppet masters. Nixon as hidden hero, as sympathetic martyr: how we wish it could be true, to dig beneath a national disgrace and find a figure of high tragedy, who sacrificed everything for America. *Secret Honor* is an awesome experiment that succeeds brilliantly—and is the kind of powerful political fiction filmmaking that Oliver Stone can only dream of creating.
Rent this one for: the performance; the conspiracy theory.
You'll (probably) like this if you liked: *All The President's Men, JFK* (gov't. conspiracy); *Nixon; Swimming to Cambodia*
Credentials: "★★★★" —Roger Ebert, Chicago *Sun-Times*

Threshold

(1983; CBS/Fox, FoxVideo; PG; 1:37)

Starring: Donald Sutherland, Jeff Goldblum, Mare Winningham
Featuring: John Marley, Sharon Acker, Michael Lerner
Written by: James Salter
Directed by: Richard Pearce

Synopsis: Dr. Thomas Vrain (Sutherland) is the finest cardiac surgeon in the world, but he's dissatisfied: Transplants are often rejected, and aren't always available when needed. He's intrigued with experimentation in artificial hearts, but wary about them—until he meets biologist Dr. Aldo Gehring (Goldblum), who has some real solutions. Vrain convinces his hospital's sponsor to hire Gehring and invest in further research. Animal tests of their prototype device are encouraging, but the hospital board denies them permission to test the mechanical pump on a human subject—until 21-year-old Carol Severance (Winningham) "dies" on the operating table when her decaying heart fails to respond to surgery. Vrain's commitment to cutting edge experimentation—and to Carol's life—is suddenly put to the ultimate test...and so is his untried, untested artificial heart.
Discussion: It's a solid, simple drama: sober, dignified, provocative and thought-provoking; emotionally tender and intense, and more detached than "serious." The film conveys the quiet excitement of envelope-pushing discovery as well as the suspense of skilled surgical procedures. (The surgery scenes, while delicately handled, are also presented in clinical detail—be warned of their graphic nature.) Even better than the story, however, are the uniformly excellent performances, turning the film into a human drama of three realistic people. Sutherland has the "surgeon personality" captured perfectly: His totally assured authority is visible in every step and gesture—but he never crosses the thin line separating his complete confidence from arrogance. Winningham is likewise perfect as the bright but vulnerable patient; the scenes between the two are painfully tender. There's a tangible sense of connection between them—and no "artificial heart" in their exceptional performances. Two small problems: Sutherland and Goldblum are both ace mumblers, so the dialog is occasionally difficult to hear; and anytime I've found this film, it's been in the "Science Fiction" section, for some bizarre reason. Check there—but do find it and rent it.
Rent this one for: its intelligent script and fine performances.
You'll (probably) like this if you liked: *ER, St. Elsewhere*
Vidbits: Produced in 1980, but unreleased because the distributors considered it "noncommercial." They changed their minds after Barney Clark's historic similar operation in 1983.

Ticket To Heaven

(1981; MGM/UA; PG; 1:47)

Starring: Nick Mancuso, Saul Rubinek, Meg Foster, Kim Cattrall
Written by: R.L. Thomas & Anne Cameron
(adapted from the book *Moonwebs* by Josh Freed)
Directed by: R.L. Thomas

Synopsis: A failed affair sends depressed David (Mancuso) from Toronto to San Francisco to visit a friend who's joined a "cooperative." But a weekend trip to the group's communal farm introduces David to a relentlessly ebullient "family" (including Cattrall in a live-wire performance) and their enforced regimen of songfests, exercise, lectures, "sharing" and precious little sleep. When David's attitude is suitably readjusted, he's allowed to go with groups into The City to sell flowers for "a Christian group." Fortunately, he has friends and family who investigate his disappearance, and when they discover the truth of his situation, they risk jail time to kidnap and deprogram him. Can they awaken him to who he was before his cult recaptures him?
Discussion: Not only is this story of cult conversion the stuff of excellent drama, but they got the details right as well: First, of classic brainwashing techniques (little food, no privacy, sleep deprivation, philosophical indoctrination), all resulting in zombification; then of the regimented daily life of the converted (being led like cattle; chanting "Bring in the money! Stay awake! Smash out Satan!"; "love bombing" dissenters until they rejoin the flock); and finally, of the tough-love deprogramming—all the more difficult as it oxymoronically involves forcing someone to think for himself. But our preview of the consequences of a failed deprogramming make David's situation all the more desperate. How could anyone submit to this seduction? Peer pressure and pleasantry: Everything is so goddamned glorious it would be downright rude to resist; the sinister psychological screwing is too ephemeral to fight. If there is a Satan, these are his most perverse coercions, preying on confused, lonely youth hungry for family, goals, inner peace. And if there *isn't* a Satan... Well, who'd need one with "religious leaders" like these? Truly a modern horror story, with its roots planted in the reality of thousands of nullified minds and extinguished souls.
Rent this one for: for the smart, seductive script: a fascinating and accurate depiction of cults' "religious conversion" process.
You'll (probably) like this if you liked: "The Prisoner," *The Manchurian Candidate, THX-1138*
Dissenting Opinion: "...a truly Archie Bunkeresque view of the phenomena of religious conversion."—from a review in Rev. Moon's Unification Church newspaper.

Tin Men

(1987; Touchstone; R; 1:52)

Starring: Richard Dreyfuss, Danny DeVito, Barbara Hershey
Featuring: John Mahoney, Bruno Kirby, J.T. Walsh, Jackie Gayle
Written and directed by: Barry Levinson

Synopsis: Baltimore, 1963: Aluminum siding salesman Bill "BB" Babowski (Dreyfuss) drives his new Cadillac off the lot—and is promptly hit by Tilley (DeVito), in his Cadillac. It's hate at first sight: "I'm gonna get even with you," BB vows. "You picked the wrong person to get even with, pal," Tilley fires back. They discover that, oddly enough, they're both "tin men"—siding salesmen for rival companies. BB's career is on a roll, though, while Tilley's is in a slump—just like his marriage to frumpy Nora (Hershey). BB and Tilley cross paths a couple more times, doing damage to each others' cars, but BB escalates his revenge by picking up and seducing Nora. Unexpected complications arise: Tilley's glad to be rid of her, for instance. And BB and Nora begin actually falling for each other. But if she ever finds out why he really seduced her in the first place...

Discussion: It's more than a car—it's a status symbol. And it's more than a dented fender—it's a bruised male ego. The men are as skilled at macho posing as they are in scamming their clients, but the minute a woman—or an emotion unfamiliar to many macho males, like tenderness, or affection—enters the picture, they're lost. *Tin Men* is a perfect example of a "character-driven" plot: the characters themselves, and no one else, are responsible for their miserable situations. Nora makes an amazing transformation in the escalating vendetta from pawn into a strong-willed woman who discovers what she wants and learns how to fight for it. And the men discover that their fates are intimately intertwined—but as two sides of a coin. The ironic reversal in the final scenes reveals they are in fact a mirror for one another, and it's difficult to love a mirror if you hate yourself. The middle act drags a bit, but it's more than made up for by the wry dialog, the undercurrent of humor, the first-rate performances, and the film's subtle ruminations on honesty and deception, whether on the job, in the home...or in the mirror.

Rent this one for: the intelligent and unpredictable character-driven script; the three-dimensional performances.

You'll (probably) like this if you liked: *Diner* (Levinson's Baltimore of a similar era); *Cadillac Man*

Credentials: Billboard ranked this in the top 10 rentals of 1988.

Dissenting Opinion: "...undermined by unresolved ideas and inconsistencies in the way the characters behave." —MMG (2.5 stars)

Truly, Madly, Deeply

(romance/fantasy)

(1991; Touchstone; PG; 1:47)

Starring: Juliet Stevenson, Alan Rickman, Michael Maloney
Written and directed by: Anthony Minghella

Synopsis: It's been a year since Nina's (Stevenson) lover died—but she's still devastated. She senses his presence; she feels watched over...but she's still depressed. Friends, family and co-workers all try to comfort her and draw her out as she drifts vaguely through the days—but to no avail. And then one day, with no warning, Jamie (Rickman) reappears, in the flesh. He's still dead, but he's back. Nina is overjoyed beyond belief. Joyously, they renew their playful relationship. Before long, however, he's up to his old bad habits, like rearranging her flat and criticizing her taste—and some new irritations, like inviting sleepless dead friends into her house to watch videos all night. The fantasy of memory begins to fade in the cold light of this fantastic reality. And when Nina meets effervescent art therapist Mark (Maloney), who pursues her relentlessly, she has an agonizing decision to make: continue living in a dead past, or embrace a living future and take a chance on a life—and on Life.

Discussion: Juliet Stevenson's virtuoso performance is the very heart of this heartfelt film—which was apparently the plan all along; playwright Minghella, in his film directing debut, allegedly wrote this as a showcase for her talents, and she fulfills the challenge admirably. Given the opportunity to express every major emotion from ecstasy to despair, she does so believably, with endearing sincerity, and with a childlike enthusiasm and unselfconsciousness. Indeed, her expertise in emotional expression actually makes the film uncomfortable to watch on occasion—as when, at her therapist's, she cries uncontrollably while the camera stares at her unflinchingly, demanding our attention, unmercifully. Such raw emotion is rare, disturbing—and precisely what we watch films for. Stevenson's goofy beauty deepens Nina into a delicate and vulnerable human with whom we can't help but feel an empathetic connection.

This is not to say that the film is an emotional endurance test. It has many moments of character-based humor, a strong undercurrent of irony (e.g., even a miracle can turn into a burden) and even the occasional touch of whimsy. (After a bitter political rant by Jamie, Nina asks in disbelief, "You've died, and you're *still* into party politics?")

Beneath Nina's story, Minghella has layered an additional level of complexity which is presented almost entirely in subtle subtext—and, ironically, Rickman's restrained performance nearly obscures this interpretation of the purpose of his reappearance. It is quite possible that Jamie has not returned in response to Nina's longing, but because her extraordinary grief required extraordinary measures—and an extraordinary sacrifice—to overcome. He returns not to carry on their relationship, but to force it to a conclusion, deposing her virtual worship of him by reminding her of his irritating idiosyncrasies, which she has forgotten in her grief, and forcing her to release him from her heart so that she can be free to love again. Jamie comes back not so she can praise him, but so she can bury him. And perhaps this act of selfless sacrifice is how Jamie (who, he admits early on, "didn't die properly") earns his own earthly release. His final, bittersweet smile, watching the final outcome of events, is one indication; the ambiguity lies in whether he's being comforted by the dead friends surrounding him—or being congratulated.

With this film full of bittersweet wisdom, Minghella has crafted a clever metaphor for the grieving process, and the healing process that accompanies it—whether the process concerns the death of a loved one or the death of a love relationship. He's managed as well to capture those rare moments when one's heart suddenly stops—from surprise, from ecstasy, or from the knife-point attack of wretched, unrequested memory. He understands the connection between love and magic, and the necessity of exchanging impossible miracles for the mundane stage magic of real life. And he illustrates this wistful wisdom with a whisper rather than a cry in this ethereal, gentle celebration, not of life, but of the decision to participate joyously in the distressing trials of life.

Rent this one for: Stevenson's performance; the poignance.

You'll (probably) like this if you liked: *Ghost, Always, Made in Heaven, To Gillian on Her 37th Birthday*

Credentials: "...truly funny and deeply moving...something very rare: a realistic fantasy." —SMV (3.5 stars) • *EW:* "A"

Dissenting Opinion: "...unable to sustain its offbeat premise to the very end." —MMG (2.5 stars)

Venice/Venice

(romance)

(1992; Orion; R; 1:48)

Starring: Nelly Alard, Henry Jaglom, David Duchovny
Featuring: Suzanne Bertish, Daphna Kastner, Zack Norman
Written and directed by: Henry Jaglom

Synopsis: Dean (Jaglom) is an independent filmmaker attending a film festival in Venice, Italy. One of his numerous interviewers is Jeanne (Alard), a Parisian journalist smitten with his films and their sensitive insights. His wheeling, dealing and schmoozing at the festival, however, shatters her romantic illusions about his screen persona, and she leaves, disenchanted and disappointed. Cut to Venice, California, some time later. Jeanne shows up unexpectedly at Dean's home to pursue their initial attraction. Problem is, Dean's already living with someone. Whose true love will overcome all obstacles?

Discussion: "It's really hard to think that real life exists independent of the movies," Jaglom-as-Dean admits. He might as well have entitled this film *Real/Reel,* as his experiments in *cinema faux verité* reach new heights of integration here. Or is that new depths of self-indulgence? The film ponders that question too, as well as more important questions, like: How do movies affect our life, especially in terms of self-concept and romantic expectation? Are movies—even "realistic" movies—an accurate reflection of life? Illustration is punctuated by discussion in a brave attempt to blur the border between life and film. The film has its flaws, which are magnified by its audacious experimental nature. It's occasionally frustrating to watch Jaglom grapple with a subject he can't *quite* seem to bring into sharp focus, for instance; and despite his defense and denial of self-indulgence, he occasionally lapses into narcissism. He must have balls big enough to fill a blimp hanger, for example, to expect to pull off a "realistic" scene in which his past, present and future lovers all share a heart-to-heart, and all end up liking, understanding and respecting one another. Now *there's* a self-indulgent fantasy!—particularly when he plays "Dean" as a cranky, obnoxious, abrasive and sometimes downright nasty little egotist. Yet despite its flaws, this is the film Jaglom has been trying to make most of his life—and it's as unique and thoughtful an attempt to fuse film and fact as has ever been committed to celluloid.

Rent this one for: its audacious experimentation.

You'll (probably) like this if you liked: *Stardust Memories, Someone To Love, The Stunt Man,* Fellini's *8-1/2*

Vidbits: Cameo: Director John Landis, at the film festival.

Flashback!

Voices

(romance)

(1979; MGM/UA; PG; 1:47)

Starring: Amy Irving, Michael Ontkean
Featuring: Alex Rocco, Viveca Lindfors
Written by: John Herzfeld
Music by: Jimmy Webb, Burton Cummings *(vocals)*
Directed by: Robert Markowitz

Synopsis: Drew (Ontkean) is a struggling singer; Rosemarie (Irving) is deaf. Not a promising combination. But it's love at first sight, and Drew is determined to make it work. She reads lips, a little; he learns a little sign language. But communication is not their problem. Their problems are social: his embarrassment, for one; and her overprotective mother (Lindfors), who insists she stick to dating successful *deaf* men. Drew is a persistent suitor, however. He watches her dance for her class of deaf kids one day and encourages her to audition for a local dance troupe. She can't hear the music, but she can feel the beat. She agrees, reluctantly. But when she's called on stage, he's desperately fighting a fire in his father's store. Will she humiliate herself and lose all her confidence, or can Drew somehow rescue his father, his lover—and her faith in herself and her dream?

Discussion: A singer and a deaf girl? A deaf dancer? Sounds like the kind of premises that can't help but turn either maudlin or ludicrous. But this heartfelt little film treads a tightrope of sincerity between these two unacceptable extremes, maintaining the high ground and a perfect balance, courtesy of the intense tenderness brought to the performances. Irving is angelic, beatific and serene, and proves her prowess as an actress by conveying every emotion, no matter how complex, with crystal clarity through the only tools Rosemarie can use: facial expressions and body language. And (although it's probably politically incorrect heresy to say so), she portrays a deaf woman more convincingly than even Marlee Matlin. Ontkean contributes a very real sense of gentleness and an almost tangible passion; in most scenes, he appears genuinely smitten.

All drama is about overcoming obstacles; all romances are about *love's* ability to overcome obstacles—or its failure to do so. The obstacle here is a gap between them as vast as an entire sense, and as visible as their different social standings. Their intense attraction for one another, however, not only bridges that gap, but seems to leap right off the screen and infect us.

Voices has one major problem: it's really only *half* a brilliant film. We've actually discussed only one side of its story so far. The other part of the plot is the loud, extraneous tale of Drew's family: three generations of men (including dad Alex Rocco) living together in a cramped Hoboken apartment, always on each others' nerves and at each others' throats. How this entirely unconnected, completely unrelated, grating and irritating tale ever attached itself like a leech onto such a delicate love story remains a mystery. Maybe writer Herzfeld was trying to achieve some kind of counterpoint; if so, he missed miserably: the men-only scenes are overbearing and obnoxious; they add nothing to the romance and actively detract from the sensitive central story. Maybe Herzfeld had a brilliant, touching script about an impossible love—but it only ran an hour, so he added some padding. I don't know. But in taping just the love scenes off a cable broadcast, I *did* discover *something:* except for one brief moment (Drew helping his family put out the fire, which makes him late for Rosemarie's audition) the two plots *never intersect.* And so I pass on to you these instructions on how to watch *Voices* as a lovely romantic movie without having to endure the pitiable peripheral plotline: After the opening, merely fast scan through any scene that doesn't include Amy Irving. It's that simple—and you won't miss anything vital.

And it's well worth the trouble, going to these lengths to see the romance unfold. Irving is a mesmerizing mime; a delicate, balletic dancer; adorable and radiant, yet capable of instilling Rosemarie with a fierce independence. Her scene with Rosemarie's overprotective mother is drama of the highest caliber: multi-leveled, smart and heartrending. *Voices* is a very enabling film, as well—one not about disability, but about the joyous expression of ability. The final scene is clever, unique, utterly original and spectacularly poignant. Drew's dilemma is how to share his first love, music, with his hearing-impaired lover. He illustrates that love is indeed the universal language as he finds a way to close the gap that's separated them since they first laid eyes on one another from a distance. If that final scene doesn't burst your heart with poignant joy, there might be nothing on earth that can move you to tears. For all its peripheral flaws, *Voices* is ultimately a very moving moving picture.

Rent this one for: its engaging, heartfelt, poignant romance, made believable by the outstanding performances of the stars.

You'll (probably) like this if you liked: *Children of a Lesser God, L.A. Story, Say Anything..., Flirting, Gas Food Lodging*

Dissenting Opinion: "Sincerely intentioned drama...compromised by Hollywood formulas." —MMG (2 stars)

Vidbits: Ontkean's singing voice is that of Burton Cummings from the '60s group Guess Who, who also wrote "Drew's" songs.

War Party

(Western)

(1989; HBO; R; 1:39)

Starring: Billy Wirth, Kevin Dillon
Featuring: Tim Sampson, Kevyn Major Howard, M. Emmet Walsh, Peggy Lipton, Jimmie Ray Weeks
Written by: Spencer Eastman
Directed by: Franc Roddam

Synopsis: It's been 100 years since the Milk River "conflict'"—only Indians call it a "massacre"—when the town council of Binger, Montana, votes to stage a reenactment to draw in tourists. It's planned as a classic Plains battle: 100 Blackfeet braves versus 100 Cavalry, all on horseback in full battle regalia. Local punk Calvin (Howard), eager to settle a barroom score with a reservation resident, loads real bullets in his six-shooter and takes advantage of the confusion to shoot him. Sonny (Wirth) whacks Calvin in response, and all hell breaks loose: it's more *deja vu* than reenactment. Sonny and friends head for the hills on horseback while a mob of mad white-eyes mounts up in their pickup trucks to pursue them. Can a handful of modern Native Americans, cut off from everything modern, remember, revive or recreate enough of the Old Ways to survive a deadly encounter with their century-old nemesis?
Discussion: The more things change, the more they stay the same. Scratch that thin veneer of civilization and you'll find many men itching for a chance to be savages; send armed authorities after the Indians and watch all promises be broken, all treaties violated. The crucible of this staged event pushes everyone back 100 years: The whites become an armed lynch mob, while each Native American must learn to become—and learn what it means to *be*—a warrior, complete with honor, loyalty and dignity. This is not your standard racial-tensions drama; its focus on the Indians is unusual, and its modern twist of sympathetic natives versus whites playing for keeps and not for *coup* predated the similar sensibilities of *Dances with Wolves*. The ending is powerful, shocking—and predestined.
Rent this one for: its sympathetic sensibilities; the scenery.
You'll (probably) like this if you liked: *Dances With Wolves, Last of the Dogmen, The Man Who Loved Cat Dancing*
Dissenting Opinion: • "...just another botched opportunity..." —MMG (2 stars) • "...not suitably developed" —VMG (2 stars) • "...impossible to take seriously." —SMV (2 stars) • "Unsubtle...therefore un-serious" —GMR (2 bones)
Vidbits: Dedicated to Spencer Eastman.

What's Eating Gilbert Grape

(1993; Paramount; PG-13; 1:58)

Starring: Johnny Depp, Leonardo DiCaprio, Juliette Lewis
Featuring: Mary Steenburgen, Crispin Glover, Darlene Cates
Written by: Peter Hedges (based on his novel)
Directed by: Lasse Hallström

Synopsis: Let's meet the Grape family! There's dad, who's dead; Momma (Cates), who weighs 500 pounds and hasn't left the house in seven years; accident-prone daughter Amy; teenage Ellen; and retarded Arnie, a 17-year-old who loves to climb trees (and the town water tower). Holding them all together in some semblance of sanity is 20-ish Gilbert (Depp)—and he's overburdened with responsibility. Good-hearted Gilbert has his hands full, stoically dealing with his megadysfunctional family—he's practically St. Gilbert of Grape. But even a saint can make mistakes—and even a saint can snap if pushed past his limit. Gilbert's limit arrives in the form of young Becky (Lewis), who's just passing through town. Her understanding and affection are the first things Gilbert's ever encountered that he wants purely for himself. But who'll hold the Grape bunch together if he chooses selfish love over his selfless duty to the family?
Discussion: "Nothing much ever happens" in rural Eudora, Iowa, Gilbert explains, "and nothing much ever will." He couldn't be more wrong—Eudora is overflowing with small-town drama; it's just all on a very humble, human scale. The plot is episodic, but it's the performances that are central—and uniformly excellent. Depp radiates melancholy, an innocent and wistful wisdom; Cates (in her film debut) hits just the right tone in a physically and emotionally demanding role; Lewis, as the wise waif, is particularly sweet and understated. Best of all is DiCaprio's sympathetic and uncannily accurate portrayal of retarded Arnie. (I worked with retarded kids for a year and can attest that his acting is gesture-perfect.) Add in some stunning photography and compassionate humor, and you've got a movie that will make you laugh out loud—and cry out loud.
Rent this one for: the performances; the sweet, oddball story.
You'll (probably) like this if you liked: *My Life As A Dog* (Hallström); *Benny & Joon* (Depp); *Running On Empty; Rain Man*
Credentials: • Oscar nomination: Supporting Actor (DiCaprio) • 1994 Golden Globe Award: Best Supporting Actor (DiCaprio) • '93 National Board of Review Award: Best Supporting Actor (DiCaprio) • "...special quality...is...its warmth." —Ebert (★★★★)
Dissenting Opinion: "You keep thinking something significant is going to happen, but nothing ever does..." —MMG (2.5)

White Hunter, Black Heart

(1990; MGM/UA; PG; 1:52)

Starring: Clint Eastwood, Jeff Fahey
Featuring: George Dzundza, Maria Berenson
Written by: Peter Viertel, James Bridges, Burt Kennedy
(based on Viertel's novel)
Directed by: Clint Eastwood

Synopsis: In the early 1950's, director John Wilson (Eastwood) packs up his cast and crew and heads for the shores of Lake Victoria to shoot an African adventure film. John develops a slightly different agenda, however; as he explains to his friend and script doctor Pete Verrill (Fahey), "We'll shoot the film after we've shot our elephants." Bagging the big game becomes his obsession, and he alienates everyone who opposes him, risking the film, his career and even his life to satisfy his twisted desire.
Discussion: "Of all the wild animals in Africa," his producer exclaims, "John Wilson is the wildest!" This thinly-veiled account of filming *The African Queen* under the capricious leadership of John Huston, based on Viertel's 1953 memoir-*cum*-novel, attempts to provide some insight into why. Discussions of Huston always use the same phrases: legendary, larger than life, full of Hemingway-style virtues like courage, nobility, honesty. And they are honor-bound to mention the other side of the Huston coin, too; i.e., his reputation as an abrasive, grandiose, bull-headed, egotistical bastard. Eastwood manages to portray every one of these character traits in this character study, while performing a low-key impersonation of the man himself, particularly the measured cadence and sing-song drawl of his speech. The intelligent dialog and Eastwood's excellent performance paint a vivid portrait of a man ruled by a passion for life and haunted by complex personal demons while remaining oddly committed to simplicity in story and deed. In addition, we attain some insight into the conflicts an artist suffers—and how these don't always result in art. The film is fascinating both as a bit of cinema history and as a character study of a rapidly vanishing breed: Not the elephant, but men like Huston, driven to explore the dark continents of their own psyches, sometimes striking oil—but sometimes striking tar.
Rent this one for: Eastwood's energetic portrayal of Huston; the unusual human story behind the creation of a classic film.
You'll (probably) like this if you liked: *African Queen, Chinatown* (Huston); *Hammett, The Stunt Man,* Huston's *Moby Dick*
Vidbits: • Filmed on location in Zimbabwe. • That must have been some shoot—Katharine Hepburn also got a book out of her experiences with Huston in Africa.

Wings of Desire

(fantasy; German and French with English subtitles)
(1988; Orion; PG-13; 2:10)

Starring: Bruno Ganz, Solveig Dommartin, Peter Falk
Written by: Wim Wenders, Peter Handke
Directed by: Wim Wenders

Synopsis: Angels walk among us. Innocent children sometimes see them. They listen in on our whispered inner monologs, often offering a comforting touch. One among them, Damiel (Ganz), is tired being a disembodied spirit, envying us our ability to touch, to feel, to love. When he becomes enamored of lonely French trapeze artist Marion (Dommartin), he decides to trade an eternity of observation for a few short mortal years of living experience. But first he must locate the missing Marion. Will destiny—or a guardian angel—allow their paths to cross again?
Discussion: Would you trade eternity for love? Renounce immortality for a transient, yet sensory, life? Evidently many angels do, as the lightness of their ethereal existence contrasts with the weight of their burden of separation. They speak, appropriately enough, in a kind of Rilkean poetry; and seeing the world through their eyes, as they pass through a library or a train car, allows us a glimpse of the ineffable sadness and longing that is our condition and their perception. With his world-weary face and deep soul-filled eyes, Ganz makes a perfect angel, and a fine human, too, responding with childlike delight to the mundane—colors, coffee, cold—and leaving us with one final question: Is it possible that a mortal life lived in love and wonder can transcend even the angelic? A lovely, somber dirge, filled with vivid imagery and a deep appreciation of the fleeting.
Rent this one for: its compassionate and contemplative inspiration; its delicately maintained tone of bittersweet poignance.
You'll (probably) like this if you liked: *Field of Dreams*
Credentials: • #2 on *Premiere* magazine's poll of 24 critics' "Best Movies of the '80s" list. • Voted #7 top foreign film of the '80s by 54 critics polled by *American Film.* • "...exquisite"—SMV (★★★★) • "A must-see" —MMG (3.5 stars) • "★★★★" —Roger Ebert
Dissenting Opinion: • "...denatured, spiritless and dull...a lifeless, joyless film..."—Barbara Shulgasser, S.F. *Examiner* • "...terribly overripe..." —Janet Maslin, *NY Times* • "...a sluggish, weary-winged fable...Sentimentality and meaninglessness: postmodern kitsch." —Pauline Kael, *New Yorker*
Vidbits: • Cinematographer Henri Alekan (for whom the film's circus is named) also shot Jean Cocteau's atmospheric *Orphée.* • Followed by a sequel, *Far Away, So Close.*

Working Girls

(slice-o'-life)

(1987; Charter Entertainment/Columbia TriStar; R; 1:33)

Starring: Louise Smith, Ellen McElduff, Amanda Goodwin, Marusia Zach, Janne Peters, Helen Nicholas
Written by: Lizzie Borden, Sandra Kay
Directed, co-produced and edited by: Lizzie Bordon

Synopsis: "Whore" is such a nasty word. They much prefer to be called "working girls." A small but classy apartment in a fashionable Manhattan district is "home" for this small business which employs a number of ladies of the evening (and afternoon). Molly (Smith), a lesbian on the verge of 30, does it to support her career as an artist. Dawn (Goodwin), a chesty blonde bimbo with an attitude problem, is putting herself through college. Gina (Zach), swarthy and sweet, knows no other life. This Day in the Life of a House (as in "of ill-repute") takes us from nooners through night shift, allowing us to sit in with the girls (who range from nervous first-timers to jaded old pros) as they "see" customers of every type: young and old; shy and cocksure; white, black and Asian; good, bad and ugly.
Discussion: Admit it: If you work for a living, you're selling your body—or at least renting it. It's the same for these "hostesses." It's just a job. They work their asses off (literally) for Lucy (McElduff), a fussy den mother full of "house rules" who still denies she runs a whorehouse, rather than "a nice place where nice people meet each other." They sit around the living room, waiting for their appointments, chatting and bitching about the boss, the job, their mates, and life in general, just like at any office. They have pet names for all their regular johns: "Fantasy Fred," "Honeymoon Joe." They share insights and tips ("One good thing about this job is that I've completely lost my fear of men," they all agree). And we sit in with them, eavesdropping on their sessions, sharing their secrets. There is plenty of drama in the interactions, along with a plethora of practical details. This fascinating film is just too matter-of-fact (and often too damn funny) to be erotic, obscene, pornographic or even very titillating. It's more akin to a documentary, in which everything you ever wondered about prostitution is revealed, stripped of all mystery and glamour. In the end, it's just another commodity.
Rent this one for: its sober, documentary-style depiction of a typical day in the life of an urban, middle-class business.
You'll (probably) like this if you liked: *Whore*
Vidbits: Funded in part by grants from the National Endowment for the Arts and the New York State Council on the Arts.

HORROR

HORROR

Blood is not horror. Blood is what passes for horror when imagination is removed. So you'll find no mad slasher flicks in these pages; no empty graves; no nightmare monsters.

What you *will* find, however, are the outlying edges of psychology and the shadowy fringes of the human mind. Fantasy asks, *What if...?* But horror asks... *What if something goes wrong?*

You'll find social commentary in a few of these films; you'll find mythology; you'll even find a bit of wit and a dollop of comedy.

You might even find that this smorgasbord of horror is a meal fit for a king—Stephen King, that is...

The Dead Zone

(1983; Paramount; R; 1:44)

Starring: Christopher Walken, Brooke Adams
Featuring: Tom Skerritt, Martin Sheen, Herbert Lom, Anthony Zerbe, Colleen Dewhurst
Written by: Jeffrey Boam (based on the novel by Stephen King)
Directed by: David Cronenberg

Synopsis: High school teacher Johnny Smith (Walken) crashes his car on a snowy road and falls into a coma—for five years. When he finally recovers, he discovers he's lost everything, including his fiancee, Sarah (Adams), who's now married and a mother. Almost as compensation, however, Johnny has gained "second sight"—the ability to foretell a person's destiny just by touching the person. This "gift," however, causes him nothing but grief; far too often, the visual flashes he receives involve violent death. He's branded a freak, and when his attempt to help a local sheriff (Skerritt) results in even deeper tragedy, he moves, changes his name, and becomes a hermit, tutoring to survive. At a political rally, a chance hand-grab by sociopathic Senate candidate Gregg Stillson (Sheen) hits Johnny with a vision he can't ignore: eventual President Stillson initiating a global nuclear war. Now Johnny's dilemma takes on a new dimension: Can he change the future as well as foresee it? Can he prevent this futureless future, or will any action he takes be frustrated and futile? And is he strong enough to do what it will take to prevent this popular lunatic from destroying the world?

Discussion: Not only is *Dead Zone* the best King adaptation to date, it's Cronenberg's best as well, here foregoing his typical gore and disgusting imagery in favor of the subdued, emotional aspects of the story. Ever-eerie Walken, with his pale skin, haunted eyes and electroshock hairdo, is perfectly cast. The sense of isolation and anguish that he suffers are tangible experiences, further enhanced by the glacial scenery of this winter's tale. And in the unpredictable, clever ending, elements of Johnny's own destiny converge in an ironic, bittersweet and satisfying manner.

Rent this one for: The chilling atmosphere; the palpable sense of isolation and anguish; the intelligent plot and twist ending.

You'll (probably) like this if you liked: *Carrie, The Shining* (good Stephen King adaptations); *Resurrection*

Dissenting Opinion: • "...ultimately promises more than it delivers" —PVG • "...slightly disappointing..." —SMV (2.5 stars)

Vidbits: Cronenberg was forced to reshoot the first premonition scene when Universal threatened to sue because a small "E.T." doll was visible in the burning bedroom.

Double Feature!

Evil Dead 2: Dead By Dawn

(1987; Vestron/LIVE; R; 1:24)

Army of Darkness

(1992; MCA; R; 1:17)

(comedy)

Starring: Bruce Campbell
Featuring: Dead 2: Sarah Berry, Dan Hicks, Theodore Raimi
Army: Embeth Davidtz, Marcus Gilbert, Theodore Raimi, Ivan Raimi
Written by: Dead 2: Sam Raimi, Scott Spiegel
Army: Sam Raimi, Ivan Raimi
Directed by: Sam Raimi

Synopsis: In *Evil Dead 2,* a weekend in a remote cabin in the mountains turns into a nightmare for Ash (Campbell) and his girlfriend Linda (Berry) when they discover a copy of *The Necronomicon,* a book of ancient magic spells left behind by an archeologist. The book has awakened Something Evil in the woods, which kills Linda then comes after Ash, who must fight off animated corpses and the possession of his own hand, among other horrors. In *Army of Darkness,* "It" returns—"big time"—and sucks Ash (and his car) back to 1300 A.D., where he is believed to be the "Promised One" destined to deliver the land from the sinister sorcery of the "Deadites." Ash embarks on a quest to recover the *Necronomicon,* his ticket home, but inadvertently awakens an army of evil undead, and reluctantly remains to fight the forces that have plagued him for so long.
Discussion: These two installments of Raimi's trilogy about housewares clerk Ash—square-jawed, hyper-serious and dirt-stupid—fighting supernatural forces are essentially live-action "Itchy and Scratchy" cartoons, and *Army,* a surreal lampoon of the swords and sorcery genre, might best be described as "Ray Harryhausen Meets the Three Stooges."

Three things make these movies memorable and worthy of multiple viewings. Least among them is the direction—but this covers so much ground it's impossible not to credit Raimi. He embraces every special effect technique ever invented, employing them in such an exaggerated manner that they become parodies of horror flick standards; and his hyperkinetic pace allows him to pack twice as much into each film as any but the most accomplished action director.

Second is the humor. Humorous horror flicks run the gamut from *Gremlins* to *Ghostbusters,* but Raimi has accomplished the impossible: making the gruesome humorous. Watching Ash laugh maniacally while gleefully lopping off his own possessed hand, for example, might be the most blood-spattered fun ever put on film. And reducing the skeletal army from mysterious supernatural menace to mundane "working stiffs" is a brilliant and witty cliché-breaker.

But the single center of gravity that elevates these freaky flicks to masterpiece status is Bruce Campbell. The movies simply would not work without his Ash, a Muppet Batman whose eyes are just a bit *too* intense and whose jaw just a bit *too* square make him anything but a comic book caricature of an action movie hero. Half dufus, half goofus; as surly as he is burly; a lunkhead punk as dumb as a box of hair with an attitude as big as his ego, Ash is the very antithesis of the stereotypical Hero (he spends much of each film screaming in mortal terror, or instance) and Campbell plays him with a deadpan intensity and a sure sense of why Ash is so damn funny. Whether he's faking an incantation, battling his demented evil twin or swaying a crowd from going Medieval on his ass with swaggering bravado and his "boom stick," he's too self-centered to let black magic best him, too modern to believe you can't fight phantoms with chainsaws and shotguns, too stupid to understand how clever he really is, too cowardly to believe he could really be a hero, and too shallow to understand that—despite all evidence to the contrary—he really is.

Rent these for: their gleefully gruesome humor.

You'll (probably) like these if you liked: *Re-Animator,* The Three Stooges, *Abbott and Costello Meet Frankenstein, Frankenhooker, Big Trouble in Little China; Darkman* (Raimi)

Credentials: "...essential viewing." —PVG

Vidbits: •• Raimi and Campbell have been friends since high school, when they often collaborated (with Sam's brother Ted) on super-8 films. •• *Evil Dead 2:* • One of Freddy Krueger's *(A Nightmare on Elm Street)* gloves hangs in the cellar of the cabin—Raimi's response to a scene from *Evil Dead* appearing on a TV set in *Nightmare.* •• *Army of Darkness:* • Bridget Fonda makes a brief appearance in a flashback in the opening sequence. • The incantation Ash must repeat to claim the *Necronomicon* ("Klaatu barada nikto") is the same phrase used to command the robot Gort in the SF classic *The Day The Earth Stood Still.* • Two endings were filmed: In the American version, Ash returns to the present where he battles the she-demon in his department store. In the version shown in Britain, he drinks a potion which will make him sleep a hundred years for each drop, then crawls to a cave to hibernate. He miscalculates and takes one drop too many, however, and wakes to a barren post-apocalyptic landscape a hundred years in the future, where he vents his wrath by screaming at the blood-red sky.

Flashback!

Exorcist II: The Heretic

(1977; Warner; R; 1:58)

Starring: Richard Burton, Linda Blair, Louise Fletcher
Featuring: Kitty Winn, James Earl Jones, Ned Beatty, Max von Sydow
Written by: William Goodhart
Music by: Ennio Morricone
Directed by: John Boorman

Synopsis: It's been four years since Father Merrin (von Sydow) exorcised a demon from Regan (Blair), now a typical teen with a gift for healing troubled youth. But Merrin's protégé, Father Lamont (Burton) has been assigned to investigate his death, which risks opening up old wounds—and summoning up old demons. Regan's psychiatrist, Dr. Tuskin (Fletcher), is wary, but allows them to use an advanced biofeedback device to hypnotize themselves into a "synchronized altered state of consciousness," where they share a virtual reality of memory. The machine proves scientifically that the demon is real—and still locked up inside her. Further "trips" convince Lamont that a tribal healer in Africa, also once possessed by this demon, holds the key to triumph over the "King of the Evil Spirits of the Air." Risking his life to find the grown boy is the easy part. But he'll risk his faith, and Regan's life, in a final confrontation—and their minds will become the battleground for this ancient evil.

Discussion: It's 20 years old and the most reviled sequel in cinema history. So what the *hell* is it doing in this book? Well, I think I know why audiences hated it—and why it should be given a second chance. People went to this sequel expecting more of the same: More turnstile heads; more pea soup puke. What they got was a philosophical treatise on science and religion working in harmony; a psychological study of a good man suffering a crisis in faith, and the trials he must endure to renew that faith; a conflict between our primal fear of ancient mysteries and our rational aspirations for human evolution; and a visionary trip through the mythological stratum of the psyche. Who wants that crap? Bring on the barf! If the movie has a weak point, it's not the script but the acting: Burton is aggressively hammy in his agony; Fletcher is a lethargic cardboard cutout; Blair, pudgy and vapid. Points in its favor, however, begin with the direction. Boorman suffuses the film with symbology, from the obvious to the subtle—Lamont under the spell of the locust-demon, for instance, "brushing wings" with the crowds on the street and in the train station. There is symbology of color and light not just in every scene, but in virtually every *shot.* Even clothing colors change to reflect the characters' psychological states. Notice the regular appearances of flashing lights—emergency vehicles, stage lights, the sun, marquee signs—subliminal repetitions of the "synchronizer" device, unconsciously cueing us that these characters are walking between two worlds: the waking world of the conscious mind and the archetype-inhabited realm of the unconscious. Watch the lights; watch the reflections; watch the way images overlap to indicate the overlapping levels consciousness. This remarkable achievement in direction gives the film an hypnotic, almost hallucinatory, tone, mirroring the interpenetration of worlds that Lamont is experiencing. His task is to enter this internal realm, face his—and Regan's—demons, and have faith that he can find his way back to rationality. Once exposed to the light of consciousness, the monsters of the unconscious cannot survive. The ending is a brilliant bringing-together of the main elements, where the action is simultaneously literal *and* symbolic. Are there "really" two Regans? Of course not. Is there "really" a plague of locusts? No: it's clear that these events are not taking place on the material plane. And the symbol system makes it very clear when they *do* re-enter "reality." "I understand now," Tuskin tells Lamont near the end of the film. "The world won't. Not yet." Maybe Boorman understood his own experiment too well. Maybe 20 years ago the world wasn't ready for a film of this mystical nature. Maybe in today's action blockbuster market, it's still not. But, if you've read any Jung or Joseph Campbell, maybe *you* are ready to appreciate this mythological movie, and to appreciate it as a thought-provoking spiritual horror story: not a bomb, but a time bomb.

Rent this one for: being modern mythology; for its central allegory of religious faith for once *cooperating* with science; for Boorman's handling of complex symbology in the imagery.

You'll (probably) like this if you liked: *The Fisher King, The Omen* (modern mythology); *Equus* (Burton as a psychiatrist, suffering a crisis of faith); *Mr. Frost, The Prophecy* (The Devil as real creature); *Paperhouse, Dreamscape, A Nightmare on Elm Street* (action in the unconscious); *8-1/2* (mid-life crisis)

Dissenting Opinion: • The 1993 edition of the GMR gave this "one bone" (out of a possible four), but upgraded it to "two bones" in the 1995 edition. • The VMG is consistent in its lowest rating: "turkey." • "Highly unsatisfactory...falls flat on its face...released in two versions and is unintelligible in either." —HFG • "Preposterous...turkey"—MMG (1.5 stars) • "...a metaphysical muddle that the director couldn't salvage despite drastic recutting after disastrous screenings." —*Premiere* (9/95) • "...may be the worst sequel in the history of film." —SMV (1/2 star) • One of "Ten Worst of Genre" —*People Magazine's Guide to Movies on Video*

Leviathan

(science fiction/ suspense)
(1989; MGM/ UA; R; 1:38)

Starring: Peter Weller, Richard Crenna, Amanda Pays, Daniel Stern, Ernie Hudson, Hector Elizondo
Featuring: Lisa Eilbacher, Meg Foster, Michael Carmine
Written by: David Peoples, Jeb Stuart
Music by: Jerry Goldsmith
Directed by: George P. Cosmatos

Synopsis: Three miles beneath the Atlantic, deep sea miners extract precious metals from the ocean floor on a 90-day "extremely hazardous" shift. When they find a sunken Russian ship, Sixpack (Stern) confiscates the safe, which is filled with the personal effects of numerous crew members who died from some mysterious malady. He also filches a bottle of vodka, which makes him deathly ill—then kills him. The Doc's (Crenna) best guess is a virus causing genetic alteration. Good call: it transforms Sixpack into a slimy, gut-crunching creature, half human, half deep-sea creature. When the thing goes on a rampage looking for new meat and tearing up the station in the process, can any of the others escape? And why is The Company dragging its feet in sending in a rescue?
Discussion: Call it *Alien from the Abyss;* when first released, the comparisons were inevitable (and fair). And how could it measure up to either? As a pastiche, however, it's entertaining enough for those who enjoyed the originals. So the script's not original? It's still a solid thriller, and the flick's main draw lies not in its oft-told story of sacrificed miners versus an alien killing machine and a corrupt corporation, but in its suitably detailed sets, its atmospheric photography, and its cast of second bananas with appeal. And it's not as though the writers were trying to put one over on us; the fact that it's a conscious homage to *Alien* is made perfectly clear with the inclusion of a slyly clever shot panning across a big bowl of popcorn just prior to the chest-chomping monster's first appearance. Enjoy it for what it is: a mutant B-remake of two superior thrillers.
Rent this one for: the cast; the atmospheric photography.
You'll (probably) like this if you liked: *The Abyss, Alien*
Dissenting Opinion: • "...leave this one alone" —VMG (2 stars) • "Yet one more dreadful *Alien* clone...Skip it." —MMG (1.5 stars)
Vidbits: Peoples wrote the final draft of *Blade Runner,* and would write the screenplays for Eastwood's *Unforgiven* and, with his wife Janet, for Gilliam's *12 Monkeys.* Stuart wrote *Die Hard* and *The Fugitive,* among other scripts.

Paperhouse

(dark psychological fantasy)
(1987; Vestron; PG-13; 1:34)

Starring: Charlotte Burke, Elliott Spiers, Glenne Headly
Written by: Matthew Jacobs
(based on the novel *Marianne Dreams* by Catherine Storr)
Directed by: Bernard Rose

Synopsis: 11-year-old Anna (Burke) is experiencing nightmares and odd fainting spells. Even more curious, whenever she's unconscious she finds herself in the same landscape: an open field in which the only structure is the strangely-shaped house she's been sketching in her notepad. As she falls more ill, her dreams continue—and evolve. She enters the house and meets its sole inhabitant: Marc (Spiers), a boy about 12, crippled from the waist down. Only when Anna's doctor mentions she's treating a boy named Marc for paralysis does Anna realize her drawings are a door into an inner world where they are bonded emotionally—and that what she draws comes true. Too bad, because she's recently added a dark stalker to her drawing—and then lost the drawing. In her fever dreams, she and Marc are able to fight off this evil figure long enough for Anna to regain her health. Marc, however, is not so lucky, and a distraught Anna must decide whether to forget him...or follow him into a world beyond drawings, beyond dreams—and beyond death.
Discussion: How thin is the membrane between fantasy and reality? Is it permeable by osmosis in both directions? One of the nicest things about this film is that we never doubt the actuality of the psychic connection between the kids; it's proven real, and its mystery is never cheapened by any pseudo-scientific explanations. The manner in which Anna's inner and waking worlds overlap, and the correspondences between them, are logical, consistent and clever: The two worlds are, we realize, not separated by fact, but only by one's state of mind. Although the film gets off to a slow start, it's worth the wait: it's filled with beautiful, honey-hued photography as well as startling and haunting imagery. The plight of the abject adolescent, dealing with grief far too deep for her tender age, is effectively poignant, and the bittersweet ending strangely satisfying.
Rent this one for: its imaginative and logical fantasy; for a visceral experience: a good scare; a good cry.
You'll (probably) like this if you liked: *A Nightmare on Elm Street; Dreamscape; Truly, Madly, Deeply;* "The Twilight Zone"
Vidbits: Director Rose got his start in music videos; this was his first feature.

Pulse

(science fiction)
(1988; RCA/Columbia; PG-13; 1:30)

Starring: Cliff De Young, Roxanne Hart, Joey Lawrence
Written and directed by: Paul Golding

Synopsis: 8-year-old David (Lawrence) isn't very happy about spending his summer vacation in suburban L.A. with his workaholic father and dad's new wife. But he's intrigued by the neighborhood mystery: The guy across the street went nuts after his wife was killed in a freak accident, and literally gutted his house in an orgy of violence. When David is left alone one night, the TV and appliances begin behaving in a very peculiar manner—just like the nutcase claimed was happening in *his* house. And when David sneaks into the ruined house looking for clues, an old electrician (Charles Tyner) tells him about the "thing" that lives in the power lines. He's just telling scary tales, daddy Bill (De Young) decides—until David nearly dies in an electrical garage mishap—and then his wife Ellen (Hart) has her own life-threatening electrical mishap. Are these events all just bizarre coincidence—or will Bill and David be forced to fight for their lives, and for their freedom, from their own home?
Discussion: What do you do—and where do you go—when your own house is trying to kill you? This suburban horror story casts a sly eye on sinister images of ordinary household items. We all take electricity for granted; the insidious center of this flick lies in investing energy itself with a malevolent intelligence, made all the more chilling by its amorphous nature and ubiquitous presence. Mesmerizing close-ups of circuits, dissolving wire wraps, and solder melting and reforming as the current reprograms the appliances make the most mundane machines appear malicious. *Pulse* begins slowly, but builds into a killer thriller in the final half hour and includes some excellent effects in the finale, as the house literally holds the humans hostage. Teen idol Joey (*"Whoa!"*) Lawrence is cute, but Tyner, as the eccentric old electrician who provides the exposition, is the real scene stealer. You'll probably want to leave a light on when you watch this one. Then again, *maybe not...*
Rent this one for: the interesting plot; the effects in the finale.
You'll (probably) like this if you liked: *Demon Seed*
Credentials: "...a genuine sci-fi sleeper." — PVG (3 diamonds)
Dissenting Opinion: "Turkey" —VMG
Vidbits: • Lawrence's little brother Matthew plays his neighbor friend. • Cop #1 at the beginning is Tim Russ, "Mr. Tuvak" on "Star Trek: Voyager."

They Live

(social satire)
(1988; MCA; R; 1:28)

Starring: "Rowdy" Roddy Piper, Keith David, Meg Foster
Written by: "Frank Armitage" *(pseudonym of John Carpenter)*
(based on the story "Eight O'Clock in the Morning" by Ray Nelson)
Music by: John Carpenter and Alan Howarth
Directed by: John Carpenter

Synopsis: Being a homeless, out-of-work drifter is a tough life. Tougher when work is scarce, unions are closed, and the rich keep getting richer while the poor suffer. "Nada" (Piper) finds all this out the hard way, and when he sneaks into a suspicious church and steals a pair of sunglasses, he finds out why: Aliens control us. The special lenses manufactured by an underground liberation movement enable real people to see through the hypnotic facade created to keep us "asleep." And what Nada sees is skull-faced aliens and subliminal messages in magazines, billboards and on TV; commands like OBEY, SUBMIT, CONFORM and WATCH TV. *They* don't like anyone who can "see," and come after Nada. Fortunately, he finds his way back to the small band of freedom fighters determined to destroy the broadcast tower transmitting *Their* hypnotic signals through our TV sets. What can a handful of working stiffs do to stop the country from being taken over by rich, powerful aliens? Plenty.
Discussion: Carpenter's working class paranoid fantasy is satire as dark, funny and violent as his *Escape From New York.* It's a throwback to grade-Z sci-fi flicks of the '50s, but with a modern twist: a parody of simple minds searching for concrete, simple-minded solutions to the complex problems of a crazy economy and a society gone insane. What simpler solution could there be than evil aliens conspiring with the greedy, traitorous "human power elite" to sell humanity out for a Rolex and a taste of the Good Life? Any literal-minded xenophobe can understand that! And of course the "lower-class cattle" have to be kept sedated with hypnotic TV and subliminal advertising. There's plenty of reactionary black humor here, played dead seriously—as well as plenty of fighting, bullets and blood. And not too many words!
Rent this one for: being the first blue-collar horror flick.
You'll (probably) like this if you liked: *Invasion of the Body Snatchers, 1984, The Hidden, The Puppet Masters,* "V"
Dissenting Opinion: • "★★" —VMG • "...doesn't take [the idea] far enough." —SMV (3 stars)
Vidbits: Look for cameos by Siskel and Ebert—as ruling class aliens, naturally—admonishing Carpenter for his violence.

Flashback!

The Wicker Man

(occult)

(1973; Magnum, Media Home Entertainment; NR; 1:43)*

Starring: Edward Woodward, Christopher Lee, Britt Ekland
Featuring: Diane Cilento, Ingrid Pitt
Written by: Anthony Shaffer
Directed by: Robin Hardy

Synopsis: Sgt. Neil Howie (Woodward) is an upright man: a good Catholic, a policeman, and a middle-aged virgin, dour and humorless. A real saint. When he visits an island off the coast of Scotland to investigate the alleged disappearance of a young girl, he is more scorned than welcomed. Summerisle is an odd place: Couples copulate in the street; near-naked nymphs dance around bonfires; young men are "presented" to beautiful Willow (Eklund) as "sacrifices to Aphrodite." Howie's response is to pray for their heathen souls. Frustrated in his investigation, he seeks the help of the island's mysterious master, Lord Summerisle (Lee), who explains the isle's religion of nature worship. Howie begins to believe that the child is not dead, but will be used as a human sacrifice in some "pagan barbarity" at the climax of the frenzied rites on their holy day of death and regeneration, May Day. Tomorrow. Can he find her in time? Or is her disappearance merely part of an even more sinister plot afoot?
Discussion: "I hope you don't think that I can be made a fool of indefinitely," Sgt. Howie growls. Well, they *are* counting on it... This intelligent primer in paganism pits a modern Christian against ancient forces of nature. Will his God forsake him? Or will he learn the hard way the parallels between the blood sacrifices of paganism and the martyrdom of Jesus? All the clues are given to Howie, and he is offered every possible chance to save himself from his fate. But he is too prig-headed to believe or accept his salvation. His fate—illustrated in the harrowing and unexpected ending—stands as a warning of the consequences of religious intolerance and a closed-minded attitude.
Rent this one for: its unique, intelligent and intriguing theme and plot; for being the only Pagan horror film—and a sympathetic one, at that! (And—boys only—for Eklund's dance scene.)
You'll (probably) like this if you liked: *Rosemary's Baby, The Fisher King, Exorcist II: The Heretic* (modern movie mythology)
Credentials: "...a must-see." —MMG (3.5 stars)
Dissenting Opinion: "...[a] disturbing sexual parable..." —SMV
Vidbits: * The 1:43 version is the restored director's cut. Beware of shorter, edited versions.

Kidvid/ Family Fare

Kidvid / Family Fare

Although it might come as a shock, the movies in this section *aren't* for kids. They just happen to be classified as "kidvid," and are most often found in the children's sections of video stores.

But the delightful surprise is that these features appeal to the child in all of us. They contain enough intelligent material to keep even the hippest adults interested—*and* they're suitable for the entire family, from six to 106.

What more could you ask for? (Sorry, no free rentals...)

Batman: Mask of the Phantasm

(animation)

(1993; Warner; PG; 1:17)

Featuring the voice talents of: Kevin Conroy (Batman), Dana Delany (Andrea Beaumont), Mark Hamill (The Joker), Stacy Keach (Carl Beaumont), Efrem Zimbalist, Jr. (Alfred)
Also featuring the voices of: Hart Bochner, Abe Vigoda, Dick Miller, John P. Ryan, Bob Hastings
Written by: Michael Reeves, Alan Burnett, Paul Dini, Martin Pako
Directed by: Eric Radomski, Bruce W. Timm

Synopsis: The one woman Bruce Wayne ever loved returns, after disappearing for a decade. But their chance at happiness is complicated by his secret life as The Batman, which he sees as incompatible with ever having a normal, private home life. Meanwhile, The Batman has his share of problems as well: A mysterious figure is killing off criminals in Gotham City—and the only connection seems to be the father of Bruce's ex-lover.
Discussion: This feature version of the Emmy Award-winning animated TV series works as well as the best of the live-action Batman movies—and better than most of them. The plot is intriguing, logical and unpredictable, and the gothic Gotham City looks like some nightmare offspring of 1930's Art Deco and '50s *film noir* angles and shadows. Although the animation is limited in places, the artists often use this to their advantage: all we really need to see sometimes to send a shiver up our spines is the silhouette of a peak-eared cape in the shadows. *B:MP* is always interesting to look at, the finale is striking, and the style perfectly matches the emotion. And that's the real unexpected bonus of this movie: *emotion.* Against all odds, it's difficult not to be affected by this flick. Anyone who's ever lost a loved one, to death or dissolution, can relate to Wayne—the "dark knight of the soul," to coin a phrase. Not bad for a kiddie cartoon! (It will, however, be best appreciated by older kids.) One minor complaint is the numerous flashback sequences, told from too many different points of view. But those involving the origin of The Batman, at any rate, are fascinating.
Rent this one for: its visual and emotional *film noir* qualities.
You'll (probably) like this if you liked: the *Batman* films.
Dissenting Opinion: "...hampered by mediocre animation" —MMG (2.5 stars)
Vidbit: • In a reversal of the typical process, this was originally intended to go straight to video, but was released theatrically instead. • According to *Premiere* (1/96), artists creating the digital Gotham City sets in *Batman Forever* used the computer database for this film as their starting point.

Cartoons For Big Kids

(animation)

What's a movie without a cartoon? While this question will make no sense to an entire generation, those of us who grew up "going to the movies" still bemoan the fact that all we get now is previews and commercials—no cartoons. It's important to remember that cartoons were originally intended for adult theatrical audiences. Only with the rise of TV did cartoons become kidvid territory. Most animated shorts made the transition smoothly (think Mickey, Bugs & pals), but there were a handful banned as too mature. They gathered dust in studio vaults until recently, when they found a new audience on video. These cartoons are violent, anarchistic, often blatantly sexual and regularly include ethnic caricatures which would be labeled racially insensitive in today's Politically Correct climate. They're packed with references to pop culture of the '40s—star caricatures, radio and movie taglines, rationing jokes—which might occasionally be unfathomable. At best, however, their humor is timeless, manic and surreal. Think of these forgotten featurettes as Mel Brooks on steroids and speed: If you don't find a gag funny, another will be along in a second (literally). Below, four collections to enhance your "home theater" experience. Just run one of the shorts from these compilations before your chosen "Killer B" feature film, and do for yourself what theaters won't. While these might not be the best cartoons ever made, they can qualify as the best cartoons you've (probably) never seen. (This entire list counts as one entry of the 237 *Killer B's*.)

• "Cartoons for Big Kids"

(1989; N/A; NR; :44)

Leonard Maltin hosts this compilation of four unusual entries, including "King-Size Canary," in which household pets takes turns swilling a super-growth formula to turn the tables on their chases; "The Great Piggy-Bank Robbery," a Dick Tracy lampoon in which Daffy Duck turns into "Duck Twacy" and encounters a parade of comic villains (and a great Carl Stalling score); "The Big Snooze," in which a finally frustrated Fudd tears up his contract, and Bugs Bunny must invade his dreams to convince him not to break up their "Rabbit & Costello" act—and which echoes such classic surreal and psychedelic sequences as Dumbo's drunk scene, Tex Avery's wolf packs and Chuck Jones' "Duck Amok." The high point, though, is Avery's risqué "Red Hot Riding Hood"—the inspiration for much of Eddie Valiant's Toontown troubles in *Who Framed Roger Rabbit?*

• "The Adventures of Superman"

(1941-43; Bridgestone Multimedia; NR; 3 volumes; :50 each)

Only three years after Superman made his comic book debut, Fleischer Studios produced this legendary series, which boasts detailed animation, cinema-style direction and fabulous noir sensibilities. As they are public domain, any number of collections of two or three of these cartoons are available—and on most, the quality sucks. Bridgestone's 50th birthday collection features all 17 original cartoons, stuck from 35mm prints, plus a bonus wartime parody, "Snafuperman." Up, up and away!

• "Beany & Cecil"

(1960; RCA/Columbia; G; 10 volumes, :40 each)

Baby boomers grew up on this TV series created by cartoon vet Bob Clampett. Cecil the Seasick Sea Serpent stars in these gentle, fun-filled pun-fests, along with Beany-boy, the cowardly "Uncle Captain" Huffenpuff, and, of course, dastardly villain, Dishonest John (perhaps Snidely Whiplash's twin brother, but with his own distinctive laugh, "*Nyah*-ah-ahhh!"). Many of the jokes went over kids' heads, and still will, but adults will roar. Vol. 1 alone features six shorts, including my own all-time favorite, "Wildman of Wildsville." The crew travels to the "Hungry i-land" to capture a beatnik Tarzan, replete with bongos, goatee, beret and a complement of cool beatnik patois, daddy-o. Proof that these are for adults: What kid could recognize the splatter backgrounds as a nod to Jackson Pollock? But what kid could resist lines like, "I'm so hip I can't even eat a square meal!"?

• "The Best of Roger Rabbit"

(1995; Disney; G & PG; :25)

Roger is unquestionably the "hare apparent" to Bugs Bunny creator Tex Avery's surreal, screwball throne. Yet you probably haven't seen these cartoons unless you were forced to escort a child to the theatrical release of a Disney kid flick. All three entries—"Tummy Trouble," "Roller Coaster Rabbit" and "Trail Mix-Up"—warp the laws of physics, pile on the gags and action at warp speed, and benefit from directing techniques even the most warped cartoonist of the '40s could never have imagined. These vivid, turbocharged tributes to the frantic energy of their predecessors are both exhilarating and exhausting.

Rent these for: their status as rediscovered adult classics.

You'll (probably) like them if you liked: *Who Framed Roger Rabbit?, The Mask, Airplane!,* "Rocky and Bullwinkle" cartoons

Explorers

(adventure/fantasy/comedy)
(1985; Paramount; PG; 1:46)

Starring: Ethan Hawke, River Phoenix, Jason Presson
Featuring: Mary Kaye Place, Dick Miller, Meshach Taylor
Written by: Eric Luke
Directed by: Joe Dante

Synopsis: Sci-fi addict Ben (Hawke), electronic genius Wolfgang (Phoenix) and tough, poor Darren (Presson) are an unlikely trio of junior high school friends, drawn together because they are outsiders. One night Ben dreams a circuit board; when Wolf builds it, a powerful force field shoots from his computer. They refine the field into an "inertialess bubble," raid a junkyard for parts, and cobble together an unsightly flying machine. Things get strange on their fun-filled test flight, and stranger still when they all dream the same dream showing them how they can use the rig to travel to space. It's as if they're being called—and what kid could resist an invitation to come out and play? After all, kids will be kids—no matter where in the galaxy they come from.
Discussion: Call it *Close Encounters for Kids.* It's a throwback to the Disney fantasy flicks of the '60s, with a bit of *TRON* tossed in for color. The SFX might not be up to today's digital ideals, but they're seamless, occasionally impressive and fill the film, keeping it visually interesting. And just because the ending doesn't fit doesn't invalidate the entire film. While the ending ignores the movie's earlier sense of wonder, it is pretty funny, as goofy as a cartoon—and does finally end upbeat and sweet.
Rent this one for: the sense of wonder in the first half.
You'll (probably) like this if you liked: *Gremlins, Flight of the Navigator, The Goonies, Escape to Witch Mountain*
Dissenting Opinion: • "...probably not for popular consumption" —HFG • "...all [the film] delivers is one—count it—*one* lame joke."—PVG (1 diamond) • "...makes disastrous wrong turn...that transforms film into a shaggy-dog joke!" —MMG (2 stars) • "... poorly structured...What starts off as an enchanting adventure turns bizarre." —SMV (2 stars) • "...too clever for its own good." —*People Magazine Guide to Movies on Video*
Vidbits: • Inside jokes: A newspaper headline reads "Kingston Falls Mystery Still Unsolved," referring to the town and events in Dante's previous flick, *Gremlins*; the junior high school is named after Bugs Bunny animator Chuck Jones; Robert Picardo, who plays the alien Wak, is also the star of *Starkiller,* the drive-in movie within the movie. Nowadays he's best known as the "emergency medical hologram" on "Star Trek: Voyager."

The 5,000 Fingers of Dr. T

(comedy)

(1953; RCA/Columbia; G; 1:29)

Starring: Hans Conried, Tommy Rettig
Featuring: Peter Lind Hayes, Mary Healy
Written by: Dr. Seuss, Allan Scott
Directed by: Roy Rowland

Synopsis: Bart (Rettig), is sevenish, fatherless and forced by his mother into endless piano practice. But key-bored Bart has a bad habit of nodding off at the ivories, and in his worst nightmare, he's a captive of Dr. Terwilliker's (Conried) "Happy Fingers Institute," a kind of keyboard concentration camp for kids, who are kept in cells and forced to perform on the world's weirdest piano. Worst of all, Bart's mom is the megalomaniacal Dr. T's right-hand gal—and fiancé! Bart gets his ally Mr. Zabladowski (Hayes) to try to put an end to this misery, but Dr. T plies Mr. Z with cigars and pickle juice, fancy dances and hypnotic trances —then orders him disintegrated at dawn. It's up to Bart to save them all, "wreck his racket," and make the world safe for play.
Discussion: The same year we lost Dr. Seuss we gained the video release of the only live-action film to recreate the singular artistic style he introduced to several generations of kids. Seuss wrote the song lyrics, co-wrote the script, and designed the look of this imaginative fantasy, ensuring it's a faithful translation of his uniquely surreal visions. Unique? What other film boasts Escher-inspired staircases, mile-high ladders ending in thin air, or roller-skating twins with a Siamese beard? Rettig, with his bulgy eyes, unruly crew-cut and goofy Seuss looks, is perfectly cast, as is "master thespian" Conried, an underrated, over-the-top living 'toon. Even Hayes is hilarious as the plumber with a deadpan delivery and a heart of a child—who knows in that heart he's only acting the role of an adult.
Rent this one for: the Seuss influence: his only non-animated movie, which captures the essence of his daring drawings and skewed humor; for a surreal peek inside a child's mind.
You'll (probably) like this if you liked: *How The Grinch Stole Christmas, Yellow Submarine, Twice Upon a Time, Willie Wonka*
Credentials: "...one of the best surrealistic fantasies ever made." —PEF
Dissenting Opinion: "Badly scripted fantasy" —HFG
Vidbits: • Rettig later starred in the "Lassie" TV series. Like many child stars who find themselves adult "has-beens," he was arrested several times on drug charges in the '70s. He later founded a computer company, and died in early 1996 at age 54.

Into The West

(1995; Touchstone; PG; 1:47)

Starring: Gabriel Byrne, Ellen Barkin, Colm Meaney
Introducing: Ruaidhi Conroy, Ciaran Fitzgerald
Written by: Jim Sheridan (based on a story by Michael Pearce)
Directed by: Mike Newell

Synopsis: A magnificent, pure white stallion appears on an Irish shore. It follows an itinerant tinker into the slums of Dublin, where the old man has come to visit his grandchildren and their father, "Papa" (Byrne). Papa was once king of the gypsies, or "Travelers," but he's turned his back on the old ways since the tragic loss of his beloved wife. Now he's determined to give his kids a better life, even if he's ill-suited for the modern world. Young Ossie (Fitzgerald) takes to the horse like a brother, and tries to hide her in their apartment. The police take her away and sell her to a rich breeder—but the boys track her down and reclaim her, then hightail it through town and country on a comic odyssey into the West, where outlaws like they've become can be free. Meanwhile, the sinister businessman, corrupt cops and worried Travelers (including Barkin and Meaney) compete to locate the kids before tragedy strikes.

Discussion: Mythology never dies. It can be forgotten, though —or change faces. For the Travelers, the ancient Irish myths are living entities. For the kids, raised in the city, Cowboys and Indians on TV have replaced the old stories. But these can be just as effective in guiding their lives. The kids are adorable and determined, agile and clever, and engage in numerous close shaves and hilarious adventures; if they're vague about their eventual destination, their horse is not. When all the pieces finally fall into place and we discover the true nature and identity of the haunting horse—and its incredible mission—we realize why the old stories never die: They live forever in our hearts. And when we're very lucky, they live in films like this heartfelt celebration of the redemptive power of love and myth. A poignant, joyous, charming, ethereal film, and one to cherish.

Rent this one for: the endearing kids; the breathtaking photography of glorious scenery; the horse's performance; the magical integration of ancient Irish myth and modern Irish life.

You'll (probably) like this if you liked: *The Black Stallion, Secret of Roan Inish, Lady In White*

Credentials: Named "one of the year's best movies" by the L.A. *Times,* the Chicago *Tribune* and *Entertainment Weekly.*

Vidbit: • Byrne and Barkin were married at the time of the production, but have since divorced. • Writer Jim Sheridan is better known as a director (*My Left Foot*).

The Journey of Natty Gann

(coming-of-age tale)
(1985; Disney; PG; 1:41)

Starring: Meredith Salenger, John Cusack, Ray Wise
Featuring: Scatman Crothers, Lainie Kazan, Verna Bloom
Written by: Jeanne Rosenberg
Music by: James Horner
Directed by: Jeremy Paul Kagan

Synopsis: Chicago, 1935: Sol Gann (Wise) gets himself a steady job—a real coup in the Depression. There's one catch, however: it's in Washington State, 2,000 miles away. He's got to take it—and when he gets some money he'll send for his adolescent daughter Natty (Salenger). But she's impatient, independent—and in trouble. She hops a west-bound freight train, and in a whistle stop town rescues a wolf from a savage dog-fighting ring. Following a train wreck which leaves her lost and alone in the Colorado wilderness, the wolf repays the debt by protecting her against the elements. They form a fond bond of mutual protection which sees them through numerous misadventures and life-threatening events, as she searches for a father who believes she's dead—a father she refuses to believe abandoned her.
Discussion: The English language has retired a number of descriptive words, like *pluck, grit* and *scrap*. Natty Gann has all these traits, in spades. Her cross-country pilgrimage is as much a journey of maturity as geography, and she eventually graduates as a resourceful and triumphant "road scholar," finding treachery everywhere and love in the least likely places. We're taught in College that anthropomorphism is a Bad Thing, but this film is not afraid of the big bad "Wolf": an unusual traveling companion, surely—but one on a search ironically similar to Natty's. Their affectionate connection is not just a high point of this film, but the one that sets it apart from similar films. Another such element is the gorgeous photography, whether of excellent recreations of the threadbare Depression-era city, or of the exquisite forest landscapes of the American West. Never maudlin or manipulative, this period adventure of a girl and her wolf, living by their grit and wits, is a heartwarming charmer.
Rent this one for: its original and ultimately uplifting story.
You'll (probably) like this if you liked: *King of the Hill, Sullivan's Travels, Dances With Wolves,* "The Waltons"
Credentials: "★★★★★" —VMG
Vidbit: • The wolf was actually played by a dog, Jed. • Hard to believe, but the same production company responsible for this family classic also produced the Demi Moore flick *Striptease.*

Little Man Tate

(1991; Orion; PG; 1:39)

Starring: Jodie Foster, Dianne Wiest, Adam Hann-Byrd
Featuring: Harry Connick, Jr., David Pearce, Debi Mazar
Written by: Scott Frank
Directed by: Jodie Foster

Synopsis: Fred (Hann-Byrd) could read at age two, and by the time he's seven, it's pretty obvious to his single mom Dede (Foster) that he isn't like the other kids. That she loves him is obvious—and that he's starving for the kind of intellectual stimulation that her working class lifestyle can't provide him with is painfully obvious. Reluctantly, she allows him to go on a three-week road trip with other brilliant kids under the care and tutelage of Dr. Jane Grierson (Wiest), head of an institute for gifted youth. Fred performs head and shoulders above the others—but learns that "you can't go home again." Against her better judgment, Dede allows Fred to live with the fastidious Dr. G. for the summer. Disappointments and a near tragedy spur a mother and child reunion, to share some practical wisdom of the heart.
Discussion: "It's not so much what he *knows*," Jane's assistant (Pearce) says of Fred with awe, "but what he *understands*." Fred is the exact opposite of the other gifted kids: Where they are arrogant, shallow overachievers, Fred just wants to be a normal kid with friends. His genius is also his curse. Hann-Byrd—pale, aged-faced, sensitive and pensive—is a welcome relief from the typical annoyingly precocious TV kid. Wiest, too, is a wonder: a fussy, disciplined, brilliant but unblossomed bookworm, with no clue how to handle a child's nightmare. And just as Fred is the flip-side of the other kids, the tough, aggressively affectionate Dede (whose wise-cracking is the only antidote to Fred's dead serious demeanor) is the diametrical opposite of Jane. Jane lives life from the neck up; Dede just lives life. Dede is fiercely protective of her precious prodigy, and her tender surrender of Fred is a visible sacrifice. She knows, though, that only together with Jane can their opposing spirits provide Fred the rounded development he needs—the only way he can become a balanced individual rather than just another warped *wunderkind*. Foster (a *wunderkind* herself in her directorial debut at age 28) goes beyond competent direction to show flashes of brilliance, as when we "see" the altered mental state of Fred's genius at work.
Rent this one for: The depth of character; the performances.
You'll (probably) like this if you liked: *Searching for Bobby Fischer*
Dissenting Opinion: "...falls just short of being special." —SMV
Vidbit: Bob Balaban plays the quizmaster in an uncredited bit.

My Neighbor Totoro

(animated adventure)

(1988; FoxVideo; G; 1:26; dubbed)

Written and directed by: Hayao Miyazaki

Synopsis: May is 5 years old and her sister Satsuki 10 or 11 when Dad moves them to a new house in rural Japan. Just because Mom is in the hospital doesn't stop them from enjoying the beautiful countryside. They love their new home—even if rumor has it that it's haunted. Well, if the house isn't, the forest nearby certainly is, as May discovers when she stumbles upon the lair of Totoro, a giant, gentle forest spirit. And when May sets off alone on a cross-country quest to visit her mom, it's up to Totoro and his strange fantasy friends to find and rescue her.
Discussion: Miyazaki has been dubbed "the Walt Disney of Japan," and if this entry doesn't quite rival Disney's detailed drawings, its photorealistic backgrounds and lovely watercolors more than compensate for its limited fluidity. Beyond the merely visual, *Totoro* proves a rare treat both in its realism and its imagination. Someone spent considerable time observing children, as their movements, reactions and expressions are superbly realistic—right down to the occasionally annoying voices. *Totoro* magically captures the essence of children—rambunctious, energetic, mercurial—and the film is childlike without ever being childish. Much of the movie isn't fantasy at all, but a pastoral idyll of childhood and its intensely-felt emotions: wonder, joy, fear. The character-driven humor is funny without being forced—even when the character is a fantasy figure. And every time fantasy is introduced, the movie simply soars. Totoro looks like some mutant hybrid between a fuzzy bunny and a blimp; he (it?) wears a wide Cheshire cat smile and makes noises like whale belches. Other characters rival the best of Dr. Seuss for surreal originality. And the scene involving trees growing like smoke under a full moon recalls Peter Pan's flight over London with the Darling children in its ecstatic magic. "Darling" is an appropriate word here, as are "sweet" and "innocent." If you find children, at their best, adorable, this film will win a space in your heart. If not—at least rent it for them. Watch it with a 4-to-6 year old, and you'll both be bewitched—and enriched.
Rent this one for: its genuine, innocent charm and magic.
You'll (probably) like this if you liked: *The 5,000 Fingers of Dr. T; The City of Lost Children; E.T.; The NeverEnding Story*
Credentials: "...magical for all ages...A real treasure...a wonderful movie..." —Roger Ebert (★★★★)
Dissenting Opinion: "...gooey..." —GMR (2.5 bones)

The NeverEnding Story

(fairy tale adventure)

(1984; Warner; PG; 1:34)

Starring: Barret Oliver, Noah Hathaway, Tami Stronach
Featuring: Gerald McRaney, Moses Gunn, Alan Oppenheimer (voice)
Written by: Wolfgang Petersen, Herman Weigel
(based on the novel by Michael Ende)
Directed by: Wolfgang Petersen

Synopsis: 8-year-old Bastian (Oliver) is taking the death of his mother very hard. He spends his days daydreaming, frightened by life, terrorized by bullies. They chase him into an antique bookstore, where he discovers and "borrows" a rare storybook entitled *The NeverEnding Story.* Hiding in his school's attic, he begins reading, fascinated by the incredible characters that populate the magical land of Fantasia, and by the adventures of young warrior Atreyu (Hathaway), sent on a quest to save Fantasia from "The Nothing," a mysterious plague which swallows reality and leaves only emptiness in its wake. Bastian finds himself irresistibly drawn into Atreyu's adventures, their fates mystically intertwined. And when the Empress (Stronach) appeals directly to Bastian from the enchanted manual, can he find the courage to *believe*—the only way to save Fantasia?
Discussion: Poet T.S. Eliot called it "the objective correlative": a metaphor so perfect and powerful that it freights with it an exact emotional experience. For Bastian, the storybook in *Story is* the objective correlative—and for the viewer, the movie serves the same purpose, as we are eerily—properly—incorporated into the action. The best fairy tales contain mystery, a moral message (here, facing your fears), a touch of darkness, and pure primal emotions—fear, despair, courage, joy—and allow us to participate in the catharsis they provide. What a rare film it is that offers all this, if only one is willing to be absorbed in the story! *Story* is both modern mythology and a loving tribute to innocence and the infinite power of the imagination; it's a film not just for children, but for the unrepentant dreamer in us all.
Rent this one for: its awe-inspiring special effects; for its unique characters and vivid visions of majestic fantasy landscapes; for its raw emotions.
You'll (probably) like this if you liked: *The Pagemaster, The Dark Crystal, The Labyrinth, Legend, The Lion, the Witch and the Wardrobe, Alice in Wonderland, The Wizard of Oz, Return to Oz*
Dissenting Opinion: "...more like the neverending movie." —SMV (2 stars)
Vidbit: • Petersen's first English language film. • The story *should* have ended: The sequel's a soulless imitation of itself.

The Secret of NIMH

(animation)

(1982; MGM/UA; G; 1:22)

Featuring the Voice Talents of: Elizabeth Hartman, John Carradine, Derek Jacobi, Dom DeLuise, Peter Strauss, Edie McClurg
Written and directed by: Don Bluth
(based on Robert C.O'Brien's book *Mrs. Frisby and the Rats of NIMH)*

Synopsis: Pity poor field mouse Mrs. Brisby! Not only was her husband Jonathan recently killed, but one of her youngsters is ill, and can't be moved before the farmer begins plowing the field where they live. To save her family from certain death, she embarks on a desperate quest, roaming from dark forest to the underworld of the rats—a subterranean civilization complete with electricity! Everywhere she travels, her deceased husband's name inspires respect. But only ancient Nicodemus, ruler of the rats, can organize them to ensure her survival. And only he can reveal the secret of NIMH, and Jonathan's role in it.
Discussion: The story behind this film is almost as interesting as the movie itself. Long before *The Little Mermaid* began a renaissance of Disney animation, artist Don Bluth and his co-workers labored away at The Mouse Factory on such best-forgotten fare as *The Black Cauldron.* Disillusioned by Disney, Bluth left in 1979 (taking 16 animators with him) to create this little gem. While not up to today's *Lion King/Hunchback*-style standards, this is probably the best animated movie Disney "produced" since *The Jungle Book* was released 15 years earlier. All the classic Disney elements are here (plucky mice, goofy birds, an evil cat), but with a special spin: While Disney 'toons often featured a missing mother, here the hero *is* a mother—and a strong woman to boot! Bluth also returned the dazzling lighting effects—detailed sparkling and flashing, and impressionistic sun-dappled, rippling water—he wasn't allowed to budget during his days at Disney. His plot contains one harrowing incident after another, building in intensity, excitement and wonder to its magical ending. "No spoilers"—but I will say that the *secret* of NIMH is clever and touching—and should have made this flick a favorite of animal rights activists.
Rent this one for: its clever story and classic animation.
You'll (probably) like this if you liked: *Babe, The Dark Crystal, The NeverEnding Story, The Rescuers, An American Tail*
Credentials: "★★★★★ — Lovers of classic...animation, rejoice! ...[M]ore than...a children's tale. Adults will enjoy it too." —VMG
Dissenting Opinion: "...not as involving, or as well paced, as it might be." —MMG (2.5 stars)
Vidbit: The voice of mouse-child Teresa is Shannen Doherty.

7 Faces of Dr. Lao

(fantasy/comedy)

(1964; MGM/UA; NR; 1:41)

Starring: Tony Randall, Barbara Eden, Arthur O'Connell
Featuring: John Ericson, Noah Beery, Jr., Royal Dano
Written by: Charles Beaumont
(based on Charles G. Finney's novel *The Circus of Dr. Lao*)
Directed by: George Pal

Synopsis: Diminutive Dr. Lao (Randall) rides into the Old West town of Abalone, circa 1912, puffing his opium pipe, ready to set up his traveling circus. He stumbles into a town crisis, however: greedy land baron Stark (O'Connell) is trying to buy up the town, while idealistic newspaper editor Ed Cunningham (Ericson) crusades for people to stay and create a community. The entire town attends Lao's show, and everyone sees something special—but few are capable of understanding what they see. Lao's center ring spectacle illustrates the fall of a great city into oblivion, cryptically revealing the fate of their town should they sell out to Stark. Will "surreal estate agent" Lao's parable open the eyes of the citizens, allowing them to save their community?
Discussion: "Are you an acrobat?" 8-year-old Mike asks the ancient Asian. "Only philosophically," Lao replies, a twinkle in his eye. His circus is a mythic mirror, specializing in wisdom. The sideshow is stocked with mythic figures: Pan; a Medusa; the Lock Ness monster; Apollonius of Tyana, cursed to tell the truth, however ugly; Merlin, the wizened wizard, slowly succumbing to senility—all played by Randall. Each visitor gravitates to the figure most likely to mirror his myth, and peering into that reflection of destiny provides a cosmic context for their petty problems. There are more things in heaven and earth than the residents can ever encounter, but the pixieish impresario provides the chance to understand that even Abalone can become an Avalon—and that the whole world is a circus, full of magic and miracles, if you just adjust your perspective. It's the role of Randall's career; a literally fabulous film, full of fun and familiar faces, poignance and timeless wisdom. And by all means read the brilliant, astonishingly original source novel!
Rent this one for: Randall; the humor; the poignant wisdom.
You'll (probably) like this if you liked: *The Wizard of Oz*
Dissenting Opinion: According to the *Psychotronic Encyclopedia,* Randall himself didn't like the film. Maybe that's why he appears as himself, sans makeup, sitting in the audience just before the final show, shaking his head, looking unimpressed.
Vidbits: • Won a Special Oscar for Makeup. • Dr. Lao's final presentation uses footage from Pal's *Atlantis, the Lost Continent.*

Tiny Toons Adventures:
How I Spent My Summer Vacation

(animation/comedy)

(1991; Warner; G; 1:20)

Featuring the Voice Talents of: Charlie Adler, Tress MacNeille, Joe Alasky, Don Messick, Jonathan Winters, Edie McClurg
Written by: Paul Dini, Nicholas Hollander, Tom Ruegger, Sherri Stoner
Directed by: Rich Arons, Byron Baughns, Alfred Gimeno, Barry Caldwell, Ken Boyer, Art Leonardi, Kent Butterworth

Synopsis: Acme Looniversity is out for the summer, and the junior versions of famous Warner 'toons have three months to whoop it up. A number of sub-plots intertwine with two main stories: In one, Buster and Babs Bunny embark on a "Huckleberry Finn"-style raft trip through the Deep South; in the other, a family road trip to "Happy World Land" turns into an endurance test for Hamton Pig and Plucky Duck.
Discussion: The original Warner Bros. cartoons were never intended for kids; they were produced for theater audiences full of adults. It's a joy to see this tradition continued. A couple of strong indications this flick isn't just for kids: the caricature cameos of Letterman, Carson, Oprah and Arsenio (as well as a row of famous faces of filmdom in the movieplex), and lampoons of *Deliverance, American Graffiti, Indiana Jones and the Temple of Doom, Friday the 13th* and *Fantasia.* The flick's funniest segment, however, is the savage skewering of Disney theme parks in the visit to "Happy World Land," an "abusement park" filled with rides like "the legendary Happy-Go-Pukey." Speaking of Disney, don't expect Disney-depth imagery. The animation isn't lush, but it's competent, and supersonically paced. (These kids apparently forgot to pack their Ritalin.) The anarchic old gags still work (they always did), and there's one in virtually every shot. (My favorite is the Babs and Buster falling through a "Plot Hole" in the ground.) And the end credits are every bit as funny as the film itself, filled with trivial disinformation like "Additional Viking Dialog: Jerry Van Dyke" and "Original Running Time: 8 Hours, 47 Minutes." (The pause and reverse buttons come in quite handy here.) All this *and* a cameo by Superman! Cool!
Rent this one for: The wild cartoon lampoons, reminiscent of the wacky early days of Warner Bros. animation.
You'll (probably) like this if you liked: Warner Bros. cartoons, "The Simpsons," *Who Framed Roger Rabbit?*
Vidbit: • The first made-for-video animated feature ever produced in the U.S. • Executive Producer: Steven Spielberg

Twice Upon A Time

(animated comedy)

(1983; HBO, Warner; PG; 1:15)

Featuring the Voice Talents of: Lorenzo Music, Marshall Efron, Judith Kahan Kampmann, James Cranna, Julie Payne, Hamilton Camp, Paul Frees
Written by: John Korty, Charles Swenson, Suella Kennedy, Bill Couterié
Directed by: John Korty, Charles Swenson
Music (includes selections by): Bruce Hornsby, The Doobie Bros.

Synopsis: Synonamess Botch (Efron), evil ruler of the Murkworks, plans to use his air force of attack-trained vultures to drop bad-dream bombs on the populace of the real world, dooming them to non-stop nightmares, while a disparate group of loony superheroes attempts to stop his dastardly plan.
Discussion: Merely saying this is an animated film is a bit like saying *Jurassic Park* is a flick about big lizards. *Twice* features virtually every style of animation ever invented, from traditional drawings to stop-motion photography of cut-out shapes ("Lumage") to combinations of animation and live action using film and photos—and much more, all to exceptional visual effect. The assorted oddballs populating this pun-filled picture are inventively exaggerated parodies of typical fantasy figures: Ralph (Music, also the voice of Garfield), for example, is a shapeshifter (an "all-purpose animal") who pals around with flaky silent human Mum ("an all-purpose nothing"). Their irascible FGM (Fairy Godmother) sports a Bronx accent—and can't keep her wings on. Then there's Rod Rescueman, apprentice superhero (he's got a learner's permit). And how bad is the fat, effete Botch? So evil he's got "Nixon/Agnew 1968" tattooed on his chest. This is one hilarious movie—wild, wacky, witty, fast-paced...and much more than a kids' film: Imagine *Yellow Submarine* directed by Terry Gilliam (*Brazil*) and written by the "Rocky and Bullwinkle" scribes. Even the end credits—a collage of photos of the cast and crew, with a few jokes thrown in—are worth sticking around for. Rare treats like *Twice* come around only once in a rare while.
Rent this one for: its rich and inventive visual tapestry; for being a wild lampoon of heroic fantasy adventures.
You'll (probably) like this if you liked: "Rocky and Bullwinkle" cartoons; *Yellow Submarine; The Wrong Trousers;* "Beany & Cecil" cartoons; "Monty Python"; *Wizards*
Vidbit: • Never released theatrically, even though George Lucas was the executive producer.

The Wizard of Speed and Time

(comedy)

(1988; SGE; PG; 1:35)

Starring: Mike Jittlov, Richard Kaye, Paige Moore
Featuring: David Conrad, Frank Laloggia, Philip Michael Thomas, Angelique Pettyjohn
Written by: Mike Jittlov, Richard Kaye, Deven Chierighino
Directed by: Mike Jittlov (credited as "The Guy in the Green Jacket")

Synopsis: A pair of sleazy movie producers is ordered by their studio to come up with a hit—*now*. They sweet-talk a struggling special effects wizard (Jittlov) into creating an eye-popping project. But "The Wizard" finds he's dealing with Holly*won't:* He's such a maverick that no union will touch him—or allow him to work. After being run through a maze of red tape and Catch-22 rules, he enlists the aid of friends in a race against time and money (and union regulations and city permits and the studio's insistence on "production values" —i.e., car chases and pretty girls) to create a film full of *very* special effects.
Discussion: "Pixilated" is the key concept here: not only as the technical term for the seamlessly smooth stop-motion effects Jittlov creates, but also in its meaning as "whimsical." Mike's house has more toys than Pee-Wee's (and his bike has a better anti-theft system), and the film is filled with sparkling, flashing, whizzing magic. The energetic overacting is totally appropriate for its "Hey kids, let's put on a show *right here!"* character. And who can resist a tale about an underappreciated underdog who proves that heart and art can triumph over big bucks and dumb fucks? Who can resist a movie that mocks itself ("the ultimate in low-tech!") or that opens with its own fake trailer ("Five years in the making—five days in the theaters!")? Who can resist a film that fools with its own credits (threatening that "violators may be forced to see this movie day and night unto perpetuity")? The fact that this is a self-produced project is fairly apparent—not that it's amateurish, but because no humorless studio or union would ever allow itself to be trashed so savagely (if gently), and because the amusing end credits read like *deja vu:* the same few names (particularly Jittlov's) popping up over and over again under dozens of job titles. Must be a union thing...
Rent this one for: The sprightly stop-motion effects; the fun.
You'll (probably) like this if you liked: Peter Gabriel's "Sledgehammer" music video; *S.O.B., Almost Hollywood*
Dissenting Opinion: "...some amateurish qualities..." —MMG
Vidbit: • Blink-and-you'll-miss-'em cameos: Sci-fi guru Forrest Ackerman (crowd scene); veteran Disney animator Ward Kimball (IRS Chief). • Final line of credits: "And have a nice day."

Mystery
Suspense
Thriller

Mystery
Suspense
Thriller

Welcome to the basement of human motivations. Steel yourself against the inevitable onslaught of fear, pain, cruelty and despair; prepare yourself for murder and mayhem; for obsession and revenge; for corruption and deduction; for risk, robbery and rewards; for double-dealing and triple-crosses; for cops, crooks and evil creeps; for blood and guns; for twisted business and sick victims; for mean spirits and nasty bastards; for mind games and deadly dames; for strange places and fast chases; for perverts and just desserts; for greed and speed; for vile threats and cigarettes; and, of course, for lust (which is its own reward).

If the edge of your seat is your favorite position...then just pick a flick, and perch on this...

After Dark, My Sweet

(modern noir)

(1990; LIVE; R; 1:54)

Starring: Jason Patric, Rachel Ward, Bruce Dern
Written by: Robert Redlin, James Foley
(based on the novel by Jim Thompson)
Music by: Maurice Jarre
Directed by: James Foley

Synopsis: Punch-drunk ex-boxer Kevin "Collie" Collins (Patric) stumbles into a dusty California desert town and is promptly picked up by beautiful, sarcastic widow Fay Anderson (Ward). She cleans him up; she gives him work; she lets him stay in a trailer out in her orchard. Enter sleazy "Uncle Bud" (Dern), who gives him some vague, sinister warnings. Even Fay advises splitting before he gets mixed up in their "scheme." He can't stay away from Fay, though; she's the first person who's ever needed him. Bud's kidnapping plan is pretty simple, but even Collie's addled brains can figure out he's being set up as the patsy, to take the fall. All he knows for sure is he's got to play this out to the end, and that he can add his own spin, as they all underestimate him so badly. Is he crazy like a fox? Or just crazy?
Discussion: Simplicity can be a very complicated thing. Uncle Bud's mistake, and Fay's as well, is in equating smarts with sanity—or with character. Even though Collie's brains might be scrambled, his insight into motivation is far more perceptive and accurate than any of the other players'. What distinguishes this movie from a standard thriller (which could be made from the simple plot) is its unusual point of view: We see situations through the eyes of a borderline lunatic, which fills the plot with unpredictable double- and triple-crosses, some of which might exist only in Collie's fevered brain. The flick wouldn't work without a brilliant central performance, and Patric pulls it off excellently. Every step his Collie takes is a prowl through the ring; every intuitive gesture, sound psychology. The movie is full of surprises, snowballing up to the ending, which contains one shocking twist after another; all logical, unpredictable and inevitable—if you've got the mind of a killer.
Rent this one for: its unusual, complex protagonist; its hard-boiled, ultimately character-driven story; Patric's performance.
You'll (probably) like this if you liked: *The Grifters, The Getaway* (Thompson adaptations); *The Last Seduction*
Dissenting Opinion: "Interesting at first, but eventually you catch on that it's heading absolutely nowhere—10 miles per hour, at that." —MMG (2.5)

Backtrack

(1989; Vestron, LIVE; R; 1:44)

Starring: Dennis Hopper, Jodie Foster, Joe Pesci
Featuring: Dean Stockwell, Vincent Price, John Turturro, Fred Ward
Written by: Rachel Kronstadt Mann, Ann Louise Bardach
Directed by: Dennis Hopper

Synopsis: Artist Anne Benton (Foster) has a flat tire on the freeway one night; as she's walking for help, she stumbles into a Mob murder. She escapes, but they're onto her—and after her. A failed hit convinces her of the seriousness of the situation, but when the cops can't protect her, she "disappears" herself. The Mob calls in Mr. Milo (Hopper), the best hitman in the business. His method of tracking is to get to know everything about the missing person, then intuit her thought process. The cops use computers. They find her simultaneously. She bolts again, this time to New Mexico. Mr. Milo finds her, but his method has finally backfired on him, and when he confronts her, he offers her a choice: He'll let her live, but she'll belong to him. The real twist is that he's such a sensitive gentleman that she might just grow to like this kinky kidnapping fantasy...

Discussion: "Murder has its sexual side," reads a line in one of Anne's "language art" machines—and that sums up this stylish modern *noir* thriller with a difference. Is Anne a victim of the Stockholm Syndrome, where kidnap victims identify with their captors—or is there something deeper and more primal at work here? What sets this film apart from most others is that it is in essence an *animus fantasy,* as delineated by Jung: A woman's fearful fancy of kidnap and seduction by a dark stranger full of sensual menace. As such, it explicates themes the original *noirs* could only hint at, like the vagaries of dominance and submission. The film goes to great lengths to show off Foster's sexy side, and when the pair become "lovers on the lam," chased by both the Mob and the cops, the humorous undercurrents bubble up—even a simple lover's spat could prove deadly. Every member of the great cast looks like he or she is having fun. And an entire essay could be written about this film's curious and circuitous history. (Simply, the vidco that produced it for theatrical release went bankrupt, and it sat on a shelf for years before going straight to tape.) *Backtrack* is a fascinating film based on the female psyche; an action flick even women can enjoy.

Rent this one for: its original approach to the *noir* thriller.

You'll (probably) like this if you liked: *Love and a .45*

Dissenting Opinion: "...clumsy...eventually falls apart" —SMV

Vidbits: • Brief appearances by Charlie Sheen (as the boyfriend) and Bob Dylan (as an artist). • Produced by Dick Clark.

Flashback!

The Big Clock

(thriller/film noir classic)
(1948; MCA; NR; 1:35; B&W)

Starring: Ray Millard, Maureen O'Sullivan, Charles Laughton
Written by: Jonathan Latimer (based on Kenneth Fearing's novel)
Directed by: John Farrow

Synopsis: Manhattan: The skyscraper housing Janoth Publications. The lobby is full of guards with orders to shoot to kill: "They mean you, George," Stroud (Milland) reminds himself. Just 36 hours ago, he was editor of *Crime Ways* magazine—and now he's wanted for murder, hiding inside the giant lobby clock and reviewing the unsettling events that led to this sorry state. Can this innocent victim of circumstance unravel the mystery and identify the real murderer before the noose of circumstantial evidence tightens around his neck once and for all?
Discussion: So what's a thriller from 1948 doing in a book about buried treasures from the 1980s and '90s? Glad I pretended you asked. The answer is simple: It's a classic film noir—and it was never available on tape until September, 1996 (just making the cut-off date for inclusion in this volume). It is necessary to suspend our disbelief that this "unidentified criminal" hunt on which the plot hinges could ever happen in these modern days of instant photography, police sketches, fax machines and TV (any combination of which would identify the suspect immediately), but once that's accomplished, the flick has much to recommend it. The air of suspense, for example, becomes almost claustrophobic by the final scenes. The plot snowballs from a battle of will and wits between arrogant autocrat Janoth (Laughton) and quick-thinking Stroud into a life-or-death chess game which turns everyone in the building into their pawns. The rat-a-tat dialog is sharp and sharky, and Stroud and company cross paths with some genuine eccentrics (notably Elsa Lanchester in a pivotal role as a comically whacked-out artist). All told, *The Big Clock* provides an engrossing 90 minutes.
Rent this one for: the suspense; as a classic noir now on tape.
You'll (probably) like this if you liked: *Out of the Past, Gun Crazy, Double Indemnity* (classic noir); *No Way Out* ('87 remake)
Dissenting Opinion: "Slick but...empty..." —HFG
Vidbits: • A young Harry Morgan (billed as "Henry" in credits) plays Bill, Janoth's silent masseuse/bodyguard. • Noel Neill, who played Lois Lane in the '50s "Superman" TV series, appears briefly as the elevator girl. • Laughton was married to Lanchester; O'Sullivan was married to director Farrow.

The Big Easy

(romance)

(1986; HBO; R; 1:40)

Starring: Dennis Quaid, Ellen Barkin
Featuring: Ned Beatty, John Goodman
Written by: Dan Petrie, Jr.
Directed by: Jim McBride

Synopsis: When a minor hood is found floating face-down in a fountain, New Orleans police Lt. Remy McSwain (Quaid) shrugs it off as a routine "wise guy" hit. But no-nonsense Asst. D.A. Anne Osborne (Barkin) demands an investigation, which leads to a clash of attitudes: his, laid-back and loose; hers, repressed and rigid. Just as his smooth Southern style begins to win her over, he's caught in a bribery sting set up to catch another cop—an event which endangers his investigation, his career and his relationship. Osborne's reaction forces Remy to question whether he can continue to overlook police corruption and still stay one of the "good guys"—a moral dilemma that escalates when he discovers that the gang war he's investigating might be a red herring covering up the police corruption she's investigating.

Discussion: "The Big Easy"—the local nickname for New Orleans—also nicely describes the attitude of the locals, and Quaid is the embodiment of that style. Smooth as *roux,* his genuinely endearing attempts to loosen Osborne up become the centerpiece of the film; the plot is merely a convenient device to push them together and pull them apart. The intriguing plot would have made an excellent movie even without this romantic capstone, but combined with a believable romance, first-rate performances, and an emotional dilemma (reminiscent of the similar work-versus-family theme of *The Godfather, Part II),* then laced with a touch of humor (like the scene divesting Goodman of his weapons), we end up with a film just as spicy and satisfying as any culinary creation from a Cajun kitchen.

Rent this one for: Quaid's charming performance (and accent); for one of the hottest non-sex scenes in recent memory; and for the superb soundtrack, featuring such Cajun superstars as Beausoliel, Buckwheat Zydeco and the Neville Brothers.

You'll (probably) like this if you liked: *Witness, Sea of Love* (mysteries with romance; the latter featuring Barkin); *Tightrope, Angel Heart, The Drowning Pool, Pretty Baby, Storyville* (New Orleans locations); *Striking Distance.*

Vidbits: Remy's case is heard before New Orleans Judge Jim Garrison, playing himself. For his story, see Oliver Stone's *JFK.*

Blood Simple

(crime drama/ modern noir)
(1984; MCA; R; 1:36)

Starring: John Getz, M. Emmet Walsh, Dan Hedaya, Frances McDormand
Written by: Ethan Coen, Joel Coen
Directed by: Joel Coen

Synopsis: Sleazeball Julian (Hedaya), owner of a seedy Texas strip bar, has hired a Private Detective (Walsh) to catch his wife (McDormand) cheating. When Julian discovers the culprit is Ray (Getz), one of his bartenders, he fires the guy—and then rehires the Detective to kill them both. The unethical Detective, however, knows there's an easier way to get the money, once Julian opens the safe... Thus begins a domino effect of double-dealing, double-crosses both real and imagined, and murderous and mistaken motives, culminating in a harrowing final confrontation between the last two left standing.
Discussion: Since enjoying the unpredictable yet somehow inevitable unfolding of events is one of this film's primary pleasures, we must leave the synopsis purposefully sketchy. Let us say merely that the plot does not disappoint. By now, we're all familiar with the Coen brothers' eccentric approach to film direction, emphasizing style and unconventional camera work. But this, their first feature film, was a stylistic surprise, and—to make an even deeper impression—they put as much effort into the plot as into the pictures. There are no insignificant details: a misplaced lighter, a delayed phone message, an innocent look —all conspire against the players in a convoluted tragedy of misinterpretation and increasingly uncomfortable, eventually deadly events. The only scenarios that exist for them are worst-case; their situations become quicksand, and any effort to extricate themselves only sucks them in deeper, until they are all in way over their heads. Walsh is wonderful as the Detective who takes to sleaze with ease, and the film is filled with electrified silences. But the real highlights are the nail-biting finale and Ray's attempt to dispose of a body in a field—a scene which will have you squirming in your seat. Five or six times.
Rent this one for: the cleverly deadly events; the field scene.
You'll (probably) like this if you liked: *Fargo, Shallow Grave*
Credentials: Grand Jury Prize—Sundance Festival • *EW:* "A-"
Dissenting Opinion: "...smart-ass. No, smart half-ass." —Stanley Kaufmann, *New Repbulic*
Vidbits: McDormand, who also starred in the Coen brother's *Fargo,* is married to the film's director Joel Coen.

Breaking In

(1989; HBO, Warner; R; 1:35)
(caper comedy)

Starring: Burt Reynolds, Casey Siemaszko
Featuring: Shiela Kelley, Maury Chaykin, Stephen Tobolowsky
Written by: John Sayles
Directed by: Bill Forsyth

Synopsis: Two stealthy figures collide in a dark house: aging cat-burglar Ernie (Reynolds), a total pro, and be-bopping Mike (Siemaszko), just bustin' in for kicks, and to raid the fridge. "I never met anyone who did crime for a living," Mike exclaims, impressed. "Need any help?" Ernie thinks it over and shares the loot: "I'd rather have a partner than a witness." They team up, and Ernie becomes both tutor and mentor to Mike, passing on details of technique—and of philosophy and discipline, which the idiot kid desperately needs. They are an odd couple, however: Ernie, serious about crime as a career; Mike, itching to live high and fast and frivolously. They bust some safes, but the kid gets cocky. They quarrel, and Mike goes it alone—with comically catastrophic results. Reconciled, the pair plans The Big Score: popping an amusement park's vault for its holiday weekend receipts. But Mike's indiscreet past is catching up with him and threatens the success of the caper. Once it goes bust, who will stay loyal to whom—and at what cost?
Discussion: You can learn a lot about crime here, but not as much as you can about criminals—and about people in general. Capers take a back seat to character in this low-key comedy, and what makes them seem real are their idiosyncrasies: Ernie always sneezing around explosives, for instance, or the colored condoms carried by Mike's "AMW" ("actress/model/whatever") girlfriend (Kelley, as an apprentice hooker; an eager amateur learning a profession just like Mike). And lest we ever forget that he can act, Burt is superb as the cranky safecracker who passes his entire career on to his precocious protégé. In this engaging entry, "Honor among thieves" is not a cliché: it's the central metaphor of the pair's fond father/son relationship.
Rent this one for: Reynolds' performance; for the rare pairing of two top-notch independent filmmakers, Forsyth and Sayles.
You'll (probably) like this if you liked: *Family Business, The Flim-Flam Man, The Brink's Job*
Credentials: "Flawless all around...a real treat." —SMV (4 stars)
Dissenting Opinion: "...script...is inventive and funny...but not enough to keep this wispy film afloat." —MMG (2.5 stars)
Vidbits: Set in San Francisco, but shot mostly in Oregon.

Flashback!

The Conversation

(1974; Paramount; PG; 1:53)

Starring: Gene Hackman, John Cazale, Allan Garfield
Featuring: Frederic Forrest, Cindy Williams, Teri Garr, Harrison Ford
Supervising Editor, Sound Montage and Re-Recording: Walter Murch
Written, produced and directed by: Francis Ford Coppola

Synopsis: Harry Caul is a good listener. The best. An expert. *The* expert in audio surveillance. 44, balding, sporting Eisenhower-era glasses, Harry plays his sax along with LPs in his off-hours, jamming with other masters of sound. Due to his profession, however, Harry's just a tiny bit ultraparanoid. Nervous. Suspicious. High-strung. But just because you're paranoid doesn't mean they *aren't* out to get you—and maybe he's got a reason this time: When he delivers the tapes of a bugged conversation to "The Director," he's warned that "those tapes are dangerous," and to be careful, as "someone may get hurt." Or maybe they don't mean him—maybe they mean the people on whose cryptic conversation he electronically eavesdropped in the first place (Forrest, Williams). Are they plotting a murder? Having an affair? Something else? Harry finds himself violating his one primary rule: *Don't get involved.*

Discussion: In watching this film, patience is a virtue, but so is observation: Little is explained, but all the clues are given. "What a stupid conversation," Harry's assistant, Stan (Cazale) observes. "What the hell they talkin' about, fer Chrissakes?" On Stan's question hinges the central conceit of this suspenseful entry: What the hell *are* they talking about? The more deeply Harry sinks into the quagmire of other peoples' plots, the more meanings the ambiguous dialog takes on. Every time the tape is repeated over a different scene, new meaning is wrung from it, until the ironic ending, which puts an unexpected twist on the entire nebulous conversation.

Hackman's Caul is a virtuoso performance, full of quiet, complex nuances. Consumed by guilt over a past tragedy, Harry is at war with himself: On one hand, his profession—and his professional ethics—demand that he remain a detached observer. This suits him just fine. No one likes to keep a lower profile. But the possibility that he could, once again, be the unwitting accomplice of suffering—even murder, perhaps—instigates a crisis of conscience which will not allow him to remain silent. The consequences of getting involved, however, are grave. First his privacy is at risk. Then his sanity. And by the time he begins to suspect that his own aural art is being used against him—that *his* wires are being tapped, and someone is "bugging the bugger"—his entire world is close to collapse. There is no privacy, no safety or security. He has lost everything that is dear to him—even his pride in being the best in the business. His skills pale in comparison to those of real pros. All that's left for Harry to do is finish the job "The Director" started.

The story behind the film is almost as intriguing as the movie itself: Coppola began writing script in 1966 (long before Watergate, which the film allegorically resembles), and finally got a chance to produce it between directing the first two installments of his epic, *The Godfather.* Sound editor Walter Murch had the thankless task of dealing with numerous alternative storylines which were developed during post-production, but he did such a thorough and brilliant job that Coppola has referred to him as the film's co-author. And in a real-life ironic twist, Coppola's wife Eleanor secretly taped many conversations with him while on location filming *Apocalypse Now,* some of which she included in her fascinating and critically acclaimed documentary about that hellish shoot, *Hearts of Darkness: A Filmmaker's Apocalypse.* (So if this film is indeed an allegory of Nixon and Watergate, and its techniques were later table-turned on its creator, *The Conversation* could be seen as a film in which art imitated life, and then became life imitating the art which imitated life. If you think this is compicated, read the discussion on *Hammett*—a film which was *also* produced by Coppola! Oh, Francis, sometimes you make me *crazy!* But I still love you...)

Rent this one for: the performances; the subtle, Kafkaesque script; the fascinating peek into the world of surveillance (even though it's all pre-digital).
You'll (probably) like this if you liked: *Rear Window, Blow Up, Blow Out, House of Games*
Credentials: • 1974 Oscar nominations: Best Picture, Original Screenplay, Sound. • 1974 Cannes Film Festival award: Best Film (Palme d'Or). • 1974 National Board of Review Awards: 10 Best Films of Year; Best Actor (Hackman); Best Director. •"★★★★★" —VMG • "brilliant" —MMG (★★★★) • "...not a false note..." —SMV (★★★★) • One of "Ten Best of Genre" *—People Magazine's Guide to Movies on Video*
Dissenting Opinion: "...more gimmicky than thoughtful." —Jon Landau, *Rolling Stone*
Vidbits: • Features Robert Duvall in an uncredited appearance as "The Director." • The Union Square mime is Robert Shields, who would have his 15 minutes of fame a few years later as half of the husband and wife TV mime team, "Shields and Yarnell."

Dead Again

(1991; Paramount; R; 1:47)

Starring: Kenneth Branagh, Emma Thompson, Andy Garcia
Featuring: Derek Jacobi, Hanna Schygulla, Wayne Knight
Written by: Scott Frank
Directed by: Kenneth Branagh

Synopsis: 1949: L.A. composer Roman Strauss (Branagh) gets the chair for murdering his wife Margaret (Thompson). He claims he loved her, though—and that "this is all far from over." Fast forward to the present, where low-rent P.I. Mike Church (Branagh) gets stuck baby-sitting amnesiac "Grace" (Thompson), who's been traumatized into silence by a pair of scissors—the Strauss murder weapon. Enter flaming antiques dealer Franklin (Jacobi), who uses hypnotic regression to help her. Under his spell, she regains her voice and her memory. But it's a memory of a past incarnation, in which she finds herself reliving the Strauss' fatal attraction. A nutjob defrocked shrink (Robin Williams) explains the "karmic credit plan," speculating that Mike and Grace might be the Strausses reincarnated—and fated to repeat their experiences. Before long, personal history is indeed repeating itself—but through a mirror, darkly. No one understands the rules of karma, however, so whose life is at risk this time around? Will it be replay, revenge—or are they both pawns in a game far more complicated than they could ever guess?

Discussion: Is it incredible coincidence or cosmic conspiracy? Even the question indicates the larger-than-life nature of this stylish thriller. Part Hitchcockian psychological suspenser (with a New Age twist), part *film noir* mystery with romance, this is a giddy, tongue-in-cheek romp played dead straight, despite its grandiose gestures. Much of its appeal lies in watching a bunch of classical actors happily slumming in a B-movie; beyond that are velvety black and white flashbacks and an ending that overlaps past and present plots to come full circle for karmic (and poetic) justice. If you just accept the born-again premise of overlapping, interlocking lives, you're in for some unpredictable intrigue and real suspense—as well as some outlandish fun.

Rent this one for: its high style and unguessably clever script.

You'll (probably) like this if you liked: *Psycho, Rebecca, Vertigo* (similar Hitchcock thrillers); *Truly, Madly, Deeply*

Credentials: • "★★★★★" —VMG • "★★★★" —SMV • *EW:* "A-"

Dissenting Opinion: "...story is too dense, and too artificial, to really work." —MMG (2.5 stars)

Vidbits: • Karmic "inside joke": Jo Anderson, who plays the nun in the contemporary opening, is "preincarnated" as a gold-digging starlet at the Hollywood party in a flashback sequence.

Dead Calm

(suspense/thriller)
(1988; Warner; R; 1:36)

Starring: Sam Neill, Nicole Kidman, Billy Zane
Written by: Terry Hayes (based on the novel by Charles Williams)
Directed by: Phillip Noyce

Synopsis: The tragic loss of their toddler son sends John and Rae Ingram (Neill and Kidman) out to sea on their sailboat for a lengthy recuperative trip of "calm days and calm seas." Four weeks out, they spot a schooner drifting in the dead calm sea. A lone man rows out in a dinghy and boards their boat. Horrified Hughie (Zane) is the only survivor of the ship's crew of six, the others, victims of botulism. So he says. John is suspicious, and while Hughie sleeps, rows over to the boat to investigate. His intuition proves true—but too late to avert disaster: Psycho Hughie has stolen his boat, taking Rae prisoner and leaving him stranded aboard the sinking schooner. What will Rae have to do—and endure—to save his life, and her own?

Discussion: There's really not a lot to say about this little thriller from Down Under, nor does a lot need to be said. It's an example of Jack Palance's *City Slickers* philosophy applied to filmmaking: "Choose one thing and do it well." The "one thing" here is *suspense,* pure and simple—and end to end. There's very little dialog, and very little needed, as fear is a universal language. The long stretches of silence enhance the atmosphere of solitude, just as the extreme long shots of the minuscule ships adrift in a vast ocean serve to accentuate the sense of isolation. It's obvious that no cops or cavalry will ride out to rescue these people; their very survival is dependent solely on their wits and skills. In contrast to the shots of the expansive sea, much of the film is shot in claustrophobic close-ups. (Thank the Goddess that Kidman is worthy of hours of close-ups!) Onboard the boat, there is nowhere to hide and certainly nowhere to run, and the intense suspense is virtually tangible. And even though the ending resorts to the "Thank God he's dead! (Not!)" gimmick borrowed from slasher flicks, the twist is that it's not a shock: we know full well what's coming, and yet still hold our breath in mesmerized suspense until it actually occurs. (That's the difference between surprise and suspense. Watch Hitchcock; he knew!) And this tension leads to a grotesquely satisfying ending.

Rent this one for: its sustained suspense and tension.

You'll (probably) like this if you liked: *Knife in the Water*

Dissenting Opinion: "Intelligently made, except for an idiotic 'shock' ending." —SMV (3 Stars)

Flashback!

Gun Crazy

(film noir; AKA Deadly is the Female*)*
(1949; FoxVideo; NR; 1:27; B&W)

Starring: Peggy Cummins, John Dall
Written by: Dalton Trumbo (based on a story by MacKinlay Kantor)
Directed by: Joseph H. Lewis

Synopsis: Call it an obsession. But Bart Tare (Dall) was always fascinated by guns—not as weapons, but because "Shooting is what I'm good at." He *is* good too—even better than carnival sharpshooter Annie Laurie Starr (Cummins). He's invited to join the show, but their mutual attraction irritates the third wheel in this romantic triangle: their boss, who fires them. Married, low on cash, with no prospects large enough to satisfy the money-hungry Laurie, Bart lets himself get talked into a series of small-time stickups. Then a bank. Then another. Bart suffers moral qualms; Laurie flatters, cajoles and threatens to leave him. Eventually he has to make a stand. He's tired of "the life," and wants out. She agrees—but only after one more heist, to set them up for life. A big one. The last one. The very last one...
Discussion: Dall is a natural on camera—lanky, likable, self-effacing; a B-movie Jimmy Stewart. And the heat between these two is palpable, from the moment they first spot each other. Technically, the direction is exceptional. If you think Scorsese invented the endless tracking shot, rewind and rewatch one of his influences: The bank robbery scene; a single, unbroken take which runs a full three minutes and seems like an eternity of suspense. (Placing the camera in the back seat of the car allows us to become accomplices in the action as an added bonus.) The classic *noir* films were existential thrillers, unafraid to tackle Big Questions: Love vs. lust; society vs. the individual; law vs. justice; free will vs. fate; the use and uselessness of morals in an unfair, uncaring world; character vs. temptation; high-minded goals vs. material desires. *Gun Crazy* addresses every one of these themes, and while it might not provide any answers, it won't let you avoid the questions. The photography might be in black and white, but its philosophy is only shades of gray.
Rent this one for: the acting, the directing, the *noir* morality.
You'll (probably) like this if you liked: *Bonnie and Clyde, True Romance, Pretty Poison, Guncrazy* ('92), *Body Heat*
Credentials: "More than just a cult classic, it's the undisputed king of the B's." —*The Reel List*
Vidbits: • Young Bart is played by Russ Tamblyn. • Former train robber Al Jennings was consultant on the robbery scenes.

Hammett

(pastiche)

(1982; Warner, Ingram Entertainment; PG; 1:38)

Starring: Frederic Forrest, Peter Boyle, Marilu Henner
Featuring: Elisha Cook, Jr., Roy Kinnear, Royal Dano, R.G. Armstrong
Written by: Ross Thomas, Dennis O'Flaherty, Thomas Pope
(based on the novel by Joe Gores)
Music by: John Barry
Directed by: Wim Wenders

Synopsis: Prohibition-era San Francisco. Jimmy Ryan (Boyle), once Sam Hammett's (Forrest) Pinkerton mentor, shows up on the writer's doorstep to call in a favor: He's been hired to find a Chinese girl, Crystal Ling (Lydia Lei), but doesn't know his way around The City. Out on the town, Sam loses the only copy of his latest pulp detective story—and Ryan. But Crystal shows up. "Quit looking for me," she advises. "I'm not lost." The cops encourage him to lay off the case as well. But Hammett and his perky neighbor Kit (Henner) doggedly pursue a twisted trail of murder masked as suicide, blackmail disguised as prostitution, perversions falsely fronted as fairy tales and betrayal played as friendship, from the smoke-filled opium dens of Chinatown to the smoke-filled back rooms of the rich and powerful. And all in search of a story...

Discussion: "Is this pure invention, or do you draw your material from real life?" one of the villains asks Hammett of his story—and this question is also the conceit on which this brilliant film revolves. Curiously, this giddy tribute to the archetypically American art form of hard-boiled pulp fiction requires French to evoke the most appropriate descriptions; words and phrases like pastiche, homage, roman á clef and mise en scène. The engaging—even thrilling—aspect of the flick is in watching Hammett living the events that would later inspire his masterwork, *The Maltese Falcon*. Or so it seems. But any good mystery delves below the surface, and this movie applies that detective attitude to its own story, delving beneath surface structure of the plot to spin a parallel story that concerns nothing less than the very nature of the roots and inspirations of storytelling itself. The surface plot and its undercurrents of reference to *The Maltese Falcon* taken together form an intricate spiral, spinning their wheels-within-wheels to carry the action forward on both levels—the "real life" events of the plot, and the story about how they served as the inspiration for a story. The film opens showing us how people from Hammett's past have worked their way into his writings of the present, forewarning us that the "real" people in his present will become characters in his future fiction. The facts that became fiction then become the "facts" which will become fiction...and this film fills in those *faux* "facts" with panache. It's a deconstruction of classic characters and familiar scenes turned into a reworked re-creation of the events, then given a final twist as the scenes are presented as a "pre-creation"—as though we were watching the "real-life" events which will inspire the familiar fiction of *Falcon*, rather than the other way around. And all the while, Sam Hammett is living his best mystery without even realizing it, biting off staccato lines of dialog like a cut-rate Bogart while inexorably circling in on the sinister center of the labyrinth that forms the surface plot. Hammett's speech to the Big Rich, in which he puts all the pieces of the puzzle together in the presence of his enemies, is a dizzying gem: a literal interpretation and complete integration of the film's structure of tightening spirals. Billed as "entirely imaginary," this stylish, stylized story of extortion and inspiration is full of crackling dialog and inside references for film buffs (check out the statue on Hammett's desk, for instance. Or his reaction to lighting a cigarette after confronting the Big Rich. Or the cabbie who bridges the films.) From the opening notes of its soulful, mournful jazz score to its tough and tender ending, *Hammett* is a thoroughly unique delight, and unjustly overlooked. Watch it as the second half of a double feature with *The Maltese Falcon*, and come away with an even deeper appreciation for "the stuff that dreams are made of."

Rent this one for: its unique pastiche; its insight into a writer's mind, collecting details and reweaving them into fiction.

You'll (probably) like this if you liked: *The Maltese Falcon, Chinatown, Julia* (1977; Jason Robards won an Oscar portraying Hammett).

Dissenting Opinion: • "Interesting but ultimately botched studio exercise" —GMR (2 bones) • "...the rather pretentious framework is largely irrelevant, leaving a detective story...indistinguishable from many others" —HFG • "...disappointing...two years in the making and hardly seems worth it...nearly incomprehensible" —VMG (2 stars) • "...confused..." —SMV (1.5 stars)

Vidbits: Francis Ford Coppola Executive Produced through his ill-fated Zoetrope Studios; the production was designed by his long-time collaborator Dean Tavoularis. • Pre-production actually began in 1975, but filming didn't begin until 1980. This first version was dumped in the rough cut stage, and some two-thirds of it was reshot in 1981 with a different crew and cast. (Sylvia Miles and Brian Keith were in the first version, for instance, but aren't in the finished film.) • Co-writer Ross Thomas appears as one of the silent Big Rich in the finale.

The Hit

(modern noir)

(1985; Sultan Entertainment; R; 1:45)

Starring: Terence Stamp, John Hurt, Tim Roth, Laura Del Sol
Featuring: Fernando Rey, Bill Hunter
Written by: Peter Prince
Title music by: Eric Clapton (assisted by Roger Waters)
Directed by: Stephen Frears

Synopsis: Small-time crook Parker (Stamp) rats out his gangster partners in exchange for immunity and a new life in Spain. Ten years later, his enemies are out and want revenge, so they send a team to kidnap and return him. Braddock (Hurt) is a total pro: sullen, humorless, no-nonsense. His partner Myron (Roth) is a dim-witted, cocky hothead. Parker is amused by the entire situation, philosophically resigned to his fate. He chats them up; suggests safer routes; cooperates completely. Police on their trail, they hole up in Madrid, only to find Harry (Hunter) and his girl Maggie (Del Sol) borrowing the flat. Wrong place, wrong time... The original trio leaves with Maggie, and the four find their allegiances reversing and reorganizing at every rest stop.
Discussion: "He's up to something!" Myron growls. "Is he?" Braddock whispers. Is Parker really as transcendentally ready for death as he seems? Or is he indeed engaged in a deadly cat and mouse game? "I haven't got any plan," he smiles, as he plants seeds of doubt in everyone's minds, intuitively knowing exactly which buttons to push in his captors to shake their complacency. *Hit* is as much a story of psychological intrigue as it is an action thriller, and it succeeds on both counts. Hurt creates a monosyllabic murderer whose very presence is a threat; Roth's Myron is a giggling goon unwittingly manipulated by everyone; Del Sol's Maggie is gorgeous and feisty, determined to be a player and not just a pawn. Their double and triple crosses—some subtle, some violent—allow us to peer beneath their cool surfaces. Is any one of them as detached as he appears? In the end, there's only one among them with any real courage—and the fun is in watching the others self-destruct. Lush direction, first-rate performances and unpredictable, intricate twists of plot combine to make this a mesmerizing modern *noir* thriller.
Rent this one for: being a road movie of the mind, where every turn, twist and curve is unexpected and potentially deadly.
You'll (probably) like this if you liked: *House of Games*
Dissenting Opinion: "Old hat thuggery...in new-style detail. Violently suspenseful but not otherwise interesting." —HFG
Vidbits: Ad line: "Even bad guys have bad days."

House of Games

(psychological thriller)
(1987; HBO; R; 1:42)

Starring: Joe Mantegna, Lindsay Crouse
Featuring: Lilia Skala, J.T. Walsh, Meshach Taylor, Ricky Jay
Written and directed by: David Mamet

Synopsis: "You just talk!" the shrink's frustrated patient complains. "The whole thing is a con game!" He's a compulsive gambler; she's Dr. Margaret Ford (Crouse), top-flight psychiatrist and author of the bestseller *Driven.* She descends into the seedy section of Seattle to the House of Games pool hall, seeking to relieve her patient of his debts and a goon's death threats. She butts heads with tough guy Mike (Mantegna), who agrees to tear up her patient's marker—*if* she helps in a minor card game scam. She's intrigued by the event, and solicits Mike to be her Virgil as she investigates the underground culture of the con man. He teaches her not only the tricks and techniques of the trade but also the psychological secrets of why they work. But when she becomes inadvertently involved in a big con which goes horribly awry, everything she knows and holds dear—including her sanity—is suddenly in jeopardy. Her only hope is to con the professional confidence men. Who'll prove the master con artist—and at what cost?

Discussion: "What's more fun than human nature?" Mike snarls cynically. And what makes for better drama than the very same? Mike and Margaret are two sides of one coin: She's got intelligence and training; he's got experience and street savvy. She's mesmerized by his skill and hooked on the gut-level thrills he provides, spicing her immaculately-ordered but essentially empty life. He admires her for her guts and sharp eye. But in a movie which openly revels in its multiple levels of deception, can we really expect anything to be what it appears? And when you pit two experts in psychological motivation against one another, the only real bottom line lies in separating the personal from the professional—and hell hath no fury like a woman scammed.

Pulitzer Prize-winning playwright Mamet's directorial debut is impressive, and his script even more so; it's sleight of hand that is anything but sleight—a gripping film worthy of superlatives. There is real intelligence here; real power and emotional intensity; real suspense and real surprise; real danger and real drama.

Oscar-winning actor Martin Landau, who teaches acting on the side, once told an interviewer words to the effect that acting is not about *showing* emotion; it's about showing people struggling to *prevent* themselves from showing emotion. Crouse's performance is a classic example of this school; her subtle portrayal of an overly-controlled obsessive compulsive slowly succumbing to her own most deeply suppressed desires is itself a masterpiece of self-control. And Mantegna deserved an Oscar for his bitter, obnoxious, edgy Mike. Neither actor has ever given a better performance—or performed in a better script.

The surface story, punctuated by Mamet's trademark precise dialog, gives us a fascinating insight into the age-old con game, revealing such insider secrets as the "tell," and providing us with a crash course in how to set up and pull off a short con or a big sting. But the film is much more than just a modern *noir.* One layer beneath this veneer is a Jungian animus fantasy: Margaret secretly yearns for a shadowy, mysterious, fascinating stranger to subdue and possess her; when she finds him, she is drawn deeply into the dark side of her own nature.

In addition to the satisfying twists and turns of the plot, the film is grounded in the psychology of its characters. To play the confidence game *requires* confidence: in one's knowledge, skills, perceptions and desires—and particularly of one's self. *House of Games* moves beyond mere mind games to raise unsettling questions about Big Issues like ethics and self-interest, right and wrong and good and evil, sanity and acceptance, and ultimately, of life and death.

House of Games is not just one of the best films in this book —it's simply one of the best films ever produced.

Rent this one for: its powerful, intelligent and suspenseful script; the exceptional performances, particularly Mantegna's.

You'll (probably) like this if you liked: *The Grifters, Body Heat, Sleuth, The Stunt Man;* comic versions include: *The Sting, Penn and Teller Get Killed*

Vidbits: • Crouse was Mamet's wife at the time of production. • Mamet shares story credit with Jonathan Katz, A.K.A. the animated "Dr. Katz, Professional Therapist" on cable's Comedy Central. • Grove Press released a book of the screenplay in 1985, which includes a fun and informative essay by Mamet about being a first-time director. ("Always a cocky lad, I had told the producer not to worry about me as a first-time director—that he would either get a good film or a sincere apology.")

Lady In White

(mystery/ supernatural)
(1988; Virgin Vision; PG-13; 1:32)

Starring: Lukas Haas, Len Cariou, Alex Rocco
Featuring: Katherine Helmond, Jason Presson, Joelle Jacobi
Music by: Frank Laloggia
Written, produced and directed by: Frank Laloggia

Synopsis: Halloween, 1962. 8-year-old Frankie (Haas) is accidentally locked in his grade school's cloakroom. In the middle of the night he sees the ghost of a girl—and watches in horror as her murder is reenacted in phantom form. A masked figure—no ghost this time—enters and attacks Frankie. He has a "near-death" experience in which he meets the girl and discovers she's a restless soul seeking her missing mother. Frankie is rescued, and the police arrest the janitor for the attack, as well as for a string of child murders—including ghost-girl Melissa (Jacobi). Frankie retrieves a piece of evidence which implicates a different suspect—who then attempts to silence him. When Frankie's life is threatened, he receives help from a most unexpected source: the mysterious Lady in White, who harbors her own secrets.
Discussion: Obviously a labor of love (check out the credits, as well as the kid's name), this quirky classic apparently had no idea what it wanted to be when it grew up: A coming-of-age tale? A tender memoir about a funny family? A slasher thriller? A supernatural fantasy? A ghost story? A lesson in racial tolerance? A gut-wrenching suspense entry? A revenge fantasy? Luckily, these disparate ingredients combine into a very special blend—a balanced buffet, rather than hash. Maybe the key is that, however eclectic the elements, both the setup and the resolution are believable and emotionally satisfying. Laloggia seamlessly weaves the most harrowingly realistic scenes (like Frankie's final flight from the legitimate killer) with sequences full of awe, wonder and spooky, otherworldly effects (Frankie's near-death experience, for instance). This is the film's real strength, the harmonious integration of opposites: light and dark, wonder and terror, fire and water, real-life monsters and angelic miracles, life and death...life and afterlife.
Rent this one for: the brave, successful experiment of blending eclectic elements of gut-wrenching suspense and ethereal supernatural fantasy.
You'll (probably) like this if you liked: *Paperhouse, The Stepfather, Blue Velvet,* "Eerie, Indiana"
Dissenting Opinion: "...way too long..." —SMV (2.5 stars)

Flashback!

The Late Show

(comedy/film noir pastiche)

(1977; Warner; PG; 1:34)

Starring: Art Carney, Lily Tomlin, Bill Macy, Eugene Roche
Featuring: Joanna Cassidy, John Considine, Howard Duff
Written and directed by: Robert Benton

Synopsis: L.A. private eye Ira Wells (Carney) used to be one of the greats. Now he's just a gray-haired old grouch with a limp, a hearing aid and an ulcer. But when his ex-partner Harry (Duff) shows up and dies on his doorstep, Ira vows revenge. Their mutual friend Charlie (Macy) introduces Ira to the "fruitcake" who hired Harry, and Ira decides to take over the case. His decision leads him into a tangled web of robbery, infidelity, double-crosses and multiple murders, all while shepherding, protecting—and enduring—his kooky client, Margo (Tomlin).
Discussion: It's a twisted mystery, and not just in the convoluted plot, but in the characters as well—notably the relationship between hard-boiled, old fashioned, tough buzzard Ira and mush-brained, motor-mouthed, New Age flake Margo. Their reluctant coupling accentuates both a generation gap ("Would it kill ya to wear a dress once in a while?" he barks) and a culture clash ("You're a slob, and I'm a Virgo," she points out). But beneath their grousing, the ditzy "dolly" and the well-past-his-prime P.I. have much in common, like loneliness and vulnerability. The performances are uniformly superb (including Cassidy in a small but hilarious role as the archetypal *noir* damsel-in-distress/femme fatale). The plot tiptoes a razor's edge between classic Chandleresque detective tale, full of snappy sniping and bloody bodies, and gentle send-up of the genre, with an undercurrent of wry wit. It's Chandler with a time-capsule twist: a '40s hero with a '70s client, viewed from the '90s—an odd experience, but one which only accentuates the film's sardonic and melancholy message that time makes everything obsolete, eventually and inevitably—except, perhaps, affectionate connection.
Rent this one for: the acting; the salute to, and spoof of, noir.
You'll (probably) like this if you liked: *The Long Goodbye* (1973); *Gumshoe; The Hit*
Credentials: • 1977 Oscar nomination: Best Original Screenplay • '77 Edgar Allan Poe Award: Best Screenplay • '77 National Board of Review Award: 10 Best Films of Year • '77 National Society of Film Critics Award: Best Actor (Carney) • [a] "...little gem." —VMG (4.5 stars) • "★★★★" — Roger Ebert
Vidbits: Produced by Robert Altman.

Lies

(psychological thriller)
(1987; Key; R; 1:34)

Starring: Ann Dusenberry, Gail Strickland, Bruce Davison
Featuring: Clu Gulager, Bert Remsen, Terence Knox
Written and directed by: Ken & Jim Wheat

Synopsis: Struggling young actress Robin (Dusenberry) is approached to play Elizabeth, a young woman who committed suicide in an insane asylum after witnessing the brutal murder of her parents. Videotaped rehearsals held in the asylum prove Robin's talent, but funding for the feature film falls through. Before she can return to L.A., however, Elizabeth's brother (Davison) convinces Robin that she is a dupe in a sinister scam to deny him his rightful—and considerable—inheritance by passing off the rehearsal tapes in a court hearing as the living, but incompetent, Elizabeth. They team up to thwart the plan—until Robin discovers an even deeper level of deception, leaving her an institutionalized pawn in a deadly game involving multiple murder and multiple millions. Her only hope for rescue lies in her jilted boyfriend and her ex-agent, who become suspicious of her disappearance and attempt to track her down.
Discussion: A quick synopsis can only scratch the surface of this intricately convoluted thriller—but revealing any more would spoil the surprises of the multiple levels of deception and double- (and triple-) crosses. Too many thrillers attempt this "Strange Loop" effect and end up muddled, illogical or incomprehensible, but *Lies* wields a deft hand at regularly ripping the rug from under our expectations in a manner thoroughly unpredictable yet immediately understandable. And even though the intelligence quotient flags a bit near the end, when the flick accelerates beyond its delicate cat-and-mouse deception-fest into an active flight-and-fight-fest, the multiple levels of plot are satisfactorily resolved, and the action is fast-paced, assuredly directed and unpredictable. (I'd enhance the irony and convolutions by adding one final line of dialog, allowing her boyfriend, a budding screenwriter, to comment, "You know, this would make one hell of a movie!")
Rent this one for: its elaborate plot contrivances that don't feel contrived; for the earnest acting; for the originality (and gallows humor) of the elevator scene.
You'll (probably) like this if you liked: *Dead of Winter, House of Games, Sleuth, Body Heat, Gaslight*
Dissenting Opinion: "Overly complicated." —SMV (2 stars)
Vidbits: Davison plays "Tom Paris" on "Star Trek: Voyager."

Love and a .45

(postmodern noir/ satire)
(1995; Vidmark; R; 1:42)

Starring: Gil Bellows, Renee Zellweger, Rory Cochrane
Featuring: Peter Fonda, Anne Wedgeworth
Written and directed by: C.M. Talkington

Synopsis: "Watty" Watts (Bellows) is polite, friendly, and full of down-home country wisdom—the kind of guy who gives the counter clerk career advice while robbing his convenience store. Life is good for him and galpal Starlene (Zellweger)—until his speed-snorting partner, Billy Mack (Cochrane) violently fucks up a holdup, then turns on Watty, who's got no choice but to incapacitate the psycho, take the money and run. Things take a turn for the worse when Watty is confronted by sadistic lawman Ranger X, which leads to more gunplay and more trouble. Suddenly, Watty's life is on the poor white trash heap. A road trip to Mexico might not be a bad idea. Then again, with half the cops in Texas, a couple of drug-addled loan sharks and a *really* pissed-off Billy on their tail...it might be a *very* bad idea.
Discussion: It's *Raising Arizona* meets *Natural Born Killers*: a wacky, violent, bloody gunfest, alternately droll and outrageous; a punky postmodern *noir* which does for movies like *Kalifornia* what the *Evil Dead* series did for (or to) horror movies; namely, give us bloodshed that is just too over the top to be taken seriously. Bellows looks like a dissolute Matthew Broderick, and his Watty (a specialist in "risk management") believes his granddad's folk wisdom that there are only two things you need to get by in life (see the title). Zellweger is a countrified Christina Applegate ("Married With Children") clone; a lusty teenage babydoll, playing "romantic outlaw lovers on the lam," always keeping an eye out for a "Polaroid moment." Together they're sympathetic kids: not evil or even bad, just victims of circumstance. ("We're not bloodthirsty killers," Starlene assures a reporter, "we're just newlyweds.") Along the way, we're treated to a mocking of tabloid TV, and Peter Fonda in a role so weird that it has to be seen (and heard) to be believed. And in the end, they prove (to Billy, anyway) that death is the biggest trip of all.
Rent this one for: its twisted black humor and original details.
You'll (probably) like this if you liked: *True Romance, Drugstore Cowboy, Raising Arizona, Blood Simple, Pulp Fiction*
Dissenting Opinion: "Derivative..." —MMG ('97 ed.; 2.5 stars)
Vidbits: Check out that flag-painted prop in the background of Fonda's dining room. Look familiar? • Zellweger made the leap to "star" in '96 by co-starring with Tom Cruise in *Jerry McGuire.*

Manhunter

(psychological/crime thriller)
(1986; Warner; R; 2:00)

Starring: William Petersen, Dennis Farina
Featuring: Kim Greist, Joan Allen, Brian Cox, Tommy Noonan
Written, produced and directed by: Michael Mann
(based on Thomas Harris' novel *Red Dragon*)

Synopsis: "The Tooth Fairy," a vicious psychokiller, has been slashing entire families in some bizarre ritual, and FBI agent Crawford (Farina) wants Will Graham (Petersen) on the case. Will's still scarred emotionally from capturing (and being cut up by) Hannibal "The Cannibal" Lecktor (as it's spelled here) (Cox). But they need his special talent: recreating a psycho's thought process, so it can be predicted and more murders prevented. Will visits Lecktor to "recover the mindset," but Lecktor, in contact with the killer, has a personal agenda. Finding his own family at risk, Will pushes his sanity to its limit, pursuing the psycho in a race against the clock with an intensity bordering on obsession.
Discussion: Grim, tense, occasionally grisly but always stylish, this is in essence a modern *noir* recast in pastels and bright primary colors. At times it's a fascinating, fast-paced police procedural, but often it offers much more, as in the scene where Will attempts to explain his psychic scars to his young son, in language he can understand but which won't pass on the same wounds; an explanation of the fringes of human experience counterpointed by the mundane setting of a grocery store cereal aisle. Mann's direction is assured and rhythmic: internal torment punctuated by crescendos of tension-relieving violence. The plot is convoluted and the logic acceptable, but these are secondary to the brooding mood and our sense of Will's agonized understanding that both physical and psychic survival is at stake—and that the only edge he has in his battle of wits with the brilliantly insane is his rapidly vanishing sanity.
Rent this one for: its moody, menacing intensity and sense of style; as a companion piece to *Silence of the Lambs.*
You'll (probably) like this if you liked: *Silence of the Lambs, Seven,* "Miami Vice," *The Stepfather*
Dissenting Opinion: "...steamy melodramatics which become actively unpleasant..." —HFG
Vidbits: • Two actors appear in both *Manhunter* and *Silence of the Lambs,* playing different characters in each: Frankie Faison plays Lt. Fisk in the former and Barney in the latter, and Dan Butler plays an FBI fingerprint expert in the former and an entomologist in the latter. • Didn't we see this same plot rewritten as an episode of "Miami Vice"?

Miracle Mile

(suspense/action)
(1989; HBO; R; 1:27)

Starring: Anthony Edwards, Mare Winningham, Denise Crosby
Music by: Tangerine Dream
Written and directed by: Steve DeJarnatt

Synopsis: When Harry (Edwards) meets Julie (Winningham), it's love at first sight. They arrange to meet again when she gets off work at an all-night eatery on the Miracle Mile, but a freak power outage causes him to oversleep and show up hours late. While trying to call her, he answers a ringing pay phone and hears a panicky confession: A soldier in a missile silo is trying to alert his dad that "the missiles are flying" and nuclear war is immanent—but he got a wrong number. Harry's convinced, though, and gets confirming clues from a strange patron of the cafe (Crosby), who sets out to arrange a survival stronghold in Antarctica. Harry's got a little over an hour to retrieve Julie and get her to the pickup point before the retaliatory warheads reach L.A., but the news—and the panic—escalates geometrically and soon all of L.A. is a chaotic jungle. Can Harry save himself and Julie from nuclear doom? *Or is there really any war at all?*
Discussion: Ever thought about the unthinkable? It might be a bit passé since the end of the Cold War, but it still makes for an engrossing film, and one which basically creates a new genre: the urban action horror movie. The key question is: Are these events real, or are they taking place in Harry's oversleeping dream? Are the missing pieces plot holes or dream logic? Either way, the film itself is a fever dream of hallucinatory imagery and nightmare-like action. In a situation this extreme, all rules are suspended, every character is on the adrenaline-edge of death, and every move is a gesture of desperation seeking survival. Like a dream, the film grows more irrational, bizarre and unreal the longer it unreels, as panic rapidly escalates into hysteria. And always nagging in the back of our mind is denial: What if Harry is wrong, and is thus responsible for this murderous mass hysteria? The suspense is intense; the panic palpable; and the ending an unbearably poignant, tender gem. If the final lines don't rip your heart out, you do not possess one.
Rent this one for: The fully believable nightmare quality; the exceptionally poignant ending.
You'll (probably) like this if you liked: *Total Recall*
Dissenting Opinion: "Artificial and overwrought from the word go...loses all credibility in its final half hour when illogic really takes over." —MMG (1.5 stars)

Mister Frost

(supernatural/psychological thriller)
(1990; SVS; R; 1:32)

Starring: Jeff Goldblum, Kathy Baker, Alan Bates
Featuring: Roland Giraud, Charley Boorman
Written by: Philip Setbon, Brad Lynch
Directed by: Philip Setbon

Synopsis: When Police Inspector Detweiler (Bates) drops by his country estate pursuing a murder, Mr. Frost (Goldblum) makes no attempt to hide the fact that he's just finished burying the body. Further investigation uncovers two dozen mutilated corpses buried on the grounds. After years of fruitless psychiatric observation, Mr. Frost is transferred to St. Clare Hospital, where he breaks his two-year silence—but only with Dr. Sarah Day (Baker). Detweiler appears, warning the staff that Frost is "the Devil himself"—a charge Frost encourages. He wants to prove his existence to the world, and chose Sarah because she's a scientist, and he needs the "confrontation with disbelief." At the risk of her career, her sanity and her life, she is compelled to continue treating him—even if he is who he claims, and even if his games trap her and Detweiler in a deadly, no-win dilemma.
Discussion: Is Mr. Frost really The Devil, or is he just a deeply disturbed individual? The film works on multiple levels; not only is it a suspense thriller and a creepy horror film (with Goldblum reveling in the chilling charm of his sinister side) but it raises provocative questions that are certainly psychological, definitely philosophical and possibly even religious, as Sarah and Mr. Frost engage in a dialog designed to illustrate the impotence of science in the face of "The Wild Side," and the failure of rationality when faced with panic. Both have persuasive arguments. (There are also strong parallels with *Exorcist II:* the same theme, some duplicate dialog; even the music and accents—not to mention Charley Boorman as a featured player here...) This pre-Dahmer fiction is less strange than the recent truth, but illustrates that we don't need a Devil to haunt us. Belief in a Devil might actually provide some comfort. After all, if a *human* is capable of such grotesque perversion, and *we're* human... In the end, the only choice is between of the lesser of two evils.
Rent this one for: Goldblum; the philosophical questions.
You'll (probably) like this if you liked: *The Omen, The Fly, The Prophecy, Exorcist II: The Heretic*
Dissenting Opinion: • "1 bone" —GMR • "A disappointment..." —SMV (2 stars) • "Goldblum is clearly having a great time, but you're not likely to." —MMG (2 stars)

Mute Witness

(thriller)

(1994; Columbia TriStar; R; 1:38)

Starring: Marina Sudina, Fay Ripley, Evan Richards
Written, directed and co-produced by: Anthony Waller

Synopsis: As the special effects expert on an American movie crew filming a slasher flick in Moscow, Billie Hughes (Sudina) knows the difference between stage murder and real murder. But when she accidentally witnesses two Russians surreptitiously using the crew's equipment after hours to shoot a snuff film, she wants to speak out. Too bad she's mute. She can *hear* just fine, but must "talk" with sign language and writing. Her protective sister Karen (Ripley) translates her story to the Russian police—but by the time they investigate, all the evidence has disappeared. All the evidence, that is, except the witness...
Discussion: What could easily have been a sub-standard, gimmicky thriller is handled deftly and with a touch of humor in this tense and suspenseful entry. Billie's muteness is not just a gimmick, for example, but a physical representation of the difficulty every one of the Americans experiences in attempting to communicate with the Russians; they all, at some point, feel her frustration at not being able to communicate. And Billie herself is no helpless handicapped heroine, but a very resourceful young woman, filled with clever methods of expressing herself (including some impressive "body language" when trying to attract the attention of a nosy neighbor). Although the film switches tracks about halfway, transforming from a murder mystery into a thriller about corrupt cops and Russian gangsters, the switch turns it into a killer thriller, where plot twists and turns and double-crosses occur every few minutes—and then every few seconds in the final minutes of the film. Add in some comic relief (mostly in the person of the inept director), a "mystery villain" and some unusual location shots of Moscow, and you've got a taut little thriller that can actually boast some originality and wit. A satisfying, suspenseful and fun little film.
Rent this one for: the snowballing suspense; the original touches; Sudina's performance.
You'll (probably) like this if you liked: *Almost Hollywood, Special Effects, Wait Until Dark*
Vidbits: • Features an appearance by a very famous actor who appears briefly as the leader of the gangster ring—but since the credits list him only as the "Mystery Guest Star," I won't spoil the surprise by revealing his identity. • A British-German-Russian co-production, filmed entirely on location in Moscow.

One False Move

(crime thriller/modern noir)
(1991; Columbia TriStar; R; 1:45)

Starring: Bill Paxton, Cynda Williams
Featuring: Billy Bob Thornton, Michael Beach
Written by: Billy Bob Thornton, Tom Epperson
Directed by: Carl Franklin *(Devil in a Blue Dress)*

Synopsis: Coke and cash—that's what Roy (Thornton) and Pluto (Beach) are after, and they don't care who they have to kill to get them, even two entire families. All signs indicate that the pair is fleeing L.A. to hide out at Roy's uncle's place in Star City, Arkansas, taking Roy's beautiful black moll, "Fantasia" (Williams), along for the ride. The backwater town's police chief, Dale Dixon (Paxton) is plumb tickled they're heading his way. This is the biggest thing that's ever happened during his 10 years on the force, and he gets to hang out with a couple of big city boys on the stakeout! Dale gets a double dose of reality, though, when he finds that the cops are mocking his countrified style—and when a photo of the killers reveals that "Fantasia" is homegirl Lila Walker. Dale tried to sway the wayward Walker from an early life of crime, but she split five years ago, leaving a young son behind her. And suddenly a second story starts, and everyone involved descends on Lila, each with his own agenda.
Discussion: Hit with both barrels of reality, Dale is suddenly sobered into proving he's not the interrupting bumpkin he appears. His motives prove complex: Is he attempting to cover up an old life come back to haunt him, or is he attempting to atone for his "one false move," made years earlier? In addition to the deft direction and compelling script, the performances are first-rate. Everyone hits precisely the right tone, particularly Paxton. A heavy sense of impending doom hangs over everyone's head in this chilling thriller, as though not one among them can escape the trajectory of their interwoven, deadly destinies. Perhaps the highest praise I can give this film is that the questions left unanswered are the most intriguing. How did Lila fall in with Roy? Is she telling the truth to Dale? And what happens after the final fadeout? We care—but we'll never know.
Rent this one for: the performances; the suspenseful script.
You'll (probably) like this if you liked: *Blood Simple, Badlands, In Cold Blood, At Close Range, Red Rock West*
Dissenting Opinion: "Wildly praised (and mildly over-praised) ...Praiseworthy—as long as you realize that Hollywood was churning out its equal a dozen or more times yearly during the heyday of film noir." —MMG (3 stars)

Red Rock West

(modern noir)

(1993; Columbia TriStar; R; 1:38)

Starring: Nicolas Cage, Dennis Hopper, Lara Flynn Boyle, J.T. Walsh
Written by: John Dahl, Rick Dahl
Directed by: John Dahl

Synopsis: Dead broke and stuck in the middle of nowhere, Mike (Cage) pulls into Red Rock, Wyoming, looking for work. Bar owner Wayne (Walsh) sees Mike's Texas plates and mistakes him for the hit man he's expecting. Mike's more than happy to take Wayne's $5K, figuring he'll skip town without doing "the job"—whacking Wayne's wife, Suzanne (Boyle). Instead, his bothersome conscience gets the better of him, and he warns the wife. She makes a counter-offer: she'll double the money if he'll whack Wayne. He hightails it out of town, but a strange accident brings him back, where he's arrested for attempted homicide by the sheriff—Wayne. He escapes, only to come across Lyle (Hopper), the real hit man—and the only one among them who might actually be who he claims he is. Mike finds himself stuck in a web of deception and greed in which alliances shift with every plot twist. Can he ever straighten out this incredible mess—or even just escape from the clutches of Red Rock?
Discussion: It's like one of those nightmares where you're running and running and the street turns to tar... Every time Mike finds a way out of town, the town itself seems to exert some strange gravitational force, pulling him back into the black hole of Red Rock—and deeper every time. His elastic escape attempts are part of the subtle fun of this low-key, stylish modern *noir* thriller. The film is filled with one unpredictably wicked plot twist after another—and ironically, many of the plot complications are caused by Mike's own misguided Good Samaritan instincts. Under its dead serious surface runs an undertow of deep, dark irony—setting the final shoot-out in a graveyard is just one example. And while the dialog is sparse, the flick is drenched in suspense. Intelligent, atmospheric and convoluted.
Rent this one for: its style; its convoluted, plot-twisted story.
You'll (probably) like this if you liked: *The Last Seduction* (Dahl), *Blood Simple, Body Heat, Shallow Grave, Love and a .45*
Credentials: "Ten Best Films of 1994" list —Gene Siskel
Dissenting Opinion: *Premiere's* profile of Dahl (3/96) says the original distributor "thought it was flat and uninteresting."
Vidbits: • Originally released on cable. • Country singer Dwight Yoakam appears as a truck driver who gives Mike a lift.

Sharky's Machine

(crime drama)

(1981; Warner; R; 1:59)

Starring: Burt Reynolds, Rachel Ward, Vittorio Gassman
Featuring: Brian Keith, Charles Durning, Bernie Casey, Richard Libertini, Henry Silva, Earl Holliman, Darryl Hickman
Written by: Gerald DiPego (based on the novel by William Diehl)
Directed by: Burt Reynolds

Synopsis: A drug bust gone bad buys Sharky (Reynolds) a demotion to Atlanta P.D.'s Vice Squad—the "snakepit," where they bust hookers and baby-sit politicians. The murder of a call girl lands him on surveillance duty, spying on sultry, smoky-voiced, $1000 prostitute Dominoe (Ward). He watches her night and day, and, inevitably, falls for her. He takes it hard when he discovers she's seeing a gubernatorial candidate (Holliman)—and that they're both owned by rich drug lord Victor (Gassman). And he takes it all the harder when she's blown away by a shotgun-wielding hitman (Silva). The Vice "machine" decides to handle this one themselves. But someone inside the P.D. is on Victor's payroll. One man on top of the town, one fink inside the department: The fix is in, and Sharky can't win. They say.
Discussion: Action, suspense, stunts, and a couple of things missing from too many similar films: humor and a heart. The high points of the movie are its quirky characters, each a true eccentric, like black Zen-master Arch (Casey), who can make himself invisible (he thinks), or Silva's drug-crazed killer, a robot zombie who screams as he shoots, or the always underused Libertini, here given rein to display his energetic comedic talent. The infusion of humor at the oddest times is a delight; even the final shoot-out has its funny moments. As for heart, Sharky is not your typical action hero. Reynolds brings surprising depth to the role, as a wistful, almost melancholy cop. Beneath their hardened masks, Sharky and Dominoe are both ruined romantics, sharing the same basic dreams and finding in each other a last chance at happiness. As an actor-turned-director, Reynolds is no Eastwood, but at worst he's eclectic in his mix of styles. The graphic violence is a bit uncomfortable, and the music is too loud, but aside from these minor problems, it's a winner.
Rent this one for: the romance; its blend of blood and humor.
You'll (probably) like this if you liked: *Heat, Stick, Tightrope, Sudden Impact, Lethal Weapon 2, Mad Dog and Glory, Laura, Dirty Harry, Someone To Watch Over Me*
Dissenting Opinion: "Jarring, loud, and extremely bloody... you'll eventually become numbed by all the sleaze..." —MMG (2)
Vidbits: Novelist Diehl appears in the vice room scene as Percy.

A Shock to the System

(black comedy)

(1990; HBO; R; 1:28)

Starring: Michael Caine, Elizabeth McGovern
Featuring: Peter Riegert, Swoozie Kurtz, Will Patton, John McMartin
Written by: Andrew Klavan (based on the novel by Simon Brett)
Directed by: Jan Egleson

Synopsis: Graham Marshall (Caine), a legitimate member of the Old Boys Network, worked hard for many years in the corporate system. He looked forward to his promotion to Head of Marketing of his New York firm. He'd *earned* it. So when he's "passed over" in favor of a smarmy subordinate (Riegert), he's hurt. And when that underhanded underling begins to undermine his power base, George wants to hurt back. A freak subway mishap convinces him that he can get away with murder—literally. And the corporate ladder suddenly sprouts some new rungs...
Discussion: Based (at least spiritually) on that corporate motto of the '80s—"Old age and treachery will overcome youth and idealism"—this very black comedy is a perfect parable for corporate war, where ruthlessness is an art and an asset. It reminds us that office power is expressed in subtle touches: who lights whose cigar; whose jokes are deemed funny. Caine, deadpan as always, suggests much more than he expresses; even his fatal charm may be sublimated rage. He seduces us with sympathy, so that when he begins to surgically eliminate boors, we root for him. *They deserve to die:* They're obnoxious, rude, a waste of space. And when we're led to believe that he might kill the *wrong* person, a *good* person—and then discover that *the thought never crossed his mind...*we realize that we're no better than Graham. Maybe worse: *We thought he'd do it.* There are too many plot twists to spoil; we can't even mention sensitive Stella (McGovern) and the seminal role she plays, or the confused Colombo trying to raise Caine. The direction is tight and sly; not a frame is wasted, and some transitions are brilliant (think "explosive orgasm"). *Shock* is a devastating satire, right up to the final shot (and sound effect): smart, sharp, subtle, sinister, subversive and cynical, undermining all expectations. We're left with one uncomfortable question, however: Is George *really* a sociopath—or is he just one small step ahead of the inevitable?
Rent this one for being a devilishly clever, wicked little thriller.
You'll (probably) like this if you liked: *Heathers, Wall Street*
Dissenting Opinion: "...so-so..." —MMG (2.5 stars)
Vidbits: The brilliant print ad campaign showed Caine glaring between Venetian blinds under the legend, "Die, Yuppie Scum!"

Silent Fall

(psychological drama)
(1995; Warner; R; 1:41)

Starring: Richard Dreyfuss, Linda Hamilton
Featuring: John Lithgow, J.T. Walsh, Ben Faulkner
"Introducing": Liv Tyler
Written by: Akiva Goldsman
Directed by: Bruce Beresford

Synopsis: Indian summer in Maryland. Retired child psychologist Dr. Jake Rainer (Dreyfuss) is brought by Sheriff Rivers (Walsh) to the scene of a grisly double murder. Why? Mom and dad's killer appears to be their autistic 9-year-old son, Timmy (Faulkner). His teenage sister, Sylvie (Tyler), is also found, unconscious, at the scene. The coroner says it couldn't be the boy—but he must have *seen* the real killer. Rivers gives Jake a chance to unlock the child's mind before resorting to Dr. Harlinger's (Lithgow) dangerous drug "therapy." Jake and his wife (Hamilton) take custody of Tim and his protective sister, but Jake has reason to be nervous: his unorthodox techniques with autistic kids apparently backfired two years earlier, resulting in tragedy. Jake discovers that Tim is indeed harboring a horrible secret. But it's not a secret anyone expects—or a secret anyone wants to hear. And discovering it could cost Jake his life.
Discussion: Dreyfuss is terrific: wounded, grieving, self-pitying —but unable to stop caring. Tim's trouble could spell salvation for them both: Jake needs to help Tim as much as Tim needs his help. Hamilton has little to do, and Lithgow less, but they do it well. The plot is involved and involving, with one intriguing surprise after another; it builds in intensity and, beneath its surface, explores the thin line between personal and professional behavior, and the risks of crossing that line. Adding electricity are the psychosexual undercurrents which figure prominently in the (multiple) resolutions. All this and the lush landscape photography we expect from Beresford. There's not a false frame in this film—so why has no one ever heard of it?
Rent this one for: its intelligent, realistic adult drama; for being a character *and* plot-driven film in a balanced blend; for Dreyfuss's performance (and little Faulkner's as well).
You'll (probably) like this if you liked: *The Stepfather, Rain Man, Paradise; What About Bob?* (comic treatment)
Dissenting Opinion: "Murky all the way, and predictable *nearly* all the way, except for an ill-advised 'light' wrap-up that'll make you take a loud fall out of your seat." —MMG (1.5 stars)
Vidbits: • Barely released to theaters before released on video.
• Liv Tyler is daughter of Aerosmith's lead singer, Steven Tyler.

Flashback!

The Silent Partner

(suspense/psychological thriller)
(1979; Vestron; R; 1:43)

Starring: Elliott Gould, Christopher Plummer, Susannah York
Featuring: Céline Lomez, Ken Pogue, John Candy
Written by: Curtis Hanson
(based on the novel *Think of a Number* by Anders Bodelson)
Directed by: Daryl Duke

Synopsis: Christmas in Canada (Toronto, precisely). Mild-mannered Miles Cullen (Gould) has a crush on fellow bank clerk Julie (York)—but her impression of him is a man whose total "is less than the sum of the parts." An odd coincidence convinces Cullen that the bank will soon be robbed by a mall Santa—and when it happens, Cullen is prepared. He sequesters most of his window's cash—nearly $50,000—in his lunch box, assuming it will be chalked up to robbery losses. What he doesn't count on is the thief catching on to his scam. And he could never have predicted that Reikle (Plummer) would turn out to be a sadistic psychopath who'll stop at nothing to get the money—and revenge. Thus begins a deadly cat-and-mouse game—only for Reikle, it's not a game...

Discussion: The robbery fuels endless speculation among the bank employees about what they'd do if the booty was theirs. "I suppose I'd use the money to buy myself another chance," Miles reveals. And this is his strength: Reikle might be greedy, but he's only after the cash. To Miles, however, this tiny sum represents his future. And it serves to symbolize his self-image, too, providing him with confidence and daring he never knew he had. Miles has other advantageous traits as well: level-headed logic, a talent for improvisation, and a history of being underestimated. When he's stalked and terrorized by Reikle, he knows he can't go to the police. But he can borrow Reikle's techniques and turn the tables on him. Although the film drags a bit once the red-herring romance is introduced (a sequence which also leads to the movie's one black mark: a gratuitously gory, eye-averting scene involving a fish tank), it picks up again near the end, as the men's deadly chess game leads Miles to take one final desperate gamble to outwit the killer—and secure a future.

Rent this one for: its clever cat-and-mouse game; for bringing civility to psychothrillers.

You'll (probably) like this if you liked: *52 Pickup*

Dissenting Opinion: "...it might have been entertaining but elected instead to be unpleasant." —*HFG*

Someone To Watch Over Me

(romance/ suspense)

(1987; Columbia TriStar; R; 1:46)

Starring: Tom Berenger, Mimi Rogers, Lorraine Bracco
Featuring: Jerry Orbach, Andreas Katsulas, John Rubenstein
Written by: Howard Franklin
Directed by: Ridley Scott

Synopsis: Mike Keegan (Berenger) is one lucky New York cop: not only is he promoted to detective, but he's transferred to the upper East side of Manhattan, home of the rich and famous. His first assignment: baby-sitting/bodyguarding beautiful rich socialite Claire Gregory (Rogers), eyewitness to a murder by mobster Joey Venza (Katsulas). Mike's a borough kinda guy, however, and feels like a fish out of water in the skyscraper society Claire inhabits. Alone, however, the two get along fine. *Too* fine, which drives a wedge between Mike and his earthy wife Ellie (Bracco). Meanwhile, Venza makes attempts on Claire's life, scaring her in ways she's unaccustomed to. A lonely woman in fear of her life; a knight in tarnished armor: Can romance be far behind? Will Mike's personal involvement help him protect Claire, or will it complicate his professional duties? And while he's protecting Claire all night, every night, who's going to protect his own family from the psychopathic antics of Venza?
Discussion: The crime plot is suspenseful, but plays second fiddle to the romantic entanglements of Mike and his two women. He's caught in the contrast between his no-nonsense wife and gritty life in Queens and the elegant, classy Uptown girl cloistered in an apartment that looks like a museum. Mike's attraction to Claire is understandable: he's drawn to her class, her calm, her beauty and intelligence—characteristics he realizes are missing at home. But what does she see in him? It's more than just opposites attracting; we get the impression that she finds him a refreshing reality check. Both are fascinated by worlds which exist only inches away, but which neither can ever inhabit or understand. And through it all runs Scott's superb eye for style, where every room becomes a luminous, smoky space and every shot a revealing photograph.
Rent this one for: its stylish visuals and emotional charge.
You'll (probably) like this if you liked: *The Bodyguard, Tequila Sunrise, Witness, Dead Again; Love At Large* (comedy)
Dissenting Opinion: "Visually dazzling but sometimes troubled tale..." —SMV (2.5 stars)
Vidbits: Features several different versions of the title song, including covers by Sting and Roberta Flack.

Flashback!

Sorcerer

(suspense thriller)
(1977; MCA; PG; 2:01)

Starring: Roy Scheider, Bruno Cremer
Written by: Walon Green (based on the film *The Wages of Fear*)
Music by: Tangerine Dream, Keith Jarrett, Charlie Parker
Directed and produced by: William Friedkin

Synopsis: Four wanted men on the run from four corners of the earth find themselves in the Amazon jungle, working on an oil rig in a shanty town. Terrorist bombs set the well on fire, and risky action is needed to cap it off: cases of aging, unstable, nitro-leaking dynamite must be transported 200 miles through the dangerous terrain of the jungle. The men become "suicide jockeys," betting their petty lives against lottery-like wages, driving antique trucks over bumpy jungle roads, mountainous terrain and decrepit bridges, and through rainforest storms, swamps, mud and felled trees. Will either truck make it? And if so, what physical and emotional toll will it take on the men?
Discussion: Once the proper adjectives are in place—harrowing, grim, suspenseful—there's really little more to say. The film knows this: there's very little dialog, and very little needed. What does stand out in this story of a desperate attempt by desperate men is the nightmarish imagery: a truck with a grill like a grinning skull or death mask, mocking them, for instance. The creepy, driving electronic score by Tangerine Dream also adds an electric charge to the thick atmosphere of menace. Scheider is excellent (as always) as the half-hardened small-time hood who understands the value of life far better than any of his companions on this wild ride—which makes the final irony of the film all the more pointed. If possible, watch this as the second half of a double feature with the original. Revel in the superior sense of suspense of the first, enhanced by the superb visual imagery of *Sorcerer.*
Rent this one for: the intense tension and suspense; the exceptional photography; the bridge-crossing sequence.
You'll (probably) like this if you liked: *The Wages of Fear*
Dissenting Opinion: • "...may have contributed to...the near demise of Friedkin's directing career." —GMR (2.5 bones) • "Why anyone should have wanted to spend twenty million dollars on a remake of *The Wages of Fear,* do it badly, and give it a misleading title is anybody's guess. The result is dire." —HFG
Vidbits: Dedicated to H-G. Clouzot, who directed the original 1955 version of the film, based on the novel by Georges Arnaud.

Special Effects

(1984; Embassy, New Line, Sultan; R; 1:46)

Starring: Zoe Tamerlis, Eric Bogosian
Written and directed by: Larry Cohen

Synopsis: Chris Neville (Bogosian) is a major film director who's fallen from grace. When he accidentally strangles struggling actress (and runaway wife) Mary Jean (Tamerlis) in his bed—and captures the killing on the "sex-cam" hidden in his bedroom—he realizes he's got the kind of real-life performance no actress could ever fake. And he conceives of a grand plan to hide his crime *and* regenerate his career: He'll frame her estranged hick hubby and make a film about the murder—starring the husband as the primary suspect. He bails out hubby, locates a Mary Jean look-alike (Tamerlis), and manipulates the cops to cooperate. Now he faces the biggest challenge of his career: To manipulate reality...not to create film, but to create an *alternate* reality that will exonerate himself—and frame an innocent man.
Discussion: A film entitled *Special Effects*—without any special effects? "I'm taking reality and making it look like make-believe," Neville tells the detective on the case. "That's a special effect, too." The film is plagued with problems: at best, it's unfocused, missing many opportunities to bring some satirical insights—and its own theme of "real vs. reel"—into sharp focus. And it starts out slow and amateurish, although it does pick up once Bogosian enters. Its merits, however, outweigh its faults enough to make the *Killer B* final cut. Tamerlis is believable in both roles (and naked much of the time); the satire that does get through often concerns the detective suckered in by Neville's presentation of the "glamour" of filmmaking (a special effect if ever there was one!), and leads to a suitably ironic result; and the convoluted plot twists as the murderous Neville frantically attempts to recreate reality to match his film are often clever, and blur the line between real-real and "reel"-real. Unfocused, but fun.
Rent this one for: the intriguing plot; Tamerlis' performances.
You'll (probably) like this if you liked: *Star 80, The Stunt Man, Almost Hollywood, Lies, Mute Witness, Ms. .45*
Credentials: "[a] rental will be money well spent." —PVG (3 ♦)
Dissenting Opinion: • "...sinks in the mire of flawed execution ...overdone script." —GMR (2 bones) • "...uneven..." —MMG (2.5 stars) • "Turkey" —VMG • "A number of witty points about Hollywood megalomania are lost in the hyperventilating plot." —SMV (2 stars)
Vidbits: Among the headshots of actresses being considered for the part of Mary Jean is Dustin Hoffman made up as "Dorothy Michaels" from *Tootsie.*

The Stepfather

(psychological thriller)
(1987; Columbia TriStar; R; 1:29)

Starring: Terry O'Quinn, Shelley Hack, Jill Schoelen
Written by: Donald E. Westlake
Music by: Patrick Moraz
Directed by: Joseph Ruben

Synopsis: It's a typical day in suburbia. A middle-aged man shaves, showers, dresses and walks out the front door—past the bloody bodies of his murdered wife and child. A year later, he's "Jerry Blake" (O'Quinn), a real estate agent married to Susan (Hack), and stepfather of troubled teen Stephanie (Schoelen). Jerry's all sweetness and light, but Steph ain't buying it—he creeps her out. Unbeknownst to any of them, the brother of "Jerry's" previous victim is tracking him down, and Steph is his unwitting assistant. If Jerry finds out, he'll be...disappointed.
Discussion: Half a century ago, we fought a viscous psychotic to protect the American Way of Life. Today, if you kill for that vision, *you're* the nut—like Jerry, a platitude-puking, pod-person paragon of '50s values, so square he makes Mike Brady look like Tim Leary. All Jerry wants is a little "order" in his life—and mere perfection from his family. There are no gray areas in his philosophy, so any violation of the whitest white deserves the blackest punishment. If one family disappoints him...Well, he'll just have to try, try again. It *is* the American way. So when his *faux* family proves to have some *real* values—like survival, self-reliance and insight—his defeat is a nail in the coffin of those vague, shallow "Family Values" we've been bombarded with for years. They always were a fantasy—and if you live in a fantasy world too long, how can you be sane? The flick is filled with wickedly witty subtle touches, like Jerry's fondness for Freddy Krueger sweaters, a parody of Rockwell's famous Thanksgiving painting, and an homage to *two* Hitchcock films in the final confrontation. It's a real "psycho" thriller, providing plenty of suspense and mind-games without the need for graphic gore.
Rent this one for: its intelligent suspense and wicked satire.
You'll (probably) like this if you liked: *Blue Velvet; Psycho*
Credentials: • One of "Ten Most Underrated Movies of the '80s" —*Premiere Guide to Movies on Video*
Vidbits: • Westlake is best known for his caper novels, many of which have been made into films (like *The Hot Rock*). • Moraz, formerly of the rock group Yes, is one of The Moody Blues. • The movie's picture-perfect American suburb is, ironically, located in Vancouver, B.C., Canada. • Skip the two lame sequels.

Thief

(crime drama)

(1981; MGM/ UA; R; 2:04)

Starring: James Caan, Tuesday Weld, Robert Prosky
Featuring: Willie Nelson, James Belushi, Dennis Farina
Music by: Tangerine Dream
Written and directed by: Michael Mann
(based on the book *The Home Invaders* by Frank Hohimer)

Synopsis: Frank (Caan) is a thief. It's what he does; who he is. Couple of scores a month; jewels and cash only. He's driven: When you've spent your twenties behind bars, you've got a lot of catching up to do. And he's got his whole life planned. Next on the list is a wife; he picks Jesse (Weld), a woman with a past herself. Things look good—until he gives in to temptation and accepts an assignment from fatherly crime boss Leo (Prosky) for one last big score. Suddenly his house is bugged, the cops are everywhere he goes, and Leo wants to run his life. Everything was easier when he was an independent—but the cost of independence now might be nothing less than everything.

Discussion: Suspenseful, gritty, absorbing and occasionally chilling, Mann's directorial debut is a masterpiece of atmosphere and style. The photography is equally gorgeous whether reflecting stark lights off cold, wet Chicago streets or spraying scathing sparks in our faces as Frank torches his way into a safe. And the film is equally compelling when providing the vicarious thrill of watching the heists or when exhibiting fascinating details of the lives, work, and insider argot of professional thieves, corrupt cops and organized crime. Beneath this surface style is a character study of Frank, a man fiercely independent, unpredictable, amoral and dangerous. It's his story, and Caan owns the film in a manner as intense and assured as Mann's direction. Everyone else is window-dressing—but Weld is attractive and effective window-dressing, and Prosky is a stand-out as the psychotic father figure who Frank unconsciously wants to replace his original father-figure, Okie (Nelson), his prison mentor and a master thief himself. The finale springs directly from Frank's character, and the film ends in a crescendo of vengeance and violence both unexpected and yet somehow inevitable.

Rent this one for: its stylish, gritty suspense.

You'll (probably) like this if you liked: *Breaking In, The Godfather, The French Connection,* "Police Story," "Miami Vice"

Dissenting Opinion: "...lacking just one vital ingredient—heart." —*People Magazine Guide to Movies on Video*

Vidbits: Look closely for William Peterson, who would later star in Mann's *Manhunter,* as a club bartender.

Flashback!

Winter Kills

(political thriller/ black comedy)
(1979; Columbia TriStar; R; 1:37)

Starring: Jeff Bridges, John Huston
Featuring: Anthony Perkins, Richard Boone, Sterling Hayden
Eli Wallach, Ralph Meeker, Belinda Bauer, Donald Moffat
Music by: Maurice Jarre
Written and directed by: William Richert
(based on "a novel" by Richard Condon)

Synopsis: On a ship in the middle of the Pacific, Nick Keegan (Bridges) hears a shocking deathbed confession: The dying man claims he was the actual assassin of Nick's half-brother, Pres. Keegan, 19 years earlier. He reveals the location of the murder weapon—and the moment Nick retrieves it, all hell breaks loose. Nick retreats to his business baron father's (Huston) expansive ranch, and the patriarch decrees that Nick will go out and blow the case wide open. He embarks on a globe-girdling odyssey of investigation, encountering strange dangers and quirky characters—and leaving a trail of bodies in his wake. It doesn't take long before Nick is the one being hunted—but by whom?
Discussion: "Who to trust," clucks the sinister Cerutti (Perkins). "Who to trust?" Nobody in this zoo, which is filled with red herrings, sleazy weasels, sitting ducks, snakes-in-the-grass, cat-and-mouse games and dog-eat-dog deals and deceptions. Not to mention a one-to-one correspondence with major players in the JFK assassination (according to some theories). (If this were a book, it would be a roman à clef.) Huston is a hoot as the ubiquitous, mega-rich megalomaniac, an amoral, foul-mouthed leering old lech, and the solution to the conspiracy is a Hitchcockian shocker. But is it really an incestuous web of treachery? Or is it just good business?
Rent this one for: the "Dead Hams Society": Huston, Boone and Hayden, each energetically attempting to chew more scenery than any of the others. (Huston wins.); for the sheer balls of turning the JFK assassination into a Marx Bros. farce: the blackest moment in recent history turned into the blackest comedy in recent memory—the JFK assassination on acid.
You'll (probably) like this if you liked: *JFK, Executive Action, Parallax View, Chinatown, The President's Analyst, Flashpoint, Three Days of the Condor, The Godfather, Part II*
Dissenting Opinion: • "...wildly uneven..." —MMG (2.5 stars) • "Heavy-going and confusing melodrama" —HFG
Vidbits: Liz Taylor is in the film (speaking not a single word) but not in the credits; allegedly she quit before completion.

SCIENCE FICTION/Fantasy

SCIENCE FICTION/Fantasy

Do you have any clue how difficult it is to find an "unseen" science fiction film? Even the worst dreck in this genre is on *somebody's* list of "cult favorites," or showed up on "Mystery Science Theater 3000." There are *entire books* devoted to discussing in great detail every science fiction, fantasy and horror flick ever produced, no matter how bad.

But *Killer B's* is about *good* unknown movies. So those guides which revel in ineptness were of little use in doing research for this section. Sure, *Plan 9 From Outer Space* is a good movie to *mock*—but it's anything *but* a good movie.

I did have a couple of advantages here, however. During my six-year stint as host of Sunday Science Fiction Night on KTEH-TV (PBS for Silicon Valley), for instance, it was incumbent upon me to do a weekly video review of a science fiction or fantasy film. So I had a good excuse to watch a *lot* of genre flicks. And second, this book was never intended for that subspecies of hard-core sci-fi fan who's seen everything but has no critical judgment about its merit. The films included in this section are movies which can be enjoyed by a general audience. Even so, I'd be *extremely* surprised if even the most hard-core SF viewer has seen all of these titles.

The great thing about SF is that it can encompass so many other film categories. In this section you'll find action epics, comedies, dramas, art house favorites, philosophical treatises, thrillers, romances and pure flights of imaginative fancy.

Something for everyone? Well...everyone except the aliens...

The Adventures of Baron Munchausen

(adventure/family fare)
(1989; Columbia TriStar; PG; 2:06)

Starring: John Neville, Eric Idle, Sarah Polley
Featuring: Jonathan Pryce, Valentina Cortese, Oliver Reed, Charles McKeown, Dennis Winston, Jack Purvis, Uma Thurman
Written and directed by: Terry Gilliam

Synopsis: "Late 18th Century. The Age of Reason. Wednesday." The stage is set—literally. A ragtag troupe of thespians attempts to perform an epic fantasy, "The Adventures of Baron Munchausen." Bad enough the city's under siege by the Turks, but then some senile old blowhard takes the stage claiming *he* is the legendary Baron (Neville)—and that *he* is responsible for this war, *and* that he is the only one who can *end* it! When the theater itself is shelled, the troupe owner's daughter Sally (Polley)—the one among them who believes his story—saves the Baron from the Grim Reaper, then stows away on his makeshift blimp, as they comb the four corners of the globe (and beyond) to reassemble his band of extraordinary servants and end the war. Or will the skeletal Spectre of Death claim him first?
Discussion: So much to say; so little space! It's an incredibly imaginative fantasy; a living storybook; an extravaganza of effects and eccentric invention; a fabulist masterpiece; an Epic Adventure film worthy of the Baron's own legendary exaggeration. Suffused with a golden glow, it's a unique visual feast, where every shot is a delicately composed painting. It's not perfect, however: it's far too long, and each sequence runs too long. And Robin Williams is not only obnoxious but embarrassingly out of place. On the other hand, Thurman's air-dancing Venus scene is wondrously perfect. Ultimately it's an exhilarating film: a glorious triumph of imagination over reason, and storytelling so vivid it transcends mundane truth to become timeless Truth.
Rent this one for: its awesome imagery; the sense of wonder.
You'll (probably) like this if you liked: *Time Bandits, The Wizard of Oz; Pinocchio, Willy Wonka; Yellow Submarine*
Credentials: "Astonishing" —Roger Ebert (3 stars)
Dissenting Opinion: "...bountiful imagination, but little control over it." —SMV (2.5 stars)
Vidbits: • According to *Variety,* the film lost $42 million, making it the second-biggest money-losing movie of the entire decade of the '80s. • Robin Williams is credited only as "Ray D. Tutto" (e.g., "rei de tutto"; "king of everything"—his film role). • Watch for Sting as the (unfortunately) heroic soldier early in the film.

Flashback!

Alphaville

(avant garde/ art/ parody)
(French with English subtitles)
(1965; Nostalgia Family Video, Home Vision; NR; 1:40; B&W)

Starring: Eddie Constantine, Anna Karina, Akim Tamiroff
Written and directed by: Jean-Luc Godard

Synopsis: Under cover as "Ivan Johnson," reporter for *Figaro-Pravda,* supertough secret agent Lemmy Caution (Constantine) drives his Ford Galaxy through intersidereal space into Alphaville, the City of Science. His mission: locate Leonard Vonbraun (formerly Prof. Nosferatu), founder of Alphaville, and bring him back—or liquidate him. Lemmy discovers that Alphaville is a fascist utopia where the denizens have lost all sense of feeling and live like emotionless robots; where a new "Bible" (i.e., dictionary) is issued daily, always with the omission of new forbidden words, like "conscience" and "tenderness"; a "galaxy" of its own, where Yes means No and where no one says "Why?; a city where one either "adapts" or is executed; where a man can be condemned to death for acting illogically—like crying when his wife dies. It is a totalitarian technocracy, all ruled by the dispassionately logical Alpha 60, the "dreadfully unique" most powerful computer ever assembled. And Prof. Vonbraun created it all. Lemmy checks into his room, fighting off attackers as well as advances by the "seductress third class" he's provided by the hotel. He attends a gala State Execution, staged as a water ballet. When he corners Vonbraun, he's beaten and taken in for interrogation by Alpha 60. Later, he debriefs the previous agent sent to do his job; dying, the broken man whispers, "Tenderness. Save those who weep." Caution finds himself falling in love with Natasha Vonbraun (Karina), the Professor's delicate and beautiful daughter; a "pretty sphinx" who might yet be saved from the soulless city. Lemmy discovers that Alphaville plans an attack on The Outlands before they destroy its logical perfection. Can Lemmy complete his mission and rescue the human race—and Natasha—before Alpha 60 destroys them all?
Discussion: "All things weird are normal in this whore of cities," Lemmy mumbles at one point. "It's not Alphaville, but Zeroville." And it's not pop art, but real cinematic art masquerading as pop art. It's the most sublime philosophy illustrated by the lowest genre forms: part detective thriller (complete with deadpan narration); part film noir; part comic strip; part sci-fi; part pop art—and part pure poignant poetry. Godard plays with the conventions and limitations of every one of these genres, using their guileless simplicity and artless blunt-

ness to deliver facts of the heart, unvarnished. And it's a totally appropriate approach. Within the city limits of Alphaville everything is exaggerated; everything falls into extreme contrasts. The perfect computer utopia looks like our worst nightmare of an Eastern Bloc hovel—yet it was filmed in Paris, the City of Lights. The stark black and white photography accentuates the black and white philosophies of both Caution and Alpha 60; of his meaningful illogic versus its logic devoid of meaning. They are engaged in a war between head and heart; between darkness and light; between the go-nowhere circle and a straight line "towards those you love."

Buuuut we're getting pretty pompous and pedantic, when this book is about pleasure. Not only is this film a rare treat, but some of the production details are fascinating as well. Why did Godard cast Constantine as Caution? According to the introduction to the published screenplay (Simon & Shuster), it's because "he's a Martian," Godard said. "He's the only one; there isn't any other. That's why I chose him." Constantine's scowling, growling delivery (a croak to match his froggy face) is only slightly less metallic than that of Alpha 60—a voice created not electronically, but performed by a man whose vocal cords were shot out in World War II, and who was retrained to speak from the diaphragm. This gave Godard's electronic slavemaster a voice that was not mechanical, but—like the citizens it controls —simultaneously human and "killed." Altogether, *Alphaville* is a wonderful oxymoron: a dead-serious parody; a deeply-feeling film easily mistaken for shallow or pretentious, when it is in fact a parody of pretentiousness; and a film filled with insight and poetry. Time capsule scenes include Caution's interview with Alpha 60 and the finale, a masterpiece of poignance, tenderness and salvation. If, in this final scene, you cannot feel, cannot intuit, the words Natasha does not know but that he's waiting for her to say...then you're as lost as the dead of Alphaville.

Rent this one for: its use of sci-fi imagery as metaphors for human emotion; for being a beautifully realized and curiously prescient fable about high-tech alienation; for the poetry.

You'll (probably) like this if you liked: *Blade Runner, 1984, THX 1138,* "The Prisoner"; *2001, Last Year At Marienbad*

Dissenting Opinion: • "Interesting but not endearing" —HFG • "...ranges from funny and perceptive to slow and pretentious" —PVG • "Jumbled...recommended for New Wave disciples only." —MMG (2 stars)

Vidbits: • Home Vision's version is letterboxed, but Nostalgia's has a more poetic translation. Quite a dilemma. • The film's full title: *Alphaville, a Strange Adventure of Lemmy Caution.* Title Godard originally wanted to use: *Tarzan vs. IBM.* • A pop quiz for the viewer: What transforms the night into day?

Android

(1982; Media Home Entertainment; PG; 1:20)

Starring: Klaus Kinski, Don Opper, Brie Howard
Written by: James Reigle, Don Opper
Directed by: Aaron Lipstadt

Synopsis: 15 October, 2036: A research station in deep space, manned by Dr. Daniel (Kinski) and "Max 404" (Opper), picks up a mayday from a spaceship in distress. The rescued spacefarers, however, are actually escaped prisoners, who see the TerraCorp logo on the station and are convinced they've stumbled into a gold mine: TerraCorp performs its most dangerous experiments in space since they built a series of androids that went on a murderous rampage in Munich. Their plan: Kill Max and Daniels and steal their secrets. Meanwhile, Dr. D. has his own problems: His project will be canceled unless he can extract the life-energy of the female prisoner, Maggie (Howard) to activate his Cassan-dra android—a model far more elegant and sophisticated than Max—into life. Then he can terminate Max, who's beginning to exhibit insolence—a symptom of the "Munich Syndrome." Caught between two warring forces that both want him dead, can Max muster enough "AI" to outwit them all? Not without some help from a most unexpected source...
Discussion: For most of the movie, Max is more like a typical teen than an emotionless robot: gawky, awkward, curious about sex, trying to establish his own identity while under the thumb of the evil Gepetto who "fathered" him; vulnerable and sensitive to a fault—and deeply into video games. Blame it on the "Munich Syndrome" if you will, but his moodswings, alternating among resentment, pride, insolence, hurt feelings, and an eager-to-please attitude, are an accurate and sensitive depiction of the struggle to separate and create one's own identity during those angst-filled years. All Max has to base his self-image on are music (like James Brown) and films (*Metropolis* in particular, with its mad scientist who even *looks* like Kinski, attempting to activate a female android). So in a very real sense this is a Gen-X coming of age story disguised as a sci-fi action flick. But it's a good SF thriller as well: a tranquil film punctuated by moments of violence and rife with psychosexual undercurrents. The ending, with its clever twist of ironic justice, is a shocker: part *Terminator,* part *Blade Runner,* but precursor of both.
Rent this one for: its agonized protagonist; its clever ending.
You'll (probably) like this if you liked: *Blade Runner,* "Star Trek: The Next Generation" (Mr. Data); *Saturn 3, Making Mr. Right, Heartbeeps, Metropolis* (to catch the many references)
Vidbits: Filmed on sets left over from *Battle Beyond the Stars.*

Flashback!

Capricorn One

(suspense/action)

(1978; FoxVideo, LIVE; R; 2:03)

Starring: Elliott Gould, James Brolin, Hal Holbrook
Featuring: Brenda Vaccaro, O.J. Simpson, Sam Waterston
Karen Black, Telly Savalas, Robert Walden, David Doyle
Music by: Jerry Goldsmith
Written and directed by: Peter Hyams

Synopsis: Minutes before the launch of America's first mission to Mars, the astronauts (Brolin, Waterston and Simpson) are plucked from their capsule and informed by the head of NASA (Holbrook) that the flight is technically impossible—and it ain't gonna happen. In order to save face, however—and keep the funding flowing—he's arranged to have the entire Martian mission staged in a hanger on an abandoned military base deep in the Southwestern desert. But when the entire world watches their spacecraft burn up on re-entry, the coerced conspirators realize that if any of them is ever seen alive again, the whole hoax will be blown. Since there's no way out for NASA but to kill them, they escape into the desert, chased by military assassins. Concurrently with their life-or-death dilemma, a beleaguered reporter (Gould), intrigued by anomalies in the official story, attempts to unravel the truth from the outside.

Discussion: It seems that there are still a number of suspicious souls out there who honestly believe that all America's moon shots were faked: that space travel proved impossible and that the moon landings never took place at all, but instead were staged for TV in a warehouse somewhere. Hyams took this legendary conspiracy theory and turned it into a simple adventure flick with no pretensions other than pure entertainment. But, as the script is filled with eminently "logical" explanations for every one of its outrageous ideas, it keeps us hooked on its virtual reality. The paranoid/conspiracy mindset is brilliantly illustrated, not just in the set-up, but in the unraveling of the scheme as well. Hyams *knows* how to direct a suspense movie, and this one is filled with solid performances, as well as an unexpected highlight: Telly Savalas' brief but hilarious appearance as the world's most obnoxious man.

Rent this one for: being a clever story well told; for the jokes.

You'll (probably) like this if you liked: *Hanger 18, Roswell, Wavelength,* "Alien Autopsy" (government space conspiracies)

Dissenting Opinion: • "...boring..." —*Sight and Sound* • "...the first SF movie without any SF" —PEF

Cast A Deadly Spell

(supernatural/ mystery parody)
(1991; HBO; PG; 1:33)

Starring: Fred Ward, David Warner, Julianne Moore
Featuring: Arnetia Walker, Alexandra Powers, Clancy Brown
Written by: Joseph Dougherty
Directed by: Martin Campbell

Synopsis: "Los Angeles, 1948," the screen reads. A second line reminds us, "Everybody used magic." Well, not quite *every*body. Not Phil Lovecraft (Ward), a hard-boiled private eye too stubborn to let magic "make things easy" for him, like everyone else. Even Phil can't escape it, though—not when he's been hired by spooky millionaire Amos Hackshaw (Warner) to find a stolen book. Not just *any* book: the *Necronomicon,* the tome of ultimate evil. Phil's crooked ex-partner Borden (Brown), is mixed up in this somehow. Figures; he also stole Phil's gal, Connie Stone (Moore), now a chanteuse in Bordon's ritzy nightclub. Worst of all, every sign, portent and planetary alignment points to something big, bad and ugly happening, and real soon. Only Phil, his wits and his gun stand between the evil creeps scheming to open the Gate to another dimension and the monstrous Old Ones they plan to unleash upon the world. Can he stop them—or will they use Phil's head for a watch fob?
Discussion: It's *Chinatown* meets *The Witches of Eastwick*—although it bears more than a passing resemblance to *Who Framed Roger Rabbit?* Set in the same post-war L.A., the flick puts a similar spin on Chandler territory, replacing living 'toons with that old black magic. And they do it so well! It's an effective genre-crossing comedy; a tongue-in-cheek tribute to both pulp horror and hard-boiled mysteries. As a detective tale, it crackles with snappy patter, and features all the requisite stereotypical characters, twisted by their reliance on sorcery (zombie bodyguards; surveillance gargoyles; "licensed witches," etc.). As horror pastiche, it's full of Lovecraftian wickedry, from virgin sacrifices to evil demons. The clever ending combines elements of both genres in a satisfying, unexpected and comically ironic resolution. *Spell* is a whimsical and affectionate recreation (in both senses of the word) of genres that just can't be done straight anymore, and a pleasant exercise in cleverly blending two distinct and distinctive forms without compromising either.
Rent this one for: its tongue-in-cheek genre-crossing.
You'll (probably) like this if you liked: *Who Framed Roger Rabbit?, Big Trouble in Little China*
Vidbits: • Made for HBO. • Credits include "unicorn wrangler."

Cherry 2000

(adventure/ satire)
(1988; Orion; PG-13; 1:39)

Starring: Melanie Griffith, David Andrews, Ben Johnson
Featuring: Tim Thomerson, Pamela Gidley, Harry Carey, Jr.
Written by: Michael Almereyda
Directed by: Steve DeJarnatt

Synopsis: Cherry (Gidley) is the perfect wife: beautiful, loving, devoted, sexy. Until she gets soap in her system and shorts out. Sam (Andrews) will do anything to replace her, but in this post-collapse America of 2017, sexbots like the Cherry 2000 just ain't made anymore—and only the best Tracker could ever find one. Sam finds the best Tracker, E. Johnson (Griffith), who's willing to go into Zone 7 and retrieve a Cherry chassis—but only if Sam rides shotgun through the dangerous no-man's land. They've got to get past Lester (Thomerson), self-proclaimed judge, jury and executioner of Zone 7, and "a total wacko." Can they avoid his fatal *faux* '50s compound, grab a Cherry and escape intact? And once Sam gets a taste of real life, real adventure—and of E. Johnson, a real woman—can he overcome his Barbie fetish?
Discussion: Most science fiction asks only that you "suspend your disbelief." Um—get yourself a *pair* of suspenders to watch this one... DeJarnatt (*Miracle Mile*) has always has a strange sci-fi vision (and an obsession with Vegas); this fun little film is by turns sci-fi spoof, Western send-up and post-apocalyptic adventure flick parody. It's full of plot holes and bad acting, but with all its faults, it's still worth watching, primarily as a visual treat. DeJarnatt located (and created) some striking and truly unusual locations: desert excavations, a sand-subsumed Vegas, and the most gargantuan drain pipe imaginable (the scene lowering their car into the latter is an eye-popper). It's also a very funny film: In this surreal, bizarro retro-future, cobbled together from 50 years of 20th century detritus, the single biggest industry is recycling, for instance. And it's full of inside jokes (Robbie and Gort both make cameos in the robot repair shop—and Sam hails from Anaheim). Equal parts *Blade Runner, Raiders* and *Road Warrior*—and lampooning them all—it's an oddball entry good for some weird, warped, mindless fun.
Rent this one for: the satire; the unusual locations.
You'll (probably) like this if you liked: *Mad Max, Escape From New York, Westworld; Blade Runner* (serious version)
Dissenting Opinion: • "...predictable mix of routine action and lazy satire." —PVG • "You actually *liked* this?" —my friend Will.
Vidbits: The club lawyer is Lawrence (aka "Larry") Fishburne.

The City of Lost Children

(1995; Columbia TriStar; R; 1:54)

Starring: Ron Perlman, Judith Vittet, Dominique Pinon, Daniel Emilfork, Jean-Louis Trintignant *(voice)*
Music by: Angelo Badalamenti
Written and directed by: Jean-Pierre Jeunet and Marc Caro

Synopsis: In a nameless, mist-enshrouded city in an ageless Victorian era, a mad scientist creates a surrogate family—but his misshapen children are all flawed and do away with their dysfunctional "father." One of his aberrant offspring, Krank (Emilfork), has a unique disease: he cannot dream. So he kidnaps the city's children and steals their dreams. The waifs are so terrified of him, however, that all he ever gets is nightmares. And he makes the mistake of his life when he kidnaps the adopted little brother of innocent, dimwitted circus strongman "One" (Perlman), who sets out to rescue his young charge with single-minded devotion. His dedicated quest attracts the assistance of precocious nine-year-old Miette (Vittet), a hardened street urchin smitten with One. Can this pair of misfits successfully steal into the nefarious Krank's floating fortress and free the youngsters? In their dreams...
Discussion: Presented for your approval: a long-lost script collaboration between Jules Verne and Robert Louis Stevenson, directed by Terry Gilliam. No, it's not true, but it's a close description of this arrestingly grotesque fantasy. The surreal seaside city is a cold Victorian horror of girders, trusses, rivets and bolts, crisscrossed with canals full of garish green water and populated with funhouse freaks, cyborg Cyclopses, Siamese sisters, clownish clones, trained fleas, hideous midgets, even a disembodied brain in a fish tank. We enter actual nightmare territory with this insanely original imagery—a singular sinister vision in the tradition of *Brazil* and Jeunet & Caro's previous film, *Delicatessen.* And as in the latter, even when integrating cutting-edge effects into the film, J&C refuse to let style dominate substance: the entire tender tale revolves around the poignant relationship between gentle giant One and the disenchanted Miette, each protecting—and oddly completing—the other. Add Pinon's inspired lunacy and Badalamenti's circus-style score, and it's an eye-popping fable which can only be called unique.
Rent this one for: its surreal, arrestingly original imagery.
You'll (probably) like this if you liked: *Time Bandits, Delicatessen, Brazil, The Nightmare Before Christmas*
Credentials: • "Ingenious! Hilarious! Imaginative, moving...a classic!" —*Newsday* • "A-" —*Entertainment Weekly* (9/26/96)
Vidbits: Caro appears as one of the Cyclops cyborgs.

Flashback!

Conquest of Space

(1955; Paramount; NR; 1:21)

Starring: Walter Brooke, Eric Fleming, Phil Foster
Featuring: Mickey Shaughnessy, Ross Martin, Benson Fong
Written by: James O'Hanlon
(based on the book by Chesley Bonestell and Willy Ley)
Directed by: Byron Haskin

Synopsis: "This is a story of tomorrow—or the day after," yells a narrator, "when we have built a station in space, constructed in the form of a giant wheel!" And so we have: *There it is!* The crew also builds an advanced spaceship to go, not to the Moon, but to *Mars!* Gen. Merritt (Brooke), commander of the station, is certain they're not ready to make the trip, but follows orders anyway. Along the way he grows more and more morose and starts thumping his Bible, pontificating about this blasphemous invasion of "the sacred domain of God." And when they lose a man in an accident, Sam goes off the deep-space end. On landing, he dumps their water supply—and they're stuck on this dry rock for a year! Religion got them into this mess—and now they'll have to rely on a miracle to survive.
Discussion: Blame them damned Russkies! *This* is what a space program might have looked like if *They* hadn't forced us into some dumb "Moon race." The upside is that this is a logical, scientific program, designed to exploit the planets to replenish earth's dwindling resources. The downside is that it's a totally military vision (even the station looks like a circular submarine in space). Or would it have been like this at all, with its Jetson-style dinner pills, its handles and switchesand non-digital dials, and its "international" crew (including a single black man and a Japanese astronaut—very daring, only a decade after WWII—but *no women*). There's quite a contrast between this and *2001,* produced just 13 years later. In the space of 81 minutes, however, look what we *do* get: A meteor shower; being chased by a "Space Mountain"-style asteroid; a cool funeral in space; a Dialog between Religion and Science; and a clever ending. This is the archetypal "true space" drama of the '50s—and a peek at a possible tomorrow that died the day after it was envisioned.
Rent this one for: being the perfect '50s space adventure flick.
You'll (probably) like this if you liked: *Destination Moon*
Dissenting Opinion: • "...hampered by a pedestrian script... A disappointment." —MMG (2.5 stars) • "...rather bloodless narrative" —SMV (2.5 stars) • "...uneasy mixture of religion and space exploration..." —GMR (1.5 bones)
Vidbits: Produced by special effects master George Pal.

Deathwatch

(AKA "Death Watch"; drama)
(1980; Embassy; R; 2:08)

Starring: Harvey Keitel, Romy Schneider, Harry Dean Stanton
Featuring: Max von Sydow
Written by: David Rayfiel, Bertrand Tavernier
(from David Compton's novel *The Continuous Katherine Mortenhoe*)
Directed by: Bertrand Tavernier

Synopsis: Katherine (Schneider) is terminally ill—and this sensation-seeking near-future world will pay to watch her die, vicariously sharing her final days. Agonizing over medical bills, she accepts money from TV network NTV to broadcast her last days live—then leaves the payment with her lover and promptly disappears. Roddy (Keitel) is an experiment at NTV: a cameraman with camera and transmitter implanted behind his eyes. Roddy finds Katherine, protects her and travels with her. She's unaware of his identity; he records her in intimate interviews. Together they set out for the countryside to visit her estranged husband, Gerald (von Sydow). But the closer Roddy grows to Katherine, the more disgusted he becomes by his own electronic voyeurism. Can Katherine accomplish a private death, or will her tragedy bring in the biggest ratings in television history?
Discussion: Is televising death an "intimate and real" event, or just another freak show? Everyone has an opinion. NTV director Vincent (Stanton) believes death is "the new pornography," and he's performing a service by raising the public's awareness. Katherine understands that on TV, "everything is of interest, but nothing matters." *Deathwatch* is an excellent example of science fiction as social commentary, and an intelligent, mature illustration of the media's intrusion into private lives—and of the public's morbid curiosity to peer into other lives. First rate performances highlight this story of the triumph of dignity and life over media's regurgitated version. It's a disturbingly prescient film, as well, predating and predicting "reality" TV, "guerrilla journalism," Tim Leary's "designer death" (originally planned as a broadcast on the Internet), and those talk shows where people revel in revealing their deepest embarrassments.
Rent this one for: the sensitive performances; the direction.
You'll (probably) like this if you liked: *My Life, Blow Up*
Dissenting Opinion: "...pretentious...Attempts at [satire]...bog down in talky muddle." —*Scheuer's Complete Guide to Videocassette Movies,* 1987 (2.5 stars—yet in the 1994 edition of his SMV, *Deathwatch* is rated 3 stars—and the objections are gone).
Vidbits: • Dedicated to director Jacques Tourneur. • Shot on location in Scotland. • Robbie Coltrane plays the limo driver.

Erik the Viking

(fantasy adventure/comedy)
(1989; Orion; PG-13; 1:44)

Starring: Tim Robbins, Terry Jones
Featuring: John Cleese, Imogen Stubbs, Mickey Rooney, Eartha Kitt
Written and directed by: Terry Jones

Synopsis: Erik (Robbins) isn't your typical Viking. Sure, he enjoys the pillaging and looting. But the raping... Well, that's rather crude. He also harbors grave philosophical doubts about all the meaningless death, violence and suffering in life. It's Ragnarok, the end of the world—and Erik is determined to end the Era. He and his mates embark on a quest to find the horn "Resounding," which will enable them to cross the Rainbow Bridge, enter Asgard and wake the sleeping Gods, ushering in an era of peace. Naturally, the warlords and weapons makers are dead set against this threat of peace, and plot to sabotage his heroic mission. But an even stranger fate awaits him in Asgard when he finally confronts the Gods themselves.
Discussion: As a team, the Monty Python troupe made some hilarious movies (*Monty Python and the Holy Grail,* for example). On their own, their record is sporadic, ranging from the brilliant (Gilliam's *Brazil*) to the gawdawful (Cleese, Idle and Chapman in *Yellowbeard*). *Erik* is one of the better ones that somehow slipped through the cracks. Even though it's based on Norse mythology (mostly), it has much more in common with *Time Bandits* than with the twisted history of *Holy Grail*...and actually resembles nothing so much as a "Mystery Science Theater 3000" parody of some old Italian Hercules flick. Although episodic, with highs (Erik wearing the "cloak of invisibility") and lows (Jones seems completely out of place in his own movie), it is, overall, an intriguing fantasy adventure filled with comic elements—most of which revolve around reducing the Epic Heroic to the mundane (endlessly discussing the seating arrangements on the longboat, for example), and imbuing the barbarians with modern sensibilities and concerns.
Rent this one for: the comedy; the eye-catching special effects.
You'll (probably) like this if you liked: *Time Bandits, The Adventures of Baron Munchausen, Monty Python and the Holy Grail; The Day the Earth Froze* (MST3K version)
Dissenting Opinion: • "...disappointing..." —SMV (2 stars) • "...unwatchable..." —MMG (BOMB)
Vidbits: Final credits include the note: "This film is *not* based on the children's book "The Saga of Erik the Viking" by Terry Jones (although he hopes it will help sales.)"

Fire in the Sky

(suspense/thriller)
(1993; Paramount; PG-13; 1:38)

Starring: D.B. Sweeney, Robert Patrick
Featuring: James Garner, Criag Sheffer, Peter Berg, Henry Thomas
Written by: Tracy Tormé
(based on Travis Walton's book, *The Walton Experience*)
Directed by: Robert Lieberman

Synopsis: On the evening of Nov. 5th, 1975, blue collar worker Travis Walton (Sweeney) and a small logging crew in the White Mountains of Arizona spotted what appeared to be a UFO. While the others cowered in fear, Travis wandered closer to get a better look—and promptly disappeared. Although the other men knew their story sounded fabricated or insane, they chose to tell the truth when interrogated by officials, including a skeptical State Investigator (Garner). Fortunately for everyone, Travis reappears five days later—scared, naked and traumatized into speechlessness—just as mysteriously as he disappeared. Even after he recuperates physically, his memory of those days remains a blank—until at last they come rushing back, and we experience along with him every horrid, horrifying, mindbending moment in which he was conscious aboard the alien spacecraft.
Discussion: Whether or not this is actually "based on a true story," as claimed, it still makes for a *good* story, and a very different kind of film. Much of the movie is the slow, folksy tale not of Walton, but of his best friend Mike Rogers (Patrick), who is hounded by the press and ostracized by the town as a liar—or a murderer. But when Rogers' personal horror ends, Walton's is just beginning. As his memories return, the film immediately and without forewarning shifts trajectories and becomes a horror flick as vivid as *Alien*—an effect cunningly calculated to viscerally indicate how Walton himself must have felt, leading a boring, normal life one moment, and the next, finding himself a guinea pig for inscrutable ETs. The special effects in Walton's anamnesia are superb—and far too realistic. If you're squeamish about mucous and medical instruments, *don't rent this movie.*
Rent this one for: its unusual structure; for the sense of wonder in asking, "What if it really *was* real?"
You'll (probably) like this if you liked: *Communion,* "X-Files"
Dissenting Opinion: "Failed sci-fi outing..." —MMG (which refers to the character twice as Travis *Wilson.* Makes you wonder if the reviewer actually watched the movie...) (2 stars)
Vidbits: • Tracy Tormé is singer Mel's daughter. • The real Walton appears in a cameo as a citizen in the town meeting.

Fortress

(action)

(1992; LIVE; R; 1:31)

Starring: Christopher Lambert, Loryn Locklyn, Kurtwood Smith
Featuring: Lincoln Kilpatrick, Tom Towles
Written by: Troy Neighbors, Steve Feinberg, David Venable, Terry Curtis Fox
Directed by: Stuart Gordon

Synopsis: In the overpopulated world of the near future, abortion is illegal and one child is the limit by law. When Brennick's (Lambert) wife Karen (Locklyn) becomes pregnant with their second, they make a run for the border—and fail. They're sentenced to 31 years in a maximum security penitentiary buried beneath a desolate desert. "The Fortress" is a torturous horror, outfitted with laser bars, AI surveillance and "intestinators"—devices embedded in their bellies to dispense pain for punishment and crowd control, and which can blow a hole in a prisoner's guts if a death sentence is issued. It's all ruled by Warden Poe (Smith), a reptilian sadist who gets his voyeuristic kicks spying on prisoners' sex dreams. When Brennick discovers that the private corporation that owns the prison also owns the inmates' children—and that they have sinister plans for his kid—he must attempt the impossible: Master the massive security, reunite with his wife and escape from this chamber of horrors.
Discussion: Warning: *Fortress* is violent, bloody, and rife with graphic physical and psychological torture—and definitely *not* recommended for the delicate. In truth, it's a mutant movie: a hybrid between action epics and slasher sadism, playing on our deepest fears: abandonment and betrayal; abortion and torture; humiliation and violation; and impotence, both physical and emotional. Yet it is precisely these disturbing elements which generate the flick's intense, gut-grabbing power. The prison itself is a marvel of effects: a gleaming chrome tube with open levels lit by smoky searchlights—a Hyatt Hotel in Hell. While the acting is uniformly mediocre, the edgy, eccentric performance by the nervous demolitions expert is fun, and Kilpatrick (a minor league Morgan Freeman) actually *acts*. The most chilling element of the film might be the long list of penology advisors in the credits. *Could they actually be designing this stuff?*
Rent this one for: its unusual action and emotional intensity.
You'll (probably) like this if you liked: *Midnight Express*
Dissenting Opinion: "...weak acting and a weaker script"—MMG
Vidbits: • Filmed at Warner Bros. Gold Coast, Australia, studio, on the same set as *Highlander II: The Quickening.*

Galaxy Express

(AKA "Galaxy 999"/ science fiction/ animation/ "animé")
(1980; New World; 1:31 / VIZ Video; 2:10; PG)

Written by: Paul Grogan, Shiro Ishimori
Directed by: Taro Rin

Synopsis: Young Joey Smith is a boy on a mission of revenge: in flashback, he recalls how the evil android Count Mecha went trophy hunting for humans—and bagged his mother. Joey is determined to travel to Andromeda, center of machine culture, return with a machine body of his own, and kill Mecha. Mysterious Maitel—a double for his mother—buys him a ticket, provided he protects her on the journey. They board Galaxy 999—an intergalactic vehicle designed to look like an old-fashioned steam train. During a stopover on Titan, Maitel is kidnapped by pirates, and Joey rescues her, with the help of a strange old woman who outfits him in a Clint Eastwood-style hat and cape, and provides him with the only gun that can kill a robot body. After other adventures, including a brush with deep space pirates, Joey and his newfound friends attack Mecha in his Time Castle. Even this isn't enough to avenge his mother's death, however: Joey now conceives the grandiose plan of destroying Andromeda, the soulless center of robot culture, for all time. Little does he realize he's being set up for betrayal—and for a fate far worse than death.
Discussion: And that's only half the plot and a quarter of the characters! This is an epic adventure in every sense, limited only in its jerky animation (which grows increasingly better through the film). The direction is excellent, the concepts mind-bending, the plot twists smart and numerous. Current interest in "Japanimation" or "animé" indicates an essential point about this film, which is that it is definitely *not* for children. It's a violent and intense revenge adventure, espousing a violent philosophy ("Shoot Mecha without mercy" is a regularly heard phrase). But there is plenty enough here to hold an adult's interest; beneath the surface story are poignant messages about what makes us human, as well as an intriguing reworking of Western cultural archetypes, providing an outsider's insight—which, in effect, holds up a mirror to our own Western souls.
Rent this one for: its strange mélange of Occidental genres—Westerns, pirate adventure, sci-fi—seen through Oriental eyes.
You'll (probably) like this if you liked: *Akira, RoboTech, Lensmen,* other Japanimation; *Star Wars, WestWorld*
Dissenting Opinion: "...too chilling for youngsters." —VMG (lowest rating: "turkey") (Right analysis; wrong rating.)

Grand Tour: Disaster in Time

(suspense/thriller)

(1992; Academy; PG-13; 1:38)

Starring: Jeff Daniels, Ariana Richards
Featuring: Emilia Crow, Jim Haynie, Nicholas Guest, George Murdock
Written and directed by: David Twohy
(based on the C.L. Moore story "Vintage Season")

Synopsis: Ben Wilson (Daniels) is attempting to recover emotionally from the tragic accident which killed his wife Carol —and for which he blames himself—by opening an inn with his daughter Hillary (Richards, pre-*Jurassic Park*). Their first guests are a mysterious tour group hiding a sinister secret: they're actually time travelers from a boring utopian future—"disaster groupies" who get their kicks by hopping from one massive catastrophe in history to another. *(Please note this is not a "spoiler": I'm not giving away anything that isn't right on the video box.)* What puzzles Ben is what they're doing in his sleepy Midwestern town. When he blackmails the black sheep of the group into an explanation, he's told simply, "Leave." But he can't: Judge Caldwell (Murdock)—who also blames Ben for the death of Carol, his daughter—has taken legal custody of Hillary, and Ben won't leave without her. When unstoppable disaster destroys half the town, a distraught Ben palms a traveler's electronic "passport" and enlists the aid of his pre-disaster self to save as many people as possible—including Hillary.
Discussion: The set-up might be simple, but no detail is insignificant; even a favorite song or a hole in a door could turn out to be important. The plot is dense enough to keep the pace snowballing—once thickie Ben finally figures out what's going on. Perhaps it's going too far to call this a parable about turning crises into opportunities, but Ben *does* exhibit some actual character development during the course of the extraordinary events. The temporal paradoxes are treated with logic and respect, and (as in the *Back to the Future* saga) can be tweaked to work in one's favor—if one has the balls to wrest control of his destiny from impassive chance. The idea that if one possessed a passport through time he could perhaps set *any* tragedy right leads to an unexpected, and unexpectedly poignant, postscript.
Rent this one for: the inventive twists on a time travel tale.
You'll (probably) like this if you liked: *Back to the Future, Parts I & II, Peggy Sue Got Married*
Dissenting Opinion: • "...too drawn-out." —MMG (2.5 stars) • "passable" —*Encyclopedia of Science Fiction* (Clute & Nicholls)
Vidbits: • Shot in Oakland, Oregon. • Originally produced for theatrical release, but demoted to a cable TV debut.

The Hidden

(action/mystery)

(1987; Media Home Entertainment; R; 1:38)

Starring: Kyle MacLachlan, Michael Nouri
Featuring: Clu Gulager, Ed O'Ross, Claudia Christian, Chris Mulkey
Written by: Bob Hunt
Directed by: Jack Sholder

Synopsis: Strange FBI agent Gallagher (MacLachlan) arrives in a Pacific Northwest town, tracking a murderous psycho who has killed a dozen people—including his partner. Things get really weird when the killer, caught and hospitalized, extrudes a snail-like alien from his mouth into the body of an unconscious patient—who then gets up and leaves. And he's got the same taste for Ferraris and heavy metal music that the first guy did as well... Gallagher explains to police detective Beck (Nouri) only that this killer "changes identities." Beck presses for details; Gallagher offers only glib answers ("I read minds"). They follow a trail of killers—serial killers, in the sense that one seems to pick up where the previous one left off. Beck is frustrated by the bizarre things he sees in a shootout with a stripper-turned-killer (Christian). "An explanation won't help you," Gallagher insists. But when Beck finally does discover the truth—it's out there.
Discussion: "I guess a career in the police didn't really prepare you for this, did it?" Gallagher chides, once Beck has discovered that they're after an alien that picks up bodies like off-the-rack suits and uses them until they're damaged to death. Although this flick might appear to be a trial run for "Twin Peaks," MacLachlan is in fact also an alien, in the tradition of *Starman*—stiff, polite, and with a comically low tolerance for alcohol. Much of the fun of the film is in the details: Gallagher trying to figure out Alka-Seltzer; the sly political commentary in the evil alien's ambitions; the odd bodies the body-hopper is forced to possess. Yes, it very bloody—but for once, the amount of lethal force is not gratuitous, but essential to the set-up. What sets this apart from many other bloody action flicks is the final compassionate sacrifices, which restore order to everyone's lives.
Rent this one for: its high-velocity, pulse-pounding suspense.
You'll (probably) like this if you liked: "Twin Peaks," *Starman, Species, The Dead Zone,* "Alien Nation," "The X Files"
Credentials: "...one of the genuine sleepers of the '80s..." *Entertainment Weekly* (3/96) Grade: "A" • One of "Ten Most Underrated Movies of the '80s" —*Premiere Guide to Movies on Video*
Dissenting Opinion: "...grows increasingly silly..." —MMG (1.5)
Vidbits: Skip the disappointing 1994 sequel.

Intruders

(1992; FoxVideo, CBS/Fox; NR; 2:42)

Starring: Richard Crenna, Mare Winningham, Susan Blakely
Featuring: Daphne Ashbrook, Ben Vereen, Robert Mandan
Written by: Barry Oringer, Tracy Tormé
(based in part on the book *Intruders* by Budd Hopkins)
Directed by: Dan Curtis

Synopsis: Were both women victimized by early sexual abuse, repressing the painful memories? Or are their memories of alien abduction actually real? These are the questions Fate throws at staid psychiatrist Chase (Crenna) when his patients' virtually identical memories are recovered under hypnosis. The gray-skinned, big-domed, evil-eyed aliens abducted Leslie (Ashbrook) from L.A. and Nebraska farm-mom Mary (Winningham) repeatedly, experimented on them (often painfully)—and now return regularly to "check up" on their human guinea pigs. Slowly, the skeptical Chase begins to believe the unbelievable. But will anyone believe him? And more importantly, can he help these people whose lives are apparently guided by *who knows what?*
Discussion: "What's happening is *real*," one character wails. Well, for sure *some* damn thing is happening these days—but damned if anyone knows *what*. A disclaimer tells us that these examples are composites "taken from scores of actual accounts" involving close encounters of the terrifying kind. Is the film objective because the subject is treated seriously? Not necessarily. But the dramatic presentations of the unsettling experiences are chilling, and the speculation—about government conspiracy and who They are and what They want—is engrossing and intriguing—whether or not one is "a believer." (Think of this as the *JFK* of UFOs.) As pure cinema, yes, it's long—and yes, it's worth it. It's long enough to delve in depth into the horrifying experiences; it's evenly-paced and never lags. It's long enough to establish the characters as humans who earn our concern—an effect enhanced by the uniformly solid performances (Winningham, with her sad, old-soul eyes is particularly effective). Does the government actually know too *little* to reveal anything? Can anyone determine whether They are angels or devils? Are Their unwilling subjects pioneers or paranoids? And if They really are interbreeding with us...*why?* These are some of the thought-provoking questions the film raises and illustrates...or reveals?
Rent this one for: the performances; the creepy abduction scenes; the interesting speculation.
You'll (probably) like this if you liked: *Communion, Fire in the Sky,* "The X-Files," *Roswell, Close Encounters*
Vidbits: • Made for TV. • Tormé's next film: *Fire in the Sky.*

Double Feature!

Le Dernier Combat

(AKA *The Final Combat* and *The Last Battle)*

(1983; Key, RCA/ Columbia; R; 1:33; B&W)

Starring: Pierre Jolivet, Fritz Wepper, Jean Reno
Written and directed by: Luc Besson

La Jetée

(1962; Festival Films; NR; :30; B&W; French with subtitles)

Written and directed by: Chris Marker

Synopsis: *Combat:* In a post-apocalyptic world where the law of survival is "Every man for himself," a loner is beaten in combat and left for dead. He's taken in by a strange scientist who heals him and eventually reveals his secret: he's captured one of the last women alive. The loner must attempt to protect them all from the attack of a vicious warrior determined to conquer their compound. *Jetée:* In a post-apocalyptic world, a man is sent back through time to the days before World War III to discover the cause of a plague destroying the remaining survivors. His mission is complicated when he falls in love, both with the time he's sent to, and with a beautiful, sensitive woman.

Discussion: They are a study in contrasts, and make a great double bill. (*Jetée* is a bonus: it's so short that I'm not counting it as one of the 237.) Both are French post-holocaust dramas filmed in stark black and white, but that is their sole point of intersection. *Combat* (Besson's directorial debut) tells its story without dialog (and therefore without the need for subtitles). It's a gritty action flick filled with wild invention and subtle touches of humor—like rains of fish, apparently the world's main source of food. It's an engaging, inventive adventure and a very successful experiment in style and silence. Follow it with *La Jetée,* the inspiration for *12 Monkeys,* but with a dozen times the emotional impact of that feature—and condensed into half an hour, at that! Where *Combat* was all silence and action, *Jetée* consists of a montage of stark, colorless stills, accompanied by the poetic narration of the tale of a man doomed to his destiny. Simultaneously harrowing and heart-wrenching, *Jetée* is a brilliant experiment in style, substance and storytelling. Taken together, they mutually illuminate one another's strengths by the contrast—and provide for an evening of artistic entertainment.

Rent these for: their style, originality and novelty.

You'll (probably) like this if you liked: • *Le Dernier Combat: Mad Max, The Road Warrior* • *La Jetée: 12 Monkeys, Alphaville*

Credentials (*Combat*): • "...stylish and subtle." —SMV (3 stars) • "...sensitive and cerebral..." —VMG (4 stars)

Dissenting Opinion (*Combat*): "Wildly overpraised..."—MMG (2)

Man Facing Southeast

(psychological mystery)
(Spanish with English subtitles)
(1986; New World, Starmaker; R; 1:45)

Starring: Hugo Soto, Lorenzo Quinteros, Ines Vernengo
Written and directed by: Eliseo Subiela

Synopsis: Dr. Denis (Quinteros) should have 32 patients in his psychiatric ward. But he has one extra, and no one knows where Rantes (Soto) came from—or where he comes from. Rantes himself claims to be from another world. What can Denis do for Rantes? What can he do for anyone, for that matter: the sick, the miserable, the defeated...including himself. Rantes stands in the garden, immobile for hours, "transmitting and receiving data." He and his kind are perfect human images (he says), except for one flaw: they cannot experience emotion. Dr. Denis is intrigued. Over a period of weeks, they engage in a dialog, Denis attempting therapy (or at least to catch him in a contradiction); Rantes weaving his story about an immanent interplanetary invasion of "Christs." The case has a profound effect on the dispirited doctor. But if Rantes is indeed a "Christ," wouldn't that make Dr. Denis his Pilate? And if Rantes is playing the archetype of Christ, can his own fate be dissimilar?
Discussion: If Rantes is a lunatic, he's a very special lunatic. He feeds the hungry, plays Bach brilliantly and moves things with his mind. The other patients follow him around like puppies and line up just to have him listen to them—which is more than the doctors ever do, and far more therapeutic than their drugs and electroshock. This Argentine entry is both thoughtful and thought-provoking, raising far more questions than it answers. In essence, they are science fiction author Philip K. Dick's "Big Questions": Who is really human, and who merely masquerading as human? What are the criteria for deciding? What behavior is insane, what rational—and what simply human? Is Rantes who he claims, or merely another mind "broken by horror"? Don't expect to be handed any answers in this haunting, introspective and sobering mystery—which is, at heart, a mystery of the heart. The concert scene alone is worth the price of admission: a scintillating spark of genius, both ecstatic and perfectly understandable—in any language.
Rent this one for: its moving philosophical questions.
You'll (probably) like this if you liked: *The Man Who Fell To Earth, Wings of Desire, King of Hearts, Alphaville*
Vidbits: Inspired by the philosophical science fiction of Philip K. Dick, as evidenced by naming the female lead "Beatriz Dick."

Max Headroom: The Original Story

(comedy)

(1985; Karl-Lorimar, Warner; NR; 1:00)

Starring: Matt Frewer, Amada Pays, Nickolas Grace
Featuring: Morgan Shepherd
Written by: Steve Roberts
Directed by: Rocky Morton, Annabel Jankel

Synopsis: The time: 20 minutes into the future. The place: A *Blade Runner*ish world in which TV is king and ratings are life—or death. Network 23's latest innovation in the ratings war is the "Blipvert," a condensed ad blast with the unfortunate side effect of causing the occasional viewer to explode—literally. When ace telejournalist Edison Carter (Frewer) gets too close to the story, jeapordizing the lucrative ad campaign, an "accident" gets him hauled off the the body-parts bank—but not before a sociopathic computer geek downloads his mind into a computer, in order to generate a digital image to cover up his disappearance. The experiment is *too* successful: The image evolves "from information to intuition," manifesting as the "Max Headroom" personality—an unruly goofball with an artificial mind of his own. Carter, meanwhile, escapes, beaten but not broken, and with his "controller" (Pays), tracks down both story and culprits.
Discussion: This pilot episode of the short-lived cult series might not live up to Max's introduction as "one of the greatest epics ever produced in the history of television," but it was a uniquely subversive series: a television program in which television itself was the villain. Frewer proved master of the task of playing both serious actor and visible Id Max, a stuttering nut and a smirking joker just a few fries short of a Happy Meal. Digital pitchman Max (Frewer in prosthetics, not real computer animation) had his 15 minutes of fame in the mid-'80s, but the subtle genius of this sly, sarcastic, cynical and quixotic series was not Max. He was magician's misdirection: a surface sneer masking the fact that each episode was pure science fiction, with intelligent plots centering on innovative technology and addressing social concerns and moral dilemmas on the horizon rather than merely recycling old action-show plots in a post-modern setting. The penalty for such intelligence, innovation and subversion? Cancellation. Or, as "Blank Reg" put it: "You know how we said there's no future? Well, this is it."
Rent this one for: the unfortunate fact that (currently, at any rate), this is all of Max that's available on video or t-t-television.
You'll (probably) like this if you liked: *Brazil, Repo Man*
Vidbits: Originally shot on video.

The Navigator

(mythic fantasy)
(1988; Trylon; PG; 1:32)

Starring: Hamish McFarlane, Bruce Lyons, Chris Haywood
Written and directed by: Vincent Ward

Synopsis: Cumbria, England, 1348 AD. Griffin (McFarlane), a young boy living in the bleak, barren landscape, has a vision: The only way to appease God and save his village from the Black Death decimating the population is to burrow from the bottom of one of the village's crude copper mines straight through the earth, where they'll find a magic land. Once there, they must raise a cross of Cumbrian copper on the spire of the Great Church. When Griffin and four men emerge, they find themselves in contemporary New Zealand—a wondrous world where the panorama of electric lights seems like a "city of celestial fire," and where simply crossing a freeway is a life and death proposition. But some things never change; they find a foundry and enlist the aid of modern blacksmiths in casting their cross, then continue their perilous journey through modern civilization to an even more perilous climb up the Cathedral spire, which leads to a shocking conclusion.
Discussion: If Ingmar Bergman directed *The Wizard of Oz,* this film might be the result. It begins in black and white, bursting into color only as the travelers reach their contemporary destination. This colorless/colorful counterpoint proves an effective method of contrasting the film's many dualities: the stark, simple life of medieval man vs. our modern world of sensory bombardment; the harsh realities of the mundane world vs. the fluid world of dreams and visions; their 14th century certainty of faith vs. our century of cynicism. Where the film excels, however, is not in its ambiguous allegory, but in its striking, dreamlike imagery. The harrowing night-sea journey, in which the men row across a harbor menaced by a "sea serpent," is as haunting, unexpected (and implausible) as any night terror. The true magic of *The Navigator* is that it seduces us into a change of perspective, enabling us to see our current world and its magical technology through new eyes.
Rent this one for: its impressive, dreamlike visual imagery.
Credentials: • Australian Film Institute Award winner. • "Astonishingly original." —VMG (4.5 stars)
Dissenting Opinion: "...what it means evaded us completely." —SMV (2.5 stars)
Vidbits: Footage from an Australian AIDS commercial was used in the Grim Reaper sequence; fitting for a film about The Plague.

Night of the Comet

(action/comedy)

(1984; FoxVideo; PG-13; 1:30)

Starring: Catherine Mary Stewart, Robert Beltran, Kelli Maroney
Featuring: Geoffrey Lewis, Mary Woronov
Written and directed by: Thom Eberhardt

Synopsis: The last time The Comet swung by Earth, the dinosaurs dropped dead. Guess what? It's *baa*-aack! And it's time to par-*tayyy!* One small problem: Passing through The Comet's tail is like a neutron bomb blast, and transforms virtually everyone into empty clothes and rusty dust. Of the handful of survivors, most are infected with a cometary plague which morphs them into bloodlusting zombies. Teenage L.A. sisters Reg (Stewart) and Sami (Maroney) are lucky enough to live—and to run into nice guy Hector (Beltran). They get guns and prepare for, like, *whatever.* What none of them realize is that a supersecret group in an underground shelter anticipated The Comet. The group is dedicated to survival—but not necessarily to *survivors.* Will these scientists pose an even greater threat to their lives?
Discussion: It's *Clueless* meets *Night of the Living Dead!* It's an action-horror-comedy, alternately silly and serious. The Val Gal sisters stand at the center of the flick, and they couldn't be more different. Reg is serious, strong-willed and self-sufficient; little sister Sami (in a delightfully perky performance) is a bubble-headed cheerleader, concerned that the last man alive hasn't made a pass at *either* of them. (He's "either a gentleman or a fag," she decides. "What are the odds, in L.A.?") So what do you do when you're the last girls alive? Shop till you drop! *Comet* is a cute film, in the best sense of the word, and a clever adventure, keeping its forward momentum by adding in a new plot twist every five minutes. (Is Sami's itch an infection that will turn her into a comet zombie, for example—or is it just a nervous rash? Her life depends on the answer, in more ways than one.) Nobody's motives are what they seem on the surface, and most are impossible to second-guess. And the charming ending even contains the punch line to a joke set up in the opening.
Rent this one for: its clever blend of sci-fi and teen silliness.
You'll (probably) like this if you liked: *A Boy and His Dog, Clueless; The Quiet Earth* (serious treatment)
Dissenting Opinion: • "...plays all its cards too soon." —MMG (2.5) • "...low-budget sci-fi quickie..." —SMV (2.5) • "...the script runs out before the movie does." —GMR (2.5)
Vidbits: Beltran and Woronov also appear together in *Eating Raoul* and *Scenes From the Class Struggle in Beverly Hills.*

Flashback!

Quest For Love

(romance)

(1971; ?; NR; 1:30)

Starring: Joan Collins, Tom Bell
Featuring: Denholm Elliott, Laurence Naismith
Written by: Terence Feely
(based on the story "Random Quest" by John Wyndham)
Directed by: Ralph Thomas

Synopsis: An accident during a demonstration of high-energy physics transports bachelor scientist Colin Trafford (Bell) into an alternate world where World War II never occurred, JFK was never assassinated, and men have never walked on the moon. In this world, he's a successful writer, but a philandering bastard, married to Ottalie (Collins), a beautiful shrew. He falls in love with her immediately, and when he realizes it was "his" own actions that made her miserable and drove her away, he determines to reform "himself" and earn her love again. No sooner is she won over than she dies of a heart condition: This parallel world might have been spared a second Great War, but at the cost of technology which lags far beyond our world, and is unable to save her. Colin's only hope for happiness is to find a way back to our world, locate the corresponding parallel Ottalie, and attempt to save her from the same certain death.
Discussion: Science fiction has traditionally been a male domain; one in which head takes precedence over heart—which might explain the relative lack of romance stories in its canon. But *Quest* successfully manages to combine the two genres in an intelligent melodrama. The SF aspects are neatly presented as a background to the romance, and the progression of the relationship itself is credible. And while the flick often threatens to become the sci-fi equivalent of a soap opera by dancing dangerously close to the maudlin (swelling music indicating swelling emotion; ubiquitous white roses symbolic of Pure Love), it never quite degenerates into a tearjerker. We all know by now that Collins can play a total bitch with the best of them; the surprise is that she once had the ability to play the other side of the virgin/whore coin: soft, sweet, vulnerable. And it's interesting that this video is so difficult to locate: In this era of Geek Rule, a flick such as this would seem to embody every miserable, lonely nerd's most secret romantic fantasy.
Rent this one for: its delicate balance of fantasy and romance.
You'll (probably) like this if you liked: *Somewhere In Time;* "The City on the Edge of Forever" episode of "Star Trek."

The Quiet Earth

(1985; FoxVideo; R; 1:31)

Starring: Bruno Lawrence, Alison Routledge, Peter Smith
Written by: Bruno Lawrence, Sam Pillsbury, Bill Baer
(based on the novel by Craig Harrison)
Directed by: Geoff Murphy

Synopsis: Middle-aged, bald, wearing only an employee I.D. badge, Zach Hobson (Lawrence) awakens to an empty world. As though a neutron bomb had dropped silently in the night, the city is devoid of people. Zach is totally alone; perhaps the last and only person on earth. No one responds to his radio broadcasts or billboards. He lives in luxury, the spoils of the depopulated world his for the taking. But that world is also his cell, in which he faces a future of solitary confinement. He goes insane. He gives speeches to life-sized cardboard cutouts on the lawn of his mansion. He proclaims himself President of "this quiet earth." He recovers and starts from scratch, rebuilding a livable life. Then one day Joanne (Routledge) wanders into his house. They embrace like lost lovers. They rejoice; they compare notes. They live a little idyll; playing, foraging, exploring. On one of his exploratory forays, Zach is captured by Api (Smith), a black activist, and the once-stable relationship becomes an awkward alliance. Two's company, but three creates an infernal triangle.
Discussion: Although this somber, leisurely-paced entry from New Zealand does contain a subplot explaining how these particular three people ended up alone on earth—and why—it's the story of their emotional dynamics that dominates the film. The science fiction aspect of a shifting, unstable reality is more of a metaphor: a mirror, on a cosmic scale, of the insecurities, instabilities and emotional struggles which define our realities, and which have always plagued people—whether alone, coupled, or in a society...even if that "society" consists of a mere three people. The actions and reactions of all three characters are believable and sincere, illustrating the best and worst aspects of being human and of attempting to make sense of the patent illogic of the heart. In this respect, the film's psychology is sound, even if the physics are fantasy. But the SF subplot does lead to the incredible conclusion, in which an attack on a research facility becomes necessary before an experiment gone awry reaches catastrophic proportions. The result of this kamikaze act—and the final shot of the film—are jawdroppers.
Rent this one for: its quiet insight into the human heart.
You'll (probably) like this if you liked: *The World, The Flesh and The Devil; Five; Glen and Randa; 12:01*
Dissenting Opinion: "The plot turns predictable..." —SMV (3)

The Stuff

(comedy/ horror)

(1985; New World; R; 1:33)

Starring: Michael Moriarty, Andrea Marcovicci, Scott Bloom
Featuring: Garrett Morris, Paul Sorvino, Patrick O'Neal, Danny Aiello
Written and directed by: Larry Cohen

Synopsis: It looks like marshmallow cream, tastes better than Ben & Jerry's—and comes bubbling up from a quarry, ready to be pumped into trucks, clumped into cartons and dumped into stores as "The Stuff." It's also addictive and alive—and if you eat enough of it, it takes over your mind then consumes you from the inside. Industrial saboteur "Moe" Rutherford (Moriarty), hired by a rival fast food chain to steal the secret recipe, discovers all of the above and more, with the help of Nicole (Marcovicci), the brain behind "The Stuff's" PR campaign, and Jason (Bloom), a kid who "saw it move" and watches it turn his family into the Cleavers from Hell. Can this intrepid trio manage to infiltrate the plant and get its evil owners to "Stuff" it?
Discussion: Ever get a craving for junk food? I've always held the theory that the "billions served" burger chain (which must remain nameless to avoid litigation) puts *a little something extra* in each burger: an undetectably small quantity of some addictive chemical that makes you crave a burger fix once a month or so... Obviously, Larry Cohen thinks likewise (and, if the packaging of "The Stuff" is any indication, also *hates* Baskin-Robbins). *The Stuff* is a throwback to old '50s flicks like *The Blob* and *Invasion of the Body Snatchers,* but done with an undercurrent of fun and a nod to modern advertising ("the stuff" if there ever was some). Morris is in great form, and Moriarty has a high old time as a good old boy, floating through the flick full of Southern charm and smarm. It's a captivating, tongue-in-cheek sci-fi adventure which is simultaneously a parable about addiction, consumerism and commercialism—and the connections that bind them all together to hold us all captive. Best of all, though, are the commercial parodies, full of delightful cameos.
Rent this one for: its goofy humor.
You'll (probably) like this if you liked: *Tremors, Attack of the Killer Tomatoes; Invasion of the Body Snatchers* (serious)
Credentials: "...a wealth of perverse surprises." —PVG
Dissenting Opinion: • "Forced, lame satire..." —GMR (1.5 bones) • "Turkey" —VMG • "...slapdash..." —MMG (2.5 stars) • "Stuff and nonsense." —SMV (1 star)
Vidbits: Don't tune out before the credits end or you'll miss the final surprise cameo.

Tremors

(action/comedy)
(1989; MCA; PG-13; 1:36)

Starring: Kevin Bacon, Fred Ward
Featuring: Finn Carter, Michael Gross, Reba McEntire, Victor Wong
Written by: S.S. Wilson, Brent Maddock
Directed by: Ron Underwood

Synopsis: Val (Bacon) and Earl (Ward) are a couple of good ol' boys; lovable, but dumb as rust; handymen who drive around in a dusty pickup doing odd jobs for the odd locals of the dusty desert town of Perfection, NV. They aspire to something—*anything*—better, but on their way out of town, they come across cars, sheep and people being sucked into the ground. And they find out why: Some kind of giant, mutated (and *stinky!*) snake on steroids is burrowing beneath their feet. Phone's out; road's out—the dozen-plus people in this isolated valley are on their own, 38 miles from the next town. They've got to get out before they become a "graboid" smorgasbord—but can anyone survive an attack that tears the entire town out from under them? With few resources, no way to run, and nowhere to hide, how do you beat an earthquake with an attitude—and a mean set of teeth?
Discussion: *Alien* meets *Airplane!* in this witty thriller, simultaneously a satire of '50s sci-fi creature features (like *The Giant Gila Monster*) and a damn good one itself. It's a tongue-in-cheek adventure, jam-packed with hair-raising escapes, special effects that are chilling, thrilling and silly (including some nice "monster point of view" shots), and buckets of technicolor blood, guts and goo (all from the squishy "sand sharks"). Much of the fun comes from their desperate and clever measures to keep off the ground and out of the maw of the Medusa-mouthed monster; from the dead-serious Survivalists (Gross and McEntire), prepared for anything—except a subterranean attack; and from their attempts to outwit the increasingly-intelligent "graboids." Don't ask too many questions (although the characters engage in some satirical speculation over their origin), just go along for the ride—it's fast, furious fun. And be glad you can't *smell* 'em!
Rent this one for: its witty spoof of '50s B-horror flicks.
You'll (probably) like this if you liked: *Matinee, Gremlins, MST3K; Jurassic Park, Alien* (serious)
Credentials: "...a small, sardonic gem in the big-bug genre...B+" —*EW* (4/12/96) • Original *EW* review: "A." Go figure.
Dissenting Opinion: "Silly, trashy, and heavily derivative... stock clichés...Not exactly memorable..." —SMV (2.5 stars)
Vidbits: • 1995 sequel • Credits list "Dirt" and "Sage" wranglers.

12:01

(1993; Columbia TriStar, New Line; PG-13; 1:32)

Starring: Jonathan Silverman, Helen Slater, Martin Landau
Written by: Philip Morton, Jonathan Heap (TV story)
(based on the short story "12:01 PM" by Richard Lupoff)
Directed by: Jack Sholder

Synopsis: Cocky screwup Barry Thomas (Silverman), low-level clerk at a high-tech research firm, has a terrible crush on one of the company's top scientists, Lisa Fredericks (Slater). But on the very day he breaks the ice with her, she's murdered. Next morning, however, she's back on the job—and Barry observes that the entire day is repeating itself. Someone has apparently sabotaged an accelerator experiment, causing a "time bounce," in which the entire universe and everyone's memory "resets" every 24 hours. Due to a freak accident, Barry is immune—and he discovers that each cycle is not *exactly* the same: his own actions change the day's events. He sets out to save Lisa's life, find out who's responsible for the accident, and prevent it. His initial attempts to persuade her of the bounce prove frustrating. But Barry is a quick study, and charms Lisa into revealing intimacies which he uses as leverage to convince her in each new cycle. How many dead ends will they have to explore before they can identify the culprit and break the circle?
Discussion: Although similar to *Groundhog Day,* where *GD* is a romantic comedy, *12:01* is a romantic thriller—with an advantage denied the typical thriller, in that the characters can go through numerous plot permutations. They're caught and killed one day, for instance, only to find themselves right back at the beginning of that same day again, ready to avoid that particular dead-end. Where the two films intersect is in the romance, and *12:01* succeeds here just as nicely as it does as a thriller. Barry has essentially a single day to meet Lisa, convince her of their situation, *and* establish a romantic relationship with her. Imagine his anguish when he accomplishes this, then is forced to start from scratch again the next day—or the greater pain of seeing her regularly murdered because something prevented him from saving her in this iteration. The tight plot (complete with satisfying "scientific" explanations) slides seamlessly from light comedy into the anxious urgency of the action, exploring along the way the evolving intimacy between lovers separated only by memory, which makes *12:01* worth watching—repeatedly.
Rent this one for: an alternate take on *Groundhog Day.*
You'll (probably) like this if you liked: *Groundhog Day*
Vidbits: • Originally made for TV. • The story was previously filmed in 1990 as a short subject, and nominated for an Oscar.

2010:
The Year We Make Contact
(1984; MGM/UA; PG; 1:56)

Starring: Roy Scheider, John Lithgow, Helen Mirren
Featuring: Bob Balaban, Kier Dullea, Dana Elcar, Madolyn Smith, Mary Jo Deschanel, Douglas Rain
Written, produced and directed by: Peter Hyams
(based on the novel by Arthur C. Clarke)

Synopsis: It's been nine years since the disappearance of the Discovery spacecraft near Jupiter (as shown Stanley Kubrick's *2001: A Space Odyssey*), and no one on earth still has a clue as to why the mission failed. But Dr. Heywood Floyd (Scheider), the brains behind the original flight, is determined to find out—as are the Russians. Both nations are building ships to recover Discovery, but the Russians will get there first—and only the Russian ship can get to Discovery before its orbit decays and it burns up in Jupiter's atmosphere. Scientists from both nations pressure the politicians to cut a deal, and three of our people (Scheider, Lithgow and Balaban) are allowed to ride along on the Russian ship. Even though the atmosphere onboard is strained due to political tensions on earth, a sense of camaraderie develops with the Comrades—especially when they discover indications of life on one of Jupiter's moons. After stabilizing Discovery's orbit and reactivating the HAL 9000 computer, an eerie appearance by the "ghost" of Discovery astronaut Dave Bowman (Dullea) warns Floyd away from Jupiter, as "something wonderful" is about to occur. The fate of their escape rests in détente between crews—and trust in a "cured" computer.

Discussion: Imagine being asked to write and direct *Citizen Kane II,* and you'll have a clue to the obstacles Hyams faced in fashioning this sequel. "I know *Citizen Kane,"* some critic is bound to write, "and you're no *Citizen Kane."*

2001 is inviolable; an absolute: hypnotic, mystical, visually brilliant; one of the finest films in the genre (perhaps in all of cinema history). *2010* naturally suffers by comparison—but *only* by comparison. Taken on its own, as a stand-alone story, *2010* has much to recommend it. At the top of that list are the flawless and beautiful special effects by Richard Edlund. And Hyams (who adapted Clarke's novel, produced, directed *and* did his own cinematography) deserves a lot of credit, not just for taking the risk of attempting a sequel to *2001,* but for making such a damn good one.

While *2001* was a detached, emotionally subdued film, *2010* concentrates on character and action, and excels at both. Not that it's devoid of ideas, however. Quite the contrary: in any other film, ideas like a computer learning noble sacrifice, or wondering if it will dream when unplugged, or of life arising elsewhere in our galactic neighborhood, would be enough to hang an entire plot on. But comparisons are inevitable, and in any contest between mystery and clever explanations, mystery always wins. Even in this contest, however, *2010* offers a subtle touch: the mystical implication that Starchild Bowman might become the *anima mundi* of the new planet, or the consciousness/life-force of its emerging species.

The real secret of *2010* is that it is essentially an old-fashioned, '50s style space adventure movie (well-)dressed up as an '80s action and effects extravaganza. (The film's political subtext sets it squarely in that Cold War era—and is the one part of the film that seems dated.) But it's a space adventure that's intellectually stimulating, emotionally compelling, visually interesting, tense and suspenseful, however—and which even touches wonder in its climax.

So it's not *2001.* So what? It's still a thrill to see our old friends the Discovery, Bowman and HAL (featuring his original voice, Douglas Rain), once again—a trio of veterans who provide the film with a poignant finale in their ultimate reunion.

Rent this one for: the engaging performances; the special effects; the clever (however mundane) solution to HAL's nervous breakdown; and for the final solution to the mystery of the Monoliths—"something wonderful," indeed.

You'll (probably) like this if you liked: *2001: A Space Odyssey, Conquest of Space, Destination Moon*

Credentials: Academy Award nomination: Art direction

Dissenting Opinion: • "Tame, almost flatfooted sequel...with none of the supposed significance and not much else to offer." —HFG • "...disappointing..." —SMV (2 stars)

Vidbits: • The credits list Syd Mead as the film's "Visual Futurist"—the same credit he received for his work on *Blade Runner.* • Author Clarke's cameo (sitting on a park bench in front of the White House) is completely lost when transferred from widescreen to small screen. But he and Kubrick appear as drawings of the leaders of the U.S. and USSR, respectively, on the Time magazine cover glimpsed in the hospital scene.

Wavelength

(1982; Embassy; PG; 1:27)

Starring: Robert Carradine, Cherie Currie, Keenan Wynn
Written and directed by: Mike Gray
Music by: Tangerine Dream

Synopsis: When an unemployed musician (Carradine) takes his new girlfriend Iris (Currie) to his house in the Hollywood hills, she begins hearing strange noises ("imagine a whale crying") that he can't hear. They comb the neighborhood for the source of the sounds until they're certain they originate from an abandoned Air Force base. But when they sneak in through a forgotten access tunnel, they discover a *very* active underground installation where four aliens are being kept in suspended animation by government investigators. The dormant visitors are apparently sending telepathic signals for help, and Iris is one of the few with an empathic connection on the right "wavelength." When the intruders are (naturally) captured by military security, we begin to see the extent of the ruthless conspiracy to keep these strange invaders on ice. It's up to our pure-hearted heroes to escape and get the childlike aliens back to the mothership—while their military captors are intent on terminating them all "with extreme prejudice," as they say.
Discussion: One reason this little flick might have been overlooked in 1982 is that it is notoriously low-budget, right down to a boom mike visible in some shots. But the real reason might be that 1982 was also the year that *E.T.* hit theaters—and who'd pay to see a third-rate version of that classic? A decade and a half later, however, *Wavelength* is a pleasant little thriller, combining elements of the Roswell UFO conspiracy with movies like *Close Encounters,* and predating *Starman* and recent fare like Fox TV's "Alien Autopsy." *Wavelength* is fast-paced; its heart is in the right place; and it's even fairly intelligent, particularly when the military men and their advisors discuss the pros and cons of hostile action against the aliens. And it has a sense of humor as well: The woman who can read the aliens' minds, for instance, knows they're not hostile—they're just lost. As she explains to her boyfriend, "If *you* could go anywhere in the universe, would *you* come to this loony bin?" Amen to that!
Rent this one for: its low-key updating of '50s B-movie clichés.
You'll (probably) like this if you liked: *E.T., Roswell, Starman, Close Encounters, Hanger 18,* "Alien Autopsy"
Dissenting Opinion: • "...steals liberally from earlier pictures for ideas." —MMG (2 stars) • "...unoriginal..." —VMR (2.5 bones)
Vidbits: Gray previously wrote another classic paranoid thriller, *The China Syndrome.* • Not to be confused with the 1996 film.

Flashback!

Zardoz

(social satire)

(1973; CBS/Fox, FoxVideo; R; 1:45)

Starring: Sean Connery, Charlotte Rampling
Featuring: John Alderton, Sara Kestelman
Written, produced and directed by: John Boorman

Synopsis: The year is 2293: A giant, scowling stone head floats over a ravaged landscape. It spews guns and a philosophy of death to its faithful followers, the Exterminators of Zardoz, who genuflect in obeisance. One among them, however, sneaks inside the head and hides. When it lands, Zed (Connery) finds himself in an idyllic community full of magical hi-tech—no place for a Webley-wielding barbarian. He's captured, disarmed and held for study by the eternally youthful, immortal inhabitants of this "Vortex"—the decadent "Eternals," who live in Eden-like luxury, cloistered away from Brutals like Zed. While the placid population of this utopian commune debates the meaning of "the monster" in their midst, Zed keeps his eyes open and his mouth shut. He soon discovers that there is trouble in paradise: dissent and dissatisfaction, deadly boredom and virtually terminal apathy. The mysterious "Tabernacle" which connects and protects them all also imprisons them all. Can the genetically-bred Zed fulfill his destiny as an Agent of Evolution and destroy the evolutionary dead-end that is The Vortex? And if he succeeds in destroying Eternity...what then?

Discussion: "What *has* Arthur been doing out there all these years?" one immortal wonders idly. Arthur Frayn, in charge of the post-apocalyptic Outlands, has spent patient generations secretly breeding the perfect killing machine, is what: a brilliant Brutal who is smart enough, strong enough, and viciously bitter enough to kill the deathlessness which holds the Eternals in evolutionary and emotional bondage. Immortality, it seems, has backfired on these "improved" humans. Sleep is obsolete and sex is history; they have become eternal children, sexless and androgynous; antecedents of the Eloi, just as the Brutals could easily be the missing link between Man and Morlock—and both types are well along Wells' *Time Machine* trajectory. Worse, even with unlimited time, the Eternals' ape's brains still can't answer the timeless Big Questions. Their mandatory immortality has turned the Vortex into, not a dystopia, but an *anti*-utopia, where ennui is their worst enemy and many among them crave the gift of sweet release from their incarcerated incarnation.

Give Boorman credit for creating a unique, well thought-out utopia, complete with its own culture and problems. It's a difficult film; to appreciate its satirical philosophy requires a reversal of our most primal and sacred beliefs. But once you accept the premise of the problem, the whole idea of Utopia becomes questionable and turned topsy-turvy. Philosophical themes are scarce in cinematic sci-fi, but *Zardoz* flaunts them in abundance, and with tongue-in-cheek twists. The hero is Death incarnate; his mission, to kill God. Heavy, heady stuff: high camp at its loftiest. It's Freudian science fiction, where eternal children rebel against their cosmic parents, attempting to kill the ultimate Father figure of the Tabernacle and sleep the sleep of oblivion in the womb of Mother Earth—who has been so subdued that the only expression left for Her is Evolution: Death and Rebirth. It's Jungian science fiction, where any trait pushed far enough becomes its own opposite. It's Nietzschean science fiction, in which humans dare to seek God (and to look behind the masks of God) in order to destroy It and end Its oppression and enslavement. It's mythological science fiction, full of dialog and imagery as psychologically primal, archetypal and raw as *Beowulf,* Camelot or Ulysses. It's science fiction as religious metaphor: a story of revenge against a god's betrayal—and of a nature god's revenge against the hubris of Humankind for creating the "offense against nature" that is The Vortex.

Zardoz is also a visually brilliant film, full of hallucinatory and hallucinogenic imagery, which peaks in the mind-bending "touch-teaching" sequence. And it's an aural experience as well, quoting Nietzsche and T.S. Eliot in the dialog, and using both the mournful and somber Second Movement of Beethoven's *Seventh Symphony* (in a haunting vocal performance) and its bright, ecstatic Third Movement in appropriate portions.

As if all this wasn't enough, *Zardoz* is also a deeply facetious film; a silly satire bursting with mock portentousness ("All that I was is gone," Connery mumbles through a porridge-thick burr), parodied pretentiousness ("In hunting you, I have become you"), pithy dialog ("It was all a joke!") and the damnedest cleverest title of any movie ever made. The secret behind the mock-god Zardoz is simultaneously obvious, unguessably brilliant and enormously amusingly—proof that self-proclaimed charlatan Arthur Frayn really *is* a wizard of gods. Even though he, like all the rest of them (and all of us!) was "bred and led" by the Evolutionary Imperative (in a cynical sense, humans might very well be merely genes' way of manufacturing more genes) he can still claim authorship of this "shaggy god story."

Rent this one for: its stunning originality; its mythic themes and dreamlike style; its high camp tragicomedy.

You'll (probably) like this if you liked: *Brazil, The Exorcist II, Alphaville, 2001* (mythic sci-fi); "The Prisoner" (final episode)
Credentials: "...stunning, thought-provoking...but don't take it too seriously." —PEF
Dissenting Opinion: • "Pompous, boring fantasy for the so-called intelligentsia" —HFG • "...pretentious." —GMR (2 bones) • "A glittering cultural trashpile...the most gloriously fatuous movie since *The Oscar.*" —*New Yorker* • "Murky plot is hard to follow..." —VMG (2.5 stars) • "...will probably leave most viewers dissatisfied." —MMG (2.5 stars) • "...gave free rein to [Boorman's] imagination...to dire effect"; "...self-indulgent fantasy...a commercial and critical flop."—*Premiere* (9/95) • "...demonstrates how one can make a cheap sci-fi flick by using mirrors and prisms as substitutes for imagination." —Judith Crist, *New York* • "No matter what goes wrong in his life, Neil [Connery, Sean's brother] can always look in the mirror and say, 'Well, at least I didn't do *Zardoz*'." —Crow T. Robot, *MST3K*
Vidbits: • The final scene (Connery and Rampling growing old together) had to be shot three times, due first to damaged film and then to accidentally exposed negatives. The stars, enduring hours of makeup for each reshoot, were reportedly not amused. • Boorman also published a "novelization" (1974).
And a little something extra for all you Boorman fans out there: Look closely at *Zardoz* and you'll see elements that would later reappear in Boorman's (also critically-lambasted) film, *Exorcist II: The Heretic* (1977). In both movies, Boorman uses science fiction as a metaphor for his philosophical and mythological musings. Both center on the split between science and religion; in *Zardoz,* the conflict is between the scientifically-created "god" of the Tabernacle and the genetically-engineered Zed (the omega in the equation "I am the alpha and omega"); in *Exorcist II,* Lamont uses cutting edge science to prove the existence of the demon. In *Zardoz,* the operating principle is Arthur C. Clarke's dictum, "Any sufficiently advanced technology is indistinguishable from magic"; in *Exorcist II,* the magical technology is the brain-wave synchronizer, allowing two people to share a hallucination. In both movies, "smoke and mirrors" figure prominently: a tribute to stage magician charlatans like Arthur Frayn and self-suspected charlatans like Fr. Lamont. And in both movies, much of the final action takes place outside of consensus reality, in the interstices between insights; the timeless archetypal universe of intuition and the unconscious. In a more concrete connection, Boorman would refine the "touch-teaching" imagery of *Zardoz*—projecting slides onto a human body "screen"—in his (critically-lambasted) 1990 film, *Where The Heart Is.* Both these films are also in this book, and I truly love all three of these "barrel-bottom Boormans".

WESTERNS

WESTERNS

"Great Westerns made since 1980?" Only a list of "Honest Politicians" would be shorter. *Dances With Wolves. Unforgiven.* That's about it, pardners—and both are highly revisionist Westerns at that, replacing the rousing action of Old Time Westerns with modern sensibilities and moral pedantry.

And yet I have managed to ferret out a short list of unknown, unsung, unseen, unadulterated Westerns which might very well send you back to the video store shelves in search of the pre-'70s classics of the genre.

So saddle up, cowboys—and give up the blues, cowgirls—while we head 'em up and rent 'em out.

Barbarosa

(1982; CBS/Fox, FoxVideo; PG; 1:30)

Starring: Willie Nelson, Gary Busey
Featuring: Gilbert Roland, Isela Vega
Written by: William D. Wittliff
Directed by: Fred Schepisi

Synopsis: Karl (Busey) never meant to kill August; it was an accident. But it tears the Texas Amish farm community apart, so Karl makes tracks for the desert. The dumb farm boy is rescued by "Barbarosa" (Nelson), a cranky old bandit also on the run from gunmen. The Savala family, headed by patriarch Don Broglio (Roland), regularly sends his sons and grandsons out to kill Barbarosa and avenge their family honor. None ever returns. Barbarosa is getting awful damn tired of having to kill them—and of the whole vendetta. The two form an odd couple team of saddle tramps, surviving by doing a little "light stealing." The seasoned pro and his thick amateur sidekick outwit a bunch of banditos and sneak into the Savala's Mexican hacienda—not for any mayhem, but to visit Josephina (Vega), Don Broglio's daughter...and Barbarosa's long-time wife. He visits when he can, risking life and limb with each clandestine tryst. This time, however, Farmboy tags along and falls for their teenage daughter. "I like her a lot," Karl informs his mentor, "and I intend to visit her again." Only when he discovers the truth about the feud does this "gringo child" realize he's already far along the road toward becoming its next target.

Discussion: They just don't make 'em like they used to—Westerns *or* legends. Luckily, this little film accomplishes both. The Savalas curse Barbarosa's name and tell exaggerated horror stories of his nefarious trespasses against their clan to their children and grandchildren, painting him as the family's personal, almost supernatural, bogeyman. They sing an epic song about the "red-bearded stranger" ("barbar rosa") and his crimes. And as they do so, they embellish his exploits and elevate him to the status of living legend. Hell, maybe he *is* a legend: his name strikes awe in most men; he escapes from his own grave; he moves in and out of the Savala compound like a ghost. Where else do legends come from but in the elaboration of fanciful exploits like his? What encourages a legend to persist and endure but regular retellings and embellishments? The deep idea within this film is that this is indeed how legends begin and propagate—and the very roots of mythology. This central conceit boosts the film up to the intellectual stature of such attempts to create Western legends as Wayne's Liberty Valence, screenwriter William Goldman's Butch and Sundance, and Clint

Eastwood's "Man With No Name" character of the Sergio Leone spaghetti-Westerns. Shepisi's insightful direction, consisting almost entirely of long shots and close-ups, reflects this philosophy of inflating the personal gesture to grand status.

It's a delightful story, as well, full of original touches which nonetheless never violate its spirit as an authentic Western. In addition, the film maintains a tongue-in-cheek comic undercurrent that acts as an abrasive to any overly intellectual pretensions. Everyone takes Barbarosa far more seriously than he ever takes himself. Nelson plays the character as a cantankerous old coot; an irascible rascal, full of piss and vinegar, and more than willing to express it to anyone. One classic scene contains a shoot-out at a horse auction, where grouchy Barbarosa desperately attempts to yell some sense into his reluctant young charge with his irritated, rapid-fire advice ("Fer Chrissake, don't let the sonovabith reload, goddamit!"). But Barbarosa is not one-dimensional in any sense: he's a wily survivor, a sly old desert rat, and a sensible mentor to the "Farmboy," providing him with the kind of fatherly guidance and "saddle-savvy" the gawky gullible desperately needs. And Barbarosa is fully aware of the irony of his situation with the Savalas, reluctantly participating in their vendetta for his own quiet reasons, which slowly unfold over the course of the film.

Busey, too, is memorable as the snaggle-toothed bumpkin who endures enough tragedy to become a man, and develops enough spirit to become an apprentice legend, heir to the mantle of the Barbarosa franchise; ready, willing and able, for his own unique reasons, to carry on the family tradition. (The one off-putting flaw in the film is Roland; he might be a screen legend, but here he chews the scenery so fiercely that he almost makes a mockery of the movie. And he was so good in a similar role in *Rustler's Rhapsody!* Hey, Gilbert! This wasn't a comedy!)

Add in a fabulous Southwestern lute and guitar score, some beautiful, panoramic scenery, and a handful of gently-presented thoughts about how love outweighs both risk and revenge, and of the mortality of men versus the immortality of legend, and what we end up with is a savvy, classic Western that pays homage to the genre without ever robbing, mocking or revising the legendary Westerns of yesteryear.

Rent this one for: its unpretentious insight into the origin of Western legends and how, by their own momentum, they can develop into myth; the original situations; the performances.

You'll (probably) like this if you liked: *Butch Cassidy and the Sundance Kid, A Fistful of Dollars, The Outlaw Josey Wales*

Dissenting Opinion: "...a ponderous and preposterous tale." —*People Magazine Guide to Movies on Video*

Vidbits: Shot in Texas' Big Bend country.

The Grey Fox

(1983; Media Home Entertainment; PG; 1:32)

Starring: Richard Farnsworth, Jackie Burroughs
Featuring: Wayne Robson, Timothy Webber, Ken Pogue
Written by: Michael Conway Baker ("John Hunter")
Directed by: Philip Borsos

Synopsis: In March, 1863, Bill Miner (Farnsworth), age 16, held up a Pony Express run. During the next 18 years he masterminded 26 daring stagecoach robberies. Dubbed "The Gentleman Bandit," he's credited with originating the phrase "Hands up!" He was captured in 1882, and on June 17, 1901, after serving 33 years in San Quentin, Bill Miner, age 67, was released into the dawning 20th century. And when he goes to a new-fangled "movie house" and sees Edwin S. Porter's "The Great Train Robbery," he's intrigued—and inspired. Entire scenes from the classic film are re-enacted in his first job—with disastrous results. He flees to Canada, picks up a new identity and a new partner, and tries again—successfully. His life is complicated when he becomes enamored of fiery, free-spirited pre-suffragette Kate (Burroughs). And it becomes too complicated when a Pinkerton tracking him rides into town. Bill agrees to meet Kate in Chicago—but only after one more job...
Discussion: Here's an oxymoron: a leisurely-paced action film. But it works, mostly because its essence is a character study of a proud man trapped in the wrong time. Most of the credit for its success must go to Farnsworth, in his first starring role—although he'd already appeared in over 300 movies as a character actor, and was a movie stuntman for 30 years. As Miner, a low-key but cunning rascal who's "just no good at work that's planned by other heads," his soulful face, handlebar mustache, sweet smile, high, quiet voice, twinkling eyes and unflagging politeness make him a charismatic charmer. (It would be no surprise to discover that this script was written expressly for him.) Although the dialog might seem a touch stiff—arch, stilted and formal—we must remember that an accurate recreation of an era involves more than just props and costumes. The photography—particularly of the trains—is breathtaking, and bookending the picture with sepia-toned, silent-era Western film footage and "title cards" is an appropriate attention-getter.
Rent this one for: its quiet, low-key charm.
You'll (probably) like this if you liked: *The Shootist*
Credentials: Winner of Canadian Genie Award.
Vidbits: Is it my imagination, or was a lot of *Back to the Future III* inspired by this film, particularly the romance and robberies?

Last of the Dogmen

(contemporary Western)
(1995; HBO; R; 1:58)

Starring: Tom Berenger, Barbara Hershey, Kurtwood Smith
Written and directed by: Tab Murphy

Synopsis: When three prisoners escape into the rugged territory of Northwest Montana, the local Sheriff (Smith) reluctantly calls in tracker Lewis Gates (Berenger), a loner who's gone into seclusion following the tragic death of his wife. Gates finds signs that Indians might still inhabit this mountainous territory, and enlists the aid of tough but lovely anthropologist Lillian Sloman (Hershey) to ferret them out. They discover a tiny, idyllic community, descended from Cheyenne "Dog Soldiers" driven into the mountains by the cavalry over a century ago, and cut off from the world since. But their commitment to protect these peaceful innocents from our savage century is challenged by a posse searching for the missing pair.
Discussion: The theme of this fascinating film is *redemption*. All three principals begin as emotional "walking wounded." Gates' spirit was broken by the death of his wife in a wilderness accident—and by his inability to save her. Her father, the Sheriff, has never forgiven Gates, and remains viciously vindictive. And anthropologist Sloman still smarts over the "unconscionable" treatment of Native Americans during the westward movement. But it takes the mystery of the hidden tribe to act as a catalyst for each to find potential redemption hidden in the others. The real mystery is why no one saw this film. The script is smart, plausible, trim but full, and ties the various themes and plot lines together into a neat and satisfying package. The direction is sure-handed, and includes some of the most breathtaking scenery since John Ford's Monument Valley Westerns. And the performers become real people, responding realistically to the psychological changes their unusual situation inspires. No one plays a heart-scarred, grumpy loner better than Berenger, and watching him slowly emerge from his shell of depression after finally meeting his match in the cocky Sloman is both amusing and touching. *Dogmen* is a thoroughly satisfying film: thought-provoking, compassionate, suspenseful and assured.
Rent this one for: its intelligent adventure; for the romance; for being a real Western merely dressed in contemporary clothes.
You'll (probably) like this if you liked: *Dances With Wolves, Emerald Forest, War Party, Lost Horizon, Brigadoon*
Vidbits: Although the action takes place in Montana, the movie was shot in Alberta, Canada and Cuernavaca, Mexico.

Appendix

Appendix

Indexes

Killer B's

The Top Ten Killer B's

(My favorites, at any rate); in alphabetical order:

1. Bedazzled
2. F For Fake
3. Funny Bones
4. House of Games
5. Joe Versus the Volcano
6. Miracle Mile
7. A Shock to the System
8. Tampopo
9. Trust
10. Where The Heart Is

The Top Ten *Percent* of Killer B's

Begin with the Top Ten, then add *(also in alphabetical order):*

11. Around the World in 80 Ways
12. Barbarosa
13. The Great Train Robbery
14. Into the West
15. L.A. Story
16. Love and a .45
17. The Nasty Girl
18. Rustler's Rhapsody
19. Secret Honor
20. The Silent Partner
21. Strictly Ballroom
22. Truly, Madly, Deeply
23. Voices
24. Zardoz

The Top Ten Most *Overrated* "Sleepers"

(i.e., the most commonly recommended sleepers, and movies that fit the "Killer B" criteria, but *just don't make the cut*); *in alphabetical order:*

1. Crossing Delancey
2. Diva
3. Dreamchild
4. Fargo
5. The Grifters
6. Local Hero
7. Melvin and Howard
8. Mona Lisa
9. My Life As A Dog
10. UFOria

Key to Film and Video Guides Quoted in *Killer B's*

The following guides are quoted so often in the "Credentials" and "Dissenting Opinion" sections of *Killer B's* that in order to conserve space (and hence pack in as much information as possible), each book has been given a code indicating the source of the quotes. In the reviews, the number of stars (or "bones," or whatever) the guide awarded the film follows this code. Space imitations of occasionally necessitated listing just the number, without the word "stars." Books are listed in alphabetical order.

I am of course deeply indebted to the heroic individuals below who have sacrificed their lives to provide viewers with the finest in modern criticism, and I heartily suggest you rush out and purchase each and every one of their invaluable books, in each and every updated edition, each and every year. No, really.

KB CODE	FULL TITLE & PARTICULARS
Ebert	**Roger Ebert's Video Companion—1995 Edition** by Roger Ebert *(Andrews & McMeel)* © 1994 by Roger Ebert Collection of Ebert's Chicago *Sun-Times* film reviews. Rates by stars, from ★ (lowest) to ★★★★ (highest)
EW	**The Entertainment Weekly Guide to the Greatest Movies Ever Made** *(© 1994 by Entertainment Weekly, Inc.)* No general editor listed; 18 editors; 47 writers (Quotes and grades have also been taken from *Entertainment Weekly* magazine; all are © 1990-96 by *Entertainment Weekly, Inc.* and/or Time Warner, Inc.) Rates by letter grade (like school) from "A+" to "F"
GMR	**VideoHound's Golden Movie Retriever 1996** *(© 1996 by Visible Ink Press™/Gale Research, Inc.)* No claim to number of entries, but easily over 20,000 12+ Editors and Contributing Editors. Rates by "bones" (equivalent to stars), from *"Woof!"* (no bones) to 4 bones (highest rating).
HFG	**Halliwell's Film Guide—7th Edition** *(Harper & Row)* © 1989 by Leslie Halliwell The last edition personally edited by Halliwell.

MMG **Leonard Maltin's Movie and Video Guide —1996 Edition**
(© 1995, Signet)
19,000+ entries
8 editors; unknown number of contributors/writers.
Rates by stars, from BOMB (=1 star) to ★★★★ (highest)

PEF **The Psychotronic Encyclopedia of Film**
by Michael Weldon
(Ballentine Books) © 1983 by Michael Weldon
No ratings, but an invaluable guide to fringe flick trivia.

PVG **The Phantom's Ultimate Video Guide**
by "The Phantom of the Movies"
(Dell) © 1989 by "The Phantom of the Movies"
Rates by diamonds, from 0 (lowest) to 4 (highest)

SMV **Movies on TV and Videocassette 1993-1994**
Conceived and Edited by Steven H. Scheuer
(© 1992, Bantam)
20,000+ entries
Staff of 8 editors; unknown number of contributors.
Rates by stars, from 0 (lowest) to ★★★★ (highest)

VMG **Video Movie Guide 1996**
by Mick Martin and Marsha Porter
Revised Edition, October, 1995 *(© 1995 Ballentine Books)*
16,000 titles
4 Editors; 24 "Chief Contributors"; 25 Writers
Rates by stars, from *Turkey* (=1 star) to ★★★★★ (highest)
*(When comparing ratings, keep in mind that the VMG's highest rating is **five** stars, versus most other guides' highest rating of **four** stars/symbols).*

By the time you read this, all of the above guides will be available in newer editions. Occasionally the editors will revise their ratings, so don't be too surprised if you look up a *Killer B* title and find a different rating. And, after reading *Killer B's*, you have a right to feel smug if the listing is revised *upward...*

Killer B's

Acknowledgments

or,

A book of this nature wouldn't be possible without blah blah blah...

I'd like to thank all those people who made *Killer B's* possible, particularly my editor (me), my publisher (also me) and my pruufwreeeder (that would be m;ee, two). (Always wanted to write an acknowledgment like that. Ha ha! Now that *that's* out of my system...)

Many thanks to:

• Scott Gracheff, my director at KTEH-TV (Silicon Valley's PBS), for his feedback, excellent suggestions and encouragement.

• Lee Grant, my original editor at the San Jose *Mercury News,* for giving me my start on the video beat.

• Van Morrison, for *Inarticulate Speech of the Heart*

• Paul Masson, for Grande Amber Brandy

• Numerous managers of Tower Video in Campbell, CA, for low-cost rentals. (And my affection and adoration to Babs Fahrney, The World's Most Beautiful Video Store Manager.)

• All those people who refused to hire me for a *real* job, allowing me to devote entire months to research and writing.

• Diana, The Beautiful Wife, for second opinions that made sure my reality checks didn't bounce; for giving me the opportunity to write this; and for making sure it was a *necessity* to write it.

As much as I am indebted to all of the above, I must accept full responsibility for any factual, stylistic, editing or proofing errors. After all, there's a limit to what you can blame on the Spell-Checker—and the downside to being a one-man publishing concern is that the only place you can point an accusatory finger is at the mirror.

Killer B's

Corrections / Suggestions

Corrections

We are not above the law! Mistakes can be made!
Not responsible! Park and lock it!

If you find an error, let me know. Don't waste your time correcting movie running times (which vary), video companies (which vary widely), or my peculiar punctuation (which varies *very* widely). Go for the gold: Misspellings, baddish grammar, wrong information in the Vidbits. And if you intend to take me to task for my information, *send evidence!*

Suggestions

If *Killer B's* is a success, you can bet there'll be second volume: *Bride of the Killer B's,* maybe, or *Son Of A (Killer) B.* Rather than limiting this second volume to films produced since 1980, let's expand the search territory to include little-known films *available on video* produced since 1960.

This is a massive task, however, and I'd certainly appreciate some help. Drop me a card and let me know what you'd like to see in a next volume. More foreign films? More animation? More art house hits? Short subjects? The *latest* buried treasures?

If you have a suggestion for consideration, drop me a note. You know the format by now; just fill in the blanks. Please include as much information as possible, and a *brief* explanation as to why you are nominating a particular film for Killer B status. If your recommendation makes the final cut (and you're the first one to recommend the title), you'll get an acknowledgment in the volume *and* a free copy! Wow! (Please check the "Don't Bother" list before sending in recommendations—in other words, don't bother trying to change my mind...)

Send all correspondence to:

The Permanent Press
Dept. KB2
P.O. Box 700305
San Jose, CA 95170

Thanks!

Killer B's

"Don't Bother" Title List

As a professional videologist, I watch a *lot* of movies. It's my *job*. The titles included in *Killer B's* represent the cream of the crop of the "buried treasures" I've discovered—but they also represent a small fraction of the films I've screened over the past dozen or more years. Even when I began serious research on this volume, and whittled down a list of thousands of titles to a few hundred prime candidates which fit the Killer B profile, *still* only about one in ten made the final cut. The 237 final choices are just the tip of the iceberg, and represent over 2,000 movies actually viewed and considered for this book.

In order to spare you the trouble of watching my rejects, below is a list of Killer B candidates that were viewed but rejected. Some of these also-rans were near-misses, while others missed the mark by a mile. Some were fine enough films, but just didn't attain "escape velocity" for me. Many were bumped from the final cut simply because I found a film I liked better, and replaced one of the semi-final 237; others were so similar to existing entries that they seemed repetitive (I chose *Lies* over the similar *Dead of Winter,* for instance, simply because *Lies* is the lesser-known title.) I've listed in **boldface** those titles which *almost* made it into this volume; those films I found *totally* worthless I've listed in *italics*—meaning "avoid at all costs."

Since tastes vary widely, I'm including this list in case you've checked through the book and decided my taste just *sucks*—in which case, the titles listed below might be more to your liking.

Exclusions: Since they don't comprise a significant portion of the *Killer B's* entries, I have deliberately excluded from this list all foreign language titles and films produced before 1980 which were considered as candidates. I've also chosen to exclude all the other titles of most of the major independent directors represented in this book (including Woody Allen, Bill Forsyth, Hal Hartley, Henry Jaglom and Alan Rudolph). Virtually everything they (and many other small, independent directors, like John Sayles) have ever produced could be considered a Killer B candidate, but their films are all, in some sense, similar works. Just assume that I viewed and considered the majority of their work and chose a representative sample entry for *Killer B's*. Only a few of their titles could be included in a general interest overview without skewing the book toward a particular director's films. But if you like what you see in *Killer B's* by a particular director, go ye forth and renteth more by him or her.

"Don't Bother" List

Adventures of Buckaroo Banzai
After Hours
Airheads
All Night Long
Amazon Women on the Moon
American Dreamer
...And God Spoke
An Angel At My Table
Apartment Zero
A.P.E.X.
Aria
Arizona Dream
At Close Range
At Play in the Fields of the Lord
Bad Influence
Ballad of Little Joe
Beer
Best Defense
Best Friends
Best Legs in the Eighth Grade
Beyond the Stars
Big Man on Campus
Bitter Moon
Boris and Natasha: The Movie
Bottle Rocket
Bound & Gagged: A Love Story
Brain Damage
Brain Dead
Brain Donors
Brief History of Time, A
Brother From Another Planet
Carnival of Souls
Carny
Cat Chaser
Catch Me If You Can
Circle of Friends
Cloak & Dagger
Closet Land
Comfort of Strangers, The
Communion
Company of Wolves, The
Cookie
Cool Runnings
Crimewave
Date with an Angel
Dazed and Confused
Dead of Winter
Deconstructing Sarah
Deepstar Six
Delirious
Desire and Hell at the Sunset Motel
Dogfight
Dominick and Eugene
Down By Law
Dream Lover
Dreamchild
Drop Dead Fred
Drowning By Numbers
Eat the Rich
Efficiency Expert, The
Electric Dreams
End of the Line
Endangered Species
Equinox
Eureka!
Even Cowgirls Get the Blues
Exotica
Fargo
Fat Man and Little Boy
Fatal Instinct
Fear of a Black Hat
Final Approach
Five Corners
Folks!
Fool and His Money, A
(AKA: Religion, Inc.)
Forbidden Choices
Four Rooms
The Freshman
Friday
Getting It Right
Great Mouse Detective
Great Santini
Hanger 18
Hangin' with the Homeboys
Happy New Year (87)
He Said, She Said
Head Office
Heart and Souls
Henry and June
Henry: Portrait of a Serial Killer
High Road to China
Hold Me, Thrill Me, Kiss Me
Hollywood Shuffle
Honeysuckle Rose
Housekeeping
I Love You To Death
Ice Pirates
Idolmaker
Impulse (84)
Impulse (90)
In the Mouth of Madness
In the Spirit
Innocent Blood
Insignificance
It's Pat: The Movie
Jack's Back
Kafka
Kill Me Again
Killing Zoe
King of the Hill
Kings and Desperate Men
Kiss Daddy Goodnight
Kiss of the Vampire
Last Polka
Late For Dinner
Let It Ride
Life is Sweet
Liquid Sky
Little Treasure
Long Riders
Loose Shoes
Love and Human Remains
Love, Cheat and Steal
Love Potion #9
Lunatics: A Love Story
Made in Heaven
Madhouse (90)
Malcolm
Man Bites Dog

"Don't Bother" List

A Man in Love
Manhattan Project, The
Map of the Human Heart
Martians Go Home!
Masquerade
Medicine Man
Melvin and Howard
Men At Work
Mi Vida Loca
Miami Rhapsody
Ms. 45
Mrs. Parker and the Vicious Circle
Mr. Destiny
Mr. Mike's Mondo Video
Mr. North
Mistress (91)
Mixed Nuts
Mom and Dad Save the World
Mona Lisa
Moon Over Parador
Mountains of the Moon
Movers and Shakers
Muriel's Wedding
My Boyfriend's Back
My New Gun
Mystery Train
Naked in New York
New York Stories
Nice Girls Don't Explode
Night Games
Night of the Running Man
Night Terror
Ninth Configuration
Noises Off
Not For Publication
Nothing But Trouble
Object of Beauty, The
O.C. and Stiggs
On Wings of Eagles
One More Saturday Night
Only the Lonely
Out Cold
Paris, Texas
Peanut Butter Solution, The
Peter's Friends
Pickle, The
Poison
Popcorn
Princess Caraboo
Public Access
Q (The Winged Serpent)
Queen of Hearts
Quest, The
Quick Change
Remote Control (88)
Repossessed
Return to Oz
Roadside Prophets
Rosencrantz and Guildenstern Are Dead
Roswell
Run
Search for Signs of Intelligent Life
in the Universe
Secret of Roan Inish
Secret Rapture, The
Seize the Day
Serial Mom
Serpent and the Rainbow, The
Shallow Grave
Shattered
Sherman's March
Shooting Party, The
Siesta
Slapstick of Another Kind
Slaves of New York
Soapdish
Songwriter
Spanking the Monkey
Stoogemania
Stormy Monday
Storyville
Strange Brew
Strange Invaders
Stuart Saves His Family
Sunset
Sweet Hearts Dance
Sweetie
Swimming with Sharks
Switch
Tall Guy, The
Tank
Tattoo
Temp, The
Teresa's Tattoo
Thank You & Good Night
Things Change
32 Short Films About Glenn Gould
To Sleep With Anger
Tom & Viv
Track 29
Trapped in Paradise
Twenty Bucks
Two Small Bodies
UFOria
UHF
Underneath, The
Until the End of the World
Vampire's Kiss
Vanya on 42nd Street
Videodrome
Watch It
Wedding Band
Where the Buffalo Roam
Whispers in the Dark
White of the Eye
Whore
Why Me?
Witches, The
Without A Clue
Wrong Is Right
Year of the Comet, The
Yellowbeard
Young Einstein
Younger & Younger
Zorro, The Gay Blade

KEY:
Boldface = mildly recommended
Italics = to be avoided

Production Information

• The text of *Killer B's* is set in 10 point Bookman Old Style, both classical and elegant.

• The Section headings used a number of miscellaneous (and hopefully appropriate-looking) fonts.

• The Indexes are set in Helvetica font of varying point sizes.

• The book was created on a Macintosh Quadra 610, using Microsoft Word 5.1a, and "typeset" on an HP LaserJet 4ML.

• The section divider page artwork was created on a Xerox machine at Office Depot, then cut and pasted to approximate real art.

About the Author

on the off chance that anyone really cares...

D. Scott Apel—the world's first and only videologist (since he invented the word)—has been writing about home video since 1983. For over a decade, he served as Video Columnist for the *San Jose* (CA) *Mercury News*, writing 534 consecutive weekly columns and more than 50 feature articles for that newspaper. During 1985, he also served as freelance video writer for the *San Francisco Examiner*, publishing monthly feature articles. His column was syndicated in several other papers, including the *Long Beach* (CA) *Press Telegram*, and his articles on home video have been published in more than 100 newspapers throughout the U.S., including the *San Francisco Chronicle*, the *Philadelphia Inquirer* and the *San Diego Tribune*, and have been picked up for national distribution by the *L.A. Times* Syndicate. He has been a frequent contributor to both *Video* and *Video Review* magazines, and, between 1990-1996, wrote and performed weekly video reviews on KTEH-TV (PBS for Silicon Valley). In addition, he is a contributing editor to Reel. Com's "Knowledge Project," a World Wide Web site devoted to film reviews.

The Anti-Bio: D. Scott Apel (the only man *on* PBS who can't *spell* "PBS") describes himself as "the world's most prolific unpublished novelist," and is the author of two previous non-fiction works, *All Works and No Plays*, and *Mein Summer Kampf*. He alleges to be the inventor of "virtual harsh reality," a graduate of Murphy's Law School and a former gift horse orthodontist. Although he is not the dumbest man on the planet, Mr. Apel claims he "can see him in line from here." And while his writing, publishing, playwrighting, television, video and film acting work have not elevated him to the status of cult figure, he *has* become a cult figurine.

Director Index

Director Index

Cast Index

Cast Index

Cast Index

Cast Index

Cast Index

Cast Index

Cast Index

** voice talent only*

Title Index

Title Index

Title Index

Title Index

Title Index